The Writings of

Henry D. Thoreau

A Week on the Concord and Merrimack Rivers

HENRY D. THOREAU

A Week on the Concord and Merrimack Rivers

EDITED BY CARL F. HOVDE
AND TEXTUAL CENTER STAFF:
WILLIAM L. HOWARTH,
ELIZABETH HALL WITHERELL

HISTORICAL INTRODUCTION BY
LINCK C. JOHNSON

PRINCETON, NEW JERSEY
PRINCETON UNIVERSITY PRESS
MCMLXXX

CENTER FOR EDITIONS OF
AMERICAN AUTHORS
AN APPROVED TEXT
MODERN LANGUAGE
ASSOCIATION OF AMERICA
®

The Center emblem means that one of a panel of textual experts serving the Center has reviewed the text and textual apparatus of the original volume by thorough and scrupulous sampling, and has approved them for sound and consistent editorial principles employed and maximum accuracy attained. The accuracy of the text has been guarded by careful and repeated proofreading of printer's copy according to standards set by the Center.

The editorial preparation of this volume, and costs associated with its publication, were supported through grants from the Editing and Publication Programs of the National Endowment for the Humanities, an independent federal agency. During the early stages of editing, support was provided by the Center for Editions of American Authors of the Modern Language Association.

Published by Princeton University Press, Princeton, New Jersey
In the United Kingdom: Princeton University Press, Guildford, Surrey

Library of Congress Cataloging in Publication Data will be found on the last printed page of this book
Clothbound editions of Princeton University Press books are printed on acid-free paper, and binding materials are chosen for strength and durability.
Printed in the United States of America by Princeton University Press, Princeton, New Jersey

The Writings

Walden, J. Lyndon Shanley (1971)

The Maine Woods, Joseph J. Moldenhauer (1972)

Reform Papers, Wendell Glick (1973)

Early Essays and Miscellanies, Joseph J. Moldenhauer and Edwin Moser, with Alexander C. Kern (1975)

A Week on the Concord and Merrimack Rivers, Carle F. Hovde (1980)

Excursions

Cape Cod

Poems

Translations

Nature Essays

Correspondence

Journal, William L. Howarth, John C. Broderick et al.

Contents

A Week on the Concord and Merrimack Rivers

Where'er thou sail'st who sailed with me,
Though now thou climbest loftier mounts,
And fairer rivers dost ascend,
Be thou my Muse, my Brother –.

I am bound, I am bound, for a distant shore,
By a lonely isle, by a far Azore,
There it is, there it is, the treasure I seek,
On the barren sands of a desolate creek.

I sailed up a river with a pleasant wind,
New lands, new people, and new thoughts to find;
Many fair reaches and headlands appeared,
And many dangers were there to be feared;
But when I remember where I have been,
And the fair landscapes that I have seen,
THOU seemest the only permanent shore,
The cape never rounded, nor wandered o'er.

Fluminaque obliquis cinxit declivia ripis;
Quæ, diversa locis, partim sorbentur ab ipsa;
In mare perveniunt partim, campoque recepta
Liberioris aquæ, pro ripis litora pulsant.

Ovid, Met. I. 39.

He confined the rivers within their sloping banks,
Which in different places are part absorbed by the earth,
Part reach the sea, and being received within the plain
Of its freer waters, beat the shore for banks.

Concord River.

> "Beneath low hills, in the broad interval
> Through which at will our Indian rivulet
> Winds mindful still of sannup and of squaw,
> Whose pipe and arrow oft the plough unburies,
> Here, in pine houses, built of new-fallen trees,
> Supplanters of the tribe, the farmers dwell."
>
> *Emerson.*

THE MUSKETAQUID, or Grass-ground River, though probably as old as the Nile or Euphrates, did not begin to have a place in civilized history, until the fame of its grassy meadows and its fish attracted settlers out of England in 1635, when it received the other but kindred name of CONCORD from the first plantation on its banks, which appears to have been commenced in a spirit of peace and harmony. It will be Grass-ground River as long as grass grows and water runs here; it will be Concord River only while men lead peaceable lives on its banks. To an extinct race it was grass-ground, where they hunted and fished, and it is still perennial grass-ground to Concord farmers, who own the Great Meadows, and get the hay from year to year. "One branch of it," according to the historian of Concord, for I love to quote so good authority, "rises in the south part of Hopkinton, and another from a pond and a large cedar swamp in Westborough," and flowing between Hopkinton and Southborough, through Framingham, and between Sudbury and Wayland, where it is sometimes called Sudbury River, it enters Concord at the south part of the town, and after receiving the North or Assabeth River, which has its source a little further to the north and west, goes out at the north-east angle, and flowing between Bedford and Carlisle, and through Billerica, empties into the Merrimack at Lowell. In Concord it is, in summer, from four to fifteen feet deep, and from one hundred to three hundred feet wide, but in the spring freshets, when it overflows its banks, it is in some places nearly a mile wide. Between Sudbury and Wayland the meadows acquire their greatest breadth, and when covered with water, they form a handsome chain of shallow vernal lakes, resorted to by numerous gulls and ducks. Just above Sherman's Bridge, between these towns, is the largest expanse, and when the wind blows freshly in a raw March day, heaving up the surface into dark and sober billows, or regular swells, skirted as it is in the distance with alder swamps and smoke-like maples, it looks like a smaller Lake Huron, and is very pleasant and exciting for a landsman to row or sail over. The farm-houses along the Sudbury shore, which rises gently to a considerable height, command fine water prospects at this season. The shore is more flat on the Wayland side, and this town is the greatest loser by the flood. Its farmers tell me that thousands of acres are flooded now, since the dams have been erected, where they remember to have seen the white honeysuckle or clover growing once, and they could go dry with shoes only in summer. Now there is nothing but blue-joint and sedge and cut-grass there, standing in water all the year round. For a long time, they made the most of the driest season to get their hay, working sometimes till nine o'clock at night, sedulously paring with their scythes in the twilight round the hummocks left by the ice; but now it is not worth the getting, when they can come at it, and they look sadly round to their wood-lots and upland as a last resource.

It is worth the while to make a voyage up this stream, if you go no farther than Sudbury, only to see how much country there is in the rear of us; great hills, and a hundred brooks, and farm-houses, and barns, and hay-stacks, you never saw before, and men every where, Sudbury, that is *Southborough* men, and Wayland, and Nine-Acre-Corner men, and Bound Rock, where four towns bound on a rock in the river, Lincoln, Wayland, Sudbury, Concord. Many waves are there agitated by the wind, keeping nature fresh, the spray blowing in your face, reeds and rushes waving; ducks by the hundred, all uneasy in the surf, in the raw wind, just ready to rise, and now going off with a clatter and a whistling like riggers, straight for Labrador, flying against the stiff gale with reefed wings, or else circling round first, with all their paddles briskly moving, just over the surf, to reconnoitre you before they leave these parts; gulls wheeling overhead, muskrats swimming for dear life, wet and cold, with no fire to warm them by, that you know of; their labored homes rising here and there like haystacks; and countless mice and moles, and winged titmice along the sunny windy shore; cranberries tossed on the waves, and heaving up on the beach, their little red skiffs beating about among the alders;—such healthy natural tumult as proves the last day is not yet at hand. And there stand all around the alders, and birches, and oaks, and maples full of glee and sap, holding in their buds until the waters subside. You shall, perhaps, run aground on Cranberry Island, only some spires of last year's pipe-grass above water, to show where the danger is, and get as good a freezing there as any where on the North-west Coast. I never voyaged so far in all my life. You shall see men you never heard of before, whose names you don't know, going away down through the meadows with long ducking guns, with water-tight boots, wading through the fowl-meadow grass, on bleak, wintry, distant shores, with guns at half cock, and they shall see teal, blue-winged, green-winged, shelldrakes, whistlers, black ducks, ospreys, and many other wild and noble sights before night, such as they who sit in parlors never dream of. You shall see rude and sturdy, experienced and wise men, keeping their castles, or teaming up their summer's wood, or chopping alone in the woods, men fuller of talk and rare adventure in the sun and wind and rain, than a chestnut is of meat; who were out not only in '75 and 1812, but have been out every day of their lives; greater men than Homer, or Chaucer, or Shakspeare, only they never got time to say so; they never took to the way of writing. Look at their fields, and imagine what they might write, if ever they should put pen to paper. Or what have they not written on the face of the earth already, clearing, and burning, and scratching, and harrowing, and plowing, and subsoiling, in and in, and out and out, and over and over, again and again, erasing what they had already written for want of parchment.

As yesterday and the historical ages are past, as the work of to-day is present, so some flitting perspectives, and demi-experiences of the life that is in nature are, in time, veritably future, or rather outside to time, perennial, young, divine, in the wind and rain which never die.

> The respectable folks,—
> Where dwell they?
> They whisper in the oaks,
> And they sigh in the hay;
> Summer and winter, night and day,
> Out on the meadow, there dwell they.

They never die,
Nor snivel, nor cry,
Nor ask our pity
With a wet eye.
A sound estate they ever mend,
To every asker readily lend;
To the ocean wealth,
To the meadow health,
To Time his length,
To the rocks strength,
To the stars light,
To the weary night,
To the busy day,
To the idle play;
And so their good cheer never ends,
For all are their debtors, and all their friends.

Concord River is remarkable for the gentleness of its current, which is scarcely perceptible, and some have referred to its influence, the proverbial moderation of the inhabitants of Concord, as exhibited in the Revolution, and on later occasions. It has been proposed, that the town should adopt for its coat of arms a field verdant, with the Concord circling nine times round. I have read that a descent of an eighth of an inch in a mile is sufficient to produce a flow. Our river has, probably, very near the smallest allowance. The story is current, at any rate, though I believe that strict history will not bear it out, that the only bridge ever carried away on the main branch, within the limits of the town, was driven up stream by the wind. But wherever it makes a sudden bend it is shallower and swifter, and asserts its title to be called a river. Compared with the other tributaries of the Merrimack, it appears to have been properly named Musketaquid, or Meadow River, by the Indians. For the most part, it creeps through broad meadows, adorned with scattered oaks, where the cranberry is found in abundance, covering the ground like a moss-bed. A row of sunken dwarf willows borders the stream on one or both sides, while at a greater distance the meadow is skirted with maples, alders, and other fluviatile trees, overrun with the grape vine, which bears fruit in its season, purple, red, white, and other grapes. Still further from the stream, on the edge of the firm land, are seen the gray and white dwellings of the inhabitants. According to the valuation of 1831, there were in Concord two thousand one hundred and eleven acres, or about one-seventh of the whole territory, in meadow; this standing next in the list after pasturage and unimproved lands, and, judging from the returns of previous years, the meadow is not reclaimed so fast as the woods are cleared.

Let us here read what old Johnson says of these meadows in his "Wonder-working Providence," which gives the account of New England from 1628 to 1652, and see how matters looked to him. He says of the Twelfth Church of Christ gathered at Concord: "This town is seated upon a fair fresh river, whose rivulets are filled with fresh marsh, and her streams with fish, it being a branch of that large river of Merrimack. Allwifes and shad in their season come up to this town, but salmon and dace cannot come up, by reason of the rocky falls, which causeth their meadows to lie much covered with water, the which these people, together with their neighbor town, have several times essayed to cut through but cannot, yet it may be turned another way with an hundred pound charge as it appeared." As to their farming he says: "Having laid out their estate upon cattle at 5 and 20 pound a cow, when they came to winter them with inland hay, and feed upon such wild fother as was never cut before, they could not hold out the winter, but, ordinarily the first or second year after their coming up to a new plantation, many of their cattle died." And this from the same author "Of the Planting of the 19th Church in the Mattachusets' Government, called Sudbury": "This year [does he mean 1654] the town and church of Christ at Sudbury began to have the first foundation stones laid, taking up her station in the inland country, as her elder sister Concord had formerly done, lying further up the same river, being furnished with great plenty of fresh marsh, but, it lying very low is much indamaged with land floods, insomuch that when the summer proves wet they lose part of their hay; yet are they so sufficiently provided that they take in cattle of other towns to winter."

The sluggish artery of the Concord meadows steals thus unobserved through the town, without a murmur or a pulse-beat, its general course from south-west to north-east, and its length about fifty miles; a huge volume of matter, ceaselessly rolling through the plains and valleys of the substantial earth, with the moccasined tread of an Indian warrior, making haste from the high places of the earth to its ancient reservoir. The murmurs of many a famous river on the other side of the globe reach even to us here, as to more distant dwellers on its banks; many a poet's stream floating the helms and shields of heroes on its bosom. The Xanthus or Scamander is not a mere dry channel and bed of a mountain torrent, but fed by the ever-flowing springs of fame;—

"And thou Simois, that as an arrowe, clere
Through Troy rennest, aie downward to the sea;—"

and I trust that I may be allowed to associate our muddy but much abused Concord river with the most famous in history.

"Sure there are poets which did never dream
Upon Parnassus, nor did taste the stream
Of Helicon; we therefore may suppose
Those made not poets, but the poets those."

The Mississippi, the Ganges, and the Nile, those journeying atoms from the Rocky Mountains, the Himmaleh, and Mountains of the Moon, have a kind of personal importance in the annals of the world. The heavens are not yet drained over their sources, but the Mountains of the Moon still send their annual tribute to the Pasha without fail, as they did to the Pharaohs, though he must collect the rest of his revenue at the point of the sword. Rivers must have been the guides which conducted the footsteps of the first travellers. They are the constant lure, when they flow by our doors, to distant enterprise and adventure, and, by a natural impulse, the dwellers on their banks will at length accompany their currents to the lowlands of the globe, or explore at their invitation the interior of continents. They are the natural highways of all nations, not only levelling the ground, and removing obstacles from the path of the traveller, quenching his thirst, and bearing him on their bosoms, but conducting him through the most interesting scenery, the most populous portions of the globe, and where the animal and vegetable kingdoms attain their greatest perfection.

I had often stood on the banks of the Concord, watching the lapse of the current, an emblem of all progress, following the same law with the system, with time, and all that is made; the weeds at the bottom gently bending down the stream, shaken by the watery wind, still planted where their seeds had sunk, but ere long to die and go down likewise; the shining pebbles, not yet anxious to better their condition, the chips and weeds, and occasional logs and stems of trees, that floated past, fulfilling their fate, were objects of singular interest to me, and at last I resolved to launch myself on its bosom, and float whither it would bear me.

Saturday.

"Come, come, my lovely fair, and let us try
These rural delicates."

Christ's Invitation to the Soul. Quarles.

AT length, on Saturday, the last day of August, 1839, we two, brothers, and natives of Concord, weighed anchor in this river port; for Concord, too, lies under the sun, a port of entry and departure for the bodies as well as the souls of men; one shore at least exempted from all duties but such as an honest man will gladly discharge. A warm drizzling rain had obscured the morning, and threatened to delay our voyage, but at length the leaves and grass were dried, and it came out a mild afternoon, as serene and fresh as if nature were maturing some greater scheme of her own. After this long dripping and oozing from every pore, she began to respire again more healthily than ever. So with a vigorous shove we launched our boat from the bank, while the flags and bullrushes curtseyed a God-speed, and dropped silently down the stream.

Our boat, which had cost us a week's labor in the spring, was in form like a fisherman's dory, fifteen feet long, by three and a half in breadth at the widest part, painted green below, with a border of blue, with reference to the two elements in which it was to spend its existence. It had been loaded the evening before at our door, half a mile from the river, with potatoes and melons from a patch which we had cultivated, and a few utensils, and was provided with wheels in order to be rolled around falls, as well as with two sets of oars, and several slender poles for shoving in shallow places, and also two masts, one of which served for a tent-pole at night; for a buffalo skin was to be our bed, and a tent of cotton cloth our roof. It was strongly built but heavy, and hardly of better model than usual. If rightly made, a boat would be a sort of amphibious animal, a creature of two elements, related by one half its structure to some swift and shapely fish, and by the other to some strong-winged and graceful bird. The fish shows where there should be the greatest breadth of beam and depth in the hold; its fins direct where to set the oars, and the tail gives some hint for the form and position of the rudder. The bird shows how to rig and trim the sails, and what form to give to the prow that it may balance the boat, and divide the air and water best. These hints we had but partially obeyed. But the eyes, though they are no sailors, will never be satisfied with any model, however fashionable, which does not answer all the requisitions of art. However, as art is all of a ship but the wood, and yet the wood alone will rudely serve the purpose of a ship, so our boat being of wood, gladly availed itself of the old law that the heavier shall float the lighter, and though a dull water fowl, proved a sufficient buoy for our purpose.

> "Were it the will of Heaven, an osier bough
> Were vessel safe enough the seas to plow."

Some village friends stood upon a promontory lower down the stream to wave us a last farewell; but we, having already performed these shore rites, with excusable reserve, as befits those who are embarked on unusual enterprises, who behold but speak not, silently glided past the firm lands of Concord, both peopled cape and lonely summer meadow with steady sweeps. And yet we did unbend so far as to let our guns speak for us, when at length we had swept out of sight, and thus left the woods to ring again with their echoes; and it may be that many russet-clad children lurking in those broad meadows with the bittern and the woodcock and the rail, though wholly concealed by brakes and hardhack and meadow-sweet, heard our salute that afternoon.

We were soon floating past the first regular battle ground of the Revolution, resting on our oars between the still visible abutments of that "North Bridge," over which in April, 1775, rolled the first faint tide of that war, which ceased not, till, as we read on the stone on our right, it "gave peace to these United States." As a Concord poet has sung,–

"By the rude bridge that arched the flood,
Their flag to April's breeze unfurled,
Here once the embattled farmers stood,
And fired the shot heard round the world.

"The foe long since in silence slept;
Alike the conqueror silent sleeps;
And Time the ruined bridge has swept
Down the dark stream which seaward creeps."

Our reflections had already acquired an historical remoteness from the scenes we had left, and we ourselves essayed to sing.

Ah, 't is in vain the peaceful din
That wakes the ignoble town,
Not thus did braver spirits win
A patriot's renown.

There is one field beside this stream,
Wherein no foot does fall,
But yet it beareth in my dream
A richer crop than all.

Let me believe a dream so dear,
  Some heart beat high that day,
Above the petty Province here,
  And Britain far away;

Some hero of the ancient mould,
  Some arm of knightly worth,
Of strength unbought, and faith unsold,
  Honored this spot of earth;

Who sought the prize his heart described,
  And did not ask release,
Whose free born valor was not bribed
  By prospect of a peace.

The men who stood on yonder height
  That day, are long since gone;
Not the same hand directs the fight
  And monumental stone.

Ye were the Grecian cities then,
  The Romes of modern birth,
Where the New England husbandmen
  Have shown a Roman worth.

In vain I search a foreign land,
  To find our Bunker Hill,
And Lexington and Concord stand
  By no Laconian rill.

With such thoughts we swept gently by this now peaceful pasture ground, on waves of Concord, in which was long since drowned the din of war.

But since we sailed
Some things have failed,
And many a dream
Gone down the stream.

Here then an aged shepherd dwelt,
Who to his flock his substance dealt,
And ruled them with a vigorous crook,
By precept of the sacred Book;
But he the pierless bridge passed o'er,
And solitary left the shore.

Anon a youthful pastor came,
Whose crook was not unknown to fame,
His lambs he viewed with gentle glance,
Spread o'er the country's wide expanse,
And fed with "Mosses from the Manse."
Here was our Hawthorne in the dale,
And here the shepherd told his tale.

That slight shaft had now sunk behind the hills, and we had floated round the neighboring bend, and under the new North Bridge between Ponkawtasset and the Poplar Hill, into the Great Meadows, which, like a broad moccasin print, have levelled a fertile and juicy place in nature.

On Ponkawtasset, since, we took our way,
Down this still stream to far Billericay,
A poet wise has settled, whose fine ray
Doth often shine on Concord's twilight day.

Like those first stars, whose silver beams on high,
Shining more brightly as the day goes by,
Most travellers cannot at first descry,
But eyes that wont to range the evening sky,

And know celestial lights, do plainly see,
And gladly hail them, numbering two or three;
For lore that's deep must deeply studied be,
As from deep wells men read star-poetry.

These stars are never pal'd, though out of sight,
But like the sun they shine forever bright;
Aye, *they* are suns, though earth must in its flight
Put out its eyes that it may see their light.

Who would neglect the least celestial sound,
Or faintest light that falls on earthly ground,
If he could know it one day would be found
That star in Cygnus whither we are bound,
And pale our sun with heavenly radiance round?

Gradually the village murmur subsided, and we seemed to be embarked on the placid current of our dreams, floating from past to future as silently as one awakes to fresh morning or evening thoughts. We glided noiselessly down the stream, occasionally driving a pickerel from the covert of the pads, or a bream from her nest, and the smaller bittern now and then sailed away on sluggish wings from some recess in the shore, or the larger lifted itself out of the long grass at our approach, and carried its precious legs away to deposit them in a place of safety. The tortoises also rapidly dropped into the water, as our boat ruffled the surface amid the willows breaking the reflections of the trees. The banks had passed the height of their beauty, and some of the brighter flowers showed by their faded tints that the season was verging towards the afternoon of the year; but this sombre tinge enhanced their sincerity, and in the still unabated heats they seemed like the mossy brink of some cool well. The narrow leaved willow (*Salix Purshiana*) lay along the surface of the water in masses of light green foliage, interspersed with the large white balls of the button-bush. The small rose-colored polygonum raised its head proudly above the water on either hand, and flowering at this season and in these localities, in front of dense fields of the white species, which skirted the sides of the stream, its little streak of red looked very rare and precious. The pure white blossoms of the arrow-head stood in the shallower parts, and a few cardinals on the margin still proudly surveyed themselves reflected in the water, though the latter, as well as the pickerel-weed, was now nearly out of blossom. The snake-head, *chelone glabra*, grew close to the shore, while a kind of coreopsis, turning its brazen face to the sun, full and rank, and a tall dull red flower, *eupatorium purpureum*, or trumpet weed, formed the rear rank of the fluvial array. The bright blue flowers of the soapwort gentian were sprinkled here and there in the adjacent meadows, like flowers which Proserpine had dropped, and still further in the fields, or higher on the bank, were seen the purple Gerardia, the Virginian rhexia, and drooping neottia or ladies'-tresses; while from the more distant waysides, which we occasionally passed, and banks where the sun had lodged, was reflected still a dull yellow beam from the ranks of tansy, now past its prime. In short, nature seemed to have adorned herself for our departure, with a profusion of fringes and curls, mingled with the bright tints of flowers, reflected in the water. But we missed the white water-lily, which is the queen of river-flowers, its reign being over for this season. He makes his voyage too late, perhaps, by a true water clock who delays so long. Many of this species inhabit our Concord water. I have passed down the river before sunrise on a summer morning, between fields of lilies still shut in sleep; and when at length the flakes of sunlight from over the bank fell on the surface of the water, whole fields of white blossoms seemed to flash open before me, as I floated along, like the unfolding of a banner, so sensible is this flower to the influence of the sun's rays.

As we were floating through the last of these familiar meadows, we observed the large and conspicuous flowers of the hibiscus, covering the dwarf willows, and mingled with the leaves of the grape, and wished that we could inform one of our friends behind of the locality of this somewhat rare and inaccessible flower, before it was too late to pluck it; but we were just gliding out of sight of the village spire before it occurred to us that the farmer in the adjacent meadow would go to church on the morrow, and would carry this news for us; and so by the Monday, while we should be floating on the Merrimack, our friend would be reaching to pluck this blossom on the bank of the Concord.

After a pause at Ball's Hill, the St. Ann's of Concord voyageurs, not to say any prayer for the success of our voyage, but to gather the few berries which were still left on the hills, hanging by very slender threads, we weighed anchor again, and were soon out of sight of our native village. The land seemed to grow fairer as we withdrew from it. Far away to the south-west lay the quiet village, left alone under its elms and button-woods in mid afternoon; and the hills, notwithstanding their blue, ethereal faces, seemed to cast a saddened eye on their old playfellows; but, turning short to the north, we bade adieu to their familiar outlines, and addressed ourselves to new scenes and adventures. Nought was familiar but the heavens, from under whose roof the voyageur never passes; but with their countenance, and the acquaintance we had with river and wood, we trusted to fare well under any circumstances.

From this point, the river runs perfectly straight for a mile or more to Carlisle Bridge, which consists of twenty wooden piers, and when we looked back over it, its surface was reduced to a line's breadth, and appeared like a cobweb gleaming in the sun. Here and there might be seen a pole sticking up, to mark the place where some fisherman had enjoyed unusual luck, and in return had consecrated his rod to the deities who preside over these shallows. It was full twice as broad as before, deep and tranquil, with a muddy bottom, and bordered with willows, beyond which spread broad lagoons covered with pads bulrushes and flags.

Late in the afternoon we passed a man on the shore fishing with a long birch pole, its silvery bark left on, and a dog at his side, rowing so near as to agitate his cork with our oars, and drive away luck for a season; and when we had rowed a mile as straight as an arrow, with our faces turned towards him, and the bubbles in our wake still visible on the tranquil surface, there stood the fisher still with his dog, like statues under the other side of the heavens, the only objects to relieve the eye in the extended meadow; and there would he stand abiding his luck, till he took his way home through the fields at evening with his fish. Thus, by one bait or another, Nature allures inhabitants into all her recesses. This man was the last of our townsmen whom we saw, and we silently through him bade adieu to our friends.

The characteristics and pursuits of various ages and races of men are always existing in epitome in every neighborhood. The pleasures of my earliest youth have become the inheritance of other men. This man is still a fisher, and belongs to an era in which I myself have lived. Perchance he is not confounded by many knowledges, and has not sought out many inventions, but how to take many fishes before the sun sets, with his slender birchen pole and flaxen line, that is invention enough for him. It is good even to be a fisherman in summer and in winter. Some men are judges these August days, sitting on benches, even till the court rises; they sit judging there honorably, between the seasons and between meals, leading a civil politic life, arbitrating in the case of Spaulding *versus* Cummings, it may be, from highest noon till the red vesper sinks into the west.

The fisherman, meanwhile, stands in three feet of water, under the same summer's sun, arbitrating in other cases between muckworm and shiner, amid the fragrance of water-lilies mint and pontederia, leading his life many rods from the dry land, within a pole's length of where the larger fishes swim. Human life is to him very much like a river,

—"renning aie downward to the sea."

This was his observation. His honor made a great discovery in bailments.

I can just remember an old brown-coated man who was the Walton of this stream, who had come over from Newcastle, England, with his son, the latter a stout and hearty man who had lifted an anchor in his day. A straight old man he was who took his way in silence through the meadows, having passed the period of communication with his fellows; his old experienced coat hanging long and straight and brown as the yellow pine bark, glittering with so much smothered sunlight, if you stood near enough, no work of art but naturalized at length. I often discovered him unexpectedly amid the pads and the gray willows when he moved, fishing in some old country method,—for youth and age then went a fishing together,—full of incommunicable thoughts, perchance about his own Tyne and Northumberland. He was always to be seen in serene afternoons haunting the river, and almost rustling with the sedge; so many sunny hours in an old man's life, entrapping silly fish, almost grown to be the sun's familar; what need had he of hat or raiment any, having served out his time, and seen through such thin disguises? I have seen how his coeval fates rewarded him with the yellow perch, and yet I thought his luck was not in proportion to his years; and I have seen when, with slow steps and weighed down with aged thoughts, he disappeared with his fish under his low-roofed house on the skirts of the village. I think nobody else saw him; nobody else remembers him now, for he soon after died, and migrated to new Tyne streams. His fishing was not a sport, nor solely a means of subsistence, but a sort of solemn sacrament and withdrawal from the world, just as the aged read their bibles.

Whether we live by the sea-side, or by the lakes and rivers, or on the prairie, it concerns us to attend to the nature of fishes, since they are not phenomena confined to certain localities only, but forms and phases of the life in nature universally dispersed. The countless shoals which annually coast the shores of Europe and America, are not so interesting to the student of nature, as the more fertile law itself, which deposits their spawn on the tops of mountains, and on the interior plains; the fish principle in nature, from which it results that they may be found in water in so many places, in greater or less numbers. The natural historian is not a fisherman, who prays for cloudy days and good luck merely, but as fishing has been styled, "a contemplative man's recreation," introducing him profitably to woods and water, so the fruit of the naturalist's observations is not in new genera or species, but in new contemplations still, and science is only a more contemplative man's recreation. The seeds of the life of fishes are every where disseminated, whether the winds waft them, or the waters float them, or the deep earth holds them; wherever a pond is dug, straightway it is stocked with this vivacious race. They have a lease of nature, and it is not yet out. The Chinese are bribed to carry their ova from province to province in jars or in hollow reeds, or the water-birds to transport them to the mountain tarns and interior lakes. There are fishes wherever there is a fluid medium, and even in clouds and in melted metals we detect their semblance. Think how in winter you can sink a line down straight in a pasture through snow and through ice, and pull up a bright, slippery, dumb, subterranean silver or golden fish! It is curious, also, to reflect how they make one family, from the largest to the smallest. The least minnow, that lies on the ice as bait for pickerel, looks like a huge sea-fish cast up on the shore. In the waters of this town there are about a dozen distinct species, though the inexperienced would expect many more.

It enhances our sense of the grand security and serenity of nature, to observe the still undisturbed economy and content of the fishes of this century, their happiness a regular fruit of the summer. The Fresh Water Sun Fish, Bream, or Ruff, *Pomotis vulgaris*, as it were, without ancestry, without posterity, still represents the Fresh Water Sun Fish in nature. It is the most common of all, and seen on every urchin's string; a simple and inoffensive fish, whose nests are visible all along the shore, hollowed in the sand, over which it is steadily poised through the summer hours on waving fin. Sometimes there are twenty or thirty nests in the space of a few rods, two feet wide by half a foot in depth, and made with no little labor, the weeds being removed, and the sand shoved up on the sides, like a bowl. Here it may be seen early in summer assiduously brooding, and driving away minnows and larger fishes, even its own species, which would disturb its ova, pursuing them a few feet, and circling round swiftly to its nest again: the minnows, like young sharks, instantly entering the empty nests, meanwhile, and swallowing the spawn, which is attached to the weeds and to the bottom, on the sunny side. The spawn is exposed to so many dangers, that a very small proportion can ever become fishes, for beside being the constant prey of birds and fishes, a great many nests are made so near the shore, in shallow water, that they are left dry in a few days, as the river goes down. These and the lamprey's are the only fishes' nests that I have observed, though the ova of some species may be seen floating on the surface. The breams are so careful of their charge that you may stand close by in the water and examine them at your leisure. I have thus stood over them half an hour at a time, and stroked them familiarly without frightening them, suffering them to nibble my fingers harmlessly, and seen them erect their dorsal fins in anger when my hand approached their ova, and have even taken them gently out of the water with my hand; though this cannot be accomplished by a sudden movement, however dexterous, for instant warning is conveyed to them through their denser element, but only by letting the fingers gradually close about them as they are poised over the palm, and with the utmost gentleness raising them slowly to the surface. Though stationary, they keep up a constant sculling or waving motion with their fins, which is exceedingly graceful, and expressive of their humble happiness; for unlike ours, the element in which they live is a stream which must be constantly resisted. From time to time they nibble the weeds at the bottom or overhanging their nests, or dart after a fly or a worm. The dorsal fin, besides answering the purpose of a keel, with the anal, serves to keep the fish upright, for in shallow water, where this is not covered, they fall on their sides. As you stand thus stooping over the bream in its nest, the edges of the dorsal and caudal fins have a singular dusty golden reflection, and its eyes, which stand out from the head, are transparent and colorless. Seen in its native element, it is a very beautiful and compact fish, perfect in all its parts, and looks like a brilliant coin fresh from the mint. It is a perfect jewel of the river, the green, red, coppery, and golden reflections of its mottled sides being the concentration of such rays as struggle through the floating pads and flowers to the sandy bottom, and in harmony with the sunlit brown and yellow pebbles. Behind its watery shield it dwells far from many accidents inevitable to human life.

There is also another species of bream found in our river, without the red spot on the operculum, which, according to M. Agassiz, is undescribed.

The Common Perch, *Perca flavescens*, which name describes well the gleaming, golden reflections of its scales as it is drawn out of the water, its red gills standing out in vain in the thin element, is one of the handsomest and most regularly formed of our fishes, and at such a moment as this reminds us of the fish in the picture, which wished to be restored to its native element until it had grown larger; and indeed most of this species that are caught are not half grown. In the ponds there is a light-colored and slender kind, which swim in shoals of many hundreds in the sunny water, in company with the shiner, averaging not more than six or seven inches in length, while only a few larger specimens are found in the deepest water, which prey upon their weaker brethren. I have often attracted these small perch to the shore at evening, by rippling the water with my fingers, and they may sometimes be caught while attempting to pass inside your hands. It is a tough and heedless fish, biting from impulse, without nibbling, and from impulse refraining to bite, and sculling indifferently past. It rather prefers the clear water and sandy bottoms, though here it has not much choice. It is a true fish, such as the angler loves to put into his basket or hang at the top of his willow twig, in shady afternoons along the banks of the stream. So many unquestionable fishes he counts, and so many shiners, which he counts and then throws away. Old Josselyn in his "New England's Rarities," published in 1672, mentions the Perch or River Partridge.

The Chivin, Dace, Roach, Cousin Trout, or whatever else it is called, *Leuciscus pulchellus*, white and red, always an unexpected prize, which, however, any angler is glad to hook for its rarity. A name that reminds us of many an unsuccessful ramble by swift streams, when the wind rose to disappoint the fisher. It is commonly a silvery soft-scaled fish, of graceful, scholarlike and classical look, like many a picture in an English book. It loves a swift current and a sandy bottom, and bites inadvertently, yet not without appetite for the bait. The minnows are used as bait for pickerel in the winter. The red chivin, according to some, is still the same fish, only older, or with its tints deepened as they think by the darker water it inhabits, as the red clouds swim in the twilight atmosphere. He who has not hooked the red chivin is not yet a complete angler. Other fishes, methinks, are slightly amphibious, but this is a denizen of the water wholly. The cork goes dancing down the swift rushing stream, amid the weeds and sands, when suddenly, by a coincidence never to be remembered, emerges this fabulous inhabitant of another element, a thing heard of but not seen, as if it were the instant creation of an eddy, a true product of the running stream. And this bright cupreous dolphin was spawned and has passed its life beneath the level of your feet in your native fields. Fishes too, as well as birds and clouds, derive their armor from the mine. I have heard of mackerel visiting the copper banks at a particular season; this fish, perchance, has its habitat in the Coppermine river. I have caught white chivin of great size in the Aboljacknagesic, where it empties into the Penobscot, at the base of Mount Ktaadn, but no red ones there. The latter variety seems not to have been sufficiently observed.

The Dace, *Leuciscus argenteus*, is a slight silvery minnow, found generally in the middle of the stream, where the current is most rapid, and frequently confounded with the last named.

The Shiner, *Leuciscus crysoleucas*, is a soft-scaled and tender fish, the victim of its stronger neighbors, found in all places, deep and shallow, clear and turbid; generally the first nibbler at the bait, but with its small mouth and nibbling propensities not easily caught. It is a gold or silver bit that passes current in the river, its limber tail dimpling the surface in sport or flight. I have seen the fry, when frightened by something thrown into the water, leap out by dozens, together with the dace, and wreck themselves upon a floating plank. It is the little light-infant of the river, with body armor of gold or silver spangles, slipping, gliding its life through with a quirk of the tail, half in the water, half in the air, upward and ever upward with flitting fin to more crystalline tides, yet still abreast of us dwellers on the bank. It is almost dissolved by the summer heats. A slighter and lighter colored shiner is found in one of our ponds.

The Pickerel, *Esox reticulatus*, the swiftest, wariest, and most ravenous of fishes, which Josselyn calls the Fresh-Water or River Wolf, is very common in the shallow and weedy lagoons along the sides of the stream. It is a solemn, stately, ruminant fish, lurking under the shadow of a pad at noon, with still, circumspect, voracious eye, motionless as a jewel set in water, or moving slowly along to take up its position, darting from time to time at such unlucky fish or frog or insect as comes within its range, and swallowing it at a gulp. I have caught one which had swallowed a brother pickerel half as large as itself, with the tail still visible in its mouth, while the head was already digested in its stomach. Sometimes a striped snake, bound to greener meadows across the stream, ends its undulatory progress in the same receptacle. They are so greedy and impetuous that they are frequently caught by being entangled in the line the moment it is cast. Fishermen also distinguish the brook pickerel, a shorter and thicker fish than the former.

The Horned Pout, *Pimelodus nebulosus*, sometimes called Minister, from the peculiar squeaking noise it makes when drawn out of the water, is a dull and blundering fellow, and like the eel vespertinal in his habits, and fond of the mud. It bites deliberately as if about its business. They are taken at night with a mass of worms strung on a thread, which catches in their teeth, sometimes three or four, with an eel, at one pull. They are extremely tenacious of life, opening and shutting their mouths for half an hour after their heads have been cut off. A bloodthirsty and bullying race of rangers, inhabiting the fertile river bottoms, with ever a lance in rest, and ready to do battle with their nearest neighbor. I have observed them in summer, when every other one had a long and bloody scar upon his back, where the skin was gone, the mark, perhaps, of some fierce encounter. Sometimes the fry, not an inch long, are seen darkening the shore with their myriads.

The Suckers, *Catostomi Bostonienses* and *tuberculati*, Common and Horned, perhaps on an average the largest of our fishes, may be seen in shoals of a hundred or more, stemming the current in the sun, on their mysterious migrations, and sometimes sucking in the bait which the fisherman suffers to float toward them. The former, which sometimes grow to a large size, are frequently caught by the hand in the brooks, or like the red chivin, are jerked out by a hook fastened firmly to the end of a stick, and placed under their jaws. They are hardly known to the mere angler, however, not often biting at his baits, though the spearer carries home many a mess in the spring. To our village eyes, these shoals have a foreign and imposing aspect, realizing the fertility of the seas.

The Common Eel, too, *Muræna Bostoniensis*, the only species of eel known in the State, a slimy, squirming creature, informed of mud, still squirming in the pan, is speared and hooked up with various success. Methinks it too occurs in picture, left after the deluge, in many a meadow high and dry.

In the shallow parts of the river, where the current is rapid, and the bottom pebbly, you may sometimes see the curious circular nests of the Lamprey Eel, *Petromyzon Americanus*, the American Stone-Sucker, as large as a cart wheel, a foot or two in height, and sometimes rising half a foot above the surface of the water. They collect these stones, of the size of a hen's egg, with their mouths, as their name implies, and are said to fashion them into circles with their tails. They ascend falls by clinging to the stones, which may sometimes be raised, by lifting the fish by the tail. As they are not seen on their way down the streams, it is thought by fishermen that they never return, but waste away and die, clinging to rocks and stumps of trees for an indefinite period; a tragic feature in the scenery of the river bottoms, worthy to be remembered with Shakspeare's description of the sea-floor. They are rarely seen in our waters at present, on account of the dams, though they are taken in great quantities at the mouth of the river in Lowell. Their nests, which are very conspicuous, look more like art than any thing in the river.

If we had leisure this afternoon, we might turn our prow up the brooks in quest of the classical trout and the minnows. Of the last alone, according to M. Agassiz, several of the species found in this town, are yet undescribed. These would, perhaps, complete the list of our finny contemporaries in the Concord waters.

Salmon, Shad, and Alewives, were formerly abundant here, and taken in weirs by the Indians, who taught this method to the whites, by whom they were used as food and as manure, until the dam, and afterward the canal at Billerica, and the factories at Lowell, put an end to their migrations hitherward; though it is thought that a few more enterprising shad may still occasionally be seen in this part of the river. It is said, to account for the destruction of the fishery, that those who at that time represented the interests of the fishermen and the fishes, remembering between what dates they were accustomed to take the grown shad, stipulated, that the dams should be left open for that season only, and the fry, which go down a month later, were consequently stopped and destroyed by myriads. Others say that the fish-ways were not properly constructed. Perchance, after a few thousands of years, if the fishes will be patient, and pass their summers elsewhere, meanwhile, nature will have levelled the Billerica dam, and the Lowell factories, and the Grass-ground River run clear again, to be explored by new migratory shoals, even as far as the Hopkinton pond and Westborough swamp.

One would like to know more of that race, now extinct, whose seines lie rotting in the garrets of their children, who openly professed the trade of fishermen, and even fed their townsmen creditably, not skulking through the meadows to a rainy afternoon sport. Dim visions we still get of miraculous draughts of fishes, and heaps uncountable by the river-side, from the tales of our seniors sent on horse-back in their childhood from the neighboring towns, perched on saddle-bags, with instructions to get the one bag filled with shad, the other with alewives. At least one memento of those days may still exist in the memory of this generation, in the familiar appellation of a celebrated train-band of this town, whose untrained ancestors stood creditably at Concord North Bridge. Their captain, a man of piscatory tastes, having duly warned his company to turn out on a certain day, they, like obedient soldiers, appeared promptly on parade at the appointed time, but, unfortunately, they went undrilled, except in the maneuvres of a soldier's wit and unlicensed jesting, that May day; for their captain, forgetting his own appointment, and warned only by the favorable aspect of the heavens, as he had often done before, went a fishing that afternoon, and his company thenceforth was known to old and young, grave and gay, as "The Shad," and by the youths of this vicinity, this was long regarded as the proper name of all the irregular militia in Christendom. But, alas, no record of these fishers' lives remains, that we know of, unless it be one brief page of hard but unquestionable history, which occurs in Day Book No. 4. of an old trader of this town, long since dead, which shows pretty plainly what constituted a fisherman's stock in trade in those days. It purports to be a Fisherman's Account Current, probably for the fishing season of the year 1805, during which months he purchased daily rum and sugar, sugar and rum, N. E. and W. I., "one cod line," "one brown mug," and "a line for the seine;" rum and sugar, sugar and rum, "good loaf sugar," and "good brown," W. I. and N. E., in short and uniform entries to the bottom of the page, all carried out in pounds shillings and pence, from March 25th to June 5th, and promptly settled by receiving "cash in full" at the last date. But perhaps not so settled altogether. These were the necessaries of life in those days; with salmon, shad, and alewives, fresh and pickled, he was thereafter independent on the groceries. Rather a preponderance of the fluid elements; but such is the fisherman's nature. I can faintly remember to have seen this same fisher in my earliest youth, still as near the river as he could get, with uncertain undulatory step, after so many things had gone down stream, swinging a scythe in the meadow, his bottle like a serpent hid in the grass; himself as yet not cut down by the Great Mower.

Surely the fates are forever kind, though Nature's laws are more immutable than any despot's, yet to man's daily life they rarely seem rigid, but permit him to relax with license in summer weather. He is not harshly reminded of the things he may not do. She is very kind and liberal to all men of vicious habits, and certainly does not deny them quarter; they do not die without priest. Still they maintain life along the way, keeping this side the Styx, still hearty, still resolute, "never better in their lives;" and again, after a dozen years have elapsed, they start up from behind a hedge, asking for work and wages for able-bodied men. Who has not met such

—"a beggar on the way,
Who sturdily could gang?" * * *
"Who cared neither for wind nor wet,
In lands where'er he past?"

"That bold adopts each house he views, his own;
Makes every pulse his checquer; and, at pleasure,
Walks forth, and taxes all the world, like Cæsar"—

As if consistency were the secret of health, while the poor inconsistent aspirant man, seeking to live a pure life, feeding on air, divided against himself, cannot stand, but pines and dies after a life of sickness, on beds of down.

The unwise are accustomed to speak as if some were not sick; but methinks the difference between men in respect to health is not great enough to lay much stress upon. Some are reputed sick and some are not. It often happens that the sicker man is the nurse to the sounder.

Shad are still taken in the basin of Concord River at Lowell, where they are said to be a month earlier than the Merrimack shad, on account of the warmth of the water. Still patiently, almost pathetically, with instinct not to be discouraged, not to be *reasoned* with, revisiting their old haunts, as if their stern fates would relent, and still met by the Corporation with its dam. Poor shad! where is thy redress? When Nature gave thee instinct, gave she thee the heart to bear thy fate? Still wandering the sea in thy scaly armor to inquire humbly at the mouths of rivers if man has perchance left them free for thee to enter. By countless shoals loitering uncertain meanwhile, merely stemming the tide there, in danger from sea foes in spite of thy bright armor, awaiting new instructions, until the sands, until the water itself, tell thee if it be so or not. Thus by whole migrating nations, full of instinct, which is thy faith, in this backward spring, turned adrift, and perchance knowest not where men do *not* dwell, where there are *not* factories, in these days. Armed with no sword, no electric shock, but mere Shad, armed only with innocence and a just cause, with tender dumb mouth only forward, and scales easy to be detached. I for one am with thee, and who knows what may avail a crow-bar against that Billerica dam?—Not despairing when whole myriads have gone to feed those sea monsters during thy suspense, but still brave, indifferent, on easy fin there, like shad reserved for higher destinies. Willing to be decimated for man's behoof after the spawning season. Away with the superficial and selfish phil-*anthropy* of men,—who knows what admirable virtue of fishes may be below low-water mark, bearing up against a hard destiny, not admired by that fellow creature who alone can appreciate it! Who hears the fishes when they cry? It will not be forgotten by some memory that we were contemporaries. Thou shalt ere long have thy way up the rivers, up all the rivers of the globe, if I am not mistaken. Yea, even thy dull watery dream shall be more than realized. If it were not so, but thou wert to be overlooked at first and at last, then would not I take their heaven. Yes, I say so, who think I know better than thou canst. Keep a stiff fin then, and stem all the tides thou mayest meet.

At length it would seem that the interests, not of the fishes only, but of the men of Wayland, of Sudbury, of Concord, demand the levelling of that dam. Innumerable acres of meadow are waiting to be made dry land, wild native grass to give place to English. The farmers stand with scythes whet, waiting the subsiding of the waters, by gravitation, by evaporation or otherwise, but sometimes their eyes do not rest, their wheels do not roll, on the quaking meadow ground during the haying season at all. So many sources of wealth inaccessible. They rate the loss hereby incurred in the single town of Wayland alone as equal to the expense of keeping a hundred yoke of oxen the year round. One year, as I learn, not long ago, the farmers standing ready to drive their teams afield as usual, the water gave no signs of falling; without new attraction in the heavens, without freshet or visible cause, still standing stagnant at an unprecedented height. All hydrometers were at fault; some trembled for their English even. But speedy emissaries revealed the unnatural secret, in the new float-board, wholly a foot in width, added to their already too high privileges by the dam proprietors. The hundred yoke of oxen, meanwhile, standing patient, gazing wishfully meadowward, at that inaccessible waving native grass, uncut but by the great mower Time, who cuts so broad a swathe, without so much as a wisp to wind about their horns.

That was a long pull from Ball's Hill to Carlisle Bridge, sitting with our faces to the south, a slight breeze rising from the north, but nevertheless water still runs and grass grows, for now, having passed the bridge between Carlisle and Bedford, we see men haying far off in the meadow, their heads waving like the grass which they cut. In the distance the wind seemed to bend all alike. As the night stole over, such a freshness was wafted across the meadow that every blade of cut-grass seemed to teem with life. Faint purple clouds began to be reflected in the water, and the cow-bells tinkled louder along the banks, while, like sly water rats, we stole along nearer the shore, looking for a place to pitch our camp.

At length, when we had made about seven miles, as far as Billerica, we moored our boat on the west side of a little rising ground which in the spring forms an island in the river. Here we found huckleberries still hanging upon the bushes, where they seemed to have slowly ripened for our especial use. Bread and sugar, and cocoa boiled in river water made our repast, and as we had drank in the fluvial prospect all day, so now we took a draught of the water with our evening meal to propitiate the river gods, and whet our vision for the sights it was to behold. The sun was setting on the one hand, while our eminence was contributing its shadow to the night, on the other. It seemed insensibly to grow lighter as the night shut in, and a distant and solitary farm-house was revealed, which before lurked in the shadows of the noon. There was no other house in sight, nor any cultivated field. To the right and left, as far as the horizon, were straggling pine woods with their plumes against the sky, and across the river were rugged hills, covered with shrub oaks, tangled with grape vines and ivy, with here and there a gray rock jutting out from the maze. The sides of these cliffs, though a quarter of a mile distant, were almost heard to rustle while we looked at them, it was such a leafy wilderness; a place for fauns and satyrs, and where bats hung all day to the rocks, and at evening flitted over the water, and fireflies husbanded their light under the grass and leaves against the night. When we had pitched our tent on the hill-side, a few rods from the shore, we sat looking through its triangular door in the twilight at our lonely mast on the shore, just seen above the alders, and hardly yet come to a stand-still from the swaying of the stream; the first encroachment of commerce on this land. There was our port, our Ostia. That straight geometrical line against the water and the sky stood for the last refinements of civilized life, and what of sublimity there is in history was there symbolized.

For the most part, there was no recognition of human life in the night, no human breathing was heard, only the breathing of the wind. As we sat up, kept awake by the novelty of our situation, we heard at intervals foxes stepping about over the dead leaves, and brushing the dewy grass close to our tent, and once a musquash fumbling among the potatoes and melons in our boat, but when we hastened to the shore we could detect only a ripple in the water ruffling the disk of a star. At intervals we were serenaded by the song of a dreaming sparrow or the throttled cry of an owl, but after each sound which near at hand broke the stillness of the night, each crackling of the twigs, or rustling among the leaves, there was a sudden pause, and deeper and more conscious silence, as if the intruder were aware that no life was rightfully abroad at that hour. There was a fire in Lowell, as we judged, this night, and we saw the horizon blazing, and heard the distant alarm bells, as it were a faint tinkling music borne to these woods. But the most constant and memorable sound of a summer's night, which we did not fail to hear every night afterward, though at no time so incessantly and so favorably as now, was the barking of the house dogs, from the loudest and hoarsest bark to the faintest aerial palpitation under the eaves of heaven, from the patient but anxious mastiff to the timid and wakeful terrier, at first loud and rapid, then faint and slow, to be imitated only in a whisper; wow-wow-wow-wow—wo ——wo——w——w. Even in a retired and uninhabited district like this, it was a sufficiency of sound for the ear of night, and more impressive than any music. I have heard the voice of a hound, just before daylight, while the stars were shining, from over the woods and river, far in the horizon, when it sounded as sweet and melodious as an instrument. The hounding of a dog pursuing a fox or other animal in the horizon, may have first suggested the notes of the hunting horn to alternate with and relieve the lungs of the dog. This natural bugle long resounded in the woods of the ancient world before the horn was invented. The very dogs that sullenly bay the moon from farm-yards in these nights, excite more heroism in our breasts than all the civil exhortations or war sermons of the age. "I had rather be a dog, and bay the moon," than many a Roman that I know. The night is equally indebted to the clarion of the cock, with wakeful hope, from the very setting of the sun, prematurely ushering in the dawn. All these sounds, the crowing of cocks, the baying of dogs, and the hum of insects at noon, are the evidence of nature's health or *sound* state. Such is the never failing beauty and accuracy of language, the most perfect art in the world; the chisel of a thousand years retouches it.

At length the antepenultimate and drowsy hours drew on, and all sounds were denied entrance to our ears.

Who sleeps by day and walks by night,
Will meet no spirit but some sprite.

Sunday.

> "The river calmly flows,
> Through shining banks, through lonely glen,
> Where the owl shrieks, though ne'er the cheer of men
> Has stirred its mute repose,
> Still if you should walk there, you would go there again."
>
> *Channing.*

> "The Indians tell us of a beautiful River lying far to the south, which they call Merrimac."
>
> *Sieur de Monts. Relations of the Jesuits*, 1604.

In the morning the river and adjacent country were covered with a dense fog, through which the smoke of our fire curled up like a still subtiler mist; but before we had rowed many rods, the sun arose and the fog rapidly dispersed, leaving a slight steam only to curl along the surface of the water. It was a quiet Sunday morning, with more of the auroral rosy and white than of the yellow light in it, as if it dated from earlier than the fall of man, and still preserved a heathenish integrity;–

> An early unconverted Saint,
> Free from noontide or evening taint,
> Heathen without reproach,
> That did upon the civil day encroach,
> And ever since its birth
> Had trod the outskirts of the earth.

But the impressions which the morning makes vanish with its dews, and not even the most "persevering mortal" can preserve the memory of its freshness to mid-day. As we passed the various islands, or what were islands in the spring, rowing with our backs down stream, we gave names to them. The one on which we had camped we called Fox Island, and one fine densely wooded island surrounded by deep water and overrun by grape vines, which looked like a mass of verdure and of flowers cast upon the waves, we named Grape Island. From Ball's Hill to Billerica meeting-house the river was still twice as broad as in Concord, a deep, dark, and dead stream, flowing between gentle hills and sometimes cliffs, and well wooded all the way. It was a long woodland lake bordered with willows. For long reaches we could see neither house nor cultivated field, nor any sign of the vicinity of man. Now we coasted along some shallow shore by the edge of a dense palisade of bulrushes, which straightly bounded the water as if clipt by art, reminding us of the reed forts of the East Indians, of which we had read; and now the bank slightly raised was overhung with graceful grasses and various species of brake, whose downy stems stood closely grouped and naked as in a vase, while their heads spread several feet on either side. The dead limbs of the willow were rounded and adorned by the climbing mikania, *mikania scandens*, which filled every crevice in the leafy bank, contrasting agreeably with the gray bark of its supporter and the balls of the button-bush. The water willow, *salix Purshiana*, when it is of large size and entire, is the most graceful and ethereal of our trees. Its masses of light green foliage, piled one upon another to the height of twenty or thirty feet, seemed to float on the surface of the water, while the slight gray stems and the shore were hardly visible between them. No tree is so wedded to the water, and harmonizes so well with still streams. It is even more graceful than the weeping willow, or any pendulous trees, which dip their branches in the stream instead of being buoyed up by it. Its limbs curved outward over the surface as if attracted by it. It had not a New England but an oriental character, reminding us of trim Persian gardens, of Haroun Alraschid, and the artificial lakes of the east.

As we thus dipped our way along between fresh masses of foliage overrun with the grape and smaller flowering vines, the surface was so calm, and both air and water so transparent, that the flight of a kingfisher or robin over the river was as distinctly seen reflected in the water below as in the air above. The birds seemed to flit through submerged groves, alighting on the yielding sprays, and their clear notes to come up from below. We were uncertain whether the water floated the land, or the land held the water in its bosom. It was such a season, in short, as that in which one of our Concord poets sailed on its stream, and sung its quiet glories.

"There is an inward voice, that in the stream
Sends forth its spirit to the listening ear,
And in a calm content it floweth on,
Like wisdom, welcome with its own respect.
Clear in its breast lie all these beauteous thoughts,
It doth receive the green and graceful trees,
And the gray rocks smile in its peaceful arms,"—

And more he sung, but too serious for our page. For every oak and birch too growing on the hill-top, as well as for these elms and willows, we knew that there was a graceful ethereal and ideal tree making down from the roots, and sometimes nature in high tides brings her mirror to its foot and makes it visible. The stillness was intense and almost conscious, as if it were a natural Sabbath, and we fancied that the morning was the evening of a celestial day. The air was so elastic and crystalline that it had the same effect on the landscape that a glass has on a picture, to give it an ideal remoteness and perfection. The landscape was clothed in a mild and quiet light, in which the woods and fences checkered and partitioned it with new regularity, and rough and uneven fields stretched away with lawn-like smoothness to the horizon, and the clouds, finely distinct and picturesque, seemed a fit drapery to hang over fairy-land. The world seemed decked for some holiday or prouder pageantry, with silken streamers flying, and the course of our lives to wind on before us like a green lane into a country maze, at the season when fruit trees are in blossom.

Why should not our whole life and its scenery be actually thus fair and distinct? All our lives want a suitable background. They should at least, like the life of the anchorite, be as impressive to behold as objects in the desert, a broken shaft or crumbling mound against a limitless horizon. Character always secures for itself this advantage, and is thus distinct and unrelated to near or trivial objects, whether things or persons. On this same stream a maiden once sailed in my boat, thus unattended but by invisible guardians, and as she sat in the prow there was nothing but herself between the steersman and the sky. I could then say with the poet;—

"Sweet falls the summer air
Over her frame who sails with me;
Her way like that is beautifully free,
Her nature far more rare,
And is her constant heart of virgin purity."

At evening still the very stars seem but this maiden's emissaries and reporters of her progress.

Low in the eastern sky
Is set thy glancing eye;
And though its gracious light
Ne'er riseth to my sight,
Yet every star that climbs
Above the gnarled limbs
Of yonder hill,
Conveys thy gentle will.

Believe I knew thy thought,
And that the zephyrs brought
Thy kindest wishes through,
As mine they bear to you,
That some attentive cloud
Did pause amid the crowd
Over my head,
While gentle things were said.

Believe the thrushes sung,
And that the flower bells rung,
That herbs exhaled their scent,
And beasts knew what was meant,
The trees a welcome waved,
And lakes their margins laved,
When thy free mind
To my retreat did wind.

It was a summer eve,
The air did gently heave,
While yet a low hung cloud
Thy eastern skies did shroud;
The lightning's silent gleam,
Startling my drowsy dream,
Seemed like the flash
Under thy dark eyelash.

Still will I strive to be
As if thou wert with me;
Whatever path I take,
It shall be for thy sake,

Of gentle slope and wide,
As thou wert by my side,
    Without a root
To trip thy gentle foot.

I'll walk with gentle pace,
And choose the smoothest place,
And careful dip the oar,
And shun the winding shore,
And gently steer my boat,
Where water lilies float,
    And cardinal flowers
Stand in their sylvan bowers.

It required some rudeness to disturb with our boat the mirror-like surface of the water, in which every twig and blade of grass was so faithfully reflected; too faithfully indeed for art to imitate, for only nature may exaggerate herself. The shallowest still water is unfathomable. Wherever the trees and skies are reflected there is more than Atlantic depth, and no danger of fancy running aground. We noticed that it required a separate intention of the eye, a more free and abstracted vision, to see the reflected trees and the sky, than to see the river bottom merely; and so are there manifold visions in the direction of every object, and even the most opaque reflect the heavens from their surface. Some men have their eyes naturally intended to the one, and some to the other object.

"A man that looks on glass,
    On it may stay his eye,
Or, if he pleaseth, through it pass,
    And the heavens espy."

Two men in a skiff, whom we passed hereabouts, floating buoyantly amid the reflections of the trees, like a feather in mid air, or a leaf which is wafted gently from its twig to the water without turning over, seemed still in their element, and to have very delicately availed themselves of the natural laws. Their floating there was a beautiful and successful experiment in natural philosophy, and it served to enoble in our eyes the art of navigation, for as birds fly and fishes swim, so these men sailed. It reminded us how much fairer and nobler all the actions of man might be, and that our life in its whole economy might be as beautiful as the fairest works of art or nature.

The sun lodged on the old gray cliffs, and glanced from every pad; the bulrushes and flags seemed to rejoice in the delicious light and air; the meadows were a drinking at their leisure; the frogs sat meditating, all sabbath thoughts, summing up their week, with one eye out on the golden sun, and one toe upon a reed, eyeing the wondrous universe in which they act their part; the fishes swam more staid and soberly, as maidens go to church; shoals of golden and silver minnows rose to the surface to behold the heavens, and then sheered off into more sombre aisles; they swept by as if moved by one mind, continually gliding past each other, and yet preserving the form of their battalion unchanged, as if they were still embraced by the transparent membrane which held the spawn; a young band of brethren and sisters, trying their new fins; now they wheeled, now shot ahead, and when we drove them to the shore and cut them off, they dexterously tacked and passed underneath the boat. Over the old wooden bridges no traveller crossed, and neither the river nor the fishes avoided to glide between the abutments.

Here was a village not far off behind the woods, Billerica, settled not long ago, and the children still bear the names of the first settlers in this late "howling wilderness;" yet to all intents and purposes it is as old as Fernay or as Mantua, an old gray town, where men grow old and sleep already under moss-grown monuments, outgrow their usefulness. This is ancient Billerica, (Villa-rica?) now in its dotage, named from the English Billericay, and whose Indian name was Shawshine. I never heard that it was young. See, is not nature here gone to decay, farms all run out, meeting-house grown gray and racked with age? If you would know of its early youth, ask those old gray rocks in the pasture. It has a bell that sounds sometimes as far as Concord woods; I have heard that,—aye, hear it now. No wonder that such a sound startled the dreaming Indian, and frightened his game, when the first bells were swung on trees, and sounded through the forest beyond the plantations of the white man. But to-day I like best the echo amid these cliffs and woods. It is no feeble imitation, but rather its original, or as if some rural Orpheus played over the strain again to show how it should sound.

Dong, sounds the brass in the east,
As if to a funeral feast,
But I like that sound the best
Out of the fluttering west.

The steeple ringeth a knell,
But the fairies' silvery bell
Is the voice of that gentle folk,
Or else the horizon that spoke.

Its metal is not of brass,
But air, and water, and glass,
And under a cloud it is swung,
And by the wind it is rung.

When the steeple tolleth the noon,
It soundeth not so soon,
Yet it rings a far earlier hour,
And the sun has not reached its tower.

On the other hand, the road runs up to Carlisle, city of the woods, which, if it is less civil, is the more natural. It does well hold the earth together. It gets laughed at because it is a small town, I know, but nevertheless it is a place where great men may be born any day, for fair winds and foul blow right on over it without distinction. It has a meeting-house and horse-sheds, a tavern and a blacksmith's shop, for centre, and a good deal of wood to cut and cord yet. And

> "Bedford, most noble Bedford,
> I shall not thee forget."

History has remembered thee; especially that meek and humble petition of thy old planters, like the wailing of the Lord's own people, "To the gentlemen, the selectmen" of Concord, praying to be erected into a separate parish. We can hardly credit that so plaintive a psalm resounded but little more than a century ago along these Babylonish waters. "In the extreme difficult seasons of heat and cold," said they, "we were ready to say of the Sabbath, Behold what a weariness is it."—"Gentlemen, if our seeking to draw off proceed from any disaffection to our present Reverend Pastor, or the Christian Society with whom we have taken such sweet counsel together, and walked unto the house of God in company, then hear us not this day, but we greatly desire, if God please, to be eased of our burden on the Sabbath, the travel and fatigue thereof, that the word of God may be nigh to us, near to our houses, and in our hearts, that we and our little ones may serve the Lord. We hope that God, who stirred up the spirit of Cyrus to set forward temple work, has stirred us up to ask, and will stir you up to grant, the prayer of our petition; so shall your humble petitioners ever pray, as in duty bound,—."

And so the temple work went forward here to a happy conclusion. Yonder in Carlisle the building of the temple was many wearisome years delayed, not that there was wanting of Shittim wood, or the gold of Ophir, but a site therefor convenient to all the worshippers; whether on "Buttrick's Plain," or rather on "Poplar Hill:" it was a tedious question.

In this Billerica solid men must have lived, select from year to year, a series of town clerks, at least, and there are old records that you may search. Some spring the white man came, built him a house, and made a clearing here, letting in the sun, dried up a farm, piled up the old gray stones in fences, cut down the pines around his dwelling, planted orchard seeds brought from the old country, and persuaded the civil apple tree to blossom next to the wild pine and the juniper, shedding its perfume in the wilderness. Their old stocks still remain. He culled the graceful elm from out the woods and from the river-side, and so refined and smoothed his village plot. He rudely bridged the stream, and drove his team afield into the river meadows, cut the wild grass, and laid bare the homes of beaver, otter, muskrat, and with the whetting of his scythe scared off the deer and bear. He set up a mill, and fields of English grain sprang in the virgin soil. And with his grain he scattered the seeds of the dandelion and the wild trefoil over the meadows, mingling his English flowers with the wild native ones. The bristling burdock, the sweet scented catnip, and the humble yarrow, planted themselves along his woodland road, they too seeking "freedom to worship God" in their way. And thus he plants a town. The white man's mullein soon reigned in Indian corn-fields, and sweet scented English grasses clothed the new soil. Where, then, could the Red

Man set his foot? The honey bee hummed through the Massachusetts' woods, and sipped the wild flowers round the Indian's wigwam, perchance unnoticed, when, with prophetic warning, it stung the Red child's hand, forerunner of that industrious tribe that was to come and pluck the wild flower of his race up by the root.

The white man comes, pale as the dawn, with a load of thought, with a slumbering intelligence as a fire raked up, knowing well what he knows, not guessing but calculating; strong in community, yielding obedience to authority; of experienced race; of wonderful, wonderful common sense; dull but capable, slow but persevering, severe but just, of little humor but genuine; a laboring man, despising game and sport; building a house that endures, a framed house. He buys the Indian's moccasins and baskets, then buys his hunting grounds, and at length forgets where he is buried, and plows up his bones. And here town records, old, tattered, time-worn, weather-stained chronicles, contain the Indian sachem's mark, perchance, an arrow or a beaver, and the few fatal words by which he deeded his hunting grounds away. He comes with a list of ancient Saxon, Norman, and Celtic names, and strews them up and down this river,—Framingham, Sudbury, Bedford, Carlisle, Billerica, Chelmsford,—and this is New Angle-land, and these are the new West Saxons, whom the Red Men call, not Angle-ish or English, but Yengeese, and so at last they are known for Yankees.

When we were opposite to the middle of Billerica, the fields on either hand had a soft and cultivated English aspect, the village spire being seen over the copses which skirt the river, and sometimes an orchard straggled down to the water side, though, generally, our course this forenoon was the wildest part of our voyage. It seemed that men led a quiet and very civil life there. The inhabitants were plainly cultivators of the earth, and lived under an organized political government. The school-house stood with a meek aspect, entreating a long truce to war and savage life. Every one finds by his own experience, as well as in history, that the era in which men cultivate the apple, and the amenities of the garden, is essentially different from that of the hunter and forest life, and neither can displace the other without loss. We have all had our day dreams, as well as more prophetic nocturnal visions, but as for farming, I am convinced that my genius dates from an older era than the agricultural. I would at least strike my spade into the earth with such careless freedom but accuracy as the woodpecker his bill into a tree. There is in my nature, methinks, a singular yearning toward all wildness. I know of no redeeming qualities in myself but a sincere love for some things, and when I am reproved I fall back on to this ground. What have I to do with plows? I cut another furrow than you see. Where the off ox treads, there is it not, it is further off; where the nigh ox walks, it will not be, it is nigher still. If corn fails, my crop fails not, and what are drought and rain to me? The rude Saxon pioneer will sometimes pine for that refinement and artificial beauty which are English, and love to hear the sound of such sweet and classical names as the Pentland and Malvern Hills, the Cliffs of Dover and the Trosachs, Richmond, Derwent, and Winandermere, which are to him now instead of the Acropolis and Parthenon, of Baiæ, and Athens with its sea walls, and Arcadia and Tempe.

Greece, who am I that should remember thee,
Thy Marathon and thy Thermopylæ?
Is my life vulgar, my fate mean,
Which on these golden memories can lean?

We are apt enough to be pleased with such books as Evelyn's Sylva, Acetarium, and Kalendarium Hortense, but they imply a relaxed nerve in the reader. Gardening is civil and social, but it wants the vigor and freedom of the forest and the outlaw. There may be an excess of cultivation as well as of any thing else, until civilization becomes pathetic. A highly cultivated man,—all whose bones can be bent! whose heaven-born virtues are but good manners! The young pines springing up in the corn-fields from year to year are to me a refreshing fact. We talk of civilizing the Indian, but that is not the name for his improvement. By the wary independence and aloofness of his dim forest life he preserves his intercourse with his native gods, and is admitted from time to time to a rare and peculiar society with nature. He has glances of starry recognition to which our saloons are strangers. The steady illumination of his genius, dim only because distant, is like the faint but satisfying light of the stars compared with the dazzling but ineffectual and short-lived blaze of candles. The Society Islanders had their day-born gods, but they were not supposed to be "of equal antiquity with the *atua fauau po*, or night-born gods." It is true, there are the innocent pleasures of country life, and it is sometimes pleasant to make the earth yield her increase, and gather the fruits in their season, but the heroic spirit will not fail to dream of remoter retirements and more rugged paths. It will have its garden plots and its parterres elsewhere than on the earth, and gather nuts and berries by the way for its subsistence, or orchard fruits with such heedlessness as berries. We would not always be soothing and taming nature, breaking the horse and the ox, but sometimes ride the horse wild and chase the buffalo. The Indian's intercourse with Nature is at least such as admits of the greatest independence of each. If he is somewhat of a stranger in her midst, the gardener is too much of a familiar. There is something vulgar and foul in the latter's closeness to his mistress, something noble and cleanly in the former's distance. In civilization, as in a southern latitude, man degenerates at length, and yields to the incursion of more northern tribes,

> "Some nation yet shut in
> With hills of ice."

There are other, savager, and more primeval aspects of nature than our poets have sung. It is only white man's poetry. Homer and Ossian even can never revive in London or Boston. And yet behold how these cities are refreshed by the mere tradition, or the imperfectly transmitted fragrance and flavor of these wild fruits. If we could listen but for an instant to the chaunt of the Indian muse, we should understand why he will not exchange his savageness for civilization. Nations are not whimsical. Steel and blankets are strong temptations; but the Indian does well to continue Indian.

After sitting in my chamber many days, reading the poets, I have been out early on a foggy morning, and heard the cry of an owl in a neighboring wood as from a nature behind the common, unexplored by science or by literature. None of the feathered race has yet realized my youthful conceptions of the woodland depths. I had seen the red Election-bird brought from their recesses on my comrades' string, and fancied that their plumage would assume stranger and more dazzling colors, like the tints of evening, in proportion as I advanced further into the darkness and solitude of the forest. Still less have I seen such strong wilderness tints on any poet's string.

These modern ingenious sciences and arts do not affect me as those more venerable arts of hunting and fishing, and even of husbandry in its primitive and simple form; as ancient and honorable trades as the sun and moon and winds pursue, coeval with the faculties of man, and invented when these were invented. We do not know their John Gutenberg, or Richard Arkwright, though the poets would fain make them to have been gradually learned and taught. According to Gower,

"And Iadahel, as saith the boke,
Firste made nette, and fishes toke.
Of huntyng eke he fond the chace,
Whiche nowe is knowe in many place;
A tent of clothe, with corde and stake,
He sette up first, and did it make."

Also, Lydgate says:

Jason first sayled, in story it is tolde,
Toward Colchos, to wynne the flees of golde.
Ceres the Goddess fond first the tilthe of londe;

* * * * * *

Also, Aristeus fonde first the usage
Of mylke, and cruddis, and of honey swote;
Peryodes, for grete avauntage,
From flyntes smote fuyre, daryng in the roote."

We read that Aristeus "obtained of Jupiter and Neptune, that the pestilential heat of the dog days, wherein was great mortality, should be mitigated with wind." This is one of those dateless benefits conferred on man, which have no record in our vulgar day, though we still find some similitude to them in our dreams, in which we have a more liberal and juster apprehension of things, unconstrained by habit, which is then in some measure put off, and divested of memory, which we call history.

According to fable, when the island of Ægina was depopulated by sickness, at the instance of Æacus, Jupiter turned the ants into men, that is, as some think, he made men of the inhabitants who lived meanly like ants. This is perhaps the fullest history of those early days extant.

The fable which is naturally and truly composed, so as to satisfy the imagination, ere it addresses the understanding, beautiful though strange as a wild flower, is to the wise man an apothegm, and admits of his most generous interpretation. When we read that Bacchus made the Tyrrhenian mariners mad, so that they leapt into the sea, mistaking it for a meadow full of flowers, and so became dolphins, we are not concerned about the historical truth of this, but rather a higher poetical truth. We seem to hear the music of a thought, and care not if the understanding be not gratified. For their beauty, consider the fables of Narcissus, of Endymion, of Memnon son of Morning, the representative of all promising youths who have died a premature death, and whose memory is melodiously prolonged to the latest morning; the beautiful stories of Phaeton, and of the Sirens whose isle shone afar off white with the bones of unburied men; the pregnant ones of Pan, Prometheus, and the Sphinx; and that long list of names which have already become part of the universal language of civilized men, and from proper are becoming common names or nouns,–the Sibyls, the Eumenides, the Parcæ, the Graces, the Muses, Nemesis, &c.

It is interesting to observe with what singular unanimity the furthest sundered nations and generations consent to give completeness and roundness to an ancient fable, of which they indistinctly appreciate the beauty or the truth. By a faint and dream-like effort, though it be only by the vote of a scientific body, the dullest posterity slowly add some trait to the mythus. As when astronomers call the lately discovered planet Neptune; or the asteroid Astræa, that the Virgin who was driven from earth to heaven at the end of the golden age, may have her local habitation in the heavens more distinctly assigned her,–for the slightest recognition of poetic worth is significant. By such slow aggregation has mythology grown from the first. The very nursery tales of this generation, were the nursery tales of primeval races. They migrate from east to west, and again from west to east; now expanded into the 'tale divine' of bards, now shrunk into a popular rhyme. This is an approach to that universal language which men have sought in vain. This fond reiteration of the oldest expressions of truth by the latest posterity, content with slightly and religiously re-touching the old material, is the most impressive proof of a common humanity.

All nations love the same jests and tales, Jews, Christians, and Mahometans, and the same translated suffice for all. All men are children, and of one family. The same tale sends them all to bed, and wakes them in the morning. Joseph Wolff, the missionary, distributed copies of Robinson Crusoe, translated into Arabic, among the Arabs, and they made a great sensation. "Robinson Crusoe's adventures and wisdom," says he, "were read by Muhammedans in the market-places of Sanaa, Hodeyda, and Loheya, and admired and believed!" On reading the book, the Arabians exclaimed, "Oh, that Robinson Crusoe must have been a great prophet!"

To some extent, mythology is only the most ancient history and biography. So far from being false or fabulous in the common sense, it contains only enduring and essential truth, the I and you, the here and there, the now and then, being omitted. Either time or rare wisdom writes it. Before printing was discovered, a century was equal to a thousand years. The poet is he who can write some pure mythology today without the aid of posterity. In how few words, for instance, the Greeks would have told the story of Abelard and Heloise, making but a sentence for our classical dictionary,—and then, perchance, have stuck up their names to shine in some corner of the firmament. We moderns, on the other hand, collect only the raw materials of biography and history, "memoirs to serve for a history," which itself is but materials to serve for a mythology. How many volumes folio would the Life and Labors of Prometheus have filled, if perchance it had fallen, as perchance it did first, in days of cheap printing! Who knows what shape the fable of Columbus will at length assume, to be confounded with that of Jason and the expedition of the Argonauts. And Franklin,—there may be a line for him in the future classical dictionary, recording what that demigod did, and referring him to some new genealogy. "Son of ——— and ———. He aided the Americans to gain their independence, instructed mankind in economy, and drew down lightning from the clouds."

The hidden significance of these fables which is sometimes thought to have been detected, the ethics running parallel to the poetry and history, are not so remarkable as the readiness with which they may be made to express a variety of truths. As if they were the skeletons of still older and more universal truths than any whose flesh and blood they are for the time made to wear. It is like striving to make the sun, or the wind, or the sea, symbols to signify exclusively the particular thoughts of our day. But what signifies it? In the mythus a superhuman intelligence uses the unconscious thoughts and dreams of men as its hieroglyphics to address men unborn. In the history of the human mind, these glowing and ruddy fables precede the noon-day thoughts of men, as Aurora the sun's rays. The matutine intellect of the poet, keeping in advance of the glare of philosophy, always dwells in this auroral atmosphere.

As we said before, the Concord is a dead stream, but its scenery is the more suggestive to the contemplative voyager, and this day its water was fuller of reflections than our pages even. Just before it reaches the falls in Billerica, it is contracted, and becomes swifter and shallower, with a yellow pebbly bottom, hardly passable for a canal boat, leaving the broader and more stagnant portion above like a lake among the hills. All through the Concord, Bedford, and Billerica meadows, we had heard no murmur from its stream, except where some tributary runnel tumbled in,

Some tumultuous little rill,
  Purling round its storied pebble,
Tinkling to the self-same tune,
From September until June,
  Which no drought doth e'er enfeeble.

Silent flows the parent stream,
  And if rocks do lie below,
Smothers with her waves the din,
As it were a youthful sin,
  Just as still, and just as slow.

But now at length we heard this staid and primitive river rushing to her fall, like any rill. We here left its channel, just above the Billerica Falls, and entered the canal, which runs, or rather is conducted, six miles through the woods to the Merrimack at Middlesex, and as we did not care to loiter in this part of our voyage, while one ran along the tow-path drawing the boat by a cord, the other kept it off the shore with a pole, so that we accomplished the whole distance in little more than an hour. This canal, which is the oldest in the country, and has even an antique look beside the more modern-railroads, is fed by the Concord, so that we were still floating on its familiar waters. It is so much water which the river *lets* for the advantage of commerce. There appeared some want of harmony in its scenery, since it was not of equal date with the woods and meadows through which it is led, and we missed the conciliatory influence of time on land and water; but in the lapse of ages, Nature will recover and indemnify herself, and gradually plant fit shrubs and flowers along its borders. Already the kingfisher sat upon a pine over the water, and the bream and pickerel swam below. Thus all works pass directly out of the hands of the architect into the hands of Nature, to be perfected.

It was a retired and pleasant route, without houses or travellers, except some young men who were lounging upon a bridge in Chelmsford, who leaned impudently over the rails to pry into our concerns, but we caught the eye of the most forward, and looked at him till he was visibly discomfited. Not that there was any peculiar efficacy in our look, but rather a sense of shame left in him which disarmed him.

It is a very true and expressive phrase, "He looked daggers at me," for the first pattern and prototype of all daggers must have been a glance of the eye. First, there was the glance of Jove's eye, then his fiery bolt, then, the material gradually hardening, tridents, spears, javelins, and finally, for the convenience of private men, daggers, krisses, and so forth, were invented. It is wonderful how we get about the streets without being wounded by these delicate and glancing weapons, a man can so nimbly whip out his rapier, or without being noticed carry it unsheathed. Yet it is rare that one gets seriously looked at.

As we passed under the last bridge over the canal, just before reaching the Merrimack, the people coming out of church paused to look at us from above, and apparently, so strong is custom, indulged in some heathenish comparisons; but we were the truest observers of this sunny day. According to Hesiod,

> "The seventh is a holy day,
> For then Latona brought forth golden-rayed Apollo,"

and by our reckoning this was the seventh day of the week, and not the first. I find among the papers of an old Justice of the Peace and Deacon of the town of Concord, this singular memorandum, which is worth preserving as a relic of an ancient custom. After reforming the spelling and grammar, it runs as follows:—"Men that travelled with teams on the Sabbath, Dec. 18th, 1803, were Jeremiah Richardson and Jonas Parker, both of Shirley. They had teams with rigging such as is used to carry barrels, and they were travelling westward. Richardson was questioned by the Hon. Ephraim Wood, Esq., and he said that Jonas Parker was his fellow traveller, and he further said that a Mr. Longley was his employer, who promised to bear him out." We were the men that were gliding northward, this Sept. 1st, 1839, with still team, and rigging not the most convenient to carry barrels, unquestioned by any Squire or Church Deacon, and ready to bear ourselves out, if need were. In the latter part of the seventeenth century, according to the historian of Dunstable, "Towns were directed to erect '*a cage*' near the meeting-house, and in this all offenders against the sanctity of the Sabbath were confined." Society has relaxed a little from its strictness, one would say, but I presume that there is not less *religion* than formerly. If the *ligature* is found to be loosened in one part, it is only drawn the tighter in another.

You can hardly convince a man of an error in a lifetime, but must content yourself with the reflection that the progress of science is slow. If he is not convinced, his grand-children may be. The geologists tell us that it took one hundred years to prove that fossils are organic, and one hundred and fifty more, to prove that they are not to be referred to the Noachian deluge. I am not sure but I should betake myself in extremities to the liberal divinities of Greece, rather than to my country's God. Jehovah, though with us he has acquired new attributes, is more absolute and unapproachable, but hardly more divine, than Jove.

He is not so much of a gentleman, not so gracious and catholic, he does not exert so intimate and genial an influence on nature, as many a god of the Greeks. I should fear the infinite power and inflexible justice of the almighty mortal, hardly as yet apotheosized, so wholly masculine, with no sister Juno, no Apollo, no Venus, nor Minerva, to intercede for me, θυμῷ φιλέουσά τε, κηδομένη τε. The Grecian are youthful and erring and fallen gods, with the vices of men, but in many important respects essentially of the divine race. In my Pantheon, Pan still reigns in his pristine glory, with his ruddy face, his flowing beard, and his shaggy body, his pipe and his crook, his nymph Echo, and his chosen daughter Iambe; for the great God Pan is not dead, as was rumored. No god ever dies. Perhaps of all the gods of New England and of ancient Greece, I am most constant at his shrine.

It seems to me that the god that is commonly worshipped in civilized countries is not at all divine, though he bears a divine name, but is the overwhelming authority and respectability of mankind combined. Men reverence one another, not yet God. If I thought that I could speak with discrimination and impartiality of the nations of Christendom, I should praise them; but it tasks me too much. They seem to be the most civil and humane, but I may be mistaken. Every people have gods to suit their circumstances; the Society Islanders had a god called Toahitu, "in shape like a dog; he saved such as were in danger of falling from rocks and trees." I think that we can do without him, as we have not much climbing to do. Among them a man could make himself a god out of a piece of wood, in a few minutes, which would frighten him out of his wits.

I fancy that some indefatigable spinster of the old school, who had the supreme felicity to be born in "days that tried men's souls," hearing this, may say with Nestor, another of the old school, "But you are younger than I. For time was when I conversed with greater men than you. For not at any time have I seen such men nor shall see them, as Perithous, and Dryas, and ποιμενα λαων," that is probably Washington, sole "Shepherd of the People." And when Apollo has now six times rolled westward, or seemed to roll, and now for the seventh time shows his face in the east, eyes well nigh glazed, long glassed, which have fluctuated only between lamb's wool and worsted, explore ceaselessly some good sermon book. For six days shalt thou labor and do all thy knitting, but on the seventh, forsooth, thy reading. Happy we who can bask in this warm September sun, which illumines all creatures, as well when they rest as when they toil, not without a feeling of gratitude; whose life is as blameless, how blame-worthy soever it may be, on the Lord's Mona-day as on his Suna-day.

There are various, nay incredible faiths; why should we be alarmed at any of them? What man believes, God believes. Long as I have lived, and many blasphemers as I have heard and seen, I have never yet heard or witnessed any direct and conscious blasphemy or irreverence; but of indirect and habitual enough. Where is the man who is guilty of direct and personal insolence to Him that made him?

One memorable addition to the old mythology is due to this era,—the Christian fable. With what pains, and tears, and blood, these centuries have woven this and added it to the mythology of mankind. The new Prometheus. With what miraculous consent, and patience, and persistency, has this mythus been stamped upon the memory of the race? It would seem as if it were in the progress of our mythology to dethrone Jehovah, and crown Christ in his stead.

If it is not a tragical life we live, I know not what to call it. Such a story as that of Jesus Christ and the history of Jerusalem, say, being a part of the Universal History. The naked, the embalmed, unburied death of Jerusalem amid its desolate hills,—think of it. In Tasso's poem I trust some things are sweetly buried. Consider the snappish tenacity with which they preach Christianity still. What are time and space to Christianity, eighteen hundred years, and a new world?—that the humble life of a Jewish peasant should have force to make a New York bishop so bigoted. Forty-four lamps, the gift of kings, now burning in a place called the Holy Sepulchre;—a church bell ringing;—some unaffected tears shed by a pilgrim on Mount Calvary within the week.—

"Jerusalem, Jerusalem, when I forget thee, may my right hand forget her cunning."

"By the waters of Babylon there we sat down, and we wept when we remembered Zion."

I trust that some may be as near and dear to Buddha, or Christ, or Swedenborg, who are without the pale of their churches. It is necessary not to be Christian, to appreciate the beauty and significance of the life of Christ. I know that some will have hard thoughts of me, when they hear their Christ named beside my Buddha, yet I am sure that I am willing they should love their Christ more than my Buddha, for the love is the main thing, and I like him too. "God is the letter Ku, as well as Khu." Why need

Christians be still intolerant and superstitious? The simple minded sailors were unwilling to cast overboard Jonah at his own request.—

> "Where is this love become in later age?
> Alas! 't is gone in endless pilgrimage
> From hence, and never to return, I doubt,
> Till revolution wheel those times about."

One man says,—

> "The world's a popular disease, that reigns
> Within the froward heart and frantic brains
> Of poor distempered mortals."

Another that

> —"all the world's a stage,
> And all the men and women merely players."

The world is a strange place for a play-house to stand within it. Old Drayton thought that a man that lived here, and would be a poet, for instance, should have in him certain "brave translunary things," and a "fine madness" should possess his brain. Certainly it were as well, that he might be up to the occasion. That is a superfluous wonder, which Dr. Johnson expresses at the assertion of Sir Thomas Browne, that "his life has been a miracle of thirty years, which to relate, were not history, but a piece of poetry, and would sound like a fable." The wonder is rather that all men do not assert as much. That would be a rare praise, if it were true, which was addressed to Francis Beaumont,—"Spectators sate part in your tragedies."

Think what a mean and wretched place this world is; that half the time we have to light a lamp that we may see to live in it. This is half our life. Who would undertake the enterprise if it were all? And, pray, what more has day to offer? A lamp that burns more clear, a purer oil, say winter-strained, that so we may pursue our idleness with less obstruction. Bribed with a little sunlight and a few prismatic tints, we bless our Maker, and stave off his wrath with hymns.

I make ye an offer,
Ye gods, hear the scoffer,
The scheme will not hurt you,
If ye will find goodness, I will find virtue.
Though I am your creature,
And child of your nature,
I have pride still unbended,
And blood undescended,
Some free independence,
And my own descendants.
I cannot toil blindly,
Though ye behave kindly,
And I swear by the rood,
I'll be slave to no God.
If ye will deal plainly,
I will strive mainly,
If ye will discover,
Great plans to your lover,
And give him a sphere
Somewhat larger than here.

"Verily, my angels! I was abashed on account of my servant, who had no Providence but me; therefore did I pardon him."–*The Gulistan of Sadi.*

Most people with whom I talk, men and women even of some originality and genius, have their scheme of the universe all cut and dried,–very *dry*, I assure you, to hear, dry enough to burn, dry-rotted and powder-post, methinks,–which they set up between you and them in the shortest intercourse; an ancient and tottering frame with all its boards blown off.

They do not walk without their bed. Some to me seemingly very unimportant and unsubstantial things and relations, are for them everlastingly settled,–as Father, Son, and Holy Ghost, and the like. These are like the everlasting hills to them. But in all my wanderings, I never came across the least vestige of authority for these things. They have not left so distinct a trace as the delicate flower of a remote geological period on the coal in my grate. The wisest man preaches no doctrines; he has no scheme; he sees no rafter, not even a cobweb, against the heavens. It is clear sky. If I ever see more clearly at one time than at another, the medium through which I see is clearer. To see from earth to heaven, and see there standing, still a fixture, that old Jewish scheme! What right have you to hold up this obstacle to my understanding you, to your understanding me? You did not invent it; it was imposed on you. Examine your authority. Even Christ, we fear, had his scheme, his conformity to tradition, which slightly vitiates his teaching. He had not swallowed all formulas. He preached some mere doctrines. As for me, Abraham, Isaac, and Jacob, are now only the subtilest imaginable essences, which would not stain the morning sky. Your scheme must be the frame-work of the universe; all other schemes will soon be ruins. The perfect God in his revelations of himself has never got to the length of one such proposition as you, his prophets, state. Have you learned the alphabet of heaven, and can count three? Do you know the number of God's family? Can you put mysteries into words? Do you presume to fable of the ineffable? Pray, what geographer are you, that speak of heaven's topography? Whose friend are you that speak of God's personality? Do you, Miles Howard, think that he has made you his confidant? Tell me of the height of the mountains of the moon, or of the diameter of space, and I may believe you, but of the secret history of the Almighty, and I shall pronounce thee mad. Yet we have a sort of family history of our God,–so have the Tahitians of theirs,–and some old poet's grand imagination is imposed on us as adamantine everlasting truth, and God's own word! Pythagoras says, truly enough, "A true assertion respecting God, is an assertion of God"; but we may well doubt if there is any example of this in literature.

The New Testament is an invaluable book, though I confess to having been slightly prejudiced against it in my very early days by the church and the Sabbath school, so that it seemed, before I read it, to be the yellowest book in the catalogue. Yet I early escaped from their meshes. It was hard to get the commentaries out of one's head, and taste its true flavor.–I think that Pilgrim's Progress is the best sermon which has been preached from this text; almost all other sermons that I have heard or heard of, have been but poor imitations of this.–It would be a poor story to be prejudiced against the Life of Christ, because the book has been edited by Christians. In fact, I love this book rarely, though it is a sort of castle in the air to me, which I am permitted to dream. Having come to it so recently and freshly, it has the greater charm, so that I cannot find any to talk with about it. I never read a novel, they have so little real life and thought in them. The reading which I love best is the scriptures of the several nations, though it happens that I am better acquainted with those of the Hindoos, the Chinese, and the Persians, than of the Hebrews, which

I have come to last. Give me one of these Bibles, and you have silenced me for a while. When I recover the use of my tongue, I am wont to worry my neighbors with the new sentences; but commonly they cannot see that there is any wit in them. Such has been my experience with the New Testament. I have not yet got to the crucifixion, I have read it over so many times. I should love dearly to read it aloud to my friends, some of whom are seriously inclined; it is so good, and I am sure that they have never heard it, it fits their case exactly, and we should enjoy it so much together,—but I instinctively despair of getting their ears. They soon show by signs not to be mistaken, that it is inexpressibly wearisome to them. I do not mean to imply that I am any better than my neighbors; for, alas! I know that I am only as good, though I love better books than they. It is remarkable, that notwithstanding the universal favor with which the New Testament is outwardly received, and even the bigotry with which it is defended, there is no hospitality shown to, there is no appreciation of, the order of truth with which it deals. I know of no book that has so few readers. There is none so truly strange, and heretical, and unpopular. To Christians, no less than Greeks and Jews, it is foolishness and a stumbling block. There are, indeed, severe things in it which no man should read aloud more than once.—"Seek first the kingdom of heaven."—"Lay not up for yourselves treasures on earth."—"If thou wilt be perfect, go and sell that thou hast, and give to the poor, and thou shalt have treasure in heaven."—"For what is a man profited, if he shall gain the whole world, and lose his own soul? or what shall a man give in exchange for his soul?"—Think of this, Yankees!—"Verily I say unto you, if ye have faith as a grain of mustard seed, ye shall say unto this mountain, Remove hence to yonder place; and it shall remove; and nothing shall be impossible unto you."–Think of repeating these things to a New England audience! thirdly, fourthly, fifteenthly, till there are three barrels of sermons! Who, without cant, can read them aloud? Who, without cant, can hear them, and not go out of the meeting-house? They never *were* read, they never *were* heard. Let but one of these sentences be rightly read from any pulpit in the land, and there would not be left one stone of that meeting-house upon another.

Yet the New Testament treats of man and man's so-called spiritual affairs too exclusively, and is too constantly moral and personal, to alone content me, who am not interested solely in man's religious or moral nature, or in man even. I have not the most definite designs on the future. Absolutely speaking, Do unto others as you would that they should do unto you, is by no means a golden rule, but the best of current silver. An honest man would have but little occasion for it. It is golden not to have any rule at all in such a case. The book has never been written which is to be accepted without any allowance. Christ was a sublime actor on the stage of the world. He knew what he was thinking of when he said, "Heaven and earth shall pass away, but my words shall not pass away." I draw near to him at such a time. Yet he taught mankind but imperfectly how to live; his thoughts were all directed toward another world. There is another kind of success than his. Even here we have a sort of living to get, and must buffet it somewhat longer. There are various tough problems yet to solve, and we must make shift to live, betwixt spirit and matter, such a human life as we can.

A healthy man, with steady employment, as wood chopping at fifty cents a cord, and a camp in the woods, will not be a good subject for Christianity. The New Testament may be a choice book to him on some, but not on all or most of his days. He will rather go a fishing in his leisure hours. The apostles, though they were fishers too, were of the solemn race of sea-fishers, and never trolled for pickerel on inland streams.

Men have a singular desire to be good without being good for any thing, because, perchance, they think vaguely that so it will be good for them in the end. The sort of morality which the priests inculcate is a very subtle policy, far finer than the politicians, and the world is very successfully ruled by them as the police-men. It is not worth the while to let our imperfections disturb us always. The conscience really does not, and ought not to, monopolize the whole of our lives, any more than the heart or the head. It is as liable to disease as any other part. I have seen some whose consciences, owing undoubtedly to former indulgence, had grown to be as irritable as spoilt children, and at length gave them no peace. They did not know when to swallow their cud, and their lives of course yielded no milk.

Conscience is instinct bred in the house,
Feeling and Thinking propagate the sin
By an unnatural breeding in and in.
I say, Turn it out doors,
Into the moors.
I love a life whose plot is simple,
And does not thicken with every pimple;
A soul so sound no sickly conscience binds it,
That makes the universe no worse than 't finds it.

I love an earnest soul,
Whose mighty joy and sorrow
Are not drowned in a bowl,
And brought to life to-morrow;
That lives one tragedy,
And not seventy;
A conscience worth keeping,
Laughing not weeping;
A conscience wise and steady,
And forever ready;
Not changing with events,
Dealing in compliments;
A conscience exercised about
Large things, where one *may* doubt.
I love a soul not all of wood,
Predestinated to be good,
But true to the backbone
Unto itself alone,
And false to none;
Born to its own affairs,
Its own joys and own cares;
By whom the work which God begun
Is finished, and not undone;
Taken up where he left off,
Whether to worship or to scoff;
If not good, why then evil,
If not good god, good devil.
Goodness!—you hypocrite, come out of that,
Live your life, do your work, then take your hat.
I have no patience towards
Such conscientious cowards.
Give me simple laboring folk,
Who love their work,
Whose virtue is a song
To cheer God along.

I was once reproved by a minister who was driving a poor beast to some meeting-house horse-sheds among the hills of New Hampshire, because I was bending my steps to a mountain-top on the Sabbath, instead of a church, when I would have gone further than he to hear a true word spoken on that or any day. He declared that I was "breaking the Lord's fourth commandment," and proceeded to enumerate, in a sepulchral tone, the disasters which had befallen him whenever he had done any ordinary work on the Sabbath. He really thought that a god was on the watch to trip up those men who followed any secular work on this day, and did not see that it was the evil conscience of the workers that did it. The country is full of this superstition, so that when one enters a village, the church, not only really but from association, is the ugliest looking building in it, because it is the one in which human nature stoops the lowest and is most disgraced. Certainly, such temples as these shall ere long cease to deform the landscape. There are few things more disheartening and disgusting than when you are walking the streets of a strange village on the Sabbath, to hear a preacher shouting like a boatswain in a gale of wind, and thus harshly profaning the quiet atmosphere of the day. You fancy him to have taken off his coat, as when men are about to do hot and dirty work.

If I should ask the minister of Middlesex to let me speak in his pulpit on a Sunday, he would object, because I do not pray as he does, or because I am not ordained. What under the sun are these things?

Really, there is no infidelity, now-a-days, so great as that which prays, and keeps the Sabbath, and rebuilds the churches. The sealer of the South Pacific preaches a truer doctrine. The church is a sort of hospital for men's souls, and as full of quackery as the hospital for their bodies. Those who are taken into it live like pensioners in their Retreat or Sailor's Snug Harbor, where you may see a row of religious cripples sitting outside in sunny weather. Let not the apprehension that he may one day have to occupy a ward therein, discourage the cheerful labors of the able-souled man. While he remembers the sick in their extremities, let him not look thither as to his goal. One is sick at heart of this pagoda worship. It is like the beating of gongs in a Hindoo subterranean temple. In dark places and dungeons the preacher's words might perhaps strike root and grow, but not in broad daylight in any part of the world that I know. The sound of the sabbath bell far away, now breaking on these shores, does not awaken pleasing associations, but melancholy and sombre ones rather. One involuntarily rests on his oar, to humor his unusually meditative mood. It is as the sound of many catechisms and religious books twanging a canting peal round the earth, seeming to issue from some Egyptian temple and echo along the shore of the Nile, right opposite to Pharoah's palace and Moses in the bulrushes, startling a multitude of storks and alligators basking in the sun.

Every where "good men" sound a retreat, and the word has gone forth to fall back on innocence. Fall forward rather on to whatever there is there. Christianity only hopes. It has hung its harp on the willows, and cannot sing a song in a strange land. It has dreamed a sad dream, and does not yet welcome the morning with joy. The mother tells her falsehoods to her child, but thank Heaven, the child does not grow up in its parent's shadow. Our mother's faith has not grown with her experience. Her experience has been too much for her. The lesson of life was too hard for her to learn.

It is remarkable, that almost all speakers and writers feel it to be incumbent on them, sooner or later, to prove or to acknowledge the personality of

God. Some Earl of Bridgewater, thinking it better late than never, has provided for it in his will. It is a sad mistake. In reading a work on agriculture, we have to skip the author's moral reflections, and the words "Providence" and "He" scattered along the page, to come at the profitable level of what he has to say. What he calls his religion is for the most part offensive to the nostrils. He should know better than expose himself, and keep his foul sores covered till they are quite healed. There is more religion in men's science than there is science in their religion. Let us make haste to the report of the committee on swine.

A man's real faith is never contained in his creed, nor is his creed an article of his faith. The last is never adopted. This it is that permits him to smile ever, and to live even as bravely as he does. And yet he clings anxiously to his creed, as to a straw, thinking that that does him good service because his sheet anchor does not drag.

In most men's religion, the ligature, which should be its umbilical cord connecting them with divinity, is rather like that thread which the accomplices of Cylon held in their hands when they went abroad from the temple of Minerva, the other end being attached to the statue of the goddess. But frequently, as in their case, the thread breaks, being stretched, and they are left without an asylum.

"A good and pious man reclined his head on the bosom of contemplation, and was absorbed in the ocean of a revery. At the instant when he awaked from his vision, one of his friends, by way of pleasantry, said; What rare gift have you brought us from that garden, where you have been recreating? He replied; I fancied to myelf and said; when I can reach the rose-bower, I will fill my lap with the flowers, and bring them as a present to my friends; but when I got there, the fragrance of the roses so intoxicated me, that the skirt dropped from my hands.——'O bird of dawn! learn the warmth of affection from the moth; for that scorched creature gave up the ghost, and uttered not a groan: These vain pretenders are ignorant of him they seek after; for of him that knew him we never heard again:—O thou! who towerest above the flights of conjecture opinion and comprehension; whatever has been reported of thee we have heard and read: the congregation is dismissed, and life drawn to a close; and we still rest at our first encomium of thee!' "—*Sadi.*

By noon we were let down into the Merrimack through the locks at Middlesex, just above Pawtucket Falls, by a serene and liberal-minded man, who came quietly from his book, though his duties, we supposed, did not require him to open the locks on Sundays. With him we had a just and equal encounter of the eyes, as between two honest men.

The movements of the eyes express the perpetual and unconscious courtesy of the parties. It is said, that a rogue does not look you in the face, neither does an honest man look at you as if he had his reputation to establish. I have seen some who did not know when to turn aside their eyes in meeting yours. A truly confident and magnanimous spirit is wiser than to contend for the mastery in such encounters. Serpents alone conquer by the steadiness of their gaze. My friend looks me in the face and sees me, that is all.

The best relations were at once established between us and this man, and though few words were spoken, he could not conceal a visible interest in us and our excursion. He was a lover of the higher mathematics, as we found, and in the midst of some vast sunny problem, when we overtook him and whispered our conjectures. By this man we were presented with the freedom of the Merrimack. We now felt as if we were fairly launched on the ocean-stream of our voyage, and were pleased to find that our boat would float on Merrimack water. We began again busily to put in practice those old arts of rowing, steering, and paddling. It seemed a strange phenomenon to us that the two rivers should mingle their waters so readily, since we had never associated them in our thoughts.

As we glided over the broad bosom of the Merrimack, between Chelmsford and Dracut, at noon, here a quarter of a mile wide, the rattling of our oars was echoed over the water to those villages, and their slight sounds to us. Their harbors lay as smooth and fairy-like as the Lido, or Syracuse, or Rhodes, in our imagination, while, like some strange roving craft, we flitted past what seemed the dwellings of noble home-staying men, seemingly as conspicuous as if on an eminence, or floating upon a tide which came up to those villagers' breasts. At a third of a mile over the water we heard distinctly some children repeating their catechism in a cottage near the shore, while in the broad shallows between, a herd of cows stood lashing their sides, and waging war with the flies.

Two hundred years ago other catechising than this was going on here; for here came the Sachem Wannalancet, and his people, and sometimes Tahatawan, our Concord Sachem, who afterwards had a church at home, to catch fish at the falls; and here also came John Elliot, with the Bible and Catechism, and Baxter's Call to the Unconverted, and other tracts, done into the Massachusetts tongue, and taught them Christianity meanwhile. "This place," says Gookin, referring to Wamesit,

"being an ancient and capital seat of Indians, they come to fish; and this good man takes this opportunity to spread the net of the gospel, to fish for their souls."—"May 5th,

1674," he continues, "according to our usual custom, Mr. Eliot and myself took our journey to Wamesit, or Pawtuckett; and arriving there that evening, Mr. Eliot preached to as many of them as could be got together, out of Matt. xxii. 1-14, the parable of the marriage of the king's son. We met at the wigwam of one called Wannalancet, about two miles from the town, near Pawtuckett falls, and bordering upon Merrimak river. This person, Wannalancet, is the eldest son of old Pasaconway, the chiefest sachem of Pawtuckett. He is a sober and grave person, and of years, between fifty and sixty. He hath been always loving and friendly to the English." As yet, however, they had not prevailed on him to embrace the Christian religion. "But at this time," says Gookin, "May 6, 1674,"—"after some deliberation and serious pause, he stood up, and made a speech to this effect:—'I must acknowledge I have, all my days, used to pass in an old canoe, (alluding to his frequent custom to pass in a canoe upon the river) and now you exhort me to change and leave my old canoe, and embark in a new canoe, to which I have hitherto been unwilling; but now I yield up myself to your advice, and enter into a new canoe, and do engage to pray to God hereafter.'" One "Mr. Richard Daniel, a gentleman that lived in Billerica," who with other "persons of quality" was present, "desired brother Eliot to tell the sachem from him, that it may be, while he went in his old canoe, he passed in a quiet stream; but the end thereof was death and destruction to soul and body. But now he went into a new canoe, perhaps he would meet with storms and trials, but yet he should be encouraged to persevere, for the end of his voyage would be everlasting rest."—"Since that time, I hear this sachem doth persevere, and is a constant and diligent hearer of God's word, and sanctifieth the Sabbath, though he doth travel to Wamesit meeting every Sabbath, which is above two miles; and though sundry of his people have deserted him, since he subjected to the gospel, yet he continues and persists."—*Gookin's Hist. Coll. of the Indians in New England*, 1674.

Already, as appears from the records, "At a General Court held at Boston in New England, the 7th of the first month, 1643-4."—"Wassamequin, Nashoonon, Kutchamaquin, Massaconomet, and Squaw Sachem, did voluntarily submit themselves" to the English; and among other things did "promise to be willing from time to time to be instructed in the knowledge of God." Being asked "Not to do any unnecessary work on the Sabbath day, especially within the gates of Christian towns," they answered, "It is easy to them; they have not much to do on any day, and they can well take their rest on that day."—"So," says Winthrop, in his Journal, "we causing them to understand the articles, and all the ten commandments of God, and they freely assenting to all, they were solemnly received, and then presented the Court with twenty-six fathom more of wampom; and the Court gave each of them a coat of two yards of cloth, and their dinner; and to them and their men, every of them, a cup of sack at their departure; so they took leave and went away."

What journeyings on foot and on horseback through the wilderness, to preach the gospel to these minks and muskrats! who first, no doubt, listened with their red ears out of a natural hospitality and courtesy, and afterward from curiosity or even interest, till at length there were "praying Indians," and, as the General Court wrote to Cromwell, the "work is brought to this perfection, that some of the Indians themselves can pray and prophesy in a comfortable manner."

It was in fact an old battle and hunting ground through which we had been floating, the ancient dwelling-place of a race of hunters and warriors. Their weirs of stone, their arrowheads and hatchets, their pestles, and the mortars in which they pounded Indian corn before the white man had tasted it, lay concealed in the mud of the river bottom. Tradition still points out the spots where they took fish in the greatest numbers, by such arts as they possessed. It is a rapid story the historian will have to put together. Miantonimo,—Winthrop,—Webster. Soon he comes from Mount Hope to Bunker Hill, from bearskins, parched corn, bows and arrows, to tiled roofs, wheat fields, guns and swords. Pawtucket and Wamesit, where the Indians resorted in the fishing season, are now Lowell, the city of spindles and Manchester of America, which sends its cotton cloth round the globe. Even we youthful voyagers had spent a part of our lives in the village of Chelmsford, when the present city, whose bells we heard, was its obscure north district only, and the giant weaver was not yet fairly born. So old are we; so young is it.

We were thus entering the State of New Hampshire on the bosom of the flood formed by the tribute of its innumerable valleys. The river was the only key which could unlock its maze, presenting its hills and valleys, its lakes and streams, in their natural order and position. The MERRIMACK, or Sturgeon River, is formed by the confluence of the Pemigewasset, which rises near the Notch of the White Mountains, and the Winnepisiogee, which drains the lake of the same name, signifying "The Smile of the Great Spirit." From their junction it runs south seventy-eight miles to Massachusetts, and thence east thirty-five miles to the sea. I have traced its stream from where it bubbles out of the rocks of the White Mountains above the clouds, to where it is lost amid the salt billows of the ocean on Plum Island beach. At first it comes on murmuring to itself by the base of stately and retired mountains, through moist primitive woods whose juices it receives, where the bear still drinks it, and the cabins of settlers are far between, and there are few to cross its stream; enjoying in solitude its cascades still unknown to fame; by long ranges of mountains of Sandwich and of Squam, slumbering like tumuli of Titans, with the peaks of

Moosehillock, the Haystack, and Kearsarge reflected in its waters; where the maple and the raspberry, those lovers of the hills, flourish amid temperate dews;—flowing long and full of meaning, but untranslatable as its name Pemigewasset, by many a pastured Pelion and Ossa, where unnamed muses haunt, tended by Oreads, Dryads, Naiads, and receiving the tribute of many an untasted Hippocrene. There are earth, air, fire, and water,—very well, this is water, and down it comes.

Such water do the gods distil,
And pour down every hill
    For their New England men;
A draught of this wild nectar bring,
And I'll not taste the spring
    Of Helicon again.

Falling all the way, and yet not discouraged by the lowest fall. By the law of its birth never to become stagnant, for it has come out of the clouds, and down the sides of precipices worn in the flood, through beaver dams broke loose, not splitting but splicing and mending itself, until it found a breathing place in this low land. There is no danger now that the sun will steal it back to heaven again before it reach the sea, for it has a warrant even to recover its own dews into its bosom again with interest at every eve.

It was already the water of Squam and Newfound Lake and Winnepisiogee, and White Mountain snow dissolved, on which we were floating, and Smith's and Baker's and Mad Rivers, and Nashua and Souhegan and Piscataquoag, and Suncook and Soucook and Contoocook, mingled in incalculable proportions, still fluid, yellowish, restless all, with an ancient, ineradicable inclination to the sea.

So it flows on down by Lowell and Haverhill, at which last place it first suffers a sea change, and a few masts betray the vicinity of the ocean. Between the towns of Amesbury and Newbury it is a broad commercial river, from a third to half a mile in width, no longer skirted with yellow and crumbling banks, but backed by high green hills and pastures, with frequent white beaches on which the fishermen draw up their nets. I have passed down this portion of the river in a steam-boat, and it was a pleasant sight to watch from its deck the fishermen dragging their seines on the distant shore, as in pictures of a foreign strand. At intervals you may meet with a schooner laden with lumber, standing up to Haverhill, or else lying at anchor or aground, waiting for wind or tide; until, at last, you glide under the famous Chain Bridge, and are landed at Newburyport. Thus she who at first was "poore of waters, naked of renowne," having received so many fair tributaries, as was said of the Forth,

> "Doth grow the greater still, the further downe;
> Till that abounding both in power and fame,
> She long doth strive to give the sea her name;"

or if not her name, in this case, at least the impulse of her stream. From the steeples of Newburyport, you may review this river stretching far up into the country, with many a white sail glancing over it like an inland sea, and behold, as one wrote who was born on its head waters, "Down out at its mouth, the dark inky main blending with the blue above. Plum Island, its sand ridges scolloping along the horizon like the sea serpent, and the distant outline broken by many a tall ship, leaning, *still*, against the sky."

Rising at an equal height with the Connecticut, the

Merrimack reaches the sea by a course only half as long, and hence has no leisure to form broad and fertile meadows like the former, but is hurried along rapids, and down numerous falls without long delay. The banks are generally steep and high, with a narrow interval reaching back to the hills, which is only rarely or partially overflown at present, and is much valued by the farmers. Between Chelmsford and Concord in New Hampshire, it varies from twenty to seventy-five rods in width. It is probably wider than it was formerly, in many places, owing to the trees having been cut down, and the consequent wasting away of its banks. The influence of the Pawtucket Dam is felt as far up as Cromwell's Falls, and many think that the banks are being abraded and the river filled up again by this cause. Like all our rivers, it is liable to freshets, and the Pemigewasset has been known to rise twenty-five feet in a few hours. It is navigable for vessels of burden about twenty miles, for canal boats by means of locks as far as Concord in New Hampshire, about seventy-five miles from its mouth, and for smaller boats to Plymouth, one hundred and thirteen miles. A small steam-boat once plied between Lowell and Nashua, before the rail road was built, and one now runs from Newburyport to Haverhill.

Unfitted to some extent for the purposes of commerce by the sand-bar at its mouth, see how this river was devoted from the first to the service of manufactures. Issuing from the iron region of Franconia, and flowing through still uncut forests, by inexhaustible ledges of granite, with Squam, and Winnepisiogee, and Newfound, and Massabesic Lakes for its mill-ponds, it falls over a succession of natural dams, where it has been offering its *privileges* in vain for ages, until at last the Yankee race came to *improve* them. Standing at its mouth, look up its sparkling stream to its source,—a silver cascade which falls all the way from the White Mountains to the sea,—and behold a city on each successive plateau, a busy colony of human beaver around every fall. Not to mention Newburyport and Haverhill, see Lawrence, and Lowell, and Nashua, and Manchester, and Concord, gleaming one above the other. When at length it has escaped from under the last of the factories it has a level and unmolested passage to the sea, a mere *waste water*, as it were, bearing little with it but its fame; its pleasant course revealed by the morning fog which hangs over it, and the sails of the few small vessels which transact the commerce of Haverhill and Newburyport. But its real vessels are railroad cars, and its true and main stream, flowing by an iron channel further south, may be traced by a long line of vapor amid the hills, which no morning wind ever disperses, to where it empties into the sea at Boston. This side is the louder murmur now. Instead of the scream of a fish-hawk scaring the fishes, is heard the whistle of the steam-engine arousing a country to its progress.

This river too was at length discovered by the white man, "trending up into the land," he knew not how far, possibly an inlet to the South Sea. Its valley, as far as the Winnepisiogee, was first surveyed in 1652. The first settlers of Massachusetts supposed that the Connecticut, in one part of its course, ran north-west, "so near the great lake as the Indians do pass their canoes into it over land." From which lake and the "hideous swamps" about it, as they supposed, came all the beaver that was traded between Virginia and Canada,—and the Potomac was thought to come out of or from very near it. Afterward the Connecticut came so near the course of the Merrimack, that with a little pains they expected to divert the current of the trade into the latter river, and its profits from their Dutch neighbors into their own pockets.

Unlike the Concord, the Merrimack is not a dead but a living stream, though it has less life within its waters and on its banks. It has a swift current, and, in this part of its course, a clayey bottom, almost no weeds, and, comparatively, few fishes. We looked down into its yellow water with the more curiosity, who were accustomed to the Nile-like blackness of the former river. Shad and alewives are taken here in their season, but salmon, though at one time more numerous than shad, are now more rare. Bass, also, are taken occasionally; but locks and dams have proved more or less destructive to the fisheries. The shad make their appearance early in May, at the same time with the blossoms of the pyrus, one of the most conspicuous early flowers, which is for this reason called the shad-blossom. An insect, called the shad-fly, also appears at the same time, covering the houses and fences. We are told that "their greatest run is when the apple trees are in full blossom. The old shad return in August; the young, three or four inches long, in September. These are very fond of flies." A rather picturesque and luxurious mode of fishing was formerly practised on the Connecticut, at Bellows Falls, where a large rock divides the stream. "On the steep sides of the island rock," says Belknap, "hang several arm chairs, fastened to ladders, and secured by a counterpoise, in which fishermen sit to catch salmon and shad with dipping nets." The remains of Indian weirs, made of large stones, are still to be seen in the Winnepisiogee, one of the headwaters of this river.

It cannot but affect our philosophy favorably to be reminded of these shoals of migratory fishes, of salmon, shad, alewives, marsh-bankers, and others, which penetrate up the innumerable rivers of our coast in the spring, even to the interior lakes, their scales gleaming in the sun; and again, of the fry, which in still greater numbers wend their way downward to the sea. "And is it not pretty sport," wrote Capt. John Smith, who was on this coast as early as 1614, "to pull up twopence, sixpence, and twelvepence, as fast as you can haul and veer a line?"—"And what sport doth yield a more pleasing content, and less hurt or charge, than angling with a hook, and crossing the sweet air from isle to isle, over the silent streams of a calm sea."

On the sandy shore, opposite the Glass-house village in Chelmsford, at the Great Bend, where we landed to rest us and gather a few wild plums, we discovered the *campanula rotundifolia*, a new flower to us, the harebell of the poets, which is common to both hemispheres, growing close to the water. Here, in the shady branches of an apple tree on the sand, we took our nooning, where there was not a zephyr to disturb the repose of this glorious Sabbath day, and we reflected serenely on the long past and successful labors of Latona.

"So silent is the cessile air,
That every cry and call,
The hills and dales, and forest fair,
Again repeats them all.

"The herds beneath some leafy trees,
Amidst the flowers they lie,
The stable ships upon the seas
Tend up their sails to dry."

As we thus rested in the shade, or rowed leisurely along, we had recourse, from time to time, to the Gazetteer, which was our Navigator, and from its bald natural facts extracted the pleasure of poetry. Beaver River comes in a little lower down, draining the meadows of Pelham, Windham, and Londonderry. The Scotch-Irish settlers of the latter town, according to this authority, were the first to introduce the potato into New England, as well as the manufacture of linen cloth.

Every thing that is printed and bound in a book contains some echo at least of the best that is in literature. Indeed, the best books have a use like sticks and stones, which is above or beside their design, not anticipated in the preface, nor concluded in the appendix. Even Virgil's poetry serves a very different use to me to-day from what it did to his contemporaries. It has often an acquired and accidental value merely, proving that man is still man in the world. It is pleasant to meet with such still lines as,

"Jam læto turgent in palmite gemmæ;"
Now the buds swell on the joyful stem;

or

"Strata jacent passim sua quæque sub arbore poma."
The apples lie scattered every where, each under its tree.

In an ancient and dead language any recognition of living nature attracts us. These are such sentences as were written while grass grew and water ran. It is no small recommendation when a book will stand the test of mere unobstructed sunshine and daylight.

What would we not give for some great poem to read now, which would be in harmony with the scenery,—for if men read aright, methinks they would never read anything but poems. No history nor philosophy can supply their place.

The wisest definition of poetry the poet will instantly prove false by setting aside its requisitions. We can, therefore, publish only our advertisement of it.

There is no doubt that the loftiest written wisdom is either rhymed, or in some way musically measured,—is, in form as well as substance, poetry; and a volume which should contain the condensed wisdom of mankind, need not have one rhythmless line.

Yet poetry, though the last and finest result, is a natural fruit. As naturally as the oak bears an acorn, and the vine a gourd, man bears a poem, either spoken or done. It is the chief and most memorable success, for history is but a prose narrative of poetic deeds. What else have the Hindoos, the Persians, the Babylonians, the Egyptians done, that can be told? It is the simplest relation of phenomena, and describes the commonest sensations with more truth than science does, and the latter at a distance slowly mimics its style and methods. The poet sings how the blood flows in his veins. He performs his functions, and is so well that he needs such stimulus to sing only as plants to put forth leaves and blossoms. He would strive in vain to modulate the remote and transient music which he sometimes hears, since his song is a vital function like breathing, and an integral result like weight. It is not the overflowing of life but its subsidence rather, and is drawn from under the feet of the poet. It is enough if Homer but say the sun sets. He is as serene as nature, and we can hardly detect the enthusiasm of the bard. It is as if nature spoke. He presents to us the simplest pictures of human life, so the child itself can understand them, and the man must not think twice to appreciate his naturalness. Each reader discovers for himself, that, with respect to the simpler features of nature, succeeding poets have done little else than copy his similes. His more memorable passages are as naturally bright as gleams of sunshine in misty weather. Nature furnishes him not only with words, but with stereotyped lines and sentences from her mint.

"As from the clouds appears the full moon,
All shining, and then again it goes behind
the shadowy clouds,
So Hector, at one time appeared among
the foremost,
And at another in the rear, commanding;
and all with brass
He shone, like to the lightning of ægis-
bearing Zeus."

He conveys the least information, even the hour of the day, with such magnificence and vast expense of natural imagery, as if it were a message from the gods.

"While it was dawn, and sacred day was
advancing,
For that space the weapons of both flew
fast, and the people fell;
But when now the woodcutter was
preparing his midday meal,
In the recesses of the mountain, and had
wearied his hands
With cutting lofty trees, and satiety came
to his mind,
And the desire of sweet food took possession
of his thoughts;
Then the Danaans, by their valor, broke
the phalanxes,
Shouting to their companions from rank
to rank."

When the army of the Trojans passed the night under arms, keeping watch lest the enemy should re-embark under cover of the dark,

"They, thinking great things, upon the
neutral ground of war
Sat all the night; and many fires burned
for them.
As when in the heavens the stars round
the bright moon
Appear beautiful, and the air is without
wind;
And all the heights, and the extreme
summits,
And the wooded sides of the mountains
appear; and from the heavens an
infinite ether is diffused,
And all the stars are seen; and the shepherd
rejoices in his heart;
So between the ships and the streams
of Xanthus
Appeared the fires of the Trojans before Ilium.
A thousand fires burned on the plain;
and by each
Sat fifty, in the light of the blazing fire;
And horses eating white barley and corn,
Standing by the chariots, awaited fair-
throned Aurora."

The "white-armed goddess Juno," sent by the Father of gods and men for Iris and Apollo,

"Went down the Idæan mountains to far
Olympus,
As when the mind of a man, who has
come over much earth,
Sallies forth, and he reflects with
rapid thoughts,
There was I, and there, and remembers
many things;
So swiftly the august Juno hastening flew
through the air,
And came to high Olympus."

His scenery is always true, and not invented. He does not leap in imagination from Asia to Greece, through mid air,

— ἐπειὴ μάλα πολλὰ μεταξὺ
Ὄυρεά τε σκιοέντα, θαλάσσα τε ἠχήεσσα.

for there are very many
Shady mountains and resounding seas between.

If his messengers repair but to the tent of Achilles, we do not wonder how they got there, but accompany them step by step along the shore of the resounding sea. Nestor's account of the march of the Pylians against the Epeians is extremely lifesome.—

"Then rose up to them sweet-worded Nestor,
the shrill orator of the Pylians,
And words sweeter than honey flowed from
his tongue."

This time, however, he addresses Patroclus alone.—"A certain river, Minyas by name, leaps seaward near to Arene, where we Pylians wait the dawn, both horse and foot. Thence with all haste we sped us on the morrow ere 't was noon-day, accoutred for the fight, even to Alpheus' sacred source, &c." We fancy that we hear the subdued murmuring of the Minyas discharging its waters into the main the live-long night, and the hollow sound of the waves breaking on the shore, —until at length we are cheered at the close of a toilsome march by the gurgling fountains of Alpheus.

There are few books which are fit to be remembered in our wisest hours, but the Iliad is brightest in the serenest days, and embodies still all the sunlight that fell on Asia Minor. No modern joy or ecstasy of ours can lower its height, or dim its lustre, but there it lies in the east of literature, as it were at once the earliest and latest production of the mind. The ruins of Egypt oppress and stifle us with their dust, foulness preserved in cassia and pitch, and swathed in linen; the death of that which never lived. But the rays of Greek poetry struggle down to us, and mingle with the sunbeams of the recent day. The statue of Memnon is cast down, but the shaft of the Iliad still meets the sun in his rising.—

> "Homer is gone; and where is Jove? and where
> The rival cities seven? His song outlives
> Time, tower, and god,—all that then was
> save Heaven."

So too, no doubt, Homer had his Homer, and Orpheus his Orpheus, in the dim antiquity which preceded them. The mythological system of the ancients, and it is still the mythology of the moderns, the poem of mankind, interwoven so wonderfully with their astronomy, and matching in grandeur and harmony the architecture of the heavens themselves, seems to point to a time when a mightier genius inhabited the earth. But after all, man is the great poet, and not Homer nor Shakspeare; and our language itself, and the common arts of life are his work. Poetry is so universally true and independent of experience, that it does not need any particular biography to illustrate it, but we refer it sooner or later to some Orpheus or Linus, and after ages to the genius of humanity, and the gods themselves.

It would be worth the while to select our reading, for books are the society we keep; to read only the serenely true; never statistics, nor fiction, nor news, nor reports, nor periodicals, but only great poems, and when they failed, read them again, or perchance write more. Instead of other sacrifice, we might offer up our perfect (τελεία) thoughts to the gods daily, in hymns or psalms. For we should be at the helm at least once a day. The whole of the day should not be day-time; there should be one hour, if no more, which the day did not bring forth. Scholars are wont to sell their birthright for a mess of learning. But is it necessary to know what the speculator prints, or the thoughtless study, or the idle read, the literature of the Russians and the Chinese, or even French philosophy and much of German criticism. Read the best books first, or you may not have a chance to read them at all. "There are the worshippers with offerings, and the worshippers with mortifications; and again the worshippers with enthusiastic devotion; so there are those, the wisdom of whose reading is their worship, men of subdued passions, and severe manners;–This world is not for him who doth not worship; and where, O Arjoon, is there another?" Certainly, we do not need to be soothed and entertained always like children. He who resorts to the easy novel, because he is languid, does no better than if he took a nap. The front aspect of great thoughts can only be enjoyed by those who stand on the side whence they arrive. Books, not which afford us a cowering enjoyment, but in which each thought is of unusual daring; such as an idle man cannot read, and a timid one would not be entertained by, which even make us dangerous to existing institutions,–such call I good books.

All that are printed and bound are not books; they do not necessarily belong to letters, but are oftener to be ranked with the other luxuries and appendages of civilized life. Base wares are palmed off under a thousand disguises. "The way to trade," as a pedler once told me, "is to *put it right through*," no matter what it is, any thing that is agreed on.—

> "You grov'ling worldlings, you whose
> wisdom trades
> Where light ne'er shot his golden ray."

By dint of able writing and pen-craft, books are cunningly compiled, and have their run and success even among the learned, as if they were the result of a new man's thinking, and their birth were attended with some natural throes. But in a little while their covers fall off, for no binding will avail, and it appears that they are not Books or Bibles at all. There are new and patented inventions in this shape, purporting to be for the elevation of the race, which many a pure scholar and genius who has learned to read is for a moment deceived by, and finds himself reading a horse-rake, or spinning jenny, or wooden nutmeg, or oak-leaf cigar, or steam-power press, or kitchen range, perchance, when he was seeking serene and biblical truths.—

> "Merchants, arise,
> And mingle conscience with your merchandise."

Paper is cheap, and authors need not now erase one book before they write another. Instead of cultivating the earth for wheat and potatoes, they cultivate literature, and fill a place in the Republic of Letters. Or they would fain write for fame merely, as others actually raise crops of grain to be distilled into brandy. Books are for the most part wilfully and hastily written, as parts of a system, to supply a want real or imagined. Books of natural history aim commonly to be hasty schedules, or inventories of God's property, by some clerk. They do not in the least teach the divine view of nature, but the popular view, or rather the popular method of studying nature, and make haste to conduct the persevering pupil only into that dilemma where the professors always dwell.—

> "To Athens gown'd he goes, and from that school
> Returns unsped, a more instructed fool."

They teach the elements really of ignorance, not of knowledge, for to speak deliberately and in view of the highest truths, it is not easy to distinguish elementary knowledge. There is a chasm between knowledge and ignorance which the arches of science can never span. A book should contain pure discoveries, glimpses of *terra firma*, though by shipwrecked mariners, and not the art of navigation by those who have never been out of sight of land. *They* must not yield wheat and potatoes, but must themselves be the unconstrained and natural harvest of their author's lives.—

> "What I have learned is mine; I've had my thought,
> And me the Muses noble truths have taught."

We do not learn much from learned books, but from true, sincere, human books, from frank and honest biographies. The life of a good man will hardly improve us more than the life of a freebooter, for the inevitable laws appear as plainly in the infringement as in the observance, and our lives are sustained by a nearly equal expense of virtue of some kind. The decaying tree, while yet it lives, demands sun wind and rain no less than the green one. It secretes sap and performs the functions of health. If we choose, we may study the alburnum only. The gnarled stump has as tender a bud as the sapling.

At least let us have healthy books, a stout horse-rake or a kitchen range which is not cracked. Let not the poet shed tears only for the public weal. He should be as vigorous as a sugar maple, with sap enough to maintain his own verdure, beside what runs into the troughs, and not like a vine, which being cut in the spring bears no fruit, but bleeds to death in the endeavor to heal its wounds. The poet is he that hath fat enough, like bears and marmots, to suck his claws all winter. He hibernates in this world, and feeds on his own marrow. We love to think in winter, as we walk over the snowy pastures, of those happy dreamers that lie under the sod, of dormice and all that race of dormant creatures, which have such a superfluity of life enveloped in thick folds of fur, impervious to cold. Alas, the poet too is, in one sense, a sort of dormouse gone into winter quarters of deep and serene thoughts, insensible to surrounding circumstances; his words are the relation of his oldest and finest memory, a wisdom drawn from the remotest experience. Other men lead a starved existence, meanwhile, like hawks, that would fain keep on the wing, and trust to pick up a sparrow now and then.

There are already essays and poems, the growth of this land, which are not in vain, all which, however, we could conveniently have stowed in the till of our chest. If the gods permitted their own inspiration to be breathed in vain, these might be overlooked in the crowd, but the accents of truth are as sure to be heard at last on earth as in heaven. They already seem ancient, and in some measure have lost the traces of their modern birth. Here are they who

> —"ask for that which is our whole life's light,
> For the perpetual, true, and clear insight."

I remember a few sentences which spring like the sward in its native pasture, where its roots were never disturbed, and not as if spread over a sandy embankment; answering to the poet's prayer,

> "Let us set so just
> A rate on knowledge, that the world may trust
> The poet's sentence, and not still aver
> Each art is to itself a flatterer."

But, above all, in our native port, did we not frequent the peaceful games of the Lyceum, from which a new era will be dated to New England, as from the games of Greece. For if Herodotus carried his history to Olympia to read, after the cestus and the race, have we not heard such histories recited there, which since our countrymen have read, as made Greece sometimes to be forgotten?–Philosophy, too, has there her grove and portico, not wholly unfrequented in these days.

Lately the victor, whom all Pindars praised, has won another palm, contending with

> "Olympian bards who sung
> Divine ideas below,
> Which always find us young,
> And always keep us so."–

What earth or sea, mountain or stream, or Muses' spring or grove, is safe from his all-searching ardent eye, who drives off Phœbus' beaten track, visits unwonted zones, makes the gelid Hyperboreans glow, and the old polar serpent writhe, and many a Nile flow back and hide his head!–

> That Phaeton of our day,
> Who'd make another milky way,
> And burn the world up with his ray;

By us an undisputed seer,–
Who'd drive his flaming car so near
Unto our shuddering mortal sphere,

Disgracing all our slender worth,
And scorching up the living earth,
To prove his heavenly birth.

The silver spokes, the golden tire,
Are glowing with unwonted fire,
And ever nigher roll and nigher;

The pins and axle melted are,
The silver radii fly afar,
Ah, he will spoil his Father's car!

Who let him have the steeds he cannot steer?
Henceforth the sun will not shine for a year.
And we shall Ethiops all appear.

From *his*

—"lips of cunning fell
The thrilling Delphic oracle."

And yet, sometimes,

We should not mind if on our ear there fell
Some less of cunning, more of oracle.

It is Apollo shining in your face. O rare Contemporary, let us have far off heats. Give us the subtler, the heavenlier though fleeting beauty, which passes through and through, and dwells not in the verse; even pure water, which but reflects those tints which wine wears in its grain. Let epic trade-winds blow, and cease this waltz of inspirations. Let us oftener feel even the gentle south-west wind upon our cheeks blowing from the Indian's heaven. What though we lose a thousand meteors from the sky, if skyey depths, if star-dust and undissolvable nebulæ remain? What though we lose a thousand wise responses of the oracle, if we may have instead some natural acres of Ionian earth?

Though we know well,

"That 't is not in the power of kings [or presidents]
to raise
A spirit for verse that is not born thereto,
Nor are they born in every prince's days;"

yet spite of all they sang in praise of their "Eliza's reign," we have evidence that poets may be born and sing in *our* day, in the presidency of James K. Polk,

"And that the utmost powers of English rhyme,"
Were not "within *her* peaceful reign confined."

The prophecy of the poet Daniel, is already how much more than fulfilled!

"And who in time knows whither we may vent
The treasure of our tongue? To what strange shores
This gain of our best glory shall be sent,
T' enrich unknowing nations with our stores?
What worlds in th' yet unformed occident,
May come refined with the accents that are ours."

Enough has been said in these days of the charm of fluent writing. We hear it complained of some works of genius, that they have fine thoughts, but are irregular and have no flow. But even the mountain peaks in the horizon are, to the eye of science, parts of one range. We should consider that the flow of thought is more like a tidal wave than a prone river, and is the result of a celestial influence, not of any declivity in its channel. The river flows because it runs down hill, and flows the faster the faster it descends. The reader who expects to float down stream for the whole voyage, may well complain of nauseating swells and choppings of the sea when his frail shore-craft gets amidst the billows of the ocean stream, which flows as much to sun and moon as lesser streams to it. But if we would appreciate the flow that is in these books, we must expect to feel it rise from the page like an exhalation, and wash away our critical brains like burr millstones, flowing to higher levels above and behind ourselves. There is many a book which ripples on like a freshet, and flows as glibly as a mill stream sucking under a causeway; and when their authors are in the full tide of their discourse, Pythagoras and Plato, and Jamblichus, halt beside them. Their long stringy slimy sentences are of that consistency that they naturally flow and run together. They read as if written for military men, for men of business, there is such a despatch in them. Compared with these, the grave thinkers and philosophers seem not to have got their swaddling clothes off; they are slower than a Roman army in its march, the rear camping to-night where the van camped last night. The wise Jamblichus eddies and gleams like a watery slough.—

"How many thousands never heard the name
  Of Sidney, or of Spenser, or their books?
And yet brave fellows, and presume of fame,
  And seem to bear down all the world with looks."

The ready writer seizes the pen, and shouts, Forward! Alamo and Fanning! and after rolls the tide of war. The very walls and fences seem to travel. But the most rapid trot is no flow after all,—and thither, reader, you and I, at least, will not follow.

A perfectly healthy sentence, it is true, is extremely rare. For the most part we miss the hue and fragrance of the thought; as if we could be satisfied with the dews of the morning or evening without their colors, or the heavens without their azure. The most attractive sentences are, perhaps, not the wisest, but the surest and roundest. They are spoken firmly and conclusively, as if the speaker had a right to know what he says, and if not wise, they have at least been well learned. Sir Walter Raleigh might well be studied if only for the excellence of his style, for he is remarkable in the midst of so many masters. There is a natural emphasis in his style, like a man's tread, and a breathing space between the sentences, which the best of modern writing does not furnish. His chapters are like English parks, or say rather like a western forest, where the larger growth keeps down the underwood, and one may ride on horseback through the openings. All the distinguished writers of that period, possess a greater vigor and naturalness than the more modern,—for it is allowed to slander our own time,—and when we read a quotation from one of them in the midst of a modern author, we seem to have come suddenly upon a greener ground, a greater depth and strength of soil. It is as if a green bough were laid across the page, and we are refreshed as by the sight of fresh grass in mid-winter or early spring. You have constantly the warrant of life and experience in what you read. The little that is said is eked out by implication of the much that was done. The sentences are verdurous and blooming as evergreen and flowers, because they are rooted in fact and experience, but our false and florid sentences have only the tints of flowers without their sap or roots. All men are really most attracted by the beauty of plain speech, and they even write in a florid style in imitation of this. They prefer to be misunderstood rather than to come short of its exuberance. Hussein Effendi praised the epistolary style of Ibrahim Pasha to the French traveller Botta, because of "the difficulty of understanding it; there was," he said, "but one person at Jidda, who was capable of understanding and explaining the Pasha's correspondence." A man's whole life is taxed for the least thing well done. It is its net result. Every sentence is the result of a long probation. Where shall we look for standard English, but to the words of a standard man? The word which is best said came nearest to not being spoken at all, for it is cousin to a deed which the speaker could have better done. Nay, almost it must have taken the place of a deed by some urgent necessity, even by some misfortune, so that the truest writer will be some captive knight, after all. And perhaps the fates had such a design, when, having stored Raleigh so richly with the substance of life and experience, they made him a fast prisoner, and compelled him to make his words his deeds, and transfer to his expression the emphasis and sincerity of his action.

Men have a respect for scholarship and learning greatly out of proportion to the use they commonly serve. We are amused to read how Ben Jonson engaged, that the dull masks with which the royal family and nobility were to be entertained, should be "grounded upon antiquity and solid learning." Can there be any greater reproach than an idle learning? Learn to split wood, at least. The necessity of labor and conversation with many men and things, to the scholar is rarely well remembered; steady labor with the hands, which engrosses the attention also, is unquestionably the best method of removing palaver and sentimentality out of one's style, both of speaking and writing. If he has worked hard from morning till night, though he may have grieved that he could not be watching the train of his thoughts during that time, yet the few hasty lines which at evening record his day's experience will be more musical and true than his freest but idle fancy could have furnished. Surely the writer is to address a world of laborers, and such therefore must be his own discipline. He will not idly dance at his work who has wood to cut and cord before night-fall in the short days of winter; but every stroke will be husbanded, and ring soberly through the wood; and so will the strokes of that scholar's pen, which at evening record the story of the day, ring soberly, yet cheerily, on the ear of the reader, long after the echoes of his axe have died away. The scholar may be sure that he writes the tougher truth for the calluses on his palms. They give firmness to the sentence. Indeed, the mind never makes a great and successful effort without a corresponding energy of the body. We are often struck by the force and precision of style to which hard-working men, unpractised in writing, easily attain, when required to make the effort. As if plainness, and vigor, and sincerity, the ornaments of style, were better learned on the farm and in the workshop than in the schools. The sentences written by such rude hands are nervous and tough, like hardened thongs, the sinews of the deer, or the roots of the pine. As for the graces of expression, a great thought is never found in a mean dress; but though it proceed from the lips of the Woloffs, the nine Muses and the three Graces will have conspired to clothe it in fit phrase. Its education has always been liberal, and its implied wit can endow a college. The world, which the Greeks called Beauty, has been made such by being gradually divested of every ornament which was not fitted to endure. The Sibyl, "speaking with inspired mouth, smileless, inornate, and unperfumed, pierces through centuries by the power of the god." The scholar might frequently emulate the propriety and emphasis of the farmer's call to his team, and confess that if that were written it would surpass his labored sentences. Whose are the truly *labored* sentences? From the weak and flimsy periods of the politician and literary man, we are glad to turn even to the description of work, the simple record of the month's labor in the farmer's almanac, to restore our tone and spirits. A sentence should read as if its author, had he held a plow instead of a pen, could have drawn a furrow deep and straight to the end. The scholar requires hard and serious labor to give an impetus to his thought. He will learn to grasp the pen firmly so, and wield it gracefully and effectively, as an axe or a sword. When we consider the weak and nerveless periods of some literary men, who perchance in feet and inches come up to the standard of their race, and are not deficient in girth also, we are amazed at the immense sacrifice of thews and sinews. What! these proportions,–these bones,–and this their work! Hands which could have felled an ox have hewed this fragile matter which would not have tasked a lady's fingers! Can this be a stalwart man's work, who has a marrow in his back and a tendon Achilles in his heel? They who set up the blocks of Stonehenge did somewhat, if they only laid out their strength for once, and stretched themselves.

Yet, after all, the truly efficient laborer will not crowd his day with work, but will saunter to his task surrounded by a wide halo of ease and leisure, and then do but what he loves best. He is anxious only about the fruitful kernels of time. Though the hen should sit all day, she could lay only one egg, and, besides, would not have picked up materials for another. Let a man take time enough for the most trivial deed, though it be but the paring of his nails. The buds swell imperceptibly, without hurry or confusion, as if the short spring days were an eternity.—

> Then spend an age in whetting thy desire,
> Thou needs't not *hasten* if thou dost *stand fast.*

Some hours seem not to be occasion for any deed, but for resolves to draw breath in. We do not directly go about the execution of the purpose that thrills us, but shut our doors behind us, and ramble with prepared mind, as if the half were already done. Our resolution is taking root or hold on the earth then, as seeds first send a shoot downward which is fed by their own albumen, ere they send one upward to the light.

There is a sort of homely truth and naturalness in some books which is very rare to find, and yet looks cheap enough. There may be nothing lofty in the sentiment, or fine in the expression, but it is careless country talk. Homeliness is almost as great a merit in a book as in a house, if the reader would abide there. It is next to beauty, and a very high art. Some have this merit only. The scholar is not apt to make his most familiar experience come gracefully to the aid of his expression. Very few men can speak of Nature, for instance, with any truth. They overstep her modesty, somehow or other, and confer no favor. They do not speak a good word for her. Most cry better than they speak, and you can get more nature out of them by pinching than by addressing them. The surliness with which the wood-chopper speaks of his woods, handling them as indifferently as his axe, is better than the mealy-mouthed enthusiasm of the lover of nature. Better that the primrose by the river's brim be a yellow primrose, and nothing more, than that it be something less. Aubrey relates of Thomas Fuller that his was "a very working head, insomuch, that walking and meditating before dinner, he would eat up a penny loaf, not knowing that he did it. His natural memory was very great, to which he added the art of memory. He would repeat to you forwards and backwards all the signs from Ludgate to Charing-cross." He says of Mr. John Hales, that "He loved Canarie," and was buried "under an altar monument of black marble —— —— with a too long epitaph;" of Edmund Halley, that he "at sixteen could make a dial, and then, he said, he thought himself a brave fellow;" of William Holder, who wrote a book upon his curing one Popham who was deaf and dumb, "he was beholding to no author; did only consult with nature." For the most part, an author consults only with all who have written before him upon a subject, and his book is but the advice of so many. But a good book will never have been forestalled, but the topic itself will in one sense be new, and its author, by consulting with nature, will consult not only with those who have gone before, but with those who may come after. There is always room and occasion enough for a true book on any subject; as there is room for more light the brightest day and more rays will not interfere with the first.

We thus worked our way up this river, gradually adjusting our thoughts to novelties, beholding from its placid bosom a new nature and new works of men, and as it were with increasing confidence, finding nature still habitable, genial, and propitious to us; not following any beaten path, but the windings of the river, as ever the nearest way for us. Fortunately we had no business in this country. The Concord had rarely been a river or *rivus*, but barely *fluvius*, or between *fluvius* and *lacus*. This Merrimack was neither *rivus* nor *fluvius* nor *lacus*, but rather *amnis* here, a gently swelling and stately rolling flood approaching the sea. We could even sympathize with its buoyant tide, going to seek its fortune in the ocean, and anticipating the time when "being received within the plain of its freer water," it should "beat the shores for banks,"—

> "campoque recepta
> Liberioris aquæ, pro ripis litora pulsant."

At length we doubled a low shrubby islet, called Rabbit Island, subjected alternately to the sun and to the waves, as desolate as if it lay some leagues within the icy sea, and found ourselves in a narrower part of the river, near the sheds and yards for picking the stone known as the Chelmsford granite, which is quarried in Westford and the neighboring towns. We passed Wicasuck Island, which contains seventy acres or more, on our right between Chelmsford and Tyngsboro'. This was a favorite residence of the Indians. According to the History of Dunstable, "About 1663, the eldest son of Passaconaway, [Chief of the Penacooks] was thrown into jail for a debt of £45, due to John Tinker, by one of his tribe, and which he had promised verbally should be paid. To relieve him from his imprisonment, his brother Wannalancet and others, who owned Wicasuck Island, sold it and paid the debt." It was, however, restored to the Indians by the General Court in 1665. After the departure of the

Indians in 1683, it was granted to Jonathan Tyng in payment for his services to the colony, in maintaining a garrison at his house. Tyng's house stood not far from Wicasuck Falls. Gookin, who, in his Epistle Dedicatory to Robert Boyle, apologizes for presenting his "matter clothed in a wilderness dress," says that on the breaking out of Philip's war in 1675, there were taken up by the Christian Indians and the English in Marlborough, and sent to Cambridge, seven "Indians belonging to Narragansett, Long Island, and Pequod, who had all been at work about seven weeks with one Mr. Jonathan Tyng, of Dunstable, upon Merrimack river; and hearing of the war, they reckoned with their master, and getting their wages, conveyed themselves away without his privity, and being afraid, marched secretly through the woods, designing to go to their own country." However, they were released soon after. Such were the hired men in those days. Tyng was the first permanent settler of Dunstable, which then embraced what is now Tyngsboro' and many other towns. In the winter of 1675, in Philip's war, every other settler left the town, but "he," says the historian of Dunstable, "fortified his house; and although 'obliged to send to Boston for his food,' sat himself down in the midst of his savage enemies, alone, in the wilderness, to defend his home. Deeming his position an important one for the defence of the frontiers, in Feb. 1676, he petitioned the Colony for aid," humbly showing, as his petition runs, that as he lived "in the uppermost house on Merrimac river, lying open to ye enemy, yet being so seated that it is, as it were, a watchhouse to the neighboring towns," he could render important service to his country if only he had some assistance, "there being," he said, "never an inhabitant left in the town but myself." Wherefore he requests that their "Honors would be pleased to order him *three or four men* to help garrison his said house," which they did. But methinks that such a garrison would be weakened by the addition of a man.—

"Make bandog thy scout watch to bark at a thief,
Make courage for life, to be capitain chief;
Make trap-door thy bulwark, make bell to begin,
Make gunstone and arrow shew who is within."

Thus he earned the title of first permanent settler. In 1694 a law was passed "that every settler who deserted a town for fear of the Indians, should forfeit all his rights therein." But now, at any rate, as I have frequently observed, a man may desert the fertile frontier territories of truth and justice, which are the State's best lands, for fear of far more insignificant foes, without forfeiting any of his civil rights therein. Nay, townships are granted to deserters, and the General Court, as I am sometimes inclined to regard it, is but a deserters' camp itself.

As we rowed along near the shore of Wicasuck Island, which was then covered with wood, in order to avoid the current, two men, who looked as if they had just run out of Lowell, where they had been waylaid by the Sabbath, meaning to go to Nashua, and who now found themselves in the strange, natural, uncultivated and unsettled part of the globe which intervenes, full of walls and barriers, a rough and uncivil place to them, seeing our boat moving so smoothly up the stream, called out from the high bank above our heads to know if we would take them as passengers, as if this were the street they had missed; that they might sit and chat and drive away the time, and so at last find themselves in Nashua. This smooth way they much preferred. But our boat was crowded with necessary furniture, and sunk low in the water, and moreover required to be worked, for even *it* did not progress against the stream without effort; so we were obliged to deny them passage. As we glided away with even sweeps, while the fates scattered oil in our course, the sun now sinking behind the alders on the distant shore, we could still see them far off over the water, running along the shore and climbing over the rocks and fallen trees like insects,—for they did not know any better than we that they were on an island,—the unsympathizing river ever flowing in an opposite direction; until, having reached the entrance of the Island Brook, which they had probably crossed upon the locks below, they found a more effectual barrier to their progress. They seemed to be learning much in a little time. They ran about like ants on a burning brand, and once more they tried the river here, and once more there, to see if water still indeed was not to be walked on, as if a new thought inspired them, and by some peculiar disposition of the limbs they could accomplish it. At length sober common sense seemed to have resumed its sway, and they concluded that what they had so long heard must be true, and resolved to ford the shallower stream. When nearly a mile distant we could see them stripping off their clothes and preparing for this experiment; yet it seemed likely that a new dilemma would arise, they were so thoughtlessly throwing away their clothes on the wrong side of the stream, as in the case of the countryman with his corn, his fox, and his goose, which had to be transported one at a time. Whether they got safely through, or went round by the locks we never learned. We could not help being struck by the seeming, though innocent indifference of Nature to these men's necessities, while elsewhere she was equally serving others. Like a true benefactress, the secret of her service is unchangeableness. Thus is the busiest merchant, though within sight of his Lowell, put to pilgrim's shifts, and soon comes to staff and scrip and scallop shell.

We, too, who held the middle of the stream, came near experiencing a pilgrim's fate, being tempted to pursue what seemed a sturgeon or larger fish, for we remembered that this was the Sturgeon River, its dark and monstrous back alternately rising and sinking in mid-stream. We kept falling behind, but the fish kept his back well out, and did not dive, and seemed to prefer to swim against the stream, so, at any rate, he would not escape us by going out to sea. At length, having got as near as was convenient, and looking out not to get a blow from his tail, now the bow-gunner delivered his charge, while the stern-man held his ground. But the halibut-skinned monster, in one of these swift-gliding pregnant moments, without ever ceasing his bobbing up and down, saw fit, without a chuckle or other prelude, to proclaim himself a huge imprisoned spar, placed there as a buoy, to warn sailors of sunken rocks. So, each casting some blame upon the other, we withdrew quickly to safer waters.

The Scene-shifter saw fit here to close the drama of this day, without regard to any unities which we mortals prize. Whether it might have proved tragedy, or comedy, or tragi-comedy, or pastoral, we cannot tell. This Sunday ended by the going down of the sun, leaving us still on the waves. But they who are on the water enjoy a longer and brighter twilight than they who are on the land, for here the water, as well as the atmosphere, absorbs and reflects the light, and some of the day seems to have sunk down into the waves. The light gradually forsook the deep water, as well as the deeper air, and the gloaming came to the fishes as well as to us, and more dim and gloomy to them, whose day is a perpetual twilight, though sufficiently bright for their weak and watery eyes. Vespers had already rung in many a dim and watery chapel down below, where the shadows of the weeds were extended in length over the sandy floor. The vespertinal pout had already begun to flit on leathern fin, and the finny gossips withdrew from the fluvial street to creeks and coves, and other private haunts, excepting a few of stronger fin, which anchored in the stream, stemming the tide even in their dreams. Meanwhile, like a dark evening cloud, we were wafted over the cope of their sky, deepening the shadows on their deluged fields.

Having reached a retired part of the river where it spread out to sixty rods in width, we pitched our tent on the east side, in Tyngsboro', just above some patches of the beach plum, which was now nearly ripe, where the sloping bank was a sufficient pillow, and with the bustle of sailors making the land, we transferred such stores as were required from boat to tent, and hung a lantern to the tent-pole, and so our house was ready. With a buffalo spread on the grass, and a blanket for our covering, our bed was soon made. A fire crackled merrily before the entrance, so near that we could tend it without stepping abroad, and when we had supped, we put out the blaze, and closed the door, and with the semblance of domestic comfort, sat up to read the gazetteer, to learn our latitude and longitude, and write the journal of the voyage, or listened to the wind and the rippling of the river till sleep overtook us. There we lay under an oak on the bank of the stream, near to some farmer's cornfield, getting sleep, and forgetting where we were; a great blessing, that we are obliged to forget our enterprises every twelve hours. Minks, muskrats, meadow-mice, woodchucks, squirrels, skunks, rabbits, foxes and weasels, all inhabit near, but keep very close while you are there. The river sucking and eddying away all night down toward the marts and the seaboard, a great wash and freshet, and no small enterprise to reflect on. Instead of the Scythian vastness of the Billerica night, and its wild musical sounds, we were kept awake by the boisterous sport of some Irish laborers on the railroad, wafted to us over the water, still unwearied and unresting on this seventh day, who would not have done with whirling up and down the track with ever increasing velocity and still reviving shouts, till late in the night.

One sailor was visited in his dreams this night by the Evil Destinies, and all those powers that are hostile to human life, which constrain and oppress the minds of men, and make their path seem difficult and narrow, and beset with dangers, so that the most innocent and worthy enterprises appear insolent and a tempting of fate, and the gods go not with us. But the other happily passed a serene and even ambrosial or immortal night, and his sleep was dreamless, or only the atmosphere of pleasant dreams remained, a happy natural sleep until the morning; and his cheerful spirit soothed and reassured his brother, for whenever they meet, the Good Genius is sure to prevail.

Monday.

"I thynke for to touche also
The worlde whiche neweth everie daie,
So as I can, so as I maie."

Gower.

"The hye sheryfe of Notynghame,
Hym holde in your mynde."

Robin Hood Ballads.

"His shoote it was but loosely shott,
Yet flewe not the arrowe in vaine,
For it mett one of the sheriffe's men,
And William a Trent was slaine."

Robin Hood Ballads.

"Gazed on the Heavens for what he missed on
Earth."

Britania's Pastorals.

WHEN the first light dawned on the earth, and the birds awoke, and the brave river was heard rippling confidently seaward, and the nimble early rising wind rustled the oak leaves about our tent, all men, having reinforced their bodies and their souls with sleep, and cast aside doubt and fear, were invited to unattempted adventures.

"All courageous knichtis
Agains the day dichtis
The breest-plate that bricht is,
To feght with their fone.
The stoned steed stampis
Throw courage and crampis,
Syne on the land lampis;
The night is neir gone."

One of us took the boat over to the opposite shore, which was flat and accessible, a quarter of a mile distant, to empty it of water and wash out the clay, while the other kindled a fire and got breakfast ready. At an early hour we were again on our way, rowing through the fog as before, the river already awake, and a million crisped waves come forth to meet the sun when he should show himself. The countrymen, recruited by their day of rest, were already stirring, and had begun to cross the ferry on the business of the week. This ferry was as busy as a beaver dam, and all the world seemed anxious to get across the Merrimack River at this particular point, waiting to get set over, —children with their two cents done up in paper, jail-birds broke loose and constable with warrant, travellers from distant lands to distant lands, men and women to whom the Merrimack river was a bar. There stands a gig in the gray morning, in the mist, the impatient traveller pacing the wet shore with whip in hand, and shouting through the fog after the regardless Charon and his retreating ark, as if he might throw that passenger overboard and return forthwith for himself; he will compensate him. He is to break his fast at some unseen place on the opposite side. It may be Ledyard or the Wandering Jew. Whence pray did he come out of the foggy night? and whither through the sunny day will he go? We observe only his transit; important to us, forgotten by him, transiting all day. There are two of them. May be, they are Virgil and Dante. But when they crossed the Styx, none were seen bound up or down the stream, that I remember. It is only a *transjectus*, a transitory voyage, like life itself, none but the long-lived gods bound up or down the stream. Many of these Monday men are ministers, no doubt, reseeking their parishes with hired horses, with sermons in their valises all read and gutted, the day after never with them. They cross each other's routes all the country over like woof and warp, making a garment of loose texture; vacation now for six days. They stop to pick nuts and berries, and gather apples by the wayside at their leisure. Good religious men, with the love of men in their hearts, and the means to pay their toll in their pockets. We got over this ferry chain without scraping, rowing athwart the tide of travel,—no toll from us that day.

The fog dispersed and we rowed leisurely along through Tyngsboro', with a clear sky and a mild atmosphere, leaving the habitations of men behind and penetrating yet further into the territory of ancient Dunstable. It was from Dunstable, then a frontier town, that the famous Capt. Lovewell, with his company, marched in quest of the Indians on the 18th of April, 1725. He was the son of "an ensign in the army of Oliver Cromwell, who came to this country, and settled at Dunstable, where he died at the great age of one hundred and twenty years." In the words of the old nursery tale, sung about a hundred years ago,—

> "He and his valiant soldiers did range the
> woods full wide,
> And hardships they endured to quell the
> Indian's pride."

In the shaggy pine forest of Pequawket they met the "rebel Indians," and prevailed, after a bloody fight, and a remnant returned home to enjoy the fame of their victory. A township called Lovewell's Town, but now, for some reason, or perhaps without reason, Pembroke, was granted them by the State.

"Of all our valiant English, there were
but thirty-four,
And of the rebel Indians, there were about
four score;
And sixteen of our English did safely home
return,
The rest were killed and wounded, for which
we all must mourn.

"Our worthy Capt. Lovewell among them
there did die,
They killed Lieut. Robbins, and wounded
good young Frye,
Who was our English Chaplin; he many
Indians slew,
And some of them he scalped while bullets
round him flew."

Our brave forefathers have exterminated all the Indians, and their degenerate children no longer dwell in garrisoned houses, nor hear any war-whoop in their path. It would be well, perchance, if many an "English Chaplin" in these days could exhibit as unquestionable trophies of his valor as did "good young Frye." We have need to be as sturdy pioneers still as Miles Standish, or Church, or Lovewell. We are to follow on another trail, it is true, but one as convenient for ambushes. What if the Indians are exterminated, are not savages as grim prowling about the clearings to-day?—

"And braving many dangers and hardships in the way,
They safe arrived at Dunstable the thirteenth (?)
day of May."

But they did not all "safe arrive in Dunstable the thirteenth," or the fifteenth, or the thirtieth "day of May." Eleazer Davis and Josiah Jones, both of Concord, for our native town had seven men in this fight, Lieutenant Farwell, of Dunstable, and Jonathan

Frye, of Andover, who were all wounded, were left behind, creeping toward the settlements. "After travelling several miles, Frye was left and lost," though a more recent poet has assigned him company in his last hours.–

"A man he was of comely form,
Polished and brave, well learned and kind;
Old Harvard's learned halls he left
Far in the wilds a grave to find.

"Ah! now his blood-red arm he lifts;
His closing lids he tries to raise;
And speak once more before he dies,
In supplication and in praise.

"He prays kind Heaven to grant success,
Brave Lovewell's men to guide and bless,
And when they've shed their heart-blood true,
To raise them all to happiness." * *

"Lieutenant Farwell took his hand,
His arm around his neck he threw,
And said, 'brave Chaplain I could wish,
That Heaven had made me die for you.' "

Farwell held out eleven days. "A tradition says," as we learn from the History of Concord, "that arriving at a pond with Lieut. Farwell, Davis pulled off one of his moccasins, cut it in strings, on which he fastened a hook, caught some fish, fried and ate them. They refreshed him, but were injurious to Farwell, who died soon after." Davis had a ball lodged in his body, and his right hand shot off; but on the whole, he seems to have been less damaged than his companion. He came into Berwick after being out fourteen days. Jones also had a ball lodged in his body, but he likewise got into Saco after fourteen days, though not in the best condition imaginable. "He had subsisted," says an old journal, "on the spontaneous vegetables of the forest; and cranberries, which he had eaten, came out of wounds he had received in his body." This was also the case with Davis. The last two reached home at length, safe if not sound, and lived many years in a crippled state to enjoy their pension.

But alas! of the crippled Indians, and their adventures in the woods,—

"For as we are informed, so thick and fast
they fell,
Scarce twenty of their number at night did
get home well,"—

how many balls lodged with them, how it fared with their cranberries, what Berwick or Saco they got into, and finally what pension or township was granted them, there is no journal to tell.

It is stated in the History of Dunstable, that just before his last march, Lovewell was warned to beware of the ambuscades of the enemy, but "he replied, 'that he did not care for them,' and bending down a small elm beside which he was standing into a bow, declared 'that he would treat the Indians in the same way.' This elm is still standing, [in Nashua] a venerable and magnificent tree."

Meanwhile, having passed the Horseshoe Interval in Tyngsboro', where the river makes a sudden bend to the northwest,—for our reflections have anticipated our progress somewhat,—we were advancing further into the country and into the day, which last proved almost as golden as the preceding, though the slight bustle and activity of the Monday seemed to penetrate even to this scenery. Now and then we had to muster all our energy to get round a point, where the river broke rippling over rocks, and the maples trailed their branches in the stream, but there was generally a backwater or eddy on the side, of which we took advantage. The river was here about forty rods wide and fifteen feet deep. Occasionally one ran along the shore, examining the country, and visiting the nearest farm-houses, while the other followed the windings of the stream alone, to meet his companion at some distant point, and hear the report of his adventures; how the farmer praised the coolness of his well, and his wife offered the stranger a draught of milk, or the children quarrelled for the only transparency in the window that they might get sight of the man at the well. For though the country seemed so new, and no house was observed by us, shut in between the high banks that sunny day, we did not have to travel far to find where men inhabited, like wild bees, and had sunk wells in the loose sand and loam of the Merrimack. There dwelt the subject of the Hebrew scriptures, and the Esprit des Lois, where a thin vaporous smoke curled up through the noon. All that is told of mankind, of the inhabitants of the Upper Nile, and the Sunderbunds, and Timbuctoo, and the Orinoko, was experience here. Every race and class of men was represented. According to Belknap, the historian of New Hampshire, who wrote sixty years ago, here too, perchance, dwelt "new lights," and free thinking men even then. "The people in general throughout the State," it is written, "are professors of the Christian religion in some form or other. There is, however, a sort of *wise men*, who pretend to reject it; but they have not yet been able to substitute a better in its place."

The other voyageur, perhaps, would in the meanwhile have seen a brown hawk, or a woodchuck, or a musquash creeping under the alders.

We occasionally rested in the shade of a maple or a willow, and drew forth a melon for our refreshment, while we contemplated at our leisure the lapse of the river and of human life; and as that current, with its floating twigs and leaves, so did all things pass in review before us, while far away in cities and marts on this very stream, the old routine was proceeding still. There is, indeed, a tide in the affairs of men, as the poet says, and yet as things flow they circulate, and the ebb always balances the flow. All streams are but tributary to the ocean, which itself does not stream, and the shores are unchanged but in longer periods than man can measure. Go where we will, we discover infinite change in particulars only, not in generals. When I go into a museum, and see the mummies wrapped in their linen bandages, I see that the lives of men began to need reform as long ago as when they walked the earth. I come out into the streets, and meet men who declare that the time is near at hand for the redemption of the race. But as men lived in Thebes, so do they live in Dunstable today. "Time drinketh up the essence of every great and noble action, which ought to be performed, and is delayed in the execution." So says Veeshnoo Sarma; and we perceive that the schemers return again and again to common sense and labor. Such is the evidence of history.–

> "Yet I doubt not thro' the ages one increasing
> purpose runs,
> And the thoughts of men are widen'd with
> the process of the Suns."

There are secret articles in our treaties with the gods, of more importance than all the rest, which the historian can never know.

There are many skilful apprentices, but few master workmen. On every hand we observe a truly wise practice, in education, in morals, and in the arts of life, the embodied wisdom of many an ancient philosopher. Who does not see that heresies have some time prevailed, that reforms have already taken place? All this worldly wisdom might be regarded as the once unamiable heresy of some wise man. Some interests have got a footing on the earth which we have not made sufficient allowance for. Even they who first built these barns, and cleared the land thus, had some valor. The abrupt epochs and chasms are smoothed down in history as the inequalities of the plain are concealed by distance. But unless we do more than simply learn the trade of our time, we are but apprentices, and not yet masters of the art of life.

Now that we are casting away these melon seeds, how can we help feeling reproach? He who eats the fruit, should at least plant the seed; aye, if possible, a better seed than that whose fruit he has enjoyed. Seeds! there are seeds enough which need only to be stirred in with the soil where they lie, by an inspired voice or pen, to bear fruit of a divine flavor. O thou spendthrift! Defray thy debt to the world; eat not the seed of institutions, as the luxurious do, but plant it rather, while thou devourest the pulp and tuber for thy subsistence; that so, perchance, one variety may at last be found worthy of preservation.

There are moments when all anxiety and stated toil are becalmed in the infinite leisure and repose of nature. All laborers must have their nooning, and at this season of the day, we are all, more or less, Asiatics, and give over all work and reform. While lying thus on our oars by the side of the stream, in the heat of the day, our boat held by an osier put through the staple in its prow, and slicing the melons, which are a fruit of the east, our thoughts reverted to Arabia, Persia, and Hindostan, the lands of contemplation and dwelling places of the ruminant nations. In the experience of this noontide we could find some apology even for the instinct of the opium, betel, and tobacco chewers. Mount Sabér, according to the French traveller and naturalist, Botta, is celebrated for producing the Kát tree, of which "the soft tops of the twigs and tender leaves are eaten," says his reviewer, "and produce an agreeable soothing excitement, restoring from fatigue, banishing sleep, and disposing to the enjoyment of conversation." We thought that we might lead a dignified oriental life along this stream as well, and the maple and alders would be our Kát trees.

It is a great pleasure to escape sometimes from the restless class of Reformers. What if these grievances exist? So do you and I. Think you that sitting hens are troubled with ennui these long summer days, sitting on and on in the crevice of a hay-loft, without active employment? By the faint cackling in distant barns, I judge that dame Nature is interested still to know how many eggs her hens lay. The Universal Soul, as it is called, has an interest in the stacking of hay, the foddering of cattle, and the draining of peat meadows. Away in Scythia, away in India, it makes butter and cheese. Suppose that all farms *are* run out, and we youths must buy old land and bring it to, still every where the relentless opponents of reform bear a strange resemblance to ourselves; or perchance, they are a few old maids and bachelors, who sit round the kitchen hearth, and listen to the singing of the kettle. "The oracles often give victory to our choice, and not to the order alone of the mundane periods. As, for instance, when they say, that our voluntary sorrows germinate in us as the growth of the particular life we lead." The reform which you talk about can be undertaken any morning before unbarring our doors. We need not call any convention. When two neighbors begin to eat corn bread, who before ate wheat, then the gods smile from ear to ear, for it is very pleasant to them. Why do you not try it? Don't let me hinder you.

There are theoretical reformers at all times, and all the world over, living on anticipation. Wolff, travelling in the deserts of Bokhara, says, "Another party of derveeshes came to me and observed, 'The time will come when there shall be no difference between rich and poor, between high and low, when property will be in common, even wives and children.' " But forever I ask of such, What then? The derveeshes in the deserts of Bokhara and the reformers in Marlboro' Chapel sing the same song. "There's a good time coming, boys," but asked one of the audience in good faith, "Can you fix the date?" Said I, "Will you help it along?"

The non-chalance and *dolce-far-niente* air of nature and society hint at infinite periods in the progress of mankind. The States have leisure to laugh from Maine to Texas at some newspaper joke, and New England shakes at the double-entendres of Australian circles, while the poor reformer cannot get a hearing.

Men do not fail commonly for want of knowledge, but for want of prudence to give wisdom the preference. What we need to know in any case is very simple. It is but too easy to establish another durable and harmonious routine. Immediately all parts of nature consent to it. Only make something to take the place of something, and men will behave as if it were the very thing they wanted. They *must* behave, at any rate, and will work up any material. There is always a present and extant life, be it better or worse, which all combine to uphold. We should be slow to mend, my friends, as slow to require mending, "Not hurling, according to the oracle, a transcendent foot towards piety." The language of excitement is at best picturesque merely. You must be calm before you can utter oracles. What was the excitement of the Delphic priestess compared with the calm wisdom of Socrates?—or whoever it was that was wise.—Enthusiasm is a supernatural serenity.

"Men find that action is another thing
 Than what they in discoursing papers read;
The world's affairs require in managing
 More arts than those wherein you clerks proceed."

As in geology, so in social institutions, we may discover the causes of all past change in the present invariable order of society. The greatest appreciable physical revolutions are the work of the light-footed air, the stealthy-paced water, and the subterranean fire. Aristotle said, "As time never fails, and the universe is eternal, neither the Tanais nor the Nile, can have flowed forever." We are independent of the change we detect. The longer the lever the less perceptible its motion. It is the slowest pulsation which is the most vital. The hero then will know how to wait, as well as to make haste. All good abides with him who waiteth *wisely*; we shall sooner overtake the dawn by remaining here than by hurrying over the hills of the west. Be assured that every man's success is in proportion to his *average* ability. The meadow flowers spring and bloom where the waters annually deposit their slime, not where they reach in some freshet only. A man is not his hope, nor his despair, nor yet his past deed. We know not yet what we have done, still less what we are doing. Wait till evening, and other parts of our day's work will shine than we had thought at noon, and we shall discover the real purport of our toil. As when the farmer has reached the end of the furrow and looks back, he can best tell where the pressed earth shines most.

To one who habitually endeavors to contemplate the true state of things, the political state can hardly be said to have any existence whatever. It is unreal, incredible and insignificant to him, and for him to endeavor to extract the truth from such lean material is like making sugar from linen rags, when sugar cane may be had. Generally speaking, the political news, whether domestic or foreign, might be written to-day for the next ten years, with sufficient accuracy. Most revolutions in society have not power to interest, still less alarm us; but tell me that our rivers are drying up, or the genus pine dying out in the country, and I might attend. Most events recorded in history are more remarkable than important, like eclipses of the sun and moon, by which all are attracted, but whose effects no one takes the trouble to calculate. But will the government never be so well administered, inquired one, that we private men shall hear nothing about it? "The king answered;–At all events, I require a prudent and able man, who is capable of managing the state affairs of my kingdom. The ex-minister said; The criterion, O Sire! of a wise and competent man, is, that he will not meddle with such like matters". Alas, that the ex-minister should have been so nearly right.

In my short experience of human life, the *outward* obstacles, if there were any such, have not been living men, but the institutions of the dead. It is grateful to make one's way through this latest generation as through dewy grass. Men are as innocent as the morning to the unsuspicious.—

> "And round about good morrows fly,
> As if day taught humanity."

Not being Reve of this Shire,

> "The early pilgrim blithe he hailed,
> That o'er the hills did stray,
> And many an early husbandman,
> That he met on his way;"—

thieves and robbers all nevertheless. I have not so surely foreseen that any Cossack or Chippeway would come to disturb the honest and simple commonwealth, as that some monster institution would at length embrace and crush its free members in its scaly folds; for it is not to be forgotten, that while the law holds fast the thief and murderer, it lets itself go loose. When I have not paid the tax which the State demanded for that protection which I did not want, itself has robbed me; when I have asserted the liberty it presumed to declare, itself has imprisoned me. Poor creature! if it knows no better I will not blame it. If it cannot live but by these means, I can. I do not wish, it happens, to be associated with Massachusetts, either in holding slaves or in conquering Mexico. I am a little better than herself in these respects.—As for

Massachusetts, that huge she Briareus, Argus and Colchian Dragon conjoined, set to watch the Heifer of the Constitution and the Golden Fleece, we would not warrant our respect for her, like some compositions, to preserve its qualities through all weathers.— Thus it has happened, that not the Arch Fiend himself has been in my way, but these toils which tradition says were originally spun to obstruct him. They are cobwebs and trifling obstacles in an earnest man's path, it is true, and at length one even becomes attached to his unswept and undusted garret. I love man—kind, but I hate the institutions of the dead unkind. Men execute nothing so faithfully as the wills of the dead, to the last codicil and letter. *They* rule this world, and the living are but their executors. Such foundation too have our lectures and our sermons commonly. They are all *Dudleian*; and piety derives its origin still from that exploit of *pius Æneas*, who bore his father, Anchises on his shoulders from the ruins of Troy. Or rather, like some Indian tribes, we bear about with us the mouldering relics of our ancestors on our shoulders. If, for instance, a man asserts the value of individual liberty over the merely political commonweal, his neighbor still tolerates him, that is he who is *living near* him, sometimes even sustains him, but never the State. Its officer, as a living man, may have human virtues and a thought in his brain, but as the tool of an institution, a jailer or constable it may be, he is not a whit superior to his prison key or his staff. Herein is the tragedy; that men doing outrage to their proper natures, even those called wise and good, lend themselves to perform the office of inferior and brutal ones. Hence come war and slavery in; and what else may not come in by this opening? But certainly there are modes by which a man may put bread into his mouth which will not prejudice him as a companion and neighbor.

> "Now turn again, turn again, said the pindèr,
> For a wrong way you have gone,
> For you have forsaken the king's highway,
> And made a path over the corn."

Undoubtedly, countless reforms are called for, because society is not animated, or instinct enough with life, but in the condition of some snakes which I have seen in early spring, with alternate portions of their bodies torpid and flexible, so that they could wriggle neither way. All men are partially buried in the grave of custom, and of some we see only the crown of the head above ground. Better are the physically dead, for they more lively rot. Even virtue is no longer such if it be stagnant. A man's life should be constantly as fresh as this river. It should be the same channel, but a new water every instant.–

> —"Virtues as rivers pass,
> But still remains that virtuous man there was."

Most men have no inclination, no rapids, no cascades, but marshes, and alligators, and miasma instead. We read that when in the expedition of Alexander, Onesicritus was sent forward to meet certain of the Indian sect of Gymnosophists, and he had told them of those new philosophers of the West, Pythagoras, Socrates, and Diogenes, and their doctrines, one of them named Dandamis answered, that "They appeared to him to have been men of genius, but to have lived with too passive a regard for the laws." The philosophers of the West are liable to this rebuke still. "They say that Lieou-hia-hoei and Chao-lien did not sustain to the end their resolutions, and that they dishonored their character. Their language was in harmony with reason and justice; while their acts were in harmony with the sentiments of men."

Chateaubriand said, "There are two things which grow stronger in the breast of man, in proportion as he advances in years; the love of country and religion. Let them be never so much forgotten in youth, they sooner or later present themselves to us arrayed in all their charms, and excite in the recesses of our hearts, an attachment justly due to their beauty." It may be so. But even this infirmity of noble minds marks the gradual decay of youthful hope and faith. It is the allowed infidelity of age. There is a saying of the Yoloffs, "He who was born first has the greatest number of old clothes," consequently M. Chateaubriand has more old clothes than I have. It is comparatively a faint and reflected beauty that is admired, not an essential and intrinsic one. It is because the old are weak, feel their mortality, and think that they have measured the strength of man. They will not boast; they will be frank and humble. Well, let them have the few poor comforts they can keep. Humility is still a very human virtue. They look back on life, and so see not into the future. The prospect of the young is forward and unbounded, mingling the future with the present. In the declining day the thoughts make haste to rest in darkness, and hardly look forward to the ensuing morning. The thoughts of the old prepare for night and slumber. The same hopes and prospects are not for him who stands upon the rosy mountain-tops of life, and him who expects the setting of his earthly day.

I must conclude that Conscience, if that be the

name of it, was not given us for no purpose, or for a hinderance. However flattering order and expediency may look, it is but the repose of a lethargy, and we will choose rather to be awake, though it be stormy, and maintain ourselves on this earth and in this life, as we may, without signing our death-warrant. Let us see if we cannot stay here where He has put us, on his own conditions. Does not his law reach as far as his light? The expedients of the nations clash with one another, only the absolutely right is expedient for all.

There are some passages in the Antigone of Sophocles, well known to scholars, of which I am reminded in this connection. Antigone has resolved to sprinkle sand on the dead body of her brother, Polynices, notwithstanding the edict of king Creon condemning to death that one who should perform this service, which the Greeks deemed so important, for the enemy of his country; but Ismene, who is of a less resolute and noble spirit, declines taking part with her sister in this work, and says,–

"I, therefore, asking those under the earth to consider me, that I am compelled to do thus, will obey those who are placed in office; for to do extreme things is not wise."

ANTIGONE.

"I would not ask you, nor would you, if you still wished, do it joyfully with me. Be such as seems good to you. But I will bury him. It is glorious for me doing this to die. I beloved will lie with him beloved, having, like a criminal, done what is holy; since the time is longer which it is necessary for me to please those below, than those here, for there I shall always lie. But if it seems good to you, hold in dishonor things which are honored by the gods."

ISMENE.

"I indeed do not hold them in dishonor; but to act in opposition to the citizens I am by nature unable."

Antigone being at length brought before King Creon, he asks,

"Did you then dare to transgress these laws?"

ANTIGONE.

"For it was not Zeus who proclaimed these to me, nor Justice who dwells with the gods below; it was not they who established these laws among men. Nor did I think that your proclamations were so strong, as, being a mortal, to be able to transcend the unwritten and immovable laws of the gods. For not something now and yesterday, but forever these live, and no one knows from what time they appeared. I was not about to pay the penalty of violating these to the gods, fearing the presumption of any man. For I well knew that I should die, and why not? even if you had not proclaimed it."

This was concerning the burial of a dead body.

The wisest conservatism is that of the Hindoos. "Immemorial custom is transcendent law," says Menu. That is, it was the custom of the gods before men used it. The fault of our New England custom is that it is memorial. What is morality but immemorial custom? Conscience is the chief of conservatives. "Perform the settled functions," says Kreeshna in the Bhagvat-Geeta, "action is preferable to inaction. The journey of thy mortal frame may not succeed from inaction."—"A man's own calling with all its faults, ought not to be forsaken. Every undertaking is involved in its faults as the fire in its smoke."—"The man who is acquainted with the whole, should not drive those from their works who are slow of comprehension, and less experienced than himself."—"Wherefore, O Arjoon, resolve to fight,"—is the advice of the God to the irresolute soldier who fears to slay his best friends. It is a sublime conservatism; as wide as the world, and as unwearied as time; preserving the universe with Asiatic anxiety, in that state in which it appeared to their minds. These philosophers dwell on the inevitability and unchangeableness of laws, on the power of temperament and constitution, the three *goon* or qualities, and the circumstances of birth and affinity. The end is an immense consolation; eternal absorption in Brahma. Their speculations never venture beyond their own table lands, though they are high and vast as they. Buoyancy, freedom, flexibility, variety, possibility, which also are qualities of the Unnamed, they deal not with. The undeserved reward is to be earned by an everlasting moral drudgery; the incalculable promise of the morrow is, as it were, weighed. And who will say that their conservatism has not been effectual. "Assuredly," says a French translator, speaking of the antiquity and durability of the Chinese and Indian nations, and of the wisdom of their legislators, "there are there some vestiges of the eternal laws which govern the world."

Christianity, on the other hand, is humane, practical, and, in a large sense, radical. So many years and ages of the gods those eastern sages sat contemplating Brahm, uttering in silence the mystic "Om," being absorbed into the essence of the Supreme Being, never going out of themselves, but subsiding further and deeper within; so infinitely wise, yet infinitely stagnant; until, at last, in that same Asia, but in the western part of it, appeared a youth, wholly unforetold by them,–not being absorbed into Brahm, but bringing Brahm down to earth and to mankind; in whom Brahm had awaked from his long sleep, and exerted himself, and the day began,–a new avatar. The Brahman had never thought to be a brother of mankind as well as a child of God. Christ is the prince of Reformers and Radicals. Many expressions in the New Testament come naturally to the lips of all protestants, and it furnishes the most pregnant and practical texts. There is no harmless dreaming, no wise speculation in it, but every where a substratum of good sense. It never *reflects*, but it *repents*. There is no poetry in it, we may say, nothing regarded in the light of beauty merely, but moral truth is its object. All mortals are convicted by its conscience.

The New Testament is remarkable for its pure morality; the best of the Hindoo Scripture, for its pure intellectuality. The reader is nowhere raised into and sustained in a higher, purer, or *rarer* region of thought than in the Bhagvat-Geeta. Warren Hastings, in his sensible letter recommending the translation of this book to the Chairman of the East India Company, declares the original to be "of a sublimity of conception, reasoning, and diction, almost unequalled," and that the writings of the Indian philosophers "will survive when the British dominion in India shall have long ceased to exist, and when the sources which it once yielded of wealth and power are lost to remembrance." It is unquestionably one of the noblest and most sacred scriptures that have come down to us. Books are to be distinguished by the grandeur of their topics, even more than by the manner in which they are treated. The oriental philosophy approaches, easily, loftier themes than the modern aspires to; and no wonder if it sometimes prattle about them. *It* only assigns their due rank respectively to Action and Contemplation, or rather does full justice to the latter. Western philosophers have not conceived of the significance of Contemplation in their sense. Speaking of the spiritual discipline to which the Brahmans subjected themselves, and the wonderful power of abstraction to which they attained, instances of which had come under his notice, Hastings says:—

"To those who have never been accustomed to the separation of the mind from the notices of the senses, it may not be easy to conceive by what means such a power is to be attained; since even the most studious men of our hemisphere will find it difficult so to restrain their attention, but that it will wander to some object of present sense or recollection; and even the buzzing of a fly will sometimes have the power to disturb it. But if we are told that there have been men who were successively, for ages past, in the daily habit of abstracted contemplation, begun in the earliest period of youth, and continued in many to the maturity of age, each adding some portion of knowledge to the store accumulated by his predecessors; it is not assuming too much to conclude, that as the mind ever gathers strength, like the body, by exercise, so in such an exercise it may in each have acquired the faculty to which they aspired, and that their collective studies may have led them to the discovery of new tracks and combinations of sentiment, totally different from the doctrines with which the learned of other nations are acquainted; doctrines, which however speculative and subtle, still, as they possess the advantage of being derived from a source so free from every adventitious mixture, may be equally founded in truth with the most simple of our own."

"The forsaking of works" was taught by Kreeshna to the most ancient of men, and handed down from age to age,

"until at length, in the course of time, the mighty art was lost.

"In wisdom is to be found every work without exception," says Kreeshna.

"Although thou wert the greatest of all offenders, thou shalt be able to cross the gulf of sin with the bark of wisdom."

"There is not any thing in this world to be compared with wisdom for purity."

"The action stands at a distance inferior to the application of wisdom."

The wisdom of a Moonee "is confirmed, when, like the tortoise, he can draw in all his members, and restrain them from their wonted purposes."

"Children only, and not the learned, speak of the speculative and the practical doctrines as two. They are but one. For both obtain the self-same end, and the place which is gained by the followers of the one, is gained by the followers of the other."

"The man enjoyeth not freedom from action, from the non-commencement of that which he hath to do; nor doth he obtain happiness from a total inactivity. No one ever resteth a moment inactive. Every man is involuntarily urged to act by those principles which are inherent in his nature. The man who restraineth his active faculties, and sitteth down with his mind attentive to the objects of his senses, is called one of an astrayed soul, and the practiser of deceit. So the man is praised, who, having subdued all his passions, performeth with his active faculties all the functions of life, unconcerned about the event."

"Let the motive be in the deed and not in the event. Be not one whose motive for action is the hope of reward. Let not thy life be spent in inaction."

"For the man who doeth that which he hath to do, without affection, obtaineth the Supreme."

"He who may behold, as it were inaction in action, and action in inaction, is wise amongst mankind. He is a perfect performer of all duty."

"Wise men call him a *Pandeet*, whose every undertaking is free from the idea of desire, and whose actions are consumed by the fire of wisdom. He abandoneth the desire of a reward of his actions; he is always contented and independent; and although he may be engaged in a work, he, as it were, doeth nothing."

"He is both a Yogee and a Sannyasee who performeth that which he hath to do independent of the fruit thereof; not he who liveth without the sacrificial fire and without action."

"He who enjoyeth but the Amreeta which is left of his offerings, obtaineth the eternal spirit of Brahm, the Supreme."

What after all does the practicalness of life amount to? The things immediate to be done are very trivial. I could postpone them all to hear this locust sing. The most glorious fact in my experience is not any thing that I have done or may hope to do, but a transient thought, or vision, or dream, which I have had. I would give all the wealth of the world, and all the deeds of all the heroes, for one true vision. But how can I communicate with the gods who am a pencil-maker on the earth, and not be insane?

"I am the same to all mankind;" says Kreeshna, "there is not one who is worthy of my love or hatred."

This teaching is not practical in the sense in which the New Testament is. It is not always sound sense in practice. The Brahman never proposes courageously to assault evil, but patiently to starve it out. His active faculties are paralyzed by the idea of cast, of impassable limits, of destiny and the tyranny of time. Kreeshna's argument, it must be allowed, is defective. No sufficient reason is given why Arjoon should fight. Arjoon may be convinced, but the reader is not, for his judgment is *not* "formed upon the speculative doctrines of the *Sankhya Sastra*." "Seek an asylum in wisdom alone,"—but what is wisdom to a western mind? The duty of which he speaks is an arbitrary one. When was it established? The Brahman's virtue consists in doing, not right, but arbitrary things. What is that which a man "hath to do?" What is "action?" What are the "settled functions?" What is "a man's own religion," which is so much better than another's? What is "a man's own particular calling?" What are the duties which are appointed by one's birth? It is a defence of the institution of casts, of what is called the "natural duty" of the Kshetree, or soldier, "to attach himself to the discipline," "not to flee from the field," and the like. But they who are unconcerned about the consequences of their actions, are not therefore unconcerned about their actions.

Behold the difference between the oriental and the occidental. The former has nothing to do in this world; the latter is full of activity. The one looks in the sun till his eyes are put out; the other follows him prone in his westward course. There is such a thing as cast, even in the West; but it is comparatively faint. It is conservatism here. It says forsake not your calling, outrage no institution, use no violence, rend no bonds, the State is thy parent. Its virtue or manhood is wholly filial. There is a struggle between the oriental and occidental in every nation; some who would be forever contemplating the sun, and some who are hastening toward the sunset. The former class says to the latter, When you have reached the sunset, you will be no nearer to the sun. To which the latter replies, But we so prolong the day. The former "walketh but in that night, when all things go to rest, the night of *time*. The contemplative Moonee sleepeth but in the day of *time*, when all things wake."

To conclude these extracts, I can say, in the words of Sanjay, "As, O mighty Prince! I recollect again and again this holy and wonderful dialogue of Kreeshna and Arjoon, I continue more and more to rejoice; and as I recall to my memory the more than miraculous form of Haree, my astonishment is great, and I marvel and rejoice again and again! Wherever Kreeshna the God of devotion may be, wherever Arjoon the mighty bowman may be, there too, without doubt, are fortune, riches, victory, and good conduct. This is my firm belief."

I would say to the readers of Scriptures, if they wish for a good book to read, Read the Bhagvat-Geeta, an episode to the Mahabharat, said to have been written by Kreeshna Dwypayen Veias,–known to have been written by ———, more than four thousand years ago,–it matters not whether three or four, or when,–translated by Charles Wilkins. It deserves to be read with reverence even by Yankees, as a part of the sacred writings of a devout people; and the intelligent Hebrew will rejoice to find in it a moral grandeur and sublimity akin to those of his own Scriptures.

To an American reader, who, by the advantage of his position, can see over that strip of Atlantic coast to Asia and the Pacific, who, as it were, sees the shore slope upward over the Alps to the Himmaleh mountains, the comparatively recent literature of Europe often appears partial and clannish, and, notwithstanding the limited range of his own sympathies and studies, the European writer who presumes that he is speaking for the world, is perceived by him to speak only for that corner of it which he inhabits. One of the rarest of England's scholars and critics, in his classification of the worthies of the world, betrays the narrowness of his European culture and the exclusiveness of his reading. None of her children has done justice to the poets and philosophers of Persia or of India. They have even been better known to her merchant scholars than to her poets and thinkers by profession. You may look in vain through English poetry for a single memorable verse inspired by these themes. Nor is Germany to be excepted, though her philological industry is indirectly serving the cause of philosophy and poetry. Even Goethe wanted that universality of genius which could have appreciated the philosophy of India, if he had more nearly approached it. His genius was more practical, dwelling much more in the regions of the understanding, and was less native to contemplation, than the genius of those sages. It is remarkable that Homer and a few Hebrews are the most oriental names which modern Europe, whose literature has taken its rise since the decline of the Persian, has admitted into her list of Worthies, and perhaps the *worthiest* of mankind, and the fathers of modern thinking,—for the contemplations of those Indian sages have influenced, and still influence, the intellectual development of mankind,—whose works even yet survive in wonderful completeness, are, for the most part, not recognized as ever having existed. If the lions had been the painters it would have been otherwise. In every one's youthful dreams philosophy is still vaguely but inseparably, and with singular truth, associated with the East, nor do after years discover its local habitation in the Western world. In comparison with the philosophers of the East, we may say that modern Europe has yet given birth to none. Beside the vast and cosmogonal philosophy of the Bhagvat-Geeta, even our Shakspeare seems sometimes youthfully green and practical merely. Some of these sublime sentences, as the Chaldæan oracles of Zoroaster, still surviving after a thousand revolutions and translations, alone make us doubt if the poetic form and dress are not transitory, and not essential to the most effective and enduring expression of thought. *Ex oriente lux* may still be the motto of scholars, for the Western world has not yet derived from the East all the light which it is destined to receive thence.

It would be worthy of the age to print together the

collected Scriptures or Sacred Writings of the several nations, the Chinese, the Hindoos, the Persians, the Hebrews, and others, as the Scripture of mankind. The New Testament is still, perhaps, too much on the lips and in the hearts of men to be called a Scripture in this sense. Such a juxtaposition and comparison might help to liberalize the faith of men. This is a work which Time will surely edit, reserved to crown the labors of the printing press. This would be the Bible, or Book of Books, which let the missionaries carry to the uttermost parts of the earth.

While engaged in these reflections, thinking ourselves the only navigators of these waters, suddenly a canal boat, with its sail set, glided round a point before us, like some huge river beast, and changed the scene in an instant; and then another and another glided into sight, and we found ourselves in the current of commerce once more. So we threw our rinds into the water for the fishes to nibble, and added our breath to the life of living men. Little did we think in the distant garden in which we had planted the seed and reared this fruit, where it would be eaten. Our melons lay at home on the sandy bottom of the Merrimack, and our potatoes in the sun and water at the bottom of the boat looked like a fruit of the country. Soon, however, we were delivered from this fleet of junks, and possessed the river in solitude, once more rowing steadily upward through the noon, between the territories of Nashua on the one hand, and Hudson, once Nottingham, on the other; from time to time we scared up a king-fisher or a summer duck, the former flying rather by vigorous impulses, than by steady and patient steering with that short rudder of his, sounding his rattle along the fluvial street.

Ere long another scow hove in sight, creeping down the river, and hailing it, we attached ourselves to its side, and floated back in company, chatting with the boatmen, and obtaining a draught of cooler water from their jug. They appeared to be green hands from far among the hills, who had taken this means to get to the seaboard, and see the world; and would possibly visit the Falkland Isles, and the China seas, before they again saw the waters of the Merrimack, or perchance, they would not return this way forever. They had already embarked the private interests of the landsman in the larger venture of the race, and were ready to mess with mankind, reserving only the till of a chest to themselves. But they too were soon lost behind a point, and we went croaking on our way alone. What grievance has its root among the New Hampshire hills? we asked; what is wanting to human life here, that these men should make such haste to the antipodes? We prayed that their bright anticipations might not be rudely disappointed.

Though all the fates should prove unkind,
Leave not your native land behind.
The ship, becalmed, at length stands still;
The steed must rest beneath the hill;
But swiftly still our fortunes pace
To find us out in every place.

The vessel, though her masts be firm,
Beneath her copper bears a worm;
Around the cape, across the line,
Till fields of ice her course confine;
It matters not how smooth the breeze,
How shallow or how deep the seas,
Whether she bears Manilla twine,

Or in her hold Madeira wine,
Or China teas, or Spanish hides,
In port or quarantine she rides;
Far from New England's blustering shore,
New England's worm her hulk shall bore,
And sink her in the Indian seas,
Twine, wine, and hides, and China teas.

We passed a small desert here on the east bank, between Tyngsboro' and Hudson, which was interesting and even refreshing to our eyes in the midst of the almost universal greenness. This sand was indeed somewhat impressive and beautiful to us. A very old inhabitant, who was at work in a field on the Nashua side, told us that he remembered when corn and grain grew there, and it was a cultivated field. But at length the fishermen, for this was a fishing place, pulled up the bushes on the shore, for greater convenience in hauling their seines, and when the bank was thus broken, the wind began to blow up the sand from the shore, until at length it had covered about fifteen acres several feet deep. We saw near the river, where the sand was blown off down to some ancient surface, the foundation of an Indian wigwam exposed, a perfect circle of burnt stones four or five feet in diameter, mingled with fine charcoal and the bones of small animals, which had been preserved in the sand. The surrounding sand was sprinkled with other burnt stones on which their fires had been built, as well as with flakes of arrow-head stone, and we found one perfect arrow-head. In one place we noticed where an Indian had sat to manufacture arrow-heads out of quartz, and the sand was sprinkled with a quart of small glass-like chips about as big as a fourpence, which he had broken off in his work. Here, then, the Indians must have fished before the whites arrived. There was another similar sandy tract about half a mile above this.

Still the noon prevailed, and we turned the prow aside to bathe, and recline ourselves under some buttonwoods by a ledge of rocks, in a retired pasture, sloping to the water's edge, and skirted with pines and hazles, in the town of Hudson. Still had India, and that old noontide philosophy, the better part of our thoughts.

It is always singular, but encouraging, to meet with common sense in very old books, as the Heetopades of Veeshnoo Sarma; a playful wisdom which has eyes behind as well as before, and oversees itself. It asserts their health and independence of the experience of later times. This pledge of sanity cannot be spared in a book, that it sometimes pleasantly reflect upon itself. The story and fabulous portion of this book winds loosely from sentence to sentence as so many oases in a desert, and is as indistinct as a camel's track between Mourzouk and Darfour. It is a comment on the flow and freshet of modern books. The reader leaps from sentence to sentence, as from one stepping stone to another, while the stream of the story rushes past unregarded. The Bhagvat-Geeta is less sententious and poetic, perhaps, but still more wonderfully sustained and developed. Its sanity and sublimity have impressed the minds even of soldiers and merchants. It is the characteristic of great poems that they will yield of their sense in due proportion to the hasty and the deliberate reader. To the practical they will be common sense, and to the wise wisdom; as either the traveller may wet his lips, or an army may fill its water casks at a full stream.

One of the most attractive of those ancient books that I have met with is the Laws of Menu. According to Sir William Jones, "Vyasa, the son of Parasara, has decided that the Veda, with its Angas, or the six compositions deduced from it, the revealed system of medicine, the Puranas, or sacred histories, and the code of Menu, were four works of supreme authority, which ought never to be shaken by arguments merely human." The last is believed by the Hindoos "to have been promulged in the beginning of time, by Menu, son or grandson of Brahma," and "first of created beings;" and Brahma is said to have "taught his laws to Menu in a hundred thousand verses, which Menu explained to the primitive world in the very words of the book now translated." Others affirm that they have undergone successive abridgments for the convenience of mortals, "while the gods of the lower heaven, and the band of celestial musicians, are engaged in studying the primary code."—"A number of glosses or comments on Menu were composed by the Munis, or old philosophers, whose treatises, together with that before us, constitute the Dherma Sastra, in a collective sense, or Body of Law." Culluca Bhatta was one of the more modern of these.

Every sacred book, successively, has been accepted in the faith that it was to be the final resting-place of the sojourning soul; but after all, it was but a caravansary which supplied refreshment to the traveller, and directed him farther on his way to Isphahan or Bagdat. Thank God, no Hindoo tyranny prevailed at the framing of the world, but we are freemen of the universe, and not sentenced to any cast.

I know of no book which has come down to us with grander pretensions than this, and it is so impersonal and sincere that it is never offensive nor ridiculous. Compare the modes in which modern literature is advertised with the prospectus of this book, and think what a reading public it addresses, what criticism it expects. It seems to have been uttered from some eastern summit, with a sober morning prescience in the dawn of time, and you cannot read a sentence without being elevated as upon the tableland of the Ghauts. It has such a rhythm as the winds of the desert, such a tide as the Ganges, and is as superior to criticism as the Himmaleh mountains. Its tone is of such unrelaxed fibre, that even at this late day, unworn by time, it wears the English and the Sanscrit dress indifferently, and its fixed sentences keep up their distant fires still like the stars, by whose dissipated rays this lower world is illumined. The whole book by noble gestures and inclinations renders many words unnecessary. English sense has toiled, but Hindoo wisdom never perspired. Though the sentences open, as we read them, unexpensively, and, at first, almost unmeaningly, as the petals of a flower, they sometimes startle us with that rare kind of wisdom which could only have been learned from the most trivial experience; but it comes to us as refined as the porcelain earth which subsides to the bottom of the ocean. They are clean and dry as fossil truths, which have been exposed to the elements for thousands of years, so impersonally and scientifically true that they are the ornament of the parlor and the cabinet. Any *moral* philosophy is exceedingly rare. This of Menu addresses our privacy more than most. It is a more private and familiar, and, at the same time, a more public and universal word than is spoken in parlor or pulpit now-a-days. As our domestic fowls are said to have their original in the wild pheasant of India, so our domestic thoughts have their prototypes in the thoughts of her philosophers. We are dabbling in the very elements of our present conventional and actual life; as if it were the primeval conventicle where how to eat and to drink and to sleep, and maintain life with adequate dignity and sincerity, were the questions to be decided. It is later and more intimate with us even than the advice of our nearest friends. And yet it is true for the widest horizon, and read out of doors has relation to the dim mountain line, and is native and aboriginal there. Most books belong to the house and street only, and in the fields their leaves feel very thin. They are bare and obvious, and have no halo nor haze about them. Nature lies far and fair behind them all. But this, as it proceeds from, so it addresses, what is deepest and most abiding in man. It belongs to the noontide of the day, the midsummer of the year, and after the snows have melted, and the waters evaporated in the spring, still its truth speaks freshly to our experience. It helps the sun to shine, and his rays fall on its page to illustrate it. It spends the mornings and the evenings, and makes such an impression on us over night as to awaken us before dawn, and its influence lingers around us like a fragrance late into the day. It conveys a new gloss to the meadows and the depths of the wood, and its spirit, like a more subtile ether, sweeps along with the prevailing winds of a country. The very locusts and crickets of a summer day are but later or earlier glosses on the Dherma Sastra of the Hindoos, a continuation of the sacred code. As we have said, there is an orientalism in the most restless pioneer, and the farthest west is but the farthest east. While we are reading these sentences, this fair modern world seems only a reprint of the Laws of Menu with the gloss of Culluca. Tried by a New England eye, or the mere practical wisdom of modern times, they are the oracles of a race already in its dotage, but held up to the sky, which is the only impartial and incorruptible ordeal, they are of a piece with its depth and serenity, and I am assured that they will have a place and significance as long as there is a sky to test them by.

Give me a sentence which no intelligence can understand. There must be a kind of life and palpitation to it, and under its words a kind of blood must circulate forever. It is wonderful that this sound should have come down to us from so far, when the voice of man can be heard so little way, and we are not now within ear-shot of any contemporary. The woodcutters have here felled an ancient pine forest, and brought to light to these distant hills a fair lake in the south-west; and now in an instant it is distinctly shown to these woods as if its image had travelled hither from eternity. Perhaps these old stumps upon the knoll remember when anciently this lake gleamed in the horizon. One wonders if the bare earth itself did not experience emotion at beholding again so fair a prospect. That fair water lies there in the sun thus revealed, so much the prouder and fairer because its beauty needed not to be seen. It seems yet lonely, sufficient to itself, and superior to observation.—So are these old sentences like serene lakes in the south-west, at length revealed to us, which have so long been reflecting our own sky in their bosom.

The great plain of India lies as in a cup between the Himmaleh and the ocean on the north and south, and the Brahmapootra and Indus, on the east and west, wherein the primeval race was received. We will not dispute the story. We are pleased to read in the natural history of the country, of the "pine, larch, spruce, and silver fir," which cover the southern face of the Himmaleh range; of the "gooseberry, raspberry, strawberry," which from an imminent temperate zone overlook the torrid plains. So did this active modern life have even then a foothold and lurking place in the midst of the stateliness and contemplativeness of those eastern plains. In another era the "lily-of-the valley, cowslip, dandelion," were to work their way down into the plain, and bloom in a level zone of their own reaching round the earth. Already has the era of the temperate zone arrived, the era of the pine and the oak, for the palm and the banian do not supply the wants of this age. The lichens on the summits of the rocks will perchance find their level ere long.

As for the tenets of the Brahmans, we are not so much concerned to know what doctrines they held, as that they were held by any. We can tolerate all philosophies, Atomists, Pneumatologists, Atheists, Theists,—Plato, Aristotle, Leucippus, Democritus, Pythagoras, Zoroaster and Confucius. It is the attitude of these men, more than any communication which they make, that attracts us. Between them and their commentators, it is true, there is an endless dispute. But if it comes to this that you compare notes, then you are all wrong. As it is, each takes us up into the serene heavens, whither the smallest bubble rises as surely as the largest, and paints earth and sky for us. Any sincere thought is irresistible. The very austerity of the Brahmans is tempting to the devotional soul, as a more refined and nobler luxury. Wants so easily and gracefully satisfied seem like a more refined pleasure. Their conception of creation is peaceful as a dream. "When that power awakes, then has this world its full expansion; but when he slumbers with a tranquil spirit, then the whole system fades away." In the very indistinctness of their theogony a sublime truth is implied. It hardly allows the reader to rest in any supreme first cause, but directly it hints at a supremer still which created the last, and the Creator is still behind increate.

Nor will we disturb the antiquity of this Scripture; "From fire, from air, and from the sun," it was "milked out." One might as well investigate the chronology of light and heat. Let the sun shine. Menu understood this matter best, when he said, "Those best know the divisions of days and nights who understand that the day of Brahma, which endures to the end of a thousand such ages, [infinite ages, nevertheless, according to mortal reckoning,] gives rise to virtuous exertions; and that his night endures as long as his day." Indeed, the Mussulman and Tartar dynasties are beyond all dating. Methinks I have lived under them myself. In every man's brain is the Sanscrit. The Vedas and their Angas are not so ancient as serene contemplation. Why will we be imposed on by antiquity? Is the babe young? When I behold it, it seems more venerable than the oldest man; it is more ancient than Nestor or the Sibyls, and bears the wrinkles of father Saturn himself. And do we live but in the present? How broad a line is that? I sit now on a stump whose rings number centuries of growth. If I look around I see that the soil is composed of the remains of just such stumps, ancestors to this. The earth is covered with mould. I thrust this stick many æons deep into its surface, and with my heel make a deeper furrow than the elements have ploughed here for a thousand years. If I listen, I hear the peep of frogs which is older than the slime of Egypt, and the distant drumming of a partridge on a log, as if it were the pulse-beat of the summer air. I raise my fairest and freshest flowers in the old mould. Why, what we would fain call new is not skin deep; the earth is not yet stained by it. It is not the fertile ground which we walk on, but the leaves that flutter over our heads. The newest is but the oldest made visible to our senses. When we dig up the soil from a thousand feet below the surface, we call it new, and the plants which spring from it; and when our vision pierces deeper into space, and detects a remoter star, we call that new also. The place where we sit is called Hudson,–once it was Nottingham,–once–

We should read history as little critically as we consider the landscape, and be more interested by the atmospheric tints and various lights and shades which the intervening spaces create, than by its groundwork and composition. It is the morning now turned evening and seen in the west,–the same sun, but a new light and atmosphere. Its beauty is like the sunset; not a fresco painting on a wall, flat and bounded, but atmospheric and roving or free. In reality, history fluctuates as the face of the landscape from morning to evening. What is of moment is its hue and color. Time hides no treasures; we want not its *then*, but its *now*. We do not complain that the mountains in the horizon are blue and indistinct; they are the more like the heavens.

Of what moment are facts that can be lost,–which need to be commemorated? The monument of death will outlast the memory of the dead. The pyramids do not tell the tale that was confided to them; the living fact commemorates itself. Why look in the dark for light? Strictly speaking, the historical societies have not recovered one fact from oblivion, but are themselves, instead of the fact, that is lost. The researcher is more memorable than the researched. The crowd stood admiring the mist and the dim outlines of the trees seen through it, when one of their number advanced to explore the phenomenon, and with fresh admiration all eyes were turned on his dimly retreating figure. It is astonishing with how little coöperation of the societies, the past is remembered. Its story has indeed had another muse than has been assigned it. There is a good instance of the manner in which all history began in Alwákidi's Arabian Chronicle, "I was informed by *Ahmed Almatîn Aljorhami*, who had it from *Rephâa Ebn Kais Alámiri*, who had it from *Saiph Ebn Jabalah Alchátgami*, who had it from *Thabet Ebn Alkamah*, who said he was present at the action." These fathers of history were not anxious to preserve, but to learn the fact; and hence it was not forgotten. Critical acumen is exerted in vain to uncover the past; the *past* cannot be *presented*; we cannot know what we are not. But one veil hangs over past, present, and future, and it is the province of the historian to find out, not what was, but what is. Where a battle has been fought, you will find nothing but the bones of men and beasts; where a battle is being fought, there are hearts beating. We will sit on a mound and muse, and not try to make these skeletons stand on their legs again. Does nature remember, think you, that they *were* men, or not rather that they *are* bones?

Ancient history has an air of antiquity. It should be more modern. It is written as if the spectator should be thinking of the backside of the picture on the wall, or as if the author expected that the dead would be his readers, and wished to detail to them their own experience. Men seem anxious to accomplish an orderly retreat through the centuries, earnestly rebuilding the works behind, as they are battered down by the encroachments of time; but while they loiter, they and their works both fall a prey to the arch enemy. History has neither the venerableness of antiquity, nor the freshness of the modern. It does as if it would go to the beginning of things, which natural history might with reason assume to do; but consider the Universal History, and then tell us—when did burdock and plantain sprout first? It has been so written for the most part, that the times it describes are with remarkable propriety called *dark ages*. They are dark, as one has observed, because we are so in the dark about them. The sun rarely shines in history, what with the dust and confusion; and when we meet with any cheering fact which implies the presence of this luminary, we excerpt and modernize it. As when we read in the history of the Saxons that Edwin of Northumbria "caused stakes to be fixed in the highways where he had seen a clear spring," and "brazen dishes were chained to them, to refresh the weary sojourner, whose fatigues Edwin had himself experienced." This is worth all Arthur's twelve battles.

> "Through the shadow of the world we sweep
>   into the younger day:
> Better fifty years of Europe than a cycle of
>   Cathay."
> Than fifty years of Europe better one New
>   England ray!

Biography, too, is liable to the same objection; it should be autobiography. Let us not, as the Germans advise, endeavor to go abroad and vex our bowels that we may be somebody else to explain him. If I am not I, who will be?

But it is fit that the Past should be dark; though the darkness is not so much a quality of the past as of tradition. It is not a distance of time, but a distance of relation, which makes thus dusky its memorials. What is near to the heart of this generation is fair and bright still. Greece lies outspread fair and sunshiny in floods of light, for there is the sun and daylight in her literature and art. Homer does not allow us to forget that the sun shone,–nor Phidias, nor the Parthenon. Yet no era has been wholly dark, nor will we too hastily submit to the historian, and congratulate ourselves on a blaze of light. If we could pierce the obscurity of those remote years, we should find it light enough; only *there* is not our day. Some creatures are made to see in the dark. There has always been the same amount of light in the world. The new and missing stars, the comets and eclipses, do not affect the general illumination, for only our glasses appreciate them. The eyes of the oldest fossil remains, they tell us, indicate that the same laws of light prevailed then as now. Always the laws of light are the same, but the modes and degrees of seeing vary. The gods are partial to no era, but steadily shines their light in the heavens, while the eye of the beholder is turned to stone. There was but the sun and the eye from the first. The ages have not added a new ray to the one, nor altered a fibre of the other.

If we will admit time into our thoughts at all, the mythologies, those vestiges of ancient poems, wrecks of poems, so to speak, the world's inheritance, still reflecting some of their original splendor, like the fragments of clouds tinted by the rays of the departed sun; reaching into the latest summer day, and allying this hour to the morning of creation; as the poet sings:–

"Fragments of the lofty strain
  Float down the tide of years,
As buoyant on the stormy main
  A parted wreck appears."–

these are the materials and hints for a history of the rise and progress of the race; how, from the condition of ants, it arrived at the condition of men, and arts were gradually invented. Let a thousand surmises shed some light on this story. We will not be confined by historical, even geological periods, which would allow us to doubt of a progress in human affairs. If we rise above this wisdom for the day, we shall expect that this morning of the race, in which it has been supplied with the simplest necessaries, with corn, and wine, and honey, and oil, and fire, and articulate speech, and agricultural and other arts, reared up, by degrees, from the condition of ants, to men, will be succeeded by a day of equally progressive splendor; that, in the lapse of the divine periods, other divine agents and godlike men will assist to elevate the race as much above its present condition. However, we do not know much about it.

Thus did one voyageur waking dream, while his companion slumbered on the bank. Suddenly, a boatman's horn was heard, echoing from shore to shore, to give notice of his approach to the farmer's wife, with whom he was to take his dinner, though in that place only muskrats and kingfishers seemed to hear. The current of our reflections and our slumbers being thus disturbed, we weighed anchor once more.

As we proceeded on our way in the afternoon, the western bank became lower, or receded further from the channel in some places, leaving a few trees only to fringe the water's edge; while the eastern rose abruptly here and there into wooded hills fifty or sixty feet high. The bass, *tilia Americana*, also called the lime or linden, which was a new tree to us, overhung the water with its broad and rounded leaf, interspersed with clusters of small hard berries, now nearly ripe, and made an agreeable shade for us sailors. The inner bark of this genus is the bast, the material of the fisherman's matting, and the ropes, and peasant's shoes, of which the Russians make so much use, and also of nets and a coarse cloth in some places. According to poets, this was once Philyra, one of the Oceanides. The ancients are said to have used its bark for the roofs of cottages, for baskets, and for a kind of paper called Philyra. They also made bucklers of its wood, "on account of its flexibility, lightness, and resiliency." It was once much used for carving, and is still in demand for sounding-boards of piano-fortes and panels of carriages, and for various uses for which toughness and flexibility are required. Baskets and cradles are made of the twigs. Its sap affords sugar, and the honey made from its flowers is said to be preferred to any other. Its leaves are in some countries given to cattle, a kind of chocolate has been made of its fruit, a medicine has been prepared from an infusion of its flowers, and finally, the charcoal made of its wood is greatly valued for gunpowder.

The sight of this tree reminded us that we had reached a strange land to us. As we sailed under this canopy of leaves we saw the sky through its chinks, and, as it were, the meaning and idea of the tree stamped in a thousand hieroglyphics on the heavens. The universe is so aptly fitted to our organization that the eye wanders and reposes at the same time. On every side there is something to soothe and refresh this sense. Look up at the tree-tops and see how finely Nature finishes off her work there. See how the pines spire without end higher and higher, and make a graceful fringe to the earth. And who shall count the finer cobwebs that soar and float away from their utmost tops, and the myriad insects that dodge between them. Leaves are of more various forms than the alphabets of all languages put together; of the oaks alone there are hardly two alike, and each expresses its own character.

In all her products Nature only develops her simplest germs. One would say that it was no great stretch of invention to create birds. The hawk, which now takes his flight over the top of the wood, was at first perchance only a leaf which fluttered in its aisles. From rustling leaves she came in the course of ages to the loftier flight and clear carol of the bird.

Salmon Brook comes in from the west under the railroad, a mile and a half below the village of Nashua. We rowed up far enough into the meadows which border it, to learn its piscatorial history from a hay-maker on its banks. He told us that the silver eel was formerly abundant here, and pointed to some sunken creels at its mouth. This man's memory and imagination were fertile in fishermen's tales of floating isles in bottomless ponds, and of lakes mysteriously stocked with fishes, and would have kept us till night-fall to listen, but we could not afford to loiter in this roadstead, and so stood out to our sea again. Though we never trod in those meadows, but only touched their margin with our hands, we still retain a pleasant memory of them.

Salmon Brook, whose name is said to be a translation from the Indian, was a favorite haunt of the aborigines. Here too the first white settlers of Nashua planted, and some dents in the earth, where their houses stood, and the wrecks of ancient apple trees are still visible. About one mile up this stream stood the house of old John Lovewell, who was an ensign in the army of Oliver Cromwell, and the father of "famous Captain Lovewell." He settled here before 1690, and died about 1754, at the age of one hundred and twenty years. He is thought to have been engaged in the famous Narragansett swamp fight, which took place in 1675, before he came here. The Indians are said to have spared him in succeeding wars on account of his kindness to them. Even in 1700 he was so old and gray-headed that his scalp was worth nothing, since the French Governor offered no bounty for such. I have stood in the dent of his cellar on the bank of the brook, and talked there with one whose grandfather had, whose father might have, talked with Lovewell. Here also he had a mill in his old age, and kept a small store. He was remembered by some who were recently living, as a hale old man who drove the boys out of his orchard with his cane.–Consider the triumphs of the mortal man, and what poor trophies it would have to show, to wit, He cobbled shoes without glasses at a hundred, and cut a handsome swathe at a hundred and five!–Lovewell's house is said to have been the first which Mrs. Dustan reached on her escape from the Indians. Here probably the hero of Pequawket was born and bred. Close by may be seen the cellar and the grave-stone of Joseph Hassell, who, as was elsewhere recorded, with his wife Anna and son Benjamin, and Mary Marks, "were slain by our Indian enemies on Sept. 2d [1691] in the evening." As Gookin observed on a previous occasion, "The Indian rod upon the English backs had not yet done God's errand." Salmon Brook near its mouth is still a solitary stream, meandering through woods and meadows, while the then uninhabited mouth of the Nashua now resounds with the din of a manufacturing town.

A stream from Otternic pond in Hudson comes in just above Salmon Brook, on the opposite side. There was a good view of Uncannunuc, the most conspicuous mountain in these parts, from the bank here, seen rising over the west end of the bridge above. We soon after passed the village of Nashua, on the river of the same name, where there is a covered bridge over the Merrimack. The Nashua, which is one of the largest tributaries, flows from Wachusett Mountain, through Lancaster, Groton and other towns, where it has formed well known elm-shaded meadows, but near its mouth it is obstructed by falls and factories, and did not tempt us to explore it.

Far away from here, in Lancaster, with another companion, I have crossed the broad valley of the Nashua, over which we had so long looked westward from the Concord hills without seeing it to the blue mountains in the horizon. So many streams, so many meadows and woods and quiet dwellings of men had lain concealed between us and those Delectable Mountains;—from yonder hill on the road to Tyngsboro' you may get a good view of them.—There where it seemed uninterrupted forest to our youthful eyes, between two neighboring pines in the horizon, lay the valley of the Nashua, and this very stream was even then winding at its bottom, and then, as now, it was here silently mingling its waters with the Merrimack. The clouds which floated over its meadows and were born there, seen far in the west, gilded by the rays of the setting sun, had adorned a thousand evening skies for us. But as it were, by a turf wall this valley was concealed, and in our journey to those hills it was first gradually revealed to us. Summer and winter our eyes had rested on the dim outline of the mountains, to which distance and indistinctness lent a grandeur not their own, so that they served to interpret all the allusions of poets and travellers. Standing on the Concord Cliffs we thus spoke our mind to them.–

With frontier strength ye stand your ground,
With grand content ye circle round,
Tumultuous silence for all sound,
Ye distant nursery of rills,
Monadnock and the Peterboro' Hills;–
Firm argument that never stirs,
Outcircling the philosophers,–
Like some vast fleet,
Sailing through rain and sleet,
Through winter's cold and summer's heat;
Still holding on upon your high emprise,
Until ye find a shore amid the skies;
Not skulking close to land,
With cargo contraband,
For they who sent a venture out by ye
Have set the Sun to see
Their honesty.
Ships of the line, each one,
Ye westward run,
Convoying clouds,
Which cluster in your shrouds,
Always before the gale,
Under a press of sail,
With weight of metal all untold,–
I seem to feel ye in my firm seat here,
Immeasurable depth of hold,
And breadth of beam, and length of running gear.

Methinks ye take luxurious pleasure
In your novel western leisure;
So cool your brows and freshly blue,
As Time had nought for ye to do;
For ye lie at your length,
An unappropriated strength,

Unhewn primeval timber,
For knees so stiff, for masts so limber;
The stock of which new earths are made,
One day to be our *western* trade,
Fit for the stanchions of a world
Which through the seas of space is hurled.

While we enjoy a lingering ray,
Ye still o'ertop the western day,
Reposing yonder on God's croft
Like solid stacks of hay;
So bold a line as ne'er was writ
On any page by human wit;
The forest glows as if
An enemy's camp-fires shone
Along the horizon,
Or the day's funeral pyre
Were lighted there;
Edged with silver and with gold,
The clouds hang o'er in damask fold,
And with such depth of amber light
The west is dight,
Where still a few rays slant,
That even Heaven seems extravagant.
Watatic Hill
Lies on the horizon's sill
Like a child's toy left over night,
And other duds to left and right,
On the earth's edge, mountains and trees,
Stand as they were on air graven,
Or as the vessels in a haven
Await the morning breeze.
I fancy even
Through your defiles windeth the way to heaven;
And yonder still, in spite of history's page,
Linger the golden and the silver age;
Upon the laboring gale
The news of future centuries is brought,
And of new dynasties of thought,
From your remotest vale.

But special I remember thee,
Wachusett, who like me
Standest alone without society.
Thy far blue eye,
A remnant of the sky,
Seen through the clearing or the gorge,
Or from the windows of the forge,
Doth leaven all it passes by.
Nothing is true
But stands 'tween me and you,
Thou western pioneer,
Who know'st not shame nor fear,
By venturous spirit driven
Under the eaves of heaven;
And canst expand thee there,
And breathe enough of air?
Even beyond the West
Thou migratest,
Into unclouded tracts,
Without a pilgrim's axe,
Cleaving thy road on high
With thy well-tempered brow,
And mak'st thyself a clearing in the sky.
Upholding heaven, holding down earth,
Thy pastime from thy birth;
Not steadied by the one, nor leaning on the other,
May I approve myself thy worthy brother!

At length, like Rasselas and other inhabitants of happy valleys, we had resolved to scale the blue wall which bounded the western horizon, though not without misgivings that thereafter no visible fairy land would exist for us. But it would be long to tell of our adventures, and we have no time this afternoon, transporting ourselves in imagination up this hazy Nashua valley, to go over again that pilgrimage. We have since made many similar excursions to the principal mountains of New England and New York, and even far in the wilderness, and have passed a night on the summit of many of them. And now when we look again westward from our native hills, Wachusett and Monadnock have retreated once more among the blue and fabulous mountains in the horizon, though our eyes rest on the very rocks on both of them, where we have pitched our tent for a night, and boiled our hasty-pudding amid the clouds.

As late as 1724 there was no house on the north side of the Nashua, but only scattered wigwams and gristly forests between this frontier and Canada. In September of that year, two men who were engaged in making turpentine on that side, for such were the first enterprises in the wilderness, were taken captive and carried to Canada by a party of thirty Indians. Ten of the inhabitants of Dunstable going to look for them, found the hoops of their barrel cut, and the turpentine spread on the ground. I have been told by an inhabitant of Tyngsboro', who had the story from his ancestors, that one of these captives, when the Indians were about to upset his barrel of turpentine, seized a pine knot and flourishing it, swore so resolutely that he would kill the first who touched it, that they refrained, and when at length he returned from Canada he found it still standing. Perhaps there was more than one barrel.–However this may have been, the scouts knew by marks on the trees, made with coal mixed with grease, that the men were not killed but taken prisoners. One of the company, named Farwell, perceiving that the turpentine had not done spreading, concluded that the Indians had been gone but a short time, and they accordingly went in instant pursuit. Contrary to the advice of Farwell, following directly on their trail up the Merrimack, they fell into an ambuscade near Thornton's Ferry, in the present town of Merrimack, and nine were killed, only one, Farwell, escaping after a vigorous pursuit. The men of Dunstable went out and picked up their bodies, and carried them all down to Dunstable and buried them. It is almost word for word as in the Robin Hood ballad:—

"They carried these foresters into fair Nottingham,
  As many there did know,
They digg'd them graves in their churchyard,
  And they buried them all a row."

Nottingham is only the other side of the river, and they were not exactly all a-row. You may read in the churchyard at Dunstable, under the "Memento Mori," and the name of one of them, how they "departed this life," and

"This man with seven more that lies in
this grave was slew all in a day by
the Indians."

The stones of some others of the company stand around the common grave with their separate inscriptions. Eight were buried here, but nine were killed, according to the best authorities.

"Gentle river, gentle river,
  Lo, thy streams are stained with gore,
Many a brave and noble captain
  Floats along thy willowed shore.

All beside thy limpid waters,
  All beside thy sands so bright,
Indian Chiefs and Christian warriors
  Joined in fierce and mortal fight."

It is related in the History of Dunstable, that on the return of Farwell the Indians were engaged by a fresh party, which they compelled to retreat, and pursued as far as the Nashua, where they fought across the stream at its mouth. After the departure of the Indians, the figure of an Indian's head was found carved by them on a large tree by the shore, which circumstance has given its name to this part of the village of Nashville,—the "Indian Head." "It was observed by some judicious," says Gookin, referring to Philip's war, "that at the beginning of the war, the English soldiers made a nothing of the Indians, and many spake words to this effect; that one Englishman was sufficient to chase ten Indians; many reckoned it was no other but *Veni, vidi, vici.*" But we may conclude that the judicious would by this time have made a different observation.

Farwell appears to have been the only one who had studied his profession, and understood the business of hunting Indians. He lived to fight another day, for the next year he was Lovewell's Lieutenant at Pequawket, but that time, as we have related, he left his bones in the wilderness. His name still reminds us of twilight days and forest scouts on Indian trails, with an uneasy scalp;—an indispensable hero to New England. As the more recent poet of Lovewell's fight has sung, halting a little but bravely still;—

"Then did the crimson streams that flowed,
Seem like the waters of the brook,
That brightly shine, that loudly dash,
Far down the cliffs of Agiochook."

These battles sound incredible to us. I think that posterity will doubt if such things ever were; if our bold ancestors who settled this land were not struggling rather with the forest shadows, and not with a copper colored race of men. They were vapors, fever and ague of the unsettled woods. Now, only a few arrow-heads are turned up by the plow. In the Pelasgic, the Etruscan, or the British story, there is nothing so shadowy and unreal.

It is a wild and antiquated looking grave-yard, overgrown with bushes, on the high road, about a quarter of a mile from and overlooking the Merrimack, with a deserted mill stream bounding it on one side, where lie the earthly remains of the ancient inhabitants of Dunstable. We passed it three or four miles below here. You may read there the names of Lovewell, Farwell, and many others whose families were distinguished in Indian warfare. We noticed there two large masses of granite more than a foot thick and rudely squared, lying flat on the ground over the remains of the first pastor and his wife.

It is remarkable that the dead lie every where under stones,–

> "Strata jacent passim *suo* quæque sub" *lapide*–

corpora, we might say, if the measure allowed. When the stone is a slight one, it does not oppress the spirits of the traveller to meditate by it; but these did seem a little heathenish to us; and so are all large monuments over men's bodies, from the pyramids down. A monument should at least be "star-y-pointing," to indicate whither the spirit is gone, and not prostrate, like the body it has deserted. There have been some nations who could do nothing but construct tombs, and these are the only traces which they have left. They are the heathen. But why these stones, so upright and emphatic, like exclamation points! What was there so remarkable that lived? Why should the monument be so much more enduring than the fame which it is designed to perpetuate,–a stone to a bone? "Here lies,"–"Here lies";–why do they not sometimes write, There rises? Is it a monument to the body only that is intended? "Having reached the term of his *natural* life;"–would it not be truer to say, Having reached the term of his *unnatural* life? The rarest quality in an epitaph is truth. If any character is given it should be as severely true as the decision of the three judges below, and not the partial testimony of friends. Friends and contemporaries should supply only the name and date, and leave it to posterity to write the epitaph.

Here lies an honest man,
Rear-Admiral Van.

Faith, then ye have
Two in one grave,
For in his favor,
Here too lies the Engraver.

Fame itself is but an epitaph; as late, as false, as true. But they only are the true epitaphs which Old Mortality retouches.

A man might well pray that he may not taboo or curse any portion of nature by being buried in it. For the most part, the best man's spirit makes a fearful sprite to haunt his grave, and it is therefore much to the credit of Little John, the famous follower of Robin Hood, and reflecting favorably on his character, that his grave was "long celebrous for the yielding of excellent whetstones." I confess that I have but little love for such collections as they have at the Catacombs, Père la Chaise, Mount Auburn, and even this Dunstable grave-yard. At any rate, nothing but great antiquity can make grave-yards interesting to me. I have no friends there. It may be that I am not competent to write the poetry of the grave. The farmer who has skimmed his farm might perchance leave his body to Nature to be plowed in, and in some measure restore its fertility. We should not retard but forward her economies.

Soon the village of Nashua was out of sight, and the woods were gained again, and we rowed slowly on before sunset, looking for a solitary place in which to spend the night. A few evening clouds began to be reflected in the water, and the surface was dimpled only here and there by a muskrat crossing the stream. We camped at length near Penichook Brook, on the confines of what is now Nashville, by a deep ravine, under the skirts of a pine wood, where the dead pine leaves were our carpet, and their tawny boughs stretched overhead. But fire and smoke soon tamed the scene; the rocks consented to be our walls, and the pines our roof. A woodside was already the fittest locality for us.

The wilderness is near, as well as dear, to every man. Even the oldest villages are indebted to the border of wild wood which surrounds them, more than to the gardens of men. There is something indescribably inspiriting and beautiful in the aspect of the forest skirting and occasionally jutting into the midst of new towns, which, like the sand-heaps of fresh fox burrows, have sprung up in their midst. The very uprightness of the pines and maples asserts the ancient rectitude and vigor of nature. Our lives need the relief of such a back-ground, where the pine flourishes and the jay still screams.

We had found a safe harbor for our boat, and as the sun was setting carried up our furniture, and soon arranged our house upon the bank, and while the kettle steamed at the tent door, we chatted of distant friends, and of the sights which we were to behold, and wondered which way the towns lay from us. Our cocoa was soon boiled, and supper set upon our chest, and we lengthened out this meal, like old voyageurs, with our talk. Meanwhile we spread the map on the ground, and read in the gazetteer when the first settlers came here and got a township granted. Then, when supper was done, and we had written the journal of our voyage, we wrapped our buffaloes about us, and lay down with our heads pillowed on our arms, listening awhile to the distant baying of a dog, or the murmurs of the river, or to the wind, which had not gone to rest,—

> The western wind came lumbering in,
> Bearing a faint Pacific din,
> Our evening mail, swift at the call
> Of its Post-Master General;
> Laden with news from Californ',
> Whate'er transpired hath since morn,
> How wags the world by brier and brake
> From hence to Athabasca lake;—

or half awake and half asleep, dreaming of a star which glimmered through our cotton roof. Perhaps at midnight one was awakened by a cricket shrilly singing on his shoulder, or by a hunting spider in his eye, and was lulled asleep again by some streamlet purling its way along at the bottom of a wooded and rocky ravine in our neighborhood. It was pleasant to lie with our heads so low in the grass, and hear what a tinkling ever-busy laboratory it was. A thousand little artisans beat on their anvils all night long.

Far in the night, as we were falling asleep on the bank of the Merrimack, we heard some tyro beating a drum incessantly, in preparation for a country muster, as we learned, and we thought of the line,

"When the drum beat at dead of night."

We could have assured him that his beat would be answered, and the forces be mustered. Fear not, thou drummer of the night, we too will be there. And still he drummed on in the silence and the dark. This stray sound from a far-off sphere came to our ears from time to time, far, sweet, and significant, and we listened with such an unprejudiced sense as if for the first time we heard at all. No doubt he was an insignificant drummer enough, but his music afforded us a prime and leisure hour, and we felt that we were in season wholly. These simple sounds related us to the stars. Aye, there was a logic in them so convincing that the combined sense of mankind could never make me doubt their conclusions. I stop my habitual thinking, as if the plow had suddenly run deeper in its furrow through the crust of the world. How can I go on, who have just stepped over such a bottomless skylight in the bog of my life. Suddenly old Time winked at me,–Ah you know me, you rogue,–and news had come that IT was well. That ancient universe is in such capital health, I think undoubtedly it will never die. Heal yourselves, doctors; by God I live.–

Then idle Time ran gadding by
And left me with Eternity alone;
I hear beyond the range of sound,
I see beyond the verge of sight,–

I see, smell, taste, hear, feel, that everlasting Something to which we are allied, at once our maker, our abode, our destiny, our very Selves; the one historic truth, the most remarkable fact which can become the distinct and uninvited subject of our thought, the actual glory of the universe; the only fact which a human being cannot avoid recognizing, or in some way forget or dispense with.—

> It doth expand my privacies
> To all, and leave me single in the crowd.

I have seen how the foundations of the world are laid, and I have not the least doubt that it will stand a good while.

> Now chiefly is my natal hour,
> And only now my prime of life.
> I will not doubt the love untold,
> Which not my worth nor want hath bought,
> Which wooed me young and wooes me old,
> And to this evening hath me brought.

What are ears? what is Time? that this particular series of sounds called a strain of music, an invisible and fairy troop which never brushed the dew from any mead, can be wafted down through the centuries from Homer to me, and he have been conversant with that same aerial and mysterious charm which now so tingles my ears? What a fine communication from age to age, of the fairest and noblest thoughts, the aspirations of ancient men, even such as were never communicated by speech, is music! It is the flower of language, thought colored and curved, fluent and flexible, its crystal fountain tinged with the sun's rays, and its purling ripples reflecting the grass and the clouds. A strain of music reminds me of a passage of the Vedas, and I associate with it the idea of infinite remoteness, as well as of beauty and serenity, for to the senses that is furthest from us which addresses the greatest depth within us. It teaches us again and again to trust the remotest and finest as the divinest instinct, and makes a dream our only real experience. We feel a sad cheer when we hear it, perchance because we that hear are not one with that which is heard.

> Therefore a torrent of sadness deep,
> Through the strains of thy triumph is heard to sweep.

The sadness is ours. The Indian poet Calidas says in the Sacontala: "Perhaps the sadness of men on seeing beautiful forms and hearing sweet music arises from some faint remembrance of past joys, and the traces of connections in a former state of existence." As polishing expresses the vein in marble and grain in wood, so music brings out what of heroic lurks any where. The hero is the sole patron of music. That harmony which exists naturally between the hero's moods and the universe the soldier would fain imitate with drum and trumpet. When we are in health all sounds fife and drum for us; we hear the notes of music in the air, or catch its echoes dying away when we awake in the dawn. Marching is when the pulse of the hero beats in unison with the pulse of Nature, and he steps to the measure of the universe; then there is true courage and invincible strength.

Plutarch says that "Plato thinks the gods never gave men music, the science of melody and harmony, for mere delectation or to tickle the ear; but that the discordant parts of the circulations and beauteous fabric of the soul, and that of it that roves about the body, and many times, for want of tune and air, breaks forth into many extravagances and excesses, might be sweetly recalled and artfully wound up to their former consent and agreement."

Music is the sound of the universal laws promulgated. It is the only assured tone. There are in it such strains as far surpass any man's faith in the loftiness of his destiny. Things are to be learned which it will be worth the while to learn. Formerly I heard these

RUMORS FROM AN ÆOLIAN HARP.

There is a vale which none hath seen,
Where foot of man has never been,
Such as here lives with toil and strife,
An anxious and a sinful life.

There every virtue has its birth,
Ere it descends upon the earth,
And thither every deed returns,
Which in the generous bosom burns.

There love is warm, and youth is young,
And poetry is yet unsung,
For Virtue still adventures there,
And freely breathes her native air.

And ever, if you hearken well,
You still may hear its vesper bell,
And tread of high-souled men go by,
Their thoughts conversing with the sky.

According to Jamblichus, "Pythagoras did not procure for himself a thing of this kind through instruments or the voice, but employing a certain ineffable divinity, and which it is difficult to apprehend, he extended his ears and fixed his intellect in the sublime symphonies of the world, he alone hearing and understanding, as it appears, the universal harmony and consonance of the spheres, and the stars that are moved through them, and which produce a fuller and more intense melody than any thing effected by mortal sounds."

Travelling on foot very early one morning due east from here about twenty miles, from Caleb Harriman's tavern in Hampstead toward Haverhill, when I reached the railroad in Plaistow, I heard at some distance a faint music in the air like an Æolian harp, which I immediately suspected to proceed from the cord of the telegraph vibrating in the just awakening morning wind, and applying my ear to one of the posts I was convinced that it was so. It was the telegraph harp singing its message through the country, its message sent not by men but by gods. Perchance, like the statue of Memnon, it resounds only in the morning when the first rays of the sun fall on it. It was like the first lyre or shell heard on the sea-shore,—that vibrating cord high in the air over the shores of earth. So have all things their higher and their lower uses. I heard a fairer news than the journals ever print. It told of things worthy to hear, and worthy of the electric fluid to carry the news of, not of the price of cotton and flour, but it hinted at the price of the world itself and of things which are priceless, of absolute truth and beauty.

Still the drum rolled on, and stirred our blood to fresh extravagance that night. The clarion sound and clang of corselet and buckler were heard from many a hamlet of the soul, and many a knight was arming for the fight behind the encamped stars.—

"Before each van
Prick forth the aery knights, and couch their spears
Till thickest legions close; with feats of arms
From either end of Heaven the welkin burns."

Away! away! away! away!
Ye have not kept your secret well,
I will abide that other day,
Those other lands ye tell.

Has time no leisure left for these,
The acts that ye rehearse?
Is not eternity a lease
For better deeds than verse?

'T is sweet to hear of heroes dead,
  To know them still alive,
But sweeter if we earn their bread,
  And in us they survive.

Our life should feed the springs of fame
  With a perennial wave,
As ocean feeds the babbling founts
  Which find in it their grave.

Ye skies drop gently round my breast,
  And be my corselet blue,
Ye earth receive my lance in rest,
  My faithful charger you;

Ye stars my spear-heads in the sky,
  My arrow-tips ye are,—
I see the routed foemen fly,
  My bright spears fixed are.

Give me an angel for a foe,
  Fix now the place and time,
And straight to meet him I will go
  Above the starry chime.

And with our clashing bucklers' clang
  The heavenly spheres shall ring,
While bright the northern lights shall hang
  Beside our tourneying.

And if she lose her champion true,
  Tell Heaven not despair,
For I will be her champion new,
  Her fame I will repair.

There was a high wind this night, which we afterwards learned had been still more violent elsewhere, and had done much injury to the cornfields far and near; but we only heard it sigh from time to time, as if it had no license to shake the foundations of our tent; the pines murmured, the water rippled, and the tent rocked a little, but we only laid our ears closer to the ground, while the blast swept on to alarm other men, and long before sunrise we were ready to pursue our voyage as usual.

Tuesday.

"On either side the river lie
Long fields of barley and of rye,
That clothe the wold and meet the sky;
And thro' the fields the road runs by
To many-towered Camelot."

Tennyson.

LONG before daylight we ranged abroad with hatchet in hand, in search of fuel, and made the yet slumbering and dreaming wood resound with our blows. Then with our fire we burned up a portion of the loitering night, while the kettle sang its homely strain to the morning star. We tramped about the shore, waked all the muskrats, and scared up the bittern and birds that were asleep upon their roosts; we hauled up and upset our boat, and washed it and rinsed out the clay, talking aloud as if it were broad day, until at length, by three o'clock, we had completed our preparations and were ready to pursue our voyage as usual; so, shaking the clay from our feet, we pushed into the fog.

Though we were enveloped in mist as usual, we trusted that there was a bright day behind it.

Ply the oars! away! away!
In each dew drop of the morning
Lies the promise of a day.

Rivers from the sunrise flow,
Springing with the dewy morn;
Voyageurs 'gainst time do row,
Idle noon nor sunset know,
Ever even with the dawn.

Belknap, the historian of this State, says that "In the neighborhood of fresh rivers and ponds, a whitish fog in the morning, lying over the water, is a sure indication of fair weather for that day; and when no fog is seen, rain is expected before night." That which seemed to us to invest the world, was only a narrow and shallow wreath of vapor stretched over the channel of the Merrimack from the sea-board to the mountains. More extensive fogs, however, have their own limits. I once saw the day break from the top of Saddle-back Mountain in Massachusetts, above the clouds. As we cannot distinguish objects through this dense fog, let me tell this story more at length.

I had come over the hills on foot and alone in serene summer days, plucking the raspberries by the way-side, and occasionally buying a loaf of bread at a farmer's house, with a knapsack on my back, which held a few traveller's books and a change of clothing, and a staff in my hand. I had that morning looked down from the Hoosack Mountain, where the road crosses it, on the village of North Adams in the valley, three miles away under my feet, showing how uneven the earth may sometimes be, and making it seem an accident that it should ever be level and convenient for the feet of man. Putting a little rice and sugar and a tin cup into my knapsack at this village, I began in the afternoon to ascend the mountain, whose summit is three thousand six hundred feet above the level of the sea, and was seven or eight miles distant by the path. My route lay up a long and spacious valley called the Bellows, because the winds rush up or down it with violence in storms, sloping up to the very clouds between the principal range and a lower mountain. There were a few farms scattered along at different elevations, each commanding a fine prospect of the mountains to the north, and a stream ran down the middle of the valley, on which near the head there was a mill. It seemed a road for the pilgrim to enter upon who would climb to the gates of heaven. Now I crossed a hay-field, and now over the brook on a slight bridge, still gradually ascending all the while, with a sort of awe, and filled with indefinite expectations as to what kind of inhabitants and what kind of nature I should come to at last. It now seemed some advantage that the earth was uneven, for one could not imagine a more noble position for a farm house than this vale afforded, further from or nearer to its head, from a glen-like seclusion overlooking the country at a great elevation between these two mountain walls.

It reminded me of the homesteads of the Hugunots, on Staten Island, off the coast of New Jersey. The hills in the interior of this island, though comparatively low, are penetrated in various directions by similar sloping valleys on a humble scale, gradually narrowing and rising to the center, and at the head of these the Hugunots, who were the first settlers, placed their houses, quite within the land, in rural and sheltered places, in leafy recesses where the breeze played with the poplar and the gum tree, from which, with equal security in calm and storm, they looked out through a widening vista, over miles of forest and stretching salt marsh, to the Hugunots' Tree, an old elm on the shore at whose root they had landed, and across the spacious outer bay of New York to Sandy Hook and the Highlands of Neversink, and thence over leagues of the Atlantic, perchance to some faint vessel in the horizon, almost a day's sail on her voyage to that Europe whence they had come. When walking in the interior there, in the midst of rural scenery, where there was as little to remind me of the ocean as amid the New Hampshire hills, I have suddenly, through a gap, a cleft or "clove road," as the Dutch settlers called it, caught sight of a ship under full sail, over a field of corn, twenty or thirty miles at sea. The effect was similar, since I had no means of measuring distances, to seeing a painted ship passed backwards and forwards through a magic lantern.

But to return to the mountain. It seemed as if he must be the most singular and heavenly-minded man whose dwelling stood highest up the valley. The thunder had rumbled at my heels all the way, but the shower passed off in another direction, though if it had not, I half believed that I should get above it. I at length reached the last house but one, where the path to the summit diverged to the right, while the summit itself rose directly in front. But I determined to follow up the valley to its head, and then find my own route up the steep, as the shorter and more adventurous way. I had thoughts of returning to this house, which was well kept and so nobly placed, the next day, and perhaps remaining a week there, if I could have entertainment. Its mistress was a frank and hospitable young woman, who stood before me in a dishabille, busily and unconcernedly combing her long black hair while she talked, giving her head the necessary toss with each sweep of the comb, with lively, sparkling eyes, and full of interest in that lower world from which I had come, talking all the while as familiarly as if she had known me for years, and reminding me of a cousin of mine. She had at first taken me for a student from Williamstown, for they went by in parties, she said, either riding or walking, almost every pleasant day, and were a pretty wild set of fellows; but they never went by the way I was going. As I passed the last house, a man called out to know what I had to sell, for seeing my knapsack, he thought that I might be a pedler, who was taking this unusual route over the ridge of the valley into South Adams. He told me that it was still four or five miles to the summit by the path which I had left, though not more than two in a straight line from where I was, but that nobody ever went this way; there was no path, and I should find it as steep as the roof of a house. But I knew that I was more used to woods and mountains than he, and went along through his cow-yard, while he, looking at the sun, shouted after me that I should not get to the top that night. I soon reached the head of the valley, but as I could not see the summit from this point, I ascended a low mountain on the opposite side, and took its bearing with my compass. I at once entered the woods, and began to climb the steep side of the mountain in a diagonal direction, taking the bearing of a tree every dozen rods. The ascent was by no means difficult or unpleasant, and occupied much less time than it would have taken to follow the path. Even country people, I have observed, magnify the difficulty of travelling in the forest, especially among mountains. They seem to lack their usual common sense in this. I have climbed several higher mountains without guide or path, and have found, as might be expected, that it takes only more time and patience commonly than to travel the smoothest highway. It is very rare that you meet with obstacles in this world, which the humblest man has not faculties to surmount. It is true, we may come to a perpendicular precipice, but we need not jump off, nor run our heads against it. A man may jump down his own cellar stairs, or dash his brains out against his chimney, if he is mad. So far as my experience goes, travellers generally exaggerate the difficulties of the way. Like most evil, the difficulty is imaginary; for what's the hurry? If a person lost would conclude that after all he is not lost, he is not beside himself, but standing in his own old shoes on the very spot where he is, and that for the time being he will live there; but the places that have known him, *they* are lost,–how much anxiety and danger would vanish. I am not alone if I stand by myself. Who knows where in space this globe is rolling? Yet we will not give ourselves up for lost, let it go where it will.

I made my way steadily upward in a straight line through a dense undergrowth of mountain laurel, until the trees began to have a scraggy and infernal look, as if contending with frost goblins, and at length I reached the summit, just as the sun was setting. Several acres here had been cleared, and were covered with rocks and stumps, and there was a rude observatory in the middle which overlooked the woods. I had one fair view of the country before the sun went down, but I was too thirsty to waste any light in viewing the prospect, and set out at once to find water. First, going down a well-beaten path for half a mile through the low scrubby wood, till I came to where the water stood in the tracks of the horses which had carried travellers up, I lay down flat, and drank these dry one after another, a pure, cold, spring-like water, but yet I could not fill my dipper, though I contrived little syphons of grass stems and ingenious aqueducts on a small scale; it was too slow a process. Then remembering that I had passed a moist place near the top on my way up, I returned to find it again, and here with sharp stones and my hands, in the twilight, I made a well about two feet deep, which was soon filled with pure cold water, and the birds too came and drank at it. So I filled my dipper, and making my way back to the observatory, collected some dry sticks and made a fire on some flat stones, which had been placed on the floor for that purpose, and so I soon cooked my supper of rice, having already whittled a wooden spoon to eat it with.

I sat up during the evening, reading by the light of the fire the scraps of newspapers in which some party had wrapped their luncheon; the prices current in New York and Boston, the advertisements, and the singular editorials which some had seen fit to publish, not foreseeing under what critical circumstances they would be read. I read these things at a vast advantage there, and it seemed to me that the advertisements, or what is called the business part of a paper, were greatly the best, the most useful, natural, and respectable. Almost all the opinions and sentiments expressed were so little considered, so shallow and flimsy, that I thought the very texture of the paper must be weaker in that part and tear the more easily. The advertisements and the prices current were more closely allied to nature, and were respectable in some measure as tide and meteorological tables are; but the reading matter, which I remembered was most prized down below, unless it was some humble record of science, or an extract from some old classic, struck me as strangely whimsical, and crude, and one-idea'd, like a school-boy's theme, such as youths write and afterward burn. The opinions were of that kind that are doomed to wear a different aspect to-morrow, like last year's fashions; as if mankind were very green indeed, and would be ashamed of themselves in a few years, when they had outgrown this verdant period. There was, moreover, a singular disposition to wit and humor, but rarely the slightest real success; and the apparent success was a terrible satire on the attempt; as if the Evil Genius of man laughed the loudest at his best jokes. The advertisements, as I have said, such as were serious, and not of the modern quack kind, suggested pleasing and poetic thoughts; for commerce is really as interesting as nature. The very names of the commodities were poetic, and as suggestive as if they had been inserted in a pleasing poem,–Lumber, Cotton, Sugar, Hides, Guano, and Logwood. Some sober, private, and original thought would have been grateful to read there, and as much in harmony with the circumstances as if it had been written on a mountain top; for it is of a fashion which never changes, and as respectable as hides and logwood, or any natural product. What an inestimable companion such a scrap of paper would have been, containing some fruit of a mature life. What a relic! What a recipe! It seemed a divine invention, by which not mere shining coin, but shining and current thoughts, could be brought up and left there.

As it was cold, I collected quite a pile of wood and lay down on a board against the side of the building, not having any blanket to cover me, with my head to the fire, that I might look after it, which is not the Indian rule. But as it grew colder towards midnight, I at length encased myself completely in boards, managing even to put a board on top of me, with a large stone on it, to keep it down, and so slept comfortably. I was reminded, it is true, of the Irish children, who inquired what their neighbors did who had no door to put over them in winter nights as they had; but I am convinced that there was nothing very strange in the inquiry. Those who have never tried it can have no idea how far a door, which keeps the single blanket down, may go toward making one comfortable. We are constituted a good deal like chickens, which taken from the hen, and put in a basket of cotton in the chimney corner, will often peep till they die nevertheless, but if you put in a book, or any thing heavy, which will press down the cotton, and feel like the hen, they go to sleep directly. My only companions were the mice, which came to pick up the crumbs that had been left in those scraps of paper; still, as every where, pensioners on man, and not unwisely improving this elevated tract for their habitation. They nibbled what was for them; I nibbled what was for me. Once or twice in the night, when I looked up, I saw a white cloud drifting through the windows, and filling the whole upper story.

This observatory was a building of considerable size, erected by the students of Williamstown College, whose buildings might be seen by daylight gleaming far down in the valley. It would be no small advantage if every college were thus located at the base of a mountain, as good at least as one well-endowed professorship. It were as well to be educated in the shadow of a mountain as in more classical shades. Some will remember, no doubt, not only that they went to the college, but that they went to the mountain. Every visit to its summit would, as it were, generalize the particular information gained below, and subject it to more catholic tests.

I was up early and perched upon the top of this tower to see the daybreak, for some time reading the names that had been engraved there before I could distinguish more distant objects. An "untameable fly" buzzed at my elbow with the same non-chalance as on a molasses hogshead at the end of Long-wharf. Even there I must attend to his stale humdrum. But now I come to the pith of this long digression.—As the light increased I discovered around me an ocean of mist, which by chance reached up exactly to the base of the tower, and shut out every vestige of the earth, while I was left floating on this fragment of the wreck of a world, on my carved plank in cloudland; a situation which required no aid from the imagination to render it impressive. As the light in the east steadily increased, it revealed to me more clearly the new world into which I had risen in the night, the new terra-firma perchance of my future life. There was not a crevice left through which the trivial places we name Massachusetts, or Vermont, or New York, could be seen, while I still inhaled the clear atmosphere of a July morning,—if it were July there. All around beneath me was spread for a hundred miles on every side, as far as the eye could reach, an undulating country of clouds, answering in the varied swell of its surface to the terrestrial world it veiled. It was such a country as we might see in dreams, with all the delights of paradise. There were immense snowy pastures, apparently smooth-shaven and firm, and shady vales between the vaporous mountains, and far in the horizon I could see where some luxurious misty timber jutted into the prairie, and trace the windings of a water course, some unimagined Amazon or Orinoko, by the misty trees on its brink. As there was wanting the symbol, so there was not the substance of impurity, no spot nor stain. It was a favor for which to be forever silent to be shown this vision. The earth beneath had become such a flitting thing of lights and shadows as the clouds had been before. It was not merely veiled to me, but it had passed away like the phantom of a shadow, σκιᾶς ὄναρ, and this new platform was gained. As I had climbed above storm and cloud, so by successive days' journeys I might reach the region of eternal day beyond the tapering shadow of the earth; aye,

> "Heaven itself shall slide,
> And roll away, like melting stars that glide
> Along their oily threads."

But when its own sun began to rise on this pure world, I found myself a dweller in the dazzling halls of Aurora, into which poets have had but a partial glance over the eastern hills,–drifting amid the saffron-colored clouds, and playing with the rosy fingers of the Dawn, in the very path of the Sun's chariot, and sprinkled with its dewy dust, enjoying the benignant smile, and near at hand the far-darting glances of the god. The inhabitants of earth behold commonly but the dark and shadowy under-side of heaven's pavement; it is only when seen at a favorable angle in the horizon, morning or evening, that some faint streaks of the rich lining of the clouds are revealed. But my muse would fail to convey an impression of the gorgeous tapestry by which I was surrounded, such as men see faintly reflected afar off in the chambers of the east. Here, as on earth, I saw the gracious god

> "Flatter the mountain tops with sovereign eye, * * *
> Gilding pale streams with heavenly alchemy."

But never here did "Heaven's sun" stain himself. But alas, owing as I think to some unworthiness in myself, my private sun did stain himself, and

> "Anon permit the basest clouds to ride
> With ugly wrack on his celestial face,"–

for before the god had reached the zenith the heavenly pavement rose and embraced my wavering virtue, or rather I sank down again into that "forlorn world," from which the celestial Sun had hid his visage.—

"How may a worm, that crawls along the dust,
Clamber the azure mountains, thrown so high,
And fetch from thence thy fair idea just,
That in those sunny courts doth hidden lie,
Cloth'd with such light, as blinds the angel's eye?
How may weak mortal ever hope to file
His unsmooth tongue, and his deprostrate style?
O, raise thou from his corse thy now entombed exile!"

In the preceding evening I had seen the summits of new and yet higher mountains, the Catskills, by which I might hope to climb to heaven again, and had set my compass for a fair lake in the south-west, which lay in my way, for which I now steered, descending the mountain by my own route, on the side opposite to that by which I had ascended, and soon found myself in the region of cloud and drizzling rain, and the inhabitants affirmed that it had been a cloudy and drizzling day wholly.

But now we must make haste back before the fog disperses to the blithe Merrimack water.—

Since that first "away! away!"
Many a lengthy reach we've rowed,
Still the sparrow on the spray
Hastes to usher in the day
With her simple stanza'd ode.

We passed a canal boat before sunrise, groping its way to the seaboard, and though we could not see it on account of the fog, the few dull, thumping, stertorous sounds which we heard, impressed us with a sense of weight and irresistible motion. One little rill of commerce already awake on this distant New Hampshire river. The fog, as it required more skill in the steering, enhanced the interest of our early voyage, and made the river seem indefinitely broad. A slight mist, through which objects are faintly visible, has the effect of expanding even ordinary streams, by a singular mirage, into arms of the sea or inland lakes. In the present instance it was even fragrant and invigorating, and we enjoyed it as a sort of earlier sunshine, or dewy and embryo light.

Low-anchored cloud,
Newfoundland air,
Fountain-head and source of rivers,
Dew cloth, dream drapery,
And napkin spread by fays;
Drifting meadow of the air,
Where bloom the daisied banks and violets,
And in whose fenny labyrinth
The bittern booms and heron wades;
Spirit of lakes and seas and rivers,
Bear only perfumes and the scent
Of healing herbs to just men's fields.

The same pleasant and observant historian whom we quoted above, says, that "In the mountainous parts of the country, the ascent of vapors, and their formation into clouds, is a curious and entertaining object. The vapors are seen rising in small columns like smoke from many chimneys. When risen to a certain height, they spread, meet, condense, and are attracted to the mountains, where they either distil in gentle dews, and replenish the springs, or descend in showers, accompanied with thunder. After short intermissions, the process is repeated many times in the course of a summer day, affording to travellers a lively illustration of what is observed in the book of Job, 'They are wet with the showers of the mountains.' "

Fogs and clouds which conceal the overshadowing mountains lend the breadth of the plains to mountain vales. Even a small-featured country acquires some grandeur in stormy weather when clouds are seen drifting between the beholder and the neighboring hills. When, in travelling toward Haverhill through Hampstead in this State, on the height of land between the Merrimack and the Piscataqua or the sea, you commence the descent eastward, the view toward the coast is so distant and unexpected, though the sea is invisible, that you at first suppose the unobstructed atmosphere to be a fog in the lowlands concealing hills of corresponding elevation to that you are upon; but it is the mist of prejudice alone, which the winds will not disperse. The most stupendous scenery ceases to be sublime when it becomes distinct, or in other words limited, and the imagination is no longer encouraged to exaggerate it. The actual height and breadth of a mountain or a water-fall are always ridiculously small; they are the imagined only that content us. Nature is not made after such a fashion as we would have her. We piously exaggerate her wonders as the scenery around our home.

Such was the heaviness of the dews along this river that we were generally obliged to leave our tent spread over the bows of the boat till the sun had dried it, to avoid mildew. We passed the mouth of Penichook Brook, a wild salmon stream, in the fog without seeing it. At length the sun's rays struggled through the mist and showed us the pines on shore dripping with dew, and springs trickling from the moist banks,–

"And now the taller sons, whom Titan warms,
Of unshorn mountains blown with easy winds,
Dandle the morning's childhood in their arms,
And, if they chanced to slip the prouder pines,
The under corylets did catch their shines,
To gild their leaves."

We rowed for some hours between glistening banks before the sun had dried the grass and leaves, or the day had established its character. Its serenity at last seemed the more profound and secure for the denseness of the morning's fog. The river became swifter, and the scenery more pleasing than before. The banks were steep and clayey for the most part, and trickling with water, and where a spring oozed out a few feet above the river, the boatmen had cut a trough out of a slab with their axes, and placed it so as to receive the water and fill their jugs conveniently. Sometimes this purer and cooler water, bursting out from under a pine or a rock, was collected into a basin close to the edge of, and level with the river, a fountain-head of the Merrimack. So near along life's stream are the fountains of innocence and youth making fertile its sandy margin; and the voyageur will do well to replenish his vessels often at these uncontaminated sources. Some youthful spring, perchance, still empties with tinkling music into the oldest river, even when it is falling into the sea, and we imagine that its music is distinguished by the river gods from the general lapse of the stream, and falls sweeter on their ears in proportion as it is nearer to the ocean. As the evaporations of the river feed thus these unsuspected springs which filter through its banks, so, perchance, our aspirations fall back again in springs on the margin of life's stream to refresh and purify it. The yellow and tepid river may float his scow, and cheer his eye with its reflections and its ripples, but the boatman quenches his thirst at this small rill alone. It is this purer and cooler element that chiefly sustains his life. The race will long survive that is thus discreet.

Our course this morning lay between the territories of Merrimack, on the west, and Litchfield, once called Brenton's Farm, on the east, which townships were anciently the Indian Naticook. Brenton was a fur trader among the Indians, and these lands were granted to him in 1656. The latter township contains about five hundred inhabitants, of whom, however, we saw none, and but few of their dwellings. Being on the river, whose banks are always high and generally conceal the few houses, the country appeared much more wild and primitive than to the traveller on the neighboring roads. The river is by far the most attractive highway, and those boatmen who have spent twenty or twenty-five years on it, must have had a much fairer, more wild and memorable experience than the dusty and jarring one of the teamster, who has driven, during the same time, on the roads which run parallel with the stream. As one ascends the Merrimack he rarely sees a village, but for the most part, alternate wood and pasture lands, and sometimes a field of corn or potatoes, of rye or oats or English grass, with a few straggling apple trees, and, at still longer intervals, a farmer's house. The soil, excepting the best of the interval, is commonly as light and sandy as a patriot could desire. Sometimes this forenoon the country appeared in its primitive state, and as if the Indian still inhabited it; and again, as if many free new settlers occupied it, their slight fences straggling down to the water's edge, and the barking of dogs, and even the prattle of children, were heard, and smoke was seen to go up from some hearth-stone, and the banks were divided into patches of pasture, mowing, tillage, and woodland. But when the river spread out broader, with an uninhabited islet, or a long low sandy shore which ran on single and devious, not answering to its opposite, but far off as if it were seashore or single coast, and the land no longer nursed the river in its bosom, but they conversed as equals, the rustling leaves with rippling waves, and few fences were seen, but high oak woods on one side, and large herds of cattle, and all tracks seemed a point to one centre, behind some statelier grove,—we imagined that the river flowed through an extensive manor, and that the few inhabitants were retainers to a lord, and a feudal state of things prevailed.

When there was a suitable reach, we caught sight of the Goffstown mountain, the Indian Uncannunuc, rising before us on the west side. It was a calm and beautiful day, with only a slight zephyr to ripple the surface of the water, and rustle the woods on shore, and just warmth enough to prove the kindly disposition of Nature to her children. With buoyant spirits and vigorous impulses we tossed our boat rapidly along into the very middle of this forenoon. The fish-hawk sailed and screamed overhead. The chipping, or striped squirrel, *sciurus striatus* (*Tamias Lysteri*, Aud.), sat upon the end of some Virginia fence or rider reaching over the stream, twirling a green nut with one paw, as in a lathe, while the other held it fast against its incisors as chisels. Like an independent russet leaf, with a will of its own, rustling whither it could; now under the fence, now over it, now peeping at the voyageurs through a crack with only its tail visible, now at its lunch deep in the toothsome kernel, and now a rod off playing at hide-and-seek, with the nut stowed away in its chops, where were half a dozen more beside, extending its cheeks to a ludicrous breadth. As if it were devising through what safe valve of frisk or somerset to let its superfluous life escape; the stream passing harmlessly off, even while it sits, in constant electric flashes through its tail; and now with a chuckling squeak it dives into the root of a hazel, and we see no more of it. Or the larger red squirrel or chickaree, sometimes called the Hudson Bay squirrel, *sciurus Hudsonius*, gave warning of our approach by that peculiar alarum of his, like the winding up of some strong clock, in the top of a pine tree, and dodged behind its stem, or leaped from tree to tree, with such caution and adroitness as if much depended on the fidelity of his scout, running along the white pine boughs sometimes twenty rods by our side, with such speed, and by such unerring routes as if it were some well-worn familiar path to him; and presently, when we have passed, he returns to his work of cutting off the pine cones, and letting them fall to the ground.

We passed Cromwell's Falls, the first we met with on this river, this forenoon, by means of locks, without using our wheels. These falls are the Nesenkeag of the Indians. Great Nesenkeag Stream comes in on the right just above, and Little Nesenkeag some distance below, both in Litchfield. We read in the gazetteer, under the head of Merrimack, that "The first house in this town was erected on the margin of the river [soon after 1665] for a house of traffic with the Indians. For some time one Cromwell carried on a lucrative trade with them, weighing their furs with his foot, till, enraged at his supposed or real deception, they formed the resolution to murder him. This intention being communicated to Cromwell, he buried his wealth and made his escape. Within a few hours after his flight, a party of the Penacook tribe arrived, and not finding the object of their resentment, burnt his habitation." Upon the top of the high bank here, close to the river, was still to be seen his cellar, now overgrown with trees. It was a convenient spot for such a traffic, at the foot of the first falls above the settlements, and commanding a pleasant view up the river, where he could see the Indians coming down with their furs. The lock-man told us that his shovel and tongs had been plowed up here, and also a stone with his name on it. But we will not vouch for the truth of this story. In the New Hampshire Historical Collections for 1815 it says, "Some time after pewter was found in the well, and an iron pot and trammel in the sand; the latter are preserved." These were the traces of the white trader. On the opposite bank, where it jutted over the stream cape-wise, we picked up four arrow-heads and a small Indian tool made of stone, as soon as we had climbed it, where plainly there had once stood a wigwam of the Indians with whom Cromwell traded, and who fished and hunted here before he came.

As usual the gossips have not been silent respecting Cromwell's buried wealth, and it is said that some years ago a farmer's plow, not far from here, slid over a flat stone which emitted a hollow sound, and on its being raised, a small hole six inches in diameter was discovered, stoned about, from which a sum of money was taken. The lock-man told us another similar story about a farmer in a neighboring town, who had been a poor man, but who suddenly bought a good farm, and was well to do in the world; and, when he was questioned, did not give a satisfactory account of the matter;—how few alas, could! This caused his hired man to remember, that one day as they were plowing together the plow struck something, and his employer going back to look, concluded not to go round again, saying that the sky looked rather louring, and so put up his team. The like urgency has caused many things to be remembered which never transpired. The truth is, there is money buried every where, and you have only to go work to find it.

Not far from these falls stands an oak tree on the interval, about a quarter of a mile from the river, on the farm of a Mr. Lund, which was pointed out to us as the spot where French, the leader of the party which went in pursuit of the Indians from Dunstable, was killed. Farwell dodged them in the thick woods near. It did not look as if men had ever had to run for their lives on this now open and peaceful interval.

Here too was another extensive desert by the side of the road in Litchfield, visible from the bank of the river. The sand was blown off in some places to the depth of ten or twelve feet, leaving small grotesque hillocks of that height where there was a clump of bushes firmly rooted. Thirty or forty years ago, as we were told, it was a sheep pasture, but the sheep being worried by the fleas, began to paw the ground, till they broke the sod, and so the sand began to blow, till now it had extended over forty or fifty acres. This evil might easily have been remedied at first, by spreading birches with their leaves on over the sand, and fastening them down with stakes, to break the wind. The fleas bit the sheep, and the sheep bit the ground, and the sore had spread to this extent. It is astonishing what a great sore a little scratch breedeth. Who knows but Sahara, where caravans and cities are buried, began with the bite of an African flea. This poor globe, how it must itch in many places! Will no god be kind enough to spread a salve of birches over its sores?—Here too we noticed where the Indians had gathered a heap of stones, perhaps for their council fire, which by their weight having prevented the sand under them from blowing away, were left on the summit of a mound. They told us that arrow-heads, and also bullets of lead and iron had been found here. We noticed several other sandy tracts in our voyage; and the course of the Merrimack can be traced from the nearest mountain by its yellow sandbanks, though the river itself is for the most part invisible. Lawsuits, as we hear, have in some cases grown out of these causes. Railroads have been made through certain irritable districts, breaking their sod, and so have set the sand to blowing, till it has converted fertile farms into deserts, and the Company has had to pay the damages.

This sand seemed to us the connecting link between land and water. It was a kind of water on which you could walk, and you could see the ripple marks on its surface, produced by the winds, precisely like those at the bottom of a brook or lake. We had read that Mussulmen are permitted by the Koran to perform their ablutions in sand when they cannot get water, a necessary indulgence in Arabia, and we now understood the propriety of this provision.

Plum Island, at the mouth of this river, to whose formation, perhaps, these very banks have sent their contribution, is a similar desert of drifting sand, of various colors, blown into graceful curves by the wind. It is a mere sand-bar exposed, stretching nine miles parallel to the coast, and, exclusive of the marsh on the inside, rarely more than half a mile wide. There are but half a dozen houses on it, and it is almost without a tree, or a sod, or any green thing with which a countryman is familiar. The thin vegetation stands half buried in sand, as in drifting snow.

The only shrub, the beach plum, which gives the island its name, grows but a few feet high; but this is so abundant that parties of a hundred at once come from the main land and down the Merrimack in September, and pitch their tents, and gather the plums, which are good to eat raw and to preserve. The graceful and delicate beach pea too grows abundantly amid the sand; and several strange moss-like and succulent plants. The island for its whole length is scolloped into low hills, not more than twenty feet high, by the wind, and excepting a faint trail on the edge of the marsh, is as trackless as Sahara. There are dreary bluffs of sand and valleys plowed by the wind, where you might expect to discover the bones of a caravan. Schooners come from Boston to load with the sand for masons' uses, and in a few hours the wind obliterates all traces of their work. Yet you have only to dig a foot or two any where to come to fresh water; and you are surprised to learn that woodchucks abound here, and foxes are found, though you see not where they can burrow or hide themselves. I have walked down the whole length of its broad beach at low tide, at which time alone you can find a firm ground to walk on, and probably Massachusetts does not furnish a more grand and dreary walk. On the sea side there are only a distant sail and a few coots to break the grand monotony. A solitary stake stuck up, or a sharper sand-hill than usual, is remarkable as a land-mark for miles; while for music you hear only the ceaseless sound of the surf, and the dreary peep of the beach birds.

There were several canal boats at Cromwell's Falls, passing through the locks, for which we waited. In the forward part of one stood a brawny New Hampshire man, leaning on his pole, bareheaded and in shirt and trousers only, a rude Apollo of a man, coming down from that "vast uplandish country" to the main; of nameless age, with flaxen hair, and vigorous, weather-bleached countenance, in whose wrinkles the sun still lodged, as little touched by the heats and frosts and withering cares of life, as a maple of the mountain; an undressed, unkempt, uncivil man, with whom we parleyed a while, and parted not without a sincere interest in one another. His humanity was genuine and instinctive, and his rudeness only a manner. He inquired, just as we were passing out of earshot, if we had killed any thing, and we shouted after him that we had shot a *buoy*, and could see him for a long while scratching his head in vain, to know if he had heard aright.

There is reason in the distinction of civil and uncivil. The manners are sometimes so rough a rind, that we doubt whether they cover any core or sapwood at all. We sometimes meet uncivil men, children of Amazons, who dwell by mountain paths, and are said to be inhospitable to strangers; whose salutation is as rude as the grasp of their brawny hands, and who deal with men as unceremoniously as they are wont to deal with the elements. They need only to extend their clearings, and let in more sunlight, to seek out the southern slopes of the hills, from which they may look down on the civil plain or ocean, and temper their diet duly with the cereal fruits, consuming less wild meat and acorns, to become like the inhabitants of cities. A true politeness does not result from any hasty and artificial polishing, it is true, but grows naturally in characters of the right grain and quality, through a long fronting of men and events, and rubbing on good and bad fortune. Perhaps I can tell a tale to the purpose while the lock is filling,—

for our voyage this forenoon furnishes but few incidents of importance.

Early one summer morning I had left the shores of the Connecticut, and for the livelong day travelled up the bank of a river, which came in from the west; now looking down on the stream, foaming and rippling through the forest a mile off, from the hills over which the road led, and now sitting on its rocky brink and dipping my feet in its rapids, or bathing adventurously in mid-channel. The hills grew more and more frequent, and gradually swelled into mountains as I advanced, hemming in the course of the river, so that at last I could not see where it came from, and was at liberty to imagine the most wonderful meanderings and descents. At noon I slept on the grass in the shade of a maple, where the river had found a broader channel than usual, and was spread out shallow, with frequent sand-bars exposed. In the names of the towns I recognized some which I had long ago read on teamsters' wagons, that had come from far up country, quiet, uplandish towns, of mountainous fame. I walked along musing, and enchanted by rows of sugar-maples, through the small and uninquisitive villages, and sometimes was pleased with the sight of a boat drawn up on a sand-bar, where there appeared no inhabitants to use it. It seemed, however, as essential to the river as a fish, and to lend a certain dignity to it. It was like the trout of mountain streams to the fishes of the sea, or like the young of the land crab born far in the interior, who have never yet heard the sound of the ocean's surf. The hills approached nearer and nearer to the stream, until at last they closed behind me, and I found myself just before night-fall, in a romantic and retired valley, about half a mile in length, and barely wide enough for the stream at its bottom. I thought that there could be no finer site for a cottage among mountains. You could any where run across the stream on the rocks, and its constant murmuring would quiet the passions of mankind forever. Suddenly the road, which seemed aiming for the mountain side, turned short to the left, and another valley opened, concealing the former, and of the same character with it. It was the most remarkable and pleasing scenery I had ever seen. I found here a few mild and hospitable inhabitants, who, as the day was not quite spent, and I was anxious to improve the light, directed me four or five miles further on my way to the dwelling of a man whose name was Rice, who occupied the last and highest of the valleys that lay in my path, and who, they said, was a rather rude and uncivil man. But, "What is a foreign country to those who have science? Who is a stranger to those who have the habit of speaking kindly?"

At length, as the sun was setting behind the mountains in a still darker and more solitary vale, I reached the dwelling of this man. Except for the narrowness of the plain, and that the stones were solid granite, it was the counterpart of that retreat to which Belphœbe bore the wounded Timias;—

> "in a pleasant glade,
> With mountains round about environed,
> And mighty woods, which did the valley shade,
> And like a stately theatre it made,
> Spreading itself into a spacious plain;
> And in the midst a little river played
> Amongst the pumy stones which seemed to plain,
> With gentle murmur that his course they did restrain."

I observed, as I drew near, that he was not so rude as I had anticipated, for he kept many cattle and dogs to watch them, and I saw where he had made maple sugar on the sides of the mountains, and above all distinguished the voices of children mingling with the murmur of the torrent before the door. As I passed his stable I met one whom I supposed to be a hired man, attending to his cattle, and inquired if they entertained travellers at that house. "Sometimes we do," he answered, gruffly, and immediately went to the farthest stall from me, and I perceived that it was Rice himself whom I had addressed. But pardoning this incivility to the wildness of the scenery, I bent my steps to the house. There was no sign-post before it, nor any of the usual invitations to the traveller, though I saw by the road that many went and came there, but the owner's name only was fastened to the outside, a sort of implied and sullen invitation, as I thought. I passed from room to room without meeting any one, till I came to what seemed the guests' apartment, which was neat, and even had an air of refinement about it, and I was glad to find a map against the wall which would direct me on my journey on the morrow. At length I heard a step in a distant apartment, which was the first I had entered, and went to see if the landlord had come in; but it proved to be only a child, one of those whose voices I had heard, probably his son, and between him and me stood in the door-way a large watch-dog, which growled at me, and looked as if he would presently spring, but the boy did not speak to him; and when I asked for a glass of water, he briefly said, "It runs in the corner." So I took a mug from the counter and went out of doors, and searched round the corner of the house, but could find neither well nor spring, nor any water but the stream which ran all along the front. I came back, therefore, and setting down the mug, asked the child if the stream was good to drink; whereupon he seized the mug and going to the corner of the room, where a cool spring which issued from the mountain behind trickled through a pipe into the apartment, filled it, and drank, and gave it to me empty again, and calling to the dog, rushed out of doors. Ere long some of the hired men made their appearance, and drank at the spring, and lazily washed themselves and combed their hair in silence, and some sat down as if weary, and fell asleep in their seats. But all the while I saw no women, though I sometimes heard a bustle in that part of the house from which the spring came.

At length Rice himself came in, for it was now dark, with an ox whip in his hand, breathing hard, and he too soon settled down into his seat not far from me, as if now that his day's work was done he had no further to travel, but only to digest his supper at his leisure. When I asked him if he could give me a bed, he said there was one ready, in such a tone as implied that I ought to have known it, and the less said about that the better. So far so good. And yet he continued to look at me as if he would fain have me say something further like a traveller. I remarked, that it was a wild and rugged country he inhabited, and worth coming many miles to see. "Not so very rough neither," said he, and appealed to his men to bear witness to the breadth and smoothness of his fields, which consisted in all of one small interval, and to the size of his crops; "and if we have some hills," added he, "there's no better pasturage any where." I then asked if this place was the one I had heard of, calling it by a name I had seen on the map, or if it was a certain other; and he answered, gruffly, that it was neither the one nor the other; that he had settled it and cultivated it, and made it what it was, and I could know nothing about it. Observing some guns and other implements of hunting hanging on brackets around the room, and his hounds now sleeping on the floor, I took occasion to change the discourse, and inquired if there was much game in that country, and he answered this question more graciously, having some glimmering of my drift; but when I inquired if there were any bears, he answered impatiently, that he was no more in danger of losing his sheep than his neighbors, he had tamed and civilized that region. After a pause, thinking of my journey on the morrow, and the few hours of daylight in that hollow and mountainous country, which would require me to be on my way betimes, I remarked, that the day must be shorter by an hour there than on the neighboring plains; at which he gruffly asked what I knew about it, and affirmed that he had as much daylight as his neighbors; he ventured to say, the days were longer there than where I lived, as I should find if I stayed; that in some way, I could not be expected to understand how, the sun came over the mountains half an hour earlier, and stayed half an hour later there than on the neighboring plains.—And more of like sort he said. He was, indeed, as rude as a fabled satyr. But I suffered him to pass for what he was, for why should I quarrel with nature? and was even pleased at the discovery of such a singular natural phenomenon. I dealt with him as if to me all manners were indifferent, and he had a sweet wild way with him. I would not question nature, and I would rather have him as he was, than as I would have him. For I had come up here not for sympathy, or kindness, or society, but for novelty and adventure, and to see what nature had produced here. I therefore did not repel his rudeness, but quite innocently welcomed it all, and knew how to appreciate it, as if I were reading in an old drama a part well sustained. He was indeed a coarse and sensual man, and, as I have said, uncivil, but he had his just quarrel with nature and mankind, I have no doubt, only he had no artificial covering to his ill humors. He was earthy enough, but yet there was good soil in him, and even a long-suffering Saxon probity at bottom. If you could represent the case to him, he would not let the race die out in him, like a red Indian.

At length I told him that he was a fortunate man, and I trusted that he was grateful for so much light, and rising, said I would take a lamp, and that I would pay him then for my lodging, for I expected to recommence my journey, even as early as the sun rose in his country; but he answered in haste, and this time civilly, that I should not fail to find some of his household stirring, however early, for they were no sluggards, and I could take my breakfast with them before I started if I chose; and as he lighted the lamp I detected a gleam of true hospitality and ancient civility, a beam of pure and even gentle humanity from his bleared and moist eyes. It was a look more intimate with me, and more explanatory, than any words of his could have been if he had tried to his dying day. It was more significant than any Rice of those parts could even comprehend, and long anticipated this man's culture,—a glance of his pure genius, which did not much enlighten him, but did impress and rule him for the moment, and faintly constrain his voice and manner. He cheerfully led the way to my apartment, stepping over the limbs of his men who were asleep on the floor in an intervening chamber, and showed me a clean and comfortable bed. For many pleasant hours, after the household was asleep, I sat at the open window, for it was a sultry night, and heard the little river

"Amongst the pumy stones, which seemed to plain
With gentle murmur that his course they did restrain."

But I arose as usual by starlight the next morning, before my host, or his men, or even his dogs, were awake; and having left a ninepence on the counter, was already half way over the mountain with the sun, before they had broken their fast.

Before I had left the country of my host, while the first rays of the sun slanted over the mountains, as I stopped by the way-side to gather some raspberries, a very old man, not far from a hundred, came along with a milking pail in his hand, and turning aside began to pluck the berries near me;—

—"his reverend locks
In comelye curles did wave;
And on his aged temples grew
The blossoms of the grave."—

But when I inquired the way, he answered in a low, rough voice, without looking up or seeming to regard my presence, which I imputed to his years; and presently, muttering to himself, he proceeded to collect his cows in a neighboring pasture; and when he had again returned near to the way-side, he suddenly stopped, while his cows went on before, and, uncovering his head, prayed aloud in the cool morning air, as if he had forgotten this exercise before, for his daily bread, and also that He who letteth his rain fall on the just and on the unjust, and without whom not a sparrow falleth to the ground, would not neglect the stranger, (meaning me,) and with even more direct and personal applications, though mainly according to the long established formula common to lowlanders and the inhabitants of mountains. When he had done praying, I made bold to ask him if he had any cheese in his hut which he would sell me, but he answered without looking up, and in the same low and repulsive voice as before, that they did not make any, and went to milking. It is written, "The stranger who turneth away from a house with disappointed hopes, leaveth there his own offences, and departeth, taking with him all the good actions of the owner."

Being now fairly in the stream of this week's commerce, we began to meet with boats more frequently, and hailed them from time to time with the freedom of sailors. The boatmen appeared to lead an easy and contented life, and we thought that we should prefer their employment ourselves to many professions which are much more sought after. They suggested how few circumstances are necessary to the well-being and serenity of man, how indifferent all employments are, and that any may seem noble and poetic to the eyes of men, if pursued with sufficient buoyancy and freedom. With liberty and pleasant weather, the simplest occupation, any unquestioned country mode of life which detains us in the open air, is alluring. The man who picks peas steadily for a living is more than respectable, he is even envied by his shop-worn neighbors. We are as happy as the birds when our Good Genius permits us to pursue any out-door work without a sense of dissipation. Our pen-knife glitters in the sun; our voice is echoed by yonder wood; if an oar drops, we are fain to let it drop again.

The canal boat is of very simple construction, requiring but little ship timber, and, as we were told, costs about two hundred dollars. They are managed by two men. In ascending the stream they use poles fourteen or fifteen feet long, pointed with iron, walking about one third the length of the boat from the forward end. Going down, they commonly keep in the middle of the stream, using an oar at each end; or if the wind is favorable they raise their broad sail, and have only to steer. They commonly carry down wood or bricks,–fifteen or sixteen cords of wood, and as many thousand bricks, at a time,–and bring back stores for the country, consuming two or three days each way between Concord and Charlestown. They sometimes pile the wood so as to leave a shelter in one part where they may retire from the rain. One can hardly imagine a more healthful employment, or one more favorable to contemplation and the observation of nature. Unlike the mariner, they have the constantly varying panorama of the shore to relieve the monotony of their labor, and it seemed to us that as they thus glided noiselessly from town to town, with all their furniture about them, for their very homestead is a moveable, they could comment on the character of the inhabitants with greater advantage and security to themselves than the traveller in a coach, who would be unable to indulge in such broadsides of wit and humor in so small a vessel, for fear of the recoil. They are not subject to great exposure, like the lumberers of Maine, in any weather, but inhale the healthfullest breezes, being slightly encumbered with clothing, frequently with the head and feet bare. When we met them at noon as they were leisurely descending the stream, their busy commerce did not look like toil, but rather like some ancient oriental game still played on a large scale, as the game of chess, for instance, handed down to this generation. From morning till night, unless the wind is so fair that his single sail will suffice without other labor than steering, the boatman walks backwards and forwards on the side of his boat, now stooping with his shoulder to the pole, then drawing it back slowly to set it again, meanwhile moving steadily forward through an endless valley and an everchanging scenery, now distinguishing his course for a mile or two, and now shut in by a sudden turn of the river in a small woodland lake. All the phenomena which surround him are simple and grand, and there is something impressive, even majestic, in the very motion he causes, which will naturally be communicated to his own character, and he feels the slow irresistible movement under him with pride, as if it were his own energy.

The news spread like wild fire among us youths, when formerly, once in a year or two, one of these boats came up the Concord river, and was seen stealing mysteriously through the meadows and past the village. It came and departed as silently as a cloud, without noise or dust, and was witnessed by few. One summer day this huge traveller might be seen moored at some meadow's wharf, and another summer day it was not there. Where precisely it came from, or who these men were who knew the rocks and soundings better than we who bathed there, we could never tell. We knew some river's bay only, but they took rivers from end to end. They were a sort of fabulous rivermen to us. It was inconceivable by what sort of mediation any mere landsman could hold communication with them. Would they heave to to gratify his wishes? No, it was favor enough to know faintly of their destination, or the time of their possible return. I have seen them in the summer, when the stream ran low, mowing the weeds in mid-channel, and with hayers' jests cutting broad swathes in three feet of water, that they might make a passage for their scow, while the grass in long windrows was carried down the stream, undried by the rarest hay weather. We admired unweariedly how their vessel would float, like a huge chip, sustaining so many casks of lime, and thousands of bricks, and such heaps of iron ore, with wheel-barrows aboard, and that when we stepped on it, it did not yield to the pressure of our feet. It gave us confidence in the prevalence of the law of buoyancy, and we imagined to what infinite uses it might be put. The men appeared to lead a kind of life on it, and it was whispered that they slept aboard. Some affirmed that it carried sail, and that such winds blew here as filled the sails of vessels on the ocean; which again others much doubted. They had been seen to sail across our Fair-Haven bay by lucky fishers who were out, but unfortunately others were not there to see. We might then say that our river was navigable,—why not? In after years I read in print, with no little satisfaction, that it was thought by some that with a little expense in removing rocks and deepening the channel, "there might be a profitable inland navigation." *I* then lived somewhere to tell of.

Such is Commerce, which shakes the cocoa-nut and bread-fruit tree in the remotest isle, and sooner or later dawns on the duskiest and most simple-minded savage. If we may be pardoned the digression,—who can help being affected at the thought of the very fine and slight, but positive relation, in which the savage inhabitants of some remote isle stand to the mysterious white mariner, the child of the sun?—As if *we* were to have dealings with an animal higher in the scale of being than ourselves. It is a barely recognised fact to the natives that he exists, and has his home far away somewhere, and is glad to buy their fresh fruits with his superfluous commodities. Under the same catholic sun glances his white ship over Pacific waves into their smooth bays, and the poor savage's paddle gleams in the air.

Man's little acts are grand,
Beheld from land to land,
There as they lie in time,
Within their native clime.
    Ships with the noon-tide weigh,
    And glide before its ray
    To some retired bay,
    Their haunt,
    Whence, under tropic sun,
    Again they run,
    Bearing gum Senegal and Tragicant.
For this was ocean meant,
For this the sun was sent,
And moon was lent,
And winds in distant caverns pent.

Since our voyage the railroad on the bank has been extended, and there is now but little boating on the Merrimack. All kinds of produce and stores were formerly conveyed by water, but now nothing is carried up the stream, and almost wood and bricks alone are carried down, and these are also carried on the railroad. The locks are fast wearing out, and will soon be impassable, since the tolls will not pay the expense of repairing them, and so in a few years there will be an end of boating on this river. The boating, at present, is principally between Merrimack and Lowell, or Hooksett and Manchester. They make two or three trips in a week, according to wind and weather, from Merrimack to Lowell and back, about twenty-five miles each way. The boatman comes singing in to shore late at night, and moors his empty boat, and gets his supper and lodging in some house near at hand, and again early in the morning, by starlight, perhaps, he pushes away up stream, and, by a shout, or the fragment of a song, gives notice of his approach to the lock-man, with whom he is to take his breakfast. If he gets up to his wood-pile before noon he proceeds to load his boat, with the help of his single "hand," and is on his way down again before night. When he gets to Lowell he unloads his boat, and gets his receipt for his cargo, and having heard the news at the public house at Middlesex or elsewhere, goes back with his empty boat and his receipt in his pocket to the owner, and to get a new load. We were frequently advertised of their approach by some faint sound behind us, and looking round saw them a mile off, creeping stealthily up the side of the stream like alligators. It was pleasant to hail these sailors of the Merrimack from time to time, and learn the news which circulated with them. We imagined that the sun shining on their bare heads had stamped a liberal and public character on their most private thoughts.

The open and sunny interval still stretched away from the river, sometimes by two or more terraces, to the distant hill country, and when we climbed the bank we commonly found an irregular copse-wood skirting the river, the primitive having floated down stream long ago to——the "King's navy." Sometimes we saw the river-road a quarter or half a mile distant, and the particolored Concord stage, with its cloud of dust, its van of earnest travelling faces, and its rear of dusty trunks, reminding us that the country had its places of rendezvous for restless Yankee men. There dwelt along at considerable distances on this interval a quiet agricultural and pastoral people, with every house its well, as we sometimes proved, and every household, though never so still and remote it appeared in the noontide, its dinner about these times. There they lived on, those New England people, farmer lives, father and grand-father and great-grand-father, on and on without noise, keeping up tradition, and expecting, beside fair weather and abundant harvests, we did not learn what. They were contented to live, since it was so contrived for them, and where their lines had fallen.—

> Our uninquiring corpses lie more low
> Than our life's curiosity doth go.

Yet these men had no need to travel to be as wise as Solomon in all his glory, so similar are the lives of men in all countries, and fraught with the same homely experiences. One half the world *knows* how the other half lives.

About noon we passed a small village in Merrimack at Thornton's Ferry, and tasted of the waters of Naticook Brook on the same side, where French and his companions, whose grave we saw in Dunstable, were ambuscaded by the Indians. The humble village of Litchfield, with its steepleless meeting-house, stood on the opposite or east bank, near where a dense grove of willows backed by maples skirted the shore. There also we noticed some shagbark trees, which, as they do not grow in Concord, were as strange a sight to us as the palm would be, whose fruit only we have seen. Our course now curved gracefully to the north, leaving a low flat shore on the Merrimack side, which forms a sort of harbor for canal boats. We observed some fair elms and particularly large and handsome white-maples standing conspicuously on this interval, and the opposite shore, a quarter of a mile below, was covered with young elms and maples six inches high, which had probably sprung from the seeds which had been washed across.

Some carpenters were at work here mending a scow on the green and sloping bank. The strokes of their mallets echoed from shore to shore, and up and down the river, and their tools gleamed in the sun a quarter of a mile from us, and we realized that boat-building was as ancient and honorable an art as agriculture, and that there might be a naval as well as a pastoral life. The whole history of commerce was made manifest in that scow turned bottom upward on the shore. Thus did men begin to go down upon the sea in ships; *quæque diu steterant in montibus altis, Fluctibus ignotis insultavêre carinæ*; "and keels which had long stood on high mountains careered insultingly (*insultavêre*) over unknown waves." (Ovid, Met. I. 133.) We thought that it would be well for the traveller to build his boat on the bank of a stream, instead of finding a ferry or a bridge. In the Adventures of Henry the fur-trader, it is pleasant to read that when with his Indians he reached the shore of Ontario, they consumed two days in making two canoes of the bark of the elm tree, in which to transport themselves to Fort Niagara. It is a worthy incident in a journey, a delay as good as much rapid travelling. A good share of our interest in Xenophon's story of his retreat is in the manœuvres to get the army safely over the rivers, whether on rafts of logs or faggots or sheep skins blown up. And where could they better afford to tarry meanwhile than on the banks of a river?

As we glided past at a distance, these out-door

workmen appeared to have added some dignity to their labor by its very publicness. It was a part of the industry of nature, like the work of hornets and mud-wasps.–

> The waves slowly beat,
> Just to keep the noon sweet,
> And no sound is floated o'er,
> Save the mallet on shore,
> Which echoing on high
> Seems a caulking the sky.

The haze, the sun's dust of travel, had a lethean influence on the land and its inhabitants, and all creatures resigned themselves to float upon the inappreciable tides of nature.

> Woof of the sun, ethereal gauze,
> Woven of Nature's richest stuffs,
> Visible heat, air-water, and dry sea,
> Last conquest of the eye;
> Toil of the day displayed, sun-dust,
> Aerial surf upon the shores of earth,
> Ethereal estuary, frith of light,
> Breakers of air, billows of heat,
> Fine summer spray on inland seas;
> Bird of the sun, transparent-winged,
> Owlet of noon, soft-pinioned,
> From heath or stubble rising without song;
> Establish thy serenity o'er the fields.

The routine which is in the sunshine and the finest days, as that which has conquered and prevailed, commends itself to us by its very antiquity and apparent solidity and necessity. Our weakness needs it, and our strength uses it. We cannot draw on our boots without bracing ourselves against it. If there were but one erect and solid standing tree in the woods, all creatures would go to rub against it and make sure of their footing. During the many hours which we spend in this waking sleep, the hand stands still on the face of the clock, and we grow like corn in the night. Men are as busy as the brooks or bees, and postpone every thing to their busy-ness; as carpenters discuss politics between the strokes of the hammer while they are shingling a roof.

This noontide was a fit occasion to make some pleasant harbor, and there read the journal of some voyageur like ourselves, not too moral nor inquisitive, and which would not disturb the noon; or else some old classic, the very flower of all reading, which we had postponed to such a season

"Of Syrian peace, immortal leisure."

But, alas, our chest, like the cabin of a coaster, contained only its well-thumbed Navigator for all literature, and we were obliged to draw on our memory for these things. We naturally remembered Alexander Henry's Adventures here, as a sort of classic among books of American travel. It contains scenery and rough sketching of men and incidents enough to inspire poets for many years, and to my fancy is as full of sounding names as any page of history,–Lake Winnipeg, Hudson's Bay, Ottaway, and portages innumerable; Chipeways, Gens de Terres, Les Pilleurs, The Weepers; with reminiscences of Hearne's journey, and the like; an immense and shaggy but sincere country summer and winter, adorned with chains of lakes and rivers, covered with snows with hemlocks and fir trees. There is a naturalness, an unpretending and cold life in this traveller, as in a Canadian winter, what life was preserved through low temperatures and frontier dangers by furs within a stout heart. He has truth and moderation worthy of the father of history, which belong only to an intimate experience, and he does not defer too much to literature. The unlearned traveller may quote his single line from the poets with as good right as the scholar. He too may speak of the stars, for he sees them shoot perhaps when the astronomer does not. The good sense of this author is very conspicuous. He is a traveller who does not exaggerate, but writes for the information of his readers, for science and for history. His story is told with as much good faith and directness as if it were a report to his brother traders, or the Directors of the Hudson Bay Company, and is fitly dedicated to Sir Joseph Banks. It reads like the argument to a great poem on the primitive state of the country and its inhabitants, and the reader imagines what in each case with the invocation of the Muse might be sung, and leaves off with suspended interest, as if the full account were to follow. In what school was this fur-trader educated? He seems to travel the immense snowy country with such purpose only as the reader who accompanies him, and to the latter's imagination, it is, as it were, momentarily created to be the scene of his adventures. What is most interesting and valuable in it, however, is not the materials for the history of Pontiac, or Braddock, or the North West, which it furnishes; not the *annals* of the country, but the natural facts, or *perennials*, which are ever without date. When out of history the truth shall be extracted, it will have shed its dates like withered leaves.

The Souhegan, or *Crooked* River, as some translate it, comes in from the west about a mile and a half above Thornton's Ferry. Babboosuck Brook empties into it near its mouth. There are said to be some of the finest water privileges in the country still unimproved on the former stream, at a short distance from the Merrimack. One spring morning, March 22, in the year 1677, an incident occurred on the banks of the river here, which is interesting to us as a slight memorial of an interview between two ancient tribes of men, one of which is now extinct, while the other, though it is still represented by a miserable remnant, has long since disappeared from its ancient hunting grounds. A Mr. James Parker at "Mr. Hinchmanne's farme ner Meremack," wrote thus "to the Honred Governer and Council at Bostown, *Hast, Post Hast.*"

"Sagamore Wanalancet come this morning to informe me, and then went to Mr. Tyng's to informe him, that his son being on ye other sid of Meremack river over against Souhegan upon the 22 day of this instant, about tene of the clock in the morning, he discovered 15 Indians on this sid the river, which he soposed to be Mohokes by ther spech. He called to them; they answered, but he could not understand ther spech; and he having a conow ther in the river, he went to breck his conow that they might not have ani ues of it. In the mean time they shot about thirty guns at him, and he being much frighted fled, and come home forthwith to Nahamcock, [Pawtucket Falls or Lowell] wher ther wigowames now stand."

Penacooks and Mohawks! *ubique gentium sunt*? In the year 1670, a Mohawk warrior scalped a Naamkeak or else a Wamesit Indian maiden near where Lowell now stands. She, however, recovered. Even as late as 1685, John Hogkins, a Penacook Indian, who describes his grandfather as having lived "at place called Malamake rever, other name chef Natukkog and Panukkog, that one rever great many names," wrote thus to the governor:—

"May 15th, 1685.

"Honor governor my friend,—

"You my friend I desire your worship and your power, because I hope you can do som great matters this one. I am poor and naked and I have no men at my place because I afraid allwayes Mohogs he will kill me every day and night. If your worship when please pray help me you no let Mohogs kill me at my place at Malamake river called Pannukkog and Natukkog, I will submit your worship and your power.—And now I want pouder and such alminishon shatt and guns, because I have forth at my hom and I plant theare.

"This all Indian hand, but pray you do consider your humble servant, JOHN HOGKINS."

Signed also by Simon Detogkom, King Hary, Sam Linis, Mr. Jorge Rodunnonukgus, John Owamosimmin, and nine other Indians, with their marks against their names.

But now, one hundred and fifty-four years having elapsed since the date of this letter, we went unalarmed on our way, without "brecking" our "conow," reading the New England Gazetteer, and seeing no traces of "Mohogs" on the banks.

The Souhegan, though a rapid river, seemed to-day to have borrowed its character from the noon.

Where gleaming fields of haze
Meet the voyageur's gaze,
And above, the heated air
Seems to make a river there,
The pines stand up with pride
By the Souhegan's side,
And the hemlock and the larch
With their triumphal arch
Are waving o'er its march
　　To the sea.
No wind stirs its waves,
But the spirits of the braves
　　Hov'ring o'er,

Whose antiquated graves
Its still water laves
    On the shore.
With an Indian's stealthy tread,
It goes sleeping in its bed,
Without joy or grief,
Or the rustle of a leaf,
Without a ripple or a billow,
Or the sigh of a willow,
From the Lyndeboro' hills
To the Merrimack mills.
With a louder din
Did its current begin,
When melted the snow
On the far mountain's brow,
And the drops came together
In that rainy weather.
Experienced river,
Hast thou flowed forever?
Souhegan soundeth old,
But the half is not told,
What names hast thou borne
In the ages far gone,
When the Xanthus and Meander
Commenced to wander,
Ere the black bear haunted
    Thy red forest-floor,
Or Nature had planted
    The pines by thy shore.

During the heat of the day, we rested on a large island a mile above the mouth of this river, pastured by a herd of cattle, with steep banks and scattered elms and oaks, and a sufficient channel for canal boats on each side. When we made a fire to boil some rice for our dinner, the flames spreading amid the dry grass, and the smoke curling silently upward and casting grotesque shadows on the ground seemed phenomena of the noon, and we fancied that we progressed up the stream without effort, and as naturally as the wind and tide went down, not outraging the calm days by unworthy bustle or impatience. The woods on the neighboring shore were alive with pigeons, which were moving south, looking for mast, but now, like ourselves, spending their noon in the shade. We could hear the slight wiry winnowing sound of their wings as they changed their roosts from time to time, and their gentle and tremulous cooing. They sojourned with us during the noontide, greater travellers far than we. You may frequently discover a single pair sitting upon the lower branches of the white pine in the depths of the wood, at this hour of the day, so silent and solitary, and with such a hermit-like appearance, as if they had never strayed beyond its skirts, while the acorn which was gathered in the forests of Maine is still undigested in their crops. We obtained one of these handsome birds, which lingered too long upon its perch, and plucked and broiled it here with some other game, to be carried along for our supper; for beside the provisions which we carried with us, we depended mainly on the river and forest for our supply. It is true, it did not seem to be putting this bird to its right use, to pluck off its feathers, and extract its entrails, and broil its carcass on the coals; but we heroically persevered, nevertheless, waiting for further information. The same regard for Nature which excited our sympathy for her creatures, nerved our hands to carry through what we had begun. For we would be honorable to the party we deserted; we would fulfil fate, and so at length, perhaps, detect the secret innocence of these incessant tragedies which Heaven allows.—

> "Too quick resolves do resolution wrong,
> What, part so soon to be divorced so long?
> Things to be done are long to be debated;
> Heaven is not day'd, Repentance is not dated."

We are double-edged blades, and every time we whet our virtue the return stroke straps our vice. Where is the skilful swordsman who can give clean wounds, and not rip up his work with the other edge?

Nature herself has not provided the most graceful end for her creatures. What becomes of all these birds that people the air and forest for our solacement? The sparrows seem always *chipper*, never infirm. We do not see their bodies lie about; yet there is a tragedy at the end of each one of their lives. They must perish miserably; not one of them is translated. True, "not a sparrow falleth to the ground without our Heavenly Father's knowledge," but they do fall, nevertheless.

The carcasses of some poor squirrels, however, the same that frisked so merrily in the morning, which we had skinned and embowelled for our dinner, we abandoned in disgust, with tardy humanity, as too wretched a resource for any but starving men. It was to perpetuate the practice of a barbarous era. If they had been larger, our crime had been less. Their small red bodies, little bundles of red tissue, mere gobbets of venison, would not have "fattened fire." With a sudden impulse we threw them away, and washed our hands, and boiled some rice for our dinner. "Behold the difference between the one who eateth flesh, and him to whom it belonged! The first hath a momentary enjoyment, whilst the latter is deprived of existence!"—"Who could commit so great a crime against a poor animal, who is fed only by the herbs which grow wild in the woods, and whose belly is burnt up with hunger?" We remembered a picture of mankind in the hunter age, chasing hares down the mountains, O me miserable! Yet sheep and oxen are but larger squirrels, whose hides are saved and meat is salted, whose souls perchance are not so large in proportion to their bodies.

There should always be some flowering and maturing of the fruits of nature in the cooking process. Some simple dishes recommend themselves to our imaginations as well as palates. In parched corn, for instance, there is a manifest sympathy between the bursting seed and the more perfect developments of vegetable life. It is a perfect flower with its petals, like the houstonia or anemone. On my warm hearth these cerealian blossoms expanded; here is the bank whereon they grew. Perhaps some such visible blessing would always attend the simple and wholesome repast.

Here was that "pleasant harbor" which we had sighed for, where the weary voyageur could read the journal of some other sailor, whose bark had plowed, perchance, more famous and classic seas. At the tables of the gods, after feasting follow music and song; we will recline now under these island trees, and for our minstrel call on

ANACREON.

"Nor has he ceased his charming song, but still that lyre,
Though he is dead, sleeps not in Hades."

Simonides' Epigram on Anacreon.

I lately met with an old volume from a London bookshop, containing the Greek Minor Poets, and it was a pleasure to read once more only the words,—Orpheus,—Linus,—Musæus,—those faint poetic sounds and echoes of a name, dying away on the ears of us modern men; and those hardly more substantial sounds, Mimnermus—Ibycus—Alcæus—Stesichorus—

Menander. They lived not in vain. We can converse with these bodiless fames without reserve or personality.

I know of no studies so composing as those of the classical scholar. When we have sat down to them, life seems as still and serene as if it were very far off, and I believe it is not habitually seen from any common platform so truly and unexaggerated as in the light of literature. In serene hours we contemplate the tour of the Greek and Latin authors with more pleasure than the traveller does the fairest scenery of Greece or Italy. Where shall we find a more refined society? That highway down from Homer and Hesiod to Horace and Juvenal is more attractive than the Appian. Reading the classics, or conversing with those old Greeks and Latins in their surviving works, is like walking amid the stars and constellations, a high and by-way serene to travel. Indeed, the true scholar will be not a little of an astronomer in his habits. Distracting cares will not be allowed to obstruct the field of his vision, for the higher regions of literature, like astronomy, are above storm and darkness.

But passing by these rumors of bards, let us pause for a moment at the Teian poet.

There is something strangely modern about him. He is very easily turned into English. Is it that our lyric poets have resounded only that lyre, which would sound only light subjects, and which Simonides tells us does not sleep in Hades? His odes are like gems of pure ivory. They possess an ethereal and evanescent beauty like summer evenings, ὅ χρή σε νοεῖν νόου ἄνθει, *which you must perceive with the flower of the mind*,–and show how slight a beauty could be expressed. You have to consider them, as the stars of lesser magnitude, with the side of the eye, and look aside from them to behold them. They charm us by their serenity and freedom from exaggeration and passion, and by a certain flower-like beauty, which does not propose itself, but must be approached and studied like a natural object. But perhaps their chief merit consists in the lightness and yet security of their tread;

> "The young and tender stalk
> Ne'er bends when *they* do walk."

True, our nerves are never strung by them;–it is too constantly the sound of the lyre, and never the note of the trumpet; but they are not gross, as has been presumed, but always elevated above the sensual.

These are some of the best that have come down to us.

ON HIS LYRE.

I wish to sing the Atridæ,
And Cadmus I wish to sing;
But my lyre sounds
Only love with its chords.
Lately I changed the strings
And all the lyre;
And I began to sing the labors
Of Hercules; but my lyre
Resounded loves.
Farewell, henceforth, for me,
Heroes! for my lyre
Sings only loves.

TO A SWALLOW.

Thou indeed, dear swallow,
Yearly going and coming,
In summer weavest thy nest,
And in winter go'st disappearing
Either to Nile or to Memphis.
But Love always weaveth
His nest in my heart. * * *

ON A SILVER CUP.

Turning the silver,
Vulcan, make for me,
Not indeed a panoply,
For what are battles to me?
But a hollow cup,
As deep as thou canst.
And make for me in it
Neither stars, nor wagons,
Nor sad Orion;
What are the Pleiades to me?
What the shining Bootes?
Make vines for me,
And clusters of grapes in it,
And of gold Love and Bathyllus
Treading the grapes
With the fair Lyæus.

ON HIMSELF.

Thou sing'st the affairs of Thebes,
And he the battles of Troy,
But I of my own defeats.
No horse have wasted me,
Nor foot, nor ships;
But a new and different host,
From eyes smiting me.

TO A DOVE.

Lovely dove,
Whence, whence dost thou fly?
Whence, running on air,
Dost thou waft and diffuse
So many sweet ointments?
Who art? What thy errand?—
Anacreon sent me
To a boy, to Bathyllus,
Who lately is ruler and tyrant of all.
Cythere has sold me
For one little song,
And I'm doing this service
For Anacreon.
And now, as you see,
I bear letters from him.

And he says that directly
He'll make me free,
But though he release me,
His slave I will tarry with him.
For why should I fly
Over mountains and fields,
And perch upon trees,
Eating some wild thing?
Now indeed I eat bread,
Plucking it from the hands
Of Anacreon himself;
And he gives me to drink
The wine which he tastes,
And drinking, I dance,
And shadow my master's
Face with my wings;
And, going to rest,
On the lyre itself I sleep.
That is all; get thee gone.
Thou hast made me more talkative,
Man, than a crow.

ON LOVE.

Love walking swiftly,
With hyacinthine staff,
Bade me to take a run with him;
And hastening through swift torrents,
And woody places, and over precipices,
A water-snake stung me.
And my heart leaped up to
My mouth, and I should have fainted;
But Love fanning my brows
With his soft wings, said,
Surely, thou art not able to love.

ON WOMEN.

Nature has given horns
To bulls, and hoofs to horses,
Swiftness to hares,
To lions yawning teeth,
To fishes swimming,
To birds flight,
To men wisdom.

For woman she had nothing beside;
What then does she give? Beauty,–
Instead of all shields,
Instead of all spears;
And she conquers even iron
And fire, who is beautiful.

ON LOVERS.

Horses have the mark
Of fire on their sides,
And some have distinguished
The Parthian men by their crests;
So I, seeing lovers,
Know them at once,
For they have a certain slight
Brand on their hearts.

TO A SWALLOW.

What dost thou wish me to do to thee–
What, thou loquacious swallow?
Dost thou wish me taking thee
Thy light pinions to clip?
Or rather to pluck out
Thy tongue from within,
As that Tereus did?
Why with thy notes in the dawn
Hast thou plundered Bathyllus
From my beautiful dreams?

TO A COLT.

Thracian colt, why at me
Looking aslant with thy eyes,
Dost thou cruelly flee,
And think that I know nothing wise?
Know I could well
Put the bridle on thee,
And holding the reins, turn
Round the bounds of the course.
But now thou browsest the meads,
And gambolling lightly dost play,
For thou hast no skilful horseman
Mounted upon thy back.

CUPID WOUNDED.

Love once among roses
Saw not
A sleeping bee, but was stung;
And being wounded in the finger
Of his hand, cried for pain.
Running as well as flying
To the beautiful Venus,
I am killed, mother, said he,
I am killed, and I die.
A little serpent has stung me,
Winged, which they call
A bee–the husbandmen.
And she said, If the sting
Of a bee afflicts you,
How, think you, are they afflicted,
Love, whom you smite?

Late in the afternoon, for we had lingered long on the island, we raised our sail for the first time, and for a short hour the south-west wind was our ally; but it did not please Heaven to abet us long. With one sail raised we swept slowly up the eastern side of the stream, steering clear of the rocks, while from the top of a hill which formed the opposite bank, some lumberers were rolling down timber to be rafted down the stream. We could see their axes and levers gleaming in the sun, and the logs came down with a dust and a rumbling sound, which was reverberated through the woods beyond us on our side, like the roar of artillery. But Zephyr soon took us out of sight and hearing of this commerce. Having passed Read's Ferry, and another island called McGaw's Island, we reached some rapids called Moore's Falls, and entered on "that section of the river, nine miles in extent, converted, by law, into the Union Canal, comprehending in that space six distinct falls; at each of which, and at several intermediate places, work has been done."

After passing Moore's Falls by means of locks, we again had recourse to our oars, and went merrily on our way, driving the small sand-piper from rock to rock before us, and sometimes rowing near enough to a cottage on the bank, though they were few and far between, to see the sun-flowers, and the seed vessels of the poppy, like small goblets filled with the water of Lethe, before the door, but without disturbing the sluggish household behind. Thus we held on, sailing or dipping our way along with the paddle up this broad river,–smooth and placid, flowing over concealed rocks, where we could see the pickerel lying low in the transparent water,–eager to double some distant cape, to make some great bend as in the life of man, and see what new perspective would open; looking far into a new country, broad and serene, the cottages of settlers seen afar for the first time, yet with the moss of a century on their roofs, and the third or fourth generation in their shadow. Strange was it to consider how the sun and the summer, the buds of spring and the seared leaves of autumn, were related to these cabins along the shore; how all the rays which paint the landscape radiate from them, and the flight of the crow and the gyrations of the hawk have reference to their roofs. Still the ever rich and fertile shores accompanied us, fringed with vines and alive with small birds and frisking squirrels, the edge of some farmer's field or widow's wood-lot, or wilder, perchance, where the muskrat, the little medicine of the river, drags itself along stealthily over the alder leaves and muscle shells, and man and the memory of man are banished far.

At length the unwearied, never sinking shore, still holding on without break, with its cool copses and serene pasture grounds, tempted us to disembark; and we adventurously landed on this remote coast, to survey it, probably without the knowledge of any human inhabitant to this day. But we still remember the gnarled and hospitable oaks which grew even there for our entertainment, and were no strangers to us, the lonely horse in his pasture, and the patient cows, whose path to the river, so judiciously chosen to overcome the difficulties of the way, we followed, and disturbed their ruminations in the shade; and, above all, the cool free aspect of the wild apple trees, generously proffering their fruit to us, though still green and crude, the hard, round, glossy fruit, which, if not ripe, still was not poison, but New English too, brought hither its ancestors by ours once. These gentler trees imparted a half-civilized and twilight aspect to the otherwise barbarian land. Still further on we scrambled up the rocky channel of a brook, which had long served nature for a sluice there, leaping like it from rock to rock through tangled woods, at the bottom of a ravine, which grew darker and darker, and more and more hoarse the murmurs of the stream, until we reached the ruins of a mill, where now the ivy grew, and the trout glanced through the crumbling flume; and there we imagined what had been the dreams and speculations of some early settler. But the waning day compelled us to embark once more, and redeem this wasted time with long and vigorous sweeps over the rippling stream.

It was still wild and solitary, except that at intervals of a mile or two the roof of a cottage might be seen over the bank. This region, as we read, was once famous for the manufacture of straw bonnets of the Leghorn kind, of which it claims the invention in these parts, and occasionally some industrious damsel tripped down to the water's edge, to put her straw a-soak, as it appeared, and stood awhile to watch the retreating voyageurs, and catch the fragment of a boat song which we had made, wafted over the water.

Thus, perchance, the Indian hunter,
 Many a lagging year agone,
Gliding o'er thy rippling waters,
 Lowly hummed a natural song.

Now the sun 's behind the willows,
 Now he gleams along the waves,
Faintly o'er the wearied billows
 Come the spirits of the braves.

Just before sundown we reached some more falls in the town of Bedford, where some stone-masons were employed repairing the locks in a solitary part of the river. They were interested in our adventures, especially one young man of our own age, who inquired at first if we were bound up to "'Skeag," and when he had heard our story, and examined our outfit, asked us other questions, but temperately still, and always turning to his work again, though as if it were become his duty. It was plain that he would like to go with us, and as he looked up the river, many a distant cape and wooded shore were reflected in his eye, as well as in his thoughts. When we were ready he left his work, and helped us through the locks with a sort of quiet enthusiasm, telling us that we were at Coos Falls, and we could still distinguish the strokes of his chisel for many sweeps after we had left him.

We wished to camp this night on a large rock in the middle of the stream, just above these falls, but the want of fuel, and the difficulty of fixing our tent firmly, prevented us; so we made our bed on the main land opposite, on the west bank, in the town of Bedford, in a retired place, as we supposed, there being no house in sight.

Wednesday.

"Man is man's foe and destiny."

Cotton.

EARLY this morning, as we were rolling up our buffaloes and loading our boat amid the dew, while our embers were still smoking, the masons who worked at the locks, and whom we had seen crossing the river in their boat the evening before while we were examining the rock, came upon us as they were going to their work, and we found that we had pitched our tent directly in their path to their boat. This was the only time that we were observed on our camping ground. Thus, far from the beaten highways and the dust and din of travel, we beheld the country privately, yet freely, and at our leisure. Other roads do some violence to Nature, and bring the traveller to stare at her, but the river steals into the scenery it traverses without intrusion, silently creating and adorning it, and is as free to come and go as the zephyr.

As we shoved away from this rocky coast, before sunrise, the smaller bittern, the genius of the shore, was moping along its edge, or stood probing the mud for its food, with ever an eye on us, though so demurely at work, or else he ran along over the wet stones like a wrecker in his storm coat, looking out for wrecks of snails and cockles. Now away he goes, with a limping flight, uncertain where he will alight, until a rod of clear sand amid the alders invites his feet; and now our steady approach compels him to seek a new retreat. It is a bird of the oldest Thalesian school, and no doubt believes in the priority of water to the other elements; the relic of a twilight ante-diluvian age which yet inhabits these bright American rivers with us Yankees. There is something venerable in this melancholy and contemplative race of birds, which may have trodden the earth while it was yet in a slimy and imperfect state. Perchance their tracks too are still visible on the stones. It still lingers into our glaring summers, bravely supporting its fate without sympathy from man, as if it looked forward to some second advent of which *he* has no assurance. One wonders if, by its patient study by rocks and sandy capes, it has wrested the whole of her secret from Nature yet. What a rich experience it must have gained, standing on one leg and looking out from its dull eye so long on sunshine and rain, moon and stars! What could it tell of stagnant pools and reeds and dank night fogs? It would be worth the while to look closely into the eye which has been open and seeing at such hours, and in such solitudes, its dull, yellowish, greenish eye. Methinks my own soul must be a bright invisible green. I have seen these birds stand by the half dozen together in the shallower water along the shore, with their bills thrust into the mud at the bottom, probing for food, the whole head being concealed, while the neck and body formed an arch above the water.

Cohass Brook, the outlet of Massabesic Pond,—which last is five or six miles distant, and contains fifteen hundred acres, being the largest body of fresh water in Rockingham county,—comes in near here from the east. Rowing between Manchester and Bedford, we passed, at an early hour, a ferry and some falls, called Goff's Falls, the Indian Cohasset, where there is a small village, and a handsome green islet in the middle of the stream. From Bedford and Merrimack have been boated the bricks of which Lowell is made. About twenty years before, as they told us, one Moore, of Bedford, having clay on his farm, contracted to furnish eight millions of bricks to the founders of that city within two years. He fulfilled his contract in one year, and since then bricks have been the principal export from these towns. The farmers found thus a market for their wood, and when they had brought a load to the kilns, they could cart a load of bricks to the shore, and so make a profitable day's work of it. Thus all parties were benefitted. It was worth the while to see the place where Lowell was "dug out." So likewise Manchester is being built of bricks made still higher up the river at Hooksett.

There might be seen here on the bank of the Merrimack, near Goff's Falls, in what is now the town of Bedford, famous "for hops and for its fine domestic manufactures," some graves of the aborigines. The land still bears this scar here, and time is slowly crumbling the bones of a race. Yet without fail every spring since they first fished and hunted here, the brown thrasher has heralded the morning from a birch or alder spray, and the undying race of reed-birds still rustles through the withering grass. But these bones rustle not. These mouldering elements are slowly preparing for another metamorphosis, to serve new masters, and what was the Indian's will ere long be the white man's sinew.

We learned that Bedford was not so famous for hops as formerly, since the price is fluctuating, and poles are now scarce. Yet if the traveller goes back a few miles from the river, the hop kilns will still excite his curiosity.

There were few incidents in our voyage this forenoon, though the river was now more rocky and the falls more frequent than before. It was a pleasant change, after rowing incessantly for many hours, to lock ourselves through in some retired place,–for commonly there was no lock-man at hand,–one sitting in the boat, while the other, sometimes with no little labor and heave-yoing, opened and shut the gates, waiting patiently to see the locks fill. We did not once use the wheels which we had provided. Taking advantage of the eddy, we were sometimes floated up to the locks almost in the face of the falls; and, by the same cause, any floating timber was carried round in a circle and repeatedly drawn into the rapids before it finally went down the stream. These old gray structures, with their quiet arms stretched over the river in the sun, appeared like natural objects in the scenery, and the king-fisher and sand-piper alighted on them as readily as on stakes or rocks.

We rowed leisurely up the stream for several hours, until the sun had got high in the sky, our thoughts monotonously beating time to our oars. For outward variety there was only the river and the receding shores, a vista continually opening behind and closing before us, as we sat with our backs up stream, and for inward such thoughts as the muses grudgingly lent us. We were always passing some low inviting shore, or some overhanging bank, on which, however, we never landed.–

Such near aspects had we
Of our life's scenery.

It might be seen by what tenure men held the earth. The smallest stream is *mediterranean* sea, a smaller ocean creek within the land, where men may steer by their farm bounds and cottage lights. For my own part, but for the geographers, I should hardly have known how large a portion of our globe is water, my life has chiefly passed within so deep a cove. Yet I have sometimes ventured as far as to the mouth of my Snug Harbor. From an old ruined fort on Staten Island, I have loved to watch all day some vessel whose name I had read in the morning through the telegraph glass, when she first came upon the coast, and her hull heaved up and glistened in the sun, from the moment when the pilot and most adventurous news-boats met her, past the Hook, and up the narrow channel of the wide outer bay, till she was boarded by the health officer, and took her station at Quarantine, or held on her unquestioned course to the wharves of New York. It was interesting, too, to watch the less adventurous news-man, who made his assault as the vessel swept through the Narrows, defying plague and quarantine law, and fastening his little cock boat to her huge side, clambered up and disappeared in the cabin. And then I could imagine what momentous news was being imparted by the captain, which no American ear had ever heard, that Asia, Africa, Europe—were all sunk; for which at length he pays the price, and is seen descending the ship's side with his bundle of newspapers, but not where he first got up, for these arrivers do not stand still to gossip,—and he hastes away with steady sweeps to dispose of his wares to the highest bidder, and we shall erelong read something startling,—"By the latest arrival,"—"by the good ship———."—On Sunday I beheld from some interior hill the long procession of vessels getting to sea, reaching from the city wharves through the Narrows, and past the Hook, quite to the ocean-stream, far as the eye could reach, with stately march and silken sails, all counting on lucky voyages, but each time some of the number, no doubt, destined to go to Davy's locker, and never come on this coast again.—

And again, in the evening of a pleasant day, it was my amusement to count the sails in sight. But as the setting sun continually brought more and more to light, still further in the horizon, the last count always had the advantage, till by the time the last rays streamed over the sea, I had doubled and trebled my first number; though I could no longer class them all under the several heads of ships, barques, brigs, schooners, and sloops, but most were faint generic *vessels* only. And then the temperate twilight light, perchance, revealed the floating home of some sailor whose thoughts were already alienated from this American coast, and directed towards the Europe of our dreams.–I have stood upon the same hill-top when a thunder shower rolling down from the Catskills and Highlands passed over the island, deluging the land, and when it had suddenly left us in sunshine, have seen it overtake successively with its huge shadow and dark descending wall of rain the vessels in the bay. Their bright sails were suddenly drooping and dark like the sides of barns, and they seemed to shrink before the storm; while still far beyond them on the sea, through this dark veil, gleamed the sunny sails of those vessels which the storm had not yet reached.–And at midnight, when all around and overhead was darkness, I have seen a field of trembling silvery light far out on the sea, the reflection of the moonlight from the ocean, as if beyond the precincts of our night, where the moon traversed a cloudless heaven,–and sometimes a dark speck in its midst, where some fortunate vessel was pursuing its happy voyage by night.

But to us river sailors the sun never rose out of ocean waves, but from some green coppice, and went down behind some dark mountain line. We, too, were but dwellers on the shore, like the bittern of the morning, and our pursuit the wrecks of snails and cockles. Nevertheless, we were contented to know the better one fair particular shore.

My life is like a stroll upon the beach,
As near the ocean's edge as I can go,
My tardy steps its waves sometimes o'erreach,
Sometimes I stay to let them overflow.

My sole employment 'tis, and scrupulous care,
To place my gains beyond the reach of tides,
Each smoother pebble, and each shell more rare,
Which ocean kindly to my hand confides.

I have but few companions on the shore,
They scorn the strand who sail upon the sea,
Yet oft I think the ocean they've sailed o'er
Is deeper known upon the strand to me.

The middle sea contains no crimson dulse,
Its deeper waves cast up no pearls to view,
Along the shore my hand is on its pulse,
And I converse with many a shipwrecked crew.

The small houses which were scattered along the river at intervals of a mile or more, were commonly out of sight to us, but sometimes when we rowed near the shore, we heard the peevish note of a hen, or some slight domestic sound, which betrayed them. The lock-men's houses were particularly well placed, retired, and high, always at falls or rapids, and commanding the pleasantest reaches of the river,—for it is generally wider and more lake-like just above a fall,—and there they wait for boats. These humble dwellings, homely and sincere, in which a hearth was still the essential part, were more pleasing to our eyes than palaces or castles would have been. In the noon of these days, as we have said, we occasionally climbed the banks and approached these houses, to get a glass of water and make acquaintance with their inhabitants. High in the leafy bank, surrounded commonly by a small patch of corn and beans, squashes and melons, with sometimes a graceful hop-yard on one side, and some running vine over the windows, they appeared like bee-hives set to gather honey for a summer. I have not read of any Arcadian life which surpasses the actual luxury and serenity of these New England dwellings. For the outward gilding, at least, the age is golden enough. As you approach the sunny door-way, awakening the echoes by your steps, still no sound from these barracks of repose, and you fear that the gentlest knock may seem rude to the oriental dreamers. The door is opened, perchance, by some Yankee-Hindoo woman, whose small-voiced but sincere hospitality, out of the bottomless depths of a quiet nature, has travelled quite round to the opposite side, and fears only to obtrude its kindness. You step over the white-scoured floor to the bright "dresser," lightly, as if afraid to disturb the devotions of the household,—for oriental dynasties appear to have passed away since the dinner table was last spread here,—and thence to the frequented curb, where you see your long-forgotten, unshaven face at the bottom, in juxta position with new-made butter and the trout in the well. "Perhaps you would like some molasses and ginger," suggests the faint noon voice. Sometimes there sits the brother who follows the sea, their representative man; who knows only how far it is to the nearest port, no more distances, all the rest is sea and distant capes,—patting the dog, or dandling the kitten in arms that were stretched by the cable and the oar, pulling against Boreas or the trade-winds. He looks up at the stranger half pleased, half astonished, with a mariner's eye, as if he were a dolphin within cast. If men will believe it, "*sua si bona nôrint*," there are no more quiet Tempes, or more poetic and Arcadian lives, than may be lived in these New England dwellings. We thought that the employment of their inhabitants by day would be to tend the flowers and herds, and at night, like the shepherds of old, to cluster and give names to the stars from the river banks.

We passed a large and densely wooded island this forenoon, between Short's and Griffith's Falls, the fairest which we had met with, with a handsome grove of elms at its head. If it had been evening we should have been glad to camp there. Not long after one or two more were passed. The boatmen told us that the current had recently made important changes here. An island always pleases my imagination, even the smallest, as a small continent and integral portion of the globe. I have a fancy for building my hut on one. Even a bare grassy isle which I can see entirely over at a glance, has some undefined and mysterious charm for me. There is commonly such a one at the junction of two rivers, whose currents bring down and deposit their respective sands in the eddy at their confluence, as it were the womb of a continent. By what a delicate and far-fetched contribution every island is made! What an enterprise of Nature thus to lay the foundations of and to build up the future continent, of golden and silver sands and the ruins of forests, with ant-like industry! Pindar gives the following account of the origin of Thera, whence, in after times, Libyan Cyrene was settled by Battus. Triton, in the form of Eurypylus, presents a clod to Euphemus, one of the Argonauts, as they are about to return home.—

"He knew of our haste,
And immediately seizing a clod
With his right hand, strove to give it
As a chance stranger's gift.
Nor did the hero disregard him, but
leaping on the shore,
Stretching hand to hand,
Received the mystic clod.
But I hear it sinking from the deck,
Go with the sea brine
At evening, accompanying the watery sea.
Often indeed I urged the careless
Menials to guard it, but their minds forgot.
And now in this island the imperishable
seed of spacious Libya
Is spilled before its hour."

It is a beautiful fable, also related by Pindar, how Helius, or the Sun, looked down into the sea one day,–when perchance his rays were first reflected from some increasing glittering sand-bar,–and saw the fair and fruitful island of Rhodes

"Springing up from the bottom,
Capable of feeding many men and suitable for flocks;

and at the nod of Zeus,

—"The island sprang from the watery
Sea; and the Genial Father of penetrating beams,
Ruler of fire-breathing horses, has it."

The shifting islands! who would not be willing that his house should be undermined by such a foe! The inhabitant of an island can tell what currents formed the land which he cultivates; and his earth is still being created or destroyed. There before his door, perchance, still empties the stream which brought down the material of his farm ages before, and is still bringing it down or washing it away,–the graceful, gentle, robber!

Not long after this we saw the Piscataquoag, or Sparkling Water, emptying in on our left, and heard the Falls of Amoskeag above. Large quantities of lumber, as we read in the gazetteer, were still annually floated down the Piscataquoag to the Merrimack, and there are many fine mill privileges on it. Just above the mouth of this river we passed the artificial falls where the canals of the Manchester Manufacturing Company discharge themselves into the Merrimack. They are striking enough to have a name, and, with the scenery of a Bashpish, would be visited from far and near. The water falls thirty or forty feet over seven or eight steep and narrow terraces of stone, to break its force, and is converted into one mass of foam. This canal water did not seem to be the worse for the wear, but foamed and fumed as purely, and boomed as savagely and impressively, as a mountain torrent, and though it came from under a factory, we saw a rainbow here. These are now the Amoskeag Falls, removed a mile down stream. But we did not tarry to examine them minutely, making haste to get past the village here collected, and out of hearing of the hammer which was laying the foundation of another Lowell on the banks. At the time of our voyage Manchester was a village of about two thousand inhabitants, where we landed for a moment to get some cool water, and where an inhabitant told us that he was accustomed to go across the river into Goffstown for his water. But now, as I have been told, and indeed have witnessed, it contains fourteen thousand inhabitants. From a hill on the road between Goffstown and Hooksett, four miles distant, I have seen a thunder shower pass over, and the sun break out and shine on a city there, where I had landed nine years before in the fields; and there was waving the flag of its museum, where "the only perfect skeleton of a Greenland or river whale in the United States" was to be seen, and I also read in its directory of a "Manchester Athenæum and Gallery of the Fine Arts."

According to the gazetteer, the descent of Amoskeag Falls, which are the most considerable in the Merrimack, is fifty-four feet in half a mile. We locked ourselves through here with much ado, surmounting the successive watery steps of this river's stair-case in the midst of a crowd of villagers, jumping into the canal to their amusement, to save our boat from upsetting, and consuming much river water in our service. Amoskeag, or Namaskeak, is said to mean "great fishing place." It was hereabouts that the Sachem Wannalancet resided. Tradition says that his tribe, when at war with the Mohawks, concealed their provisions in the cavities of the rocks in the upper part of these falls. The Indians who hid their provisions in these holes, and affirmed "that God had cut them out for that purpose," understood their origin and use better than the Royal Society, who in their Transactions, in the last century, speaking of these very holes, declare that "they seem plainly to be artificial." Similar "potholes," may be seen at the Stone Flume on this river, on the Ottaway, at Bellows' Falls on the Connecticut, and in the limestone rock at Shelburne Falls on Deerfield river in Massachusetts, and more or less generally about all falls. Perhaps the most remarkable curiosity of this kind in New England is the well known Basin on the Pemigewasset, one of the head-waters of this river, twenty by thirty feet in extent and proportionably deep, with a smooth and rounded brim, and filled with a cold pellucid and greenish water. At Amoskeag the river is divided into many separate torrents and trickling rills by the rocks, and its volume is so much reduced by the drain of the canals that it does not fill its bed. There are many pot-holes here on a rocky island which the river washes over in high freshets. As at Shelburne Falls, where I first observed them, they are from one foot to four or five in diameter, and as many in depth, perfectly round and regular, with smooth and gracefully curved brims, like goblets. Their origin is apparent to the most careless observer. A stone which the current has washed down, meeting with obstacles, revolves as on a pivot where it lies, gradually sinking in the course of centuries deeper and deeper into the rock, and in new freshets receiving the aid of fresh stones which are drawn into this trap and doomed to revolve there for an indefinite period, doing Sisyphus-like penance for stony sins, until they either wear out, or wear through the bottom of their prison, or else are released by some revolution of nature. There lie the stones of various sizes, from a pebble to a foot or two in diameter, some of which have rested from their labor only since the spring, and some higher up which have lain still and dry for ages,–we noticed some here at least sixteen feet above the present level of the water,–while others are still revolving, and enjoy no respite at any season. In one instance, at Shelburne Falls, they have worn quite through the rock, so that a portion of the river leaks through in anticipation of the fall. Some of these pot-holes at Amoskeag, in a very hard brown stone, had an oblong cylindrical stone of the same material loosely fitting them. One, as much as fifteen feet deep and seven or eight in diameter, which was worn quite through to the water, had a huge rock of the same material, smooth but of irregular form, lodged in it. Every where there were the rudiments or the wrecks of a dimple in the rock; the rocky shells of whirlpools.

As if, by force of example and sympathy after so many lessons, the rocks, the hardest material, had been endeavoring to whirl or flow into the forms of the most fluid. The finest workers in stone are not copper or steel tools, but the gentle touches of air and water working at their leisure with a liberal allowance of time.

Not only have some of these basins been forming for countless ages, but others exist which must have been completed in a former geological period. In deepening the Pawtucket Canal, in 1822, the workmen came to ledges with pot-holes in them, where probably was once the bed of the river, and there are some, we are told, in the town of Canaan in this State, with the stones still in them, on the height of land between the Merrimack and Connecticut, and nearly a thousand feet above these rivers, proving that the mountains and the rivers have changed places. There lie the stones which completed their revolutions perhaps before thoughts began to revolve in the brain of man. The periods of Hindoo and Chinese history, though they reach back to the time when the race of mortals is confounded with the race of gods, are as nothing compared with the periods which these stones have inscribed. That which commenced a rock when time was young, shall conclude a pebble in the unequal contest. With such expense of time and natural forces are our very paving stones produced. They teach us lessons, these dumb workers; verily there are "sermons in stones, and books in the running streams." In these very holes the Indians hid their provisions; but now there is no bread, but only its old neighbor stones at the bottom. Who knows how many races they have served thus? By as simple a law, some accidental by-law, perchance, our system itself was made ready for its inhabitants.

These, and such as these, must be our antiquities, for lack of human vestiges. The monuments of heroes and the temples of the gods which may once have stood on the banks of this river, are now, at any rate, returned to dust and primitive soil. The murmur of unchronicled nations has died away along these shores, and once more Lowell and Manchester are on the trail of the Indian.

The fact that Romans once inhabited her reflects no little dignity on Nature herself; that from some particular hill the Roman once looked out on the sea. She need not be ashamed of the vestiges of her children. How gladly the antiquary informs us that their vessels penetrated into this frith, or up that river of some remote isle! Their military monuments still remain on the hills and under the sod of the valleys. The oft-repeated Roman story is written in still legible characters in every quarter of the old world, and but to-day, perchance, a new coin is dug up whose inscription repeats and confirms their fame. Some "*Judæa Capta*," with a woman mourning under a palm tree, with silent argument and demonstration confirms the pages of history.

> "Rome living was the world's sole ornament;
> And dead is now the world's sole monument."
>
> *   *   *   *   *
>
> "With her own weight down pressed now she lies,
> And by her heaps her hugeness testifies."

If one doubts whether Grecian valor and patriotism are not a fiction of the poets, he may go to Athens and see still upon the walls of the temple of Minerva the circular marks made by the shields taken from the enemy in the Persian war, which were suspended there. We have not far to seek for living and unquestionable evidence. The very dust takes shape and confirms some story which we had read. As Fuller said, commenting on the zeal of Camden, "A broken urn is a whole evidence; or an old gate still surviving out of which the city is run out." When Solon endeavored to prove that Salamis had formerly belonged to the Athenians, and not to the Megareans, he caused the tombs to be opened, and showed that the inhabitants of Salamis turned the faces of their dead to the same side with the Athenians, but the Megareans to the opposite side. There they were to be interrogated.

Some minds are as little logical or argumentative as nature; they can offer no reason or "guess," but they exhibit the solemn and incontrovertible fact. If a historical question arises, they cause the tombs to be opened. Their silent and practical logic convinces the reason and the understanding at the same time. Of such sort is always the only pertinent question and the only satisfactory reply.

Our own country furnishes antiquities as ancient and durable, and as useful, as any; rocks at least as well covered with lichens, and a soil which if it is virgin, is but virgin mould, the very dust of nature. What if we cannot read Rome, or Greece, Etruria, or Carthage, or Egypt, or Babylon, on these; are our cliffs bare? The lichen on the rocks is a rude and simple shield which beginning and imperfect Nature suspended there. Still hangs her wrinkled trophy. And here too the poet's eye may still detect the brazen nails which fastened Time's inscriptions, and if he has the gift, decipher them by this clue. The walls that fence our fields, as well as modern Rome, and not less the Parthenon itself, are all built of *ruins*. Here may be heard the din of rivers, and ancient winds which have long since lost their names sough through our woods;—the first faint sounds of spring, older than the summer of Athenian glory, the titmouse lisping in the wood, the jay's scream, and blue-bird's warble, and the hum of

"bees that fly
About the laughing blossoms of sallowy."

Here is the gray dawn for antiquity, and our to-morrow's future should be at least paulo-post to theirs which we have put behind us. There are the red-maple and birchen leaves, old runes which are not yet deciphered; catkins, pine-cones, vines, oak-leaves, and acorns; the very things themselves, and not their forms in stone,—so much the more ancient and venerable. And even to the current summer there has come down tradition of a hoary-headed master of all art, who once filled every field and grove with statues and god-like architecture, of every design which Greece has lately copied; whose ruins are now mingled with the dust, and not one block remains upon another. The century sun and unwearied rain have wasted them, till not one fragment from that quarry now exists; and poets perchance will feign that gods sent down the material from heaven.

What though the traveller tell us of the ruins of Egypt, are we so sick or idle, that we must sacrifice our America and to-day to some man's ill-remembered and indolent story? Carnac and Luxor are but names, or if their skeletons remain, still more desert sand, and at length a wave of the Mediterranean sea, are needed to wash away the filth that attaches to their grandeur. Carnac! Carnac! here is Carnac for me. I behold the columns of a larger and purer temple.

This is my Carnac, whose unmeasured dome
Shelters the measuring art and measurer's home.
Behold these flowers, let us be up with time,
Not dreaming of three thousand years ago,
Erect ourselves and let those columns lie,
Not stoop to raise a foil against the sky.
Where is the spirit of that time but in
This present day, perchance this present line?
Three thousand years ago are not agone,
They are still lingering in this summer morn,
And Memnon's Mother sprightly greets us now,
Wearing her youthful radiance on her brow.
If Carnac's columns still stand on the plain,
To enjoy our opportunities they remain.

In these parts dwelt the famous Sachem Passaconaway, who was seen by Gookin "at Pawtucket, when he was about one hundred and twenty years old." He was reputed a wise man and a powwow, and restrained his people from going to war with the English. They believed "that he could make water burn, rocks move, and trees dance, and metamorphose himself into a flaming man; that in winter he could raise a green leaf out of the ashes of a dry one, and produce a living snake from the skin of a dead one, and many similar miracles." In 1660, according to Gookin, at a great feast and dance, he made his farewell speech to his people, in which he said, that as he was not likely to see them met together again, he would leave them this word of advice, to take heed how they quarrelled with their English neighbors, for though they might do them much mischief at first, it would prove the means of their own destruction. He himself, he said, had been as much an enemy to the English at their first coming as any, and had used all his arts to destroy them, or at least to prevent their settlement, but could by no means effect it. Gookin thought that he "possibly might have such a kind of spirit upon him as was upon Balaam, who in xxiii. Numbers, 23, said 'Surely, there is no enchantment against Jacob, neither is there any divination against Israel.' " His son Wannalancet carefully followed his advice, and when Philip's War broke out, he withdrew his followers to Penacook, now Concord in New Hampshire, from the scene of the war. On his return afterwards he visited the minister of Chelmsford, and, as is stated in the history of that town, "wished to know whether Chelmsford had suffered much during the war; and being informed that it had not, and that God should be thanked for it, Wannalancet replied, 'Me next.' "

Manchester was the residence of John Stark, a hero of two wars, and survivor of a third, and at his death the last but one of the American generals of the Revolution. He was born in the adjoining town of Londonderry, then Nutfield, in 1728. As early as 1752, he was taken prisoner by the Indians while hunting in the wilderness near Baker's River; he performed notable service as a captain of rangers in the French war; commanded a regiment of the New Hampshire militia at the battle of Bunker Hill; and fought and won the battle of Bennington in 1777. He was past service in the last war, and died here in 1822, at the age of 94. His monument stands upon the second bank of the river, about a mile and a half above the falls, and commands a prospect several miles up and down the Merrimack. It suggested how much more impressive in the landscape is the tomb of a hero than the dwellings of the inglorious living. Who is most dead,—a hero by whose monument you stand, or his descendants of whom you have never heard?

The graves of Passaconaway and Wannalancet are marked by no monument on the bank of their native river.

Every town which we passed, if we may believe the gazetteer, had been the residence of some great man. But though we knocked at many doors, and even made particular inquiries, we could not find that there were any now living. Under the head of Litchfield we read,—

"The Hon. Wyseman Clagett closed his life in this town." According to another, "He was a classical scholar, a good lawyer, a wit, and a poet." We saw his old gray house just below Great Nesenkeag Brook.—Under the head of Merrimac,—"Hon. Mathew Thornton, one of the signers of the Declaration of American Independence, resided many years in this town." His house too we saw from the river.—"Dr. Jonathan Gove, a man distinguished for his urbanity, his talents and professional skill, resided in this town [Goffstown.] He was one of the oldest practitioners of medicine in the county. He was many years an active member of the legislature."—"Hon. Robert Means, who died Jan. 24, 1823, at the age of 80, was for a long period a resident in Amherst. He was a native of Ireland. In 1764 he came to this country, where by his industry and application to business, he acquired a large property, and great respect."—"William Stinson, [one of the first settlers of Dunbarton,] born in Ireland, came to Londonderry with his father. He was much respected and was a useful man. James Rogers was from Ireland, and father to Major Robert Rogers. He was shot in the woods, being mistaken for a bear."—"Rev. Matthew Clark, second minister of Londonderry, was a native of Ireland, who had in early life been an officer in the army, and distinguished himself in the defence of the city of Londonderry, when besieged by the army of King James II.

A. D. 1688–9. He afterwards relinquished a military life for the clerical profession. He possessed a strong mind, marked by a considerable degree of eccentricity. He died Jan. 25, 1735, and was borne to the grave, at his particular request, by his former companions in arms, of whom there were a considerable number among the early settlers of this town; several of whom had been made free from taxes throughout the British dominions by King William, for their bravery in that memorable siege."—Col. George Reid and Capt. David M'Clary, also citizens of Londonderry, were "distinguished and brave" officers.—"Major Andrew M'Clary, a native of this town [Epsom,] fell at the battle of Breed's Hill."—Many of these heroes, like the illustrious Roman, were plowing when the news of the massacre at Lexington arrived, and straightway left their plows in the furrow, and repaired to the scene of action. Some miles from where we now were, there once stood a guide-post on which were the words, "3 miles to Squire MacGaw's."—

But generally speaking, the land is now, at any rate, very barren of men, and we doubt if there are as many hundreds as we read of. It may be that we stood too near.

Uncannunuc Mountain in Goffstown was visible from Amoskeag, five or six miles westward. It is the north-easternmost in the horizon, which we see from our native town, but seen from there is too ethereally blue to be the same which the like of us have ever climbed. Its name is said to mean "The Two Breasts," there being two eminences some distance apart. The highest, which is about fourteen hundred feet above the sea, probably affords a more extensive view of the Merrimack valley and the adjacent country than any other hill, though it is somewhat obstructed by woods. Only a few short reaches of the river are visible, but you can trace its course far down stream by the sandy tracts on its banks.

A little south of Uncannunuc, about sixty years ago, as the story goes, an old woman who went out to gather pennyroyal, tript her foot in the bail of a small brass kettle in the dead grass and bushes. Some say that flints and charcoal and some traces of a camp were also found. This kettle, holding about four quarts, is still preserved and used to dye thread in. It is supposed to have belonged to some old French or Indian hunter, who was killed in one of his hunting or scouting excursions, and so never returned to look after his kettle.

But we were most interested to hear of the pennyroyal, it is so soothing to be reminded that wild nature produces any thing ready for the use of man. Men know that *something* is good. One says that it is yellow-dock, another that it is bitter-sweet, another that it is slippery-elm bark, burdock, catnip, calamint, elicampane, thoroughwort, or pennyroyal. A man may esteem himself happy when that which is his food is also his medicine. There is no kind of herb, but somebody or other says that it is good. I am very glad to hear it. It reminds me of the first chapter of Genesis. But how should they know that it is good? That is the mystery to me. I am always agreeably disappointed; it is incredible that they should have found it out. Since all things are good, men fail at last to distinguish which is the bane, and which the antidote. There are sure to be two prescriptions diametrically opposite. Stuff a cold and starve a cold are but two ways. They are the two practices both always in full blast. Yet you must take advice of the one school as if there was no other. In respect to religion and the healing art, all nations are still in a state of barbarism. In the most civilized countries the priest is still but a Powwow, and the physician a Great Medicine. Consider the deference which is everywhere paid to a doctor's opinion. Nothing more strikingly betrays the credulity of mankind than medicine. Quackery is a thing universal, and universally successful. In this case it becomes literally true that no imposition is too great for the credulity of men. Priests and physicians should never look one another in the face. They have no common ground, nor is there any to mediate between them. When the one comes, the other goes. They could not come together without laughter, or a significant silence, for the one's profession is a satire on the other's, and either's success would be the other's failure. It is wonderful that the physician should ever die, and that the priest should ever live. Why is it that the priest is never called to consult with the physician? It is because men believe practically that matter is independent of spirit. But what is quackery? It is commonly an attempt to cure the diseases of a man by addressing his body alone. There is need of a physician who shall minister to both soul and body at once, that is to man. Now he falls between two stools.

After passing through the locks, we had poled ourselves through the canal here, about half a mile in length, to the boatable part of the river. Above Amoskeag the river spreads out into a lake reaching a mile or two without a bend. There were many canal boats here bound up to Hooksett, about eight miles, and as they were going up empty with a fair wind, one boatman offered to take us in tow if we would wait. But when we came along-side, we found that they meant to take us on board, since otherwise we should clog their motions too much; but as our boat was too heavy to be lifted aboard, we pursued our way up the stream, as before, while the boatmen were at their dinner, and came to anchor at length under some alders on the opposite shore, where we could take our lunch. Though far on one side every sound was wafted over to us from the opposite bank, and from the harbor of the canal, and we could see every thing that passed. By and by came several canal boats, at intervals of a quarter of a mile, standing up to Hooksett with a light breeze, and one by one disappeared round a point above. With their broad sails set, they moved slowly up the stream in the sluggish and fitful breeze, like one-winged antediluvian birds, and as if impelled by some mysterious counter current. It was a grand motion, so slow and stately, this "standing out," as the phrase is, expressing the gradual and steady progress of a vessel, as if it were by mere rectitude and disposition, without shuffling. Their sails, which stood so still, were like chips cast into the current of the air to show which way it set. At length the boat which we had spoken came along, keeping the middle of the stream, and when within speaking distance the steersman called out ironically to say, that if we would come along-side now he would take us in tow; but not heeding his taunt, we still loitered in the shade till we had finished our lunch, and when the last boat had disappeared round the point with flapping sail, for the breeze had now sunk to a zephyr, with our own sails set, and plying our oars, we shot rapidly up the stream in pursuit, and as we glided close alongside, while they were vainly invoking Æolus to their aid, we returned their compliment by proposing, if they would throw us a rope, to "take them in tow," to which these Merrimack sailors had no suitable answer ready. Thus we gradually overtook and passed each boat in succession until we had the river to ourselves again.

Our course this afternoon was between Manchester and Goffstown.

While we float here, far from that tributary stream on whose banks our friends and kindred dwell, our thoughts, like the stars, come out of their horizon still; for there circulates a finer blood than Lavoisier has discovered the laws of,–the blood, not of kindred merely, but of kindness, whose pulse still beats at any distance and forever.

True kindness is a pure divine affinity,
Not founded upon human consanguinity.
It is a spirit, not a blood relation,
Superior to family and station.

After years of vain familiarity, some distant gesture or unconscious behavior, which we remember, speaks to us with more emphasis than the wisest or kindest words. We are sometimes made aware of a kindness long passed, and realize that there have been times when our friends' thoughts of us were of so pure and lofty a character that they passed over us like the winds of heaven unnoticed; when they treated us not as what we were, but as what we aspired to be. There has just reached us, it may be, the nobleness of some such silent behavior, not to be forgotten, not to be remembered, and we shudder to think how it fell on us cold, though in some true but tardy hour we endeavor to wipe off these scores.

In my experience, persons, when they are made the subject of conversation, though with a friend, are commonly the most prosaic and trivial of facts. The universe seems bankrupt as soon as we begin to discuss the character of individuals. Our discourse all runs to slander, and our limits grow narrower as we advance. How is it that we are impelled to treat our old friends so ill when we obtain new ones? The housekeeper says, I never had any new crockery but I began to break the old. I say, let us speak of mushrooms and forest trees rather. Yet we can sometimes afford to remember them in private.—

Lately, alas, I knew a gentle boy,
  Whose features all were cast in Virtue's mould,
As one she had designed for Beauty's toy,
  But after manned him for her own stronghold.

On every side he open was as day,
  That you might see no lack of strength within,
For walls and ports do only serve alway
  For a pretence to feebleness and sin.

Say not that Cæsar was victorious,
  With toil and strife who stormed the
    House of Fame,
In other sense this youth was glorious,
  Himself a kingdom wheresoe'er he came.

No strength went out to get him victory,
  When all was income of its own accord;
For where he went none other was to see,
  But all were parcel of their noble lord.

He forayed like the subtil haze of summer,
  That stilly shows fresh landscapes to our eyes,
And revolutions works without a murmur,
  Or rustling of a leaf beneath the skies.

So was I taken unawares by this,
  I quite forgot my homage to confess;
Yet now am forced to know, though hard it is,
  I might have loved him had I loved him less.

Each moment as we nearer drew to each,
   A stern respect withheld us further yet,
So that we seemed beyond each other's reach,
   And less acquainted than when first we met.

We two were one while we did sympathize,
   So could we not the simplest bargain drive;
And what avails it now that we are wise,
   If absence doth this doubleness contrive?

Eternity may not the chance repeat,
   But I must tread my single way alone,
In sad remembrance that we once did meet,
   And know that bliss irrevocably gone.

The spheres henceforth my elegy shall sing,
   For elegy has other subject none;
Each strain of music in my ears shall ring
   Knell of departure from that other one.

Make haste and celebrate my tragedy;
   With fitting strain resound ye woods and fields;
Sorrow is dearer in such case to me
   Than all the joys other occasion yields.

Is't then too late the damage to repair?
   Distance, forsooth, from my weak grasp hath reft
The empty husk, and clutched the useless tare,
   But in my hands the wheat and kernel left.

If I but love that virtue which he is,
   Though it be scented in the morning air,
Still shall we be truest acquaintances,
   Nor mortals know a sympathy more rare.

Friendship is evanescent in every man's experience, and remembered like heat lightning in past summers. Fair and flitting like a summer cloud;—there is always some vapor in the air, no matter how long the drought; there are even April showers. Surely from time to time, for its vestiges never depart, it floats through our atmosphere. It takes place, like vegetation in so many materials, because there is such a law, but always without permanent form, though ancient and familiar as the sun and moon, and as sure to come again. The heart is forever inexperienced. They silently gather as by magic, these never failing, never quite deceiving visions, like the bright and fleecy clouds in the calmest and clearest days. The Friend is some fair floating isle of palms eluding the mariner in Pacific seas. Many are the dangers to be encountered, equinoctial gales and coral reefs, ere he may sail before the constant trades. But who would not sail through mutiny and storm even over Atlantic waves, to reach the fabulous retreating shores of some continent man? The imagination still clings to the faintest tradition of

THE ATLANTIDES.

The smothered streams of love, which flow
More bright than Phlegethon, more low,
Island us ever, like the sea,
In an Atlantic mystery.
Our fabled shores none ever reach,
No mariner has found our beach,
Only our mirage now is seen,
And neighboring waves with floating green,
Yet still the oldest charts contain
Some dotted outline of our main;
In ancient times midsummer days
Unto the western islands' gaze,
To Teneriffe and the Azores,
Have shown our faint and cloud-like shores.

But sink not yet, ye desolate isles,
Anon your coast with commerce smiles,
And richer freights ye'll furnish far
Than Africa or Malabar.
Be fair, be fertile evermore,

Ye rumored but untrodden shore,
Princes and monarchs will contend
Who first unto your land shall send,
And pawn the jewels of the crown
To call your distant soil their own.

Columbus has sailed westward of these isles by the mariner's compass, but neither he nor his successors have found them. We are no nearer than Plato was. The earnest seeker and hopeful discoverer of this New World always haunts the outskirts of his time, and walks through the densest crowd uninterrupted, and as it were in a straight line.—

Sea and land are but his neighbors,
And companions in his labors,
Who on the ocean's verge and firm land's end
Doth long and truly seek his Friend.
Many men dwell far inland,
But he alone sits on the strand.
Whether he ponders men or books,
Always still he seaward looks,
Marine news he ever reads,
And the slightest glances heeds,
Feels the sea breeze on his cheek
At each word the landsmen speak,
In every companion's eye
A sailing vessel doth descry;
In the ocean's sullen roar
From some distant port he hears,
Of wrecks upon a distant shore,
And the ventures of past years.

Who does not walk on the plain as amid the columns of Tadmore of the desert? There is on the earth no institution which Friendship has established; it is not taught by any religion; no scripture contains its maxims. It has no temple, nor even a solitary column. There goes a rumor that the earth is inhabited, but the shipwrecked mariner has not seen a foot-print on the shore. The hunter has found only fragments of pottery and the monuments of inhabitants.

However, our fates at least are social. Our courses do not diverge; but as the web of destiny is woven it is fulled, and we are cast more and more into the centre. Men naturally, though feebly, seek this alliance, and their actions faintly foretell it. We are inclined to lay the chief stress on likeness and not on difference, and in foreign bodies we admit that there are many degrees of warmth below blood heat, but none of cold above it.

Mencius says: "If one loses a fowl or a dog, he knows well how to seek them again; if one loses the sentiments of his heart, he does not know how to seek them again. . . . . The duties of practical philosophy consist only in seeking after those sentiments of the heart which we have lost; that is all."

One or two persons come to my house from time to time, there being proposed to them the faint possibility of intercourse. They are as full as they are silent, and wait for my plectrum to stir the strings of their lyre. If they could ever come to the length of a sentence, or hear one, on that ground which they are dreaming of! They speak faintly, and do not obtrude themselves. They have heard some news, which none, not even they themselves, can impart. It is a wealth they can bear about them which can be expended in various ways. What came they out to seek?

No word is oftener on the lips of men than Friendship, and indeed no thought is more familiar to their aspirations. All men are dreaming of it, and its drama, which is always a tragedy, is enacted daily. It is the secret of the universe. You may thread the town, you may wander the country, and none shall ever speak of it, yet thought is every where busy about it, and the idea of what is possible in this respect affects our behavior toward all new men and women, and a great many old ones. Nevertheless, I can remember only two or three essays on this subject in all literature. No wonder that the Mythology, and Arabian Nights, and Shakspeare, and Scott's novels, entertain us,–we are poets and fablers and dramatists and novelists ourselves. We are continually acting a part in a more interesting drama than any written. We are dreaming that our Friends are our *Friends*, and that we are our Friends' *Friends*. Our actual Friends are but distant relations of those to whom we are pledged. We never exchange more than three words with a Friend in our lives, on that level to which our thoughts and feelings almost habitually rise. One goes forth prepared to say "Sweet Friends!" and the salutation is "Damn your eyes!" But never mind; faint heart never won true Friend. O my Friend, may it come to pass, once, that when you are my Friend I may be yours.

Of what use the friendliest disposition even, if there are no hours given to Friendship, if it is forever postponed to unimportant duties and relations? Friendship is first, Friendship last. But it is equally impossible to forget our Friends, and to make them answer to our ideal. When they say farewell, then indeed we begin to keep them company. How often we find ourselves turning our backs on our actual Friends, that we may go and meet their ideal cousins. I would that I were worthy to be any man's Friend.

What is commonly honored with the name of Friendship is no very profound or powerful instinct. Men do not, after all, *love* their Friends greatly. I do not often see the farmers made seers and wise to the verge of insanity by their Friendship for one another. They are not often transfigured and translated by love in each other's presence. I do not observe them purified, refined, and elevated by the love of a man. If one abates a little the price of his wood, or gives a neighbor his vote at town-meeting, or a barrel of apples, or lends him his wagon frequently, it is esteemed a rare instance of Friendship. Nor do the farmers' wives lead lives consecrated to Friendship. I do not see the pair of farmer Friends of either sex prepared to stand against the world. There are only two or three couples in history. To say that a man is your Friend, means commonly no more than this, that he is not your enemy. Most contemplate only what would be the accidental and trifling advantages of Friendship, as that the Friend can assist in time of need, by his substance, or his influence, or his counsel; but he who foresees such advantages in this relation proves himself blind to its real advantage, or indeed wholly inexperienced in the relation itself. Such services are particular and menial, compared with the perpetual and all-embracing service which it is. Even the utmost good-will and harmony and practical kindness are not sufficient for Friendship, for Friends do not live in harmony merely, as some say, but in melody. We do not wish for Friends to feed and clothe our bodies,—neighbors are kind enough for that,—but to do the like office to our spirits. For this few are rich enough, however well disposed they may be. For the most part we stupidly confound one man with another. The dull distinguish only races or nations, or at most classes, but the wise man, individuals. To his Friend a man's peculiar character appears in every feature and in every action, and it is thus drawn out and improved by him.

Think of the importance of Friendship in the education of men.

> "He that hath love and judgment too,
> Sees more than any other doe."

It will make a man honest; it will make him a hero; it will make him a saint. It is the state of the just dealing with the just, the magnanimous with the magnanimous, the sincere with the sincere, man with man.—

And it is well said by another poet,

> "Why love among the virtues is not known,
> Is that love is them all contract in one."

All the abuses which are the object of reform with the philanthropist, the statesman, and the housekeeper, are unconsciously amended in the intercourse of Friends. A Friend is one who incessantly pays us the compliment of expecting from us all the virtues, and who can appreciate them in us. It takes two to speak the truth,—one to speak, and another to hear. How can one treat with magnanimity mere wood and stone? If we dealt only with the false and dishonest, we should at last forget how to speak truth. Only lovers know the value and magnanimity of truth, while traders prize a cheap honesty, and neighbors and acquaintance a cheap civility. In our daily intercourse with men, our nobler faculties are dormant and suffered to rust. None will pay us the compliment to expect nobleness from us. Though we have gold to give, they demand only copper. We ask our neighbor to suffer himself to be dealt with truly, sincerely, nobly; but he answers no by his deafness. He does not even hear this prayer. He says practically,–I will be content if you treat me as no better than I should be, as deceitful, mean, dishonest and selfish. For the most part, we are contented so to deal and to be dealt with, and we do not think that for the mass of men there is any truer and nobler relation possible. A man may have *good* neighbors, so called, and acquaintances, and even companions, wife, parents, brothers, sisters, children, who meet himself and one another on this ground only. The State does not demand justice of its members, but thinks that it succeeds very well with the least degree of it, hardly more than rogues practise; and so do the neighborhood and the family. What is commonly called Friendship even is only a little more honor among rogues.

But sometimes we are said to *love* another, that is to stand in a true relation to him, so that we give the best to, and receive the best from, him. Between whom there is hearty truth there is love; and in proportion to our truthfulness and confidence in one another, our lives are divine and miraculous, and answer to our ideal. There are passages of affection in our intercourse with mortal men and women, such as no prophecy had taught us to expect, which transcend our earthly life, and anticipate heaven for us. What is this Love that may come right into the middle of a prosaic Goffstown day, equal to any of the gods? that discovers a new world, fair and fresh and eternal, occupying the place of this old one, when to the common eye a dust has settled on the universe? which world cannot else be reached, and does not exist. What other words, we may almost ask, are memorable and worthy to be repeated than those which love has inspired? It is wonderful that they were ever uttered.

They are few and rare, indeed, but, like a strain of music, they are incessantly repeated and modulated by the memory. All other words crumble off with the stucco which overlies the heart. We should not dare to repeat them now aloud. We are not competent to hear them at all times.

The books for young people say a great deal about the *selection* of Friends; it is because they really have nothing to say about *Friends*. They mean associates and confidants merely. "Know that the contrariety of foe and Friend proceeds from God." Friendship takes place between those who have an affinity for one another, and is a perfectly natural and inevitable result. No professions nor advances will avail. Even speech, at first, necessarily has nothing to do with it; but it follows after silence, as the buds in the graft do not put forth into leaves till long after the graft has taken. It is a drama in which the parties have no part to act. We are all Mussulmen and fatalists in this respect. Impatient and uncertain lovers think that they must say or do something kind whenever they meet; they must never be cold. But they who are Friends, do not do what they *think* they must, but what they *must*. Even their Friendship is to some extent but a sublime phenomenon to them.

The true and not despairing Friend will address his Friend in some such terms as these.

"I never asked thy leave to let me love thee,–I have a right. I love thee not as something private and personal, which is *your own*, but as something universal and worthy of love, *which I have found.* O how I think of you! You are purely good,–you are infinitely good. I can trust you forever. I did not think that humanity was so rich. Give me an opportunity to live."

"You are the fact in a fiction,–you are the truth more strange and admirable than fiction. Consent only to be what you are. I alone will never stand in your way."

"This is what I would like,–to be as intimate with you as our spirits are intimate,–respecting you as I respect my ideal. Never to profane one another by word or action, even by a thought. Between us, if necessary, let there be no acquaintance."

"I have discovered you; how can you be concealed from me?"

The Friend asks no return but that his Friend will religiously accept and wear and not disgrace his apotheosis of him. They cherish each other's hopes. They are kind to each other's dreams.

Though the poet says, " 'T is the pre-eminence of Friendship to impute excellence," yet we can never praise our Friend, nor esteem him praiseworthy, nor let him think that he can please us by any *behavior*, or ever *treat* us well enough. That kindness which has so good a reputation elsewhere can least of all consist with this relation, and no such affront can be offered to a Friend, as a conscious good-will, a friendliness which is not a necessity of the Friend's nature.

The sexes are naturally most strongly attracted to one another, by constant constitutional differences, and are most commonly and surely the complements of each other. How natural and easy it is for man to secure the attention of woman to what interests himself. Men and women of equal culture, thrown together, are sure to be of a certain value to one another, more than men to men. There exists already a natural disinterestedness and liberality in such society, and I think that any man will more confidently carry his favorite books to read to some circle of intelligent women, than to one of his own sex. The visit of man to man is wont to be an interruption, but the sexes naturally expect one another. Yet Friendship is no respecter of sex; and perhaps it is more rare between the sexes, than between two of the same sex.

Friendship is, at any rate, a relation of perfect equality. It cannot well spare any outward sign of equal obligation and advantage. The nobleman can never have a Friend among his retainers, nor the king among his subjects. Not that the parties to it are in all respects equal, but they are equal in all that respects or affects their Friendship. The one's love is exactly balanced and represented by the other's. Persons are only the vessels which contain the nectar, and the hydrostatic paradox is the symbol of love's law. It finds its level and rises to its fountain-head in all breasts, and its slenderest column balances the ocean.—

"And love as well the shepherd can
As can the mighty nobleman."

The one sex is not, in this respect, more tender than the other. A hero's love is as delicate as a maiden's.

Confucius said, "Never contract Friendship with a man that is not better than thyself." It is the merit and preservation of Friendship, that it takes place on a level higher than the actual characters of the parties would seem to warrant. The rays of light come to us in such a curve that every man whom we meet appears to be taller than he actually is. Such foundation has civility. My Friend is that one whom I can associate with my choicest thought. I always assign to him a nobler employment in my absence than I ever find him engaged in; and I imagine that the hours which he devotes to me were snatched from a higher society. The sorest insult which I ever received from a Friend was, when he behaved with the license which only long and cheap acquaintance allows to one's faults, in my presence, without shame, and still addressed me in friendly accents. Beware, lest thy Friend learn at last to tolerate one frailty of thine, and so an obstacle be raised to the progress of thy love. There are times when we have had enough even of our Friends, when we begin inevitably to profane one another, and must withdraw religiously into solitude and silence, the better to prepare ourselves for a loftier intimacy. Silence is the ambrosial night in the intercourse of Friends, in which their sincerity is recruited and takes deeper root.

Friendship is never established as an understood relation. Do you demand that I be less your Friend that you may know it? Yet what right have I to think that another cherishes so rare a sentiment for me? It is a miracle which requires constant proofs. It is an exercise of the purest imagination and the rarest faith. It says by a silent but eloquent behavior,—"I will be so related to thee as thou canst imagine; even so thou mayest believe. I will spend truth,—all my wealth on thee,"—and the Friend responds silently through his nature and life, and treats his Friend with the same divine courtesy. He knows us literally through thick and thin. He never asks for a sign of love, but can distinguish it by the features which it naturally wears. We never need to stand upon ceremony with him with regard to his visits. Wait not till I invite thee, but observe that I am glad to see thee when thou comest. It would be paying too dear for thy visit to ask for it. Where my Friend lives there are all riches and every attraction, and no slight obstacle can keep me from him. Let me never have to tell thee what I have not to tell. Let our intercourse be wholly above ourselves, and draw us up to it. The language of Friendship is not words but meanings. It is an intelligence above language. One imagines endless conversations with his Friend, in which the tongue shall be loosed, and thoughts be spoken without hesitancy, or end; but the experience is commonly far otherwise. Acquaintances may come and go, and have a word ready for every occasion; but what puny word shall he utter whose very breath is thought and meaning? Suppose you go to bid farewell to your Friend who is setting out on a journey; what other outward sign do you know of than to shake his hand? Have you any palaver ready for him then? any box of salve to commit to his pocket? any particular message to send by him? any statement which you had forgotten to make?–as if you could forget any thing.–No, it is much that you take his hand and say Farewell; that you could easily omit; so far custom has prevailed. It is even painful, if he is to go, that he should linger so long. If he must go, let him go quickly. Have you any *last* words? Alas, it is only the word of words, which you have so long sought and found not; *you* have not a *first* word yet. There are few even whom I should venture to call earnestly by their most proper names. A name pronounced is the recognition of the individual to whom it belongs. He who can pronounce my name aright, he can call me, and is entitled to my love and service. Yet reserve is the freedom and abandonment of lovers. It is the reserve of what is hostile or indifferent in their natures, to give place to what is kindred and harmonious.

The violence of love is as much to be dreaded as that of hate. When it is durable it is serene and equable. Even its famous pains begin only with the ebb of love, for few are indeed lovers, though all would fain be. It is one proof of a man's fitness for Friendship that he is able to do without that which is cheap and passionate. A true Friendship is as wise as it is tender. The parties to it yield implicitly to the guidance of their love, and know no other law nor kindness. It is not extravagant and insane, but what it says is something established henceforth, and will bear to be stereotyped. It is a truer truth, it is better and fairer news, and no time will ever shame it, or prove it false. This is a plant which thrives best in a temperate zone, where summer and winter alternate with one another. The Friend is a *necessarius*, and meets his Friend on homely ground; not on carpets and cushions, but on the ground and on rocks they will sit, obeying the natural and primitive laws. They will meet without any outcry, and part without loud sorrow. Their relation implies such qualities as the warrior prizes; for it takes a valor to open the hearts of men as well as the gates of castles. It is not an idle sympathy and mutual consolation merely, but a heroic sympathy of aspiration and endeavor.

"When manhood shall be matched so
That fear can take no place,
Then weary *works* make warriors
Each other to embrace."

The Friendship which Wawatam testified for Henry the fur-trader, as described in the latter's "Adventures," so almost bare and leafless, yet not blossomless nor fruitless, is remembered with satisfaction and security. The stern imperturbable warrior, after fasting, solitude, and mortification of body, comes to the white man's lodge, and affirms that he is the white brother whom he saw in his dream, and adopts him henceforth. He buries the hatchet as it regards his friend, and they hunt and feast and make maple-sugar together. "Metals unite from fluxility; birds and beasts from motives of convenience; fools from fear and stupidity; and just men at sight." If Wawatam would taste the "white man's milk" with his tribe, or take his bowl of human broth made of the trader's fellow-countrymen, he first finds a place of safety for his Friend, whom he has rescued from a similar fate. At length, after a long winter of undisturbed and happy intercourse in the family of the chieftain in the wilderness, hunting and fishing, they return in the spring to Michilimackinac to dispose of their furs; and it becomes necessary for Wawatam to take leave of his Friend at the Isle aux Outardes, when the latter, to avoid his enemies, proceeded to the Sault de Sainte Marie, supposing that they were to be separated for a short time only. "We now exchanged farewells," says Henry, "with an emotion entirely reciprocal. I did not quit the lodge without the most grateful sense of the many acts of goodness which I had experienced in it, nor without the sincerest respect for the virtues which I had witnessed among its members. All the family accompanied me to the beach; and the canoe had no sooner put off than Wawatam commenced an address to the Kichi Manito, beseeching him to take care of me, his brother, till we should next meet.—We had proceeded to too great a distance to allow of our hearing his voice, before Wawatam had ceased to offer up his prayers." We never hear of him again.

Friendship is not so kind as is imagined; it has not much human blood in it, but consists with a certain disregard for men and their erections, the Christian duties and humanities, while it purifies the air like electricity. There may be the sternest tragedy in the relation of two who are more than usually innocent and true to their highest instincts. We may call it an essentially heathenish intercourse, free and irresponsible in its nature, and practising all the virtues gratuitously. It is not the highest sympathy merely, but a pure and lofty society, a fragmentary and godlike intercourse of ancient date, still kept up at intervals, which, remembering itself, does not hesitate to disregard the humbler rights and duties of humanity. It requires immaculate and godlike qualities full-grown, and exists at all only by condescension and anticipation of the remotest future. We love nothing which is merely good and not fair, if such a thing is possible. Nature puts some kind of blossom before every fruit, not simply a calix behind it. When the Friend comes out of his heathenism and superstition, and breaks his idols, being converted by the precepts of a newer testament; when he forgets his mythology, and treats his Friend like a Christian, or as he can afford; then Friendship ceases to be Friendship, and becomes charity; that principle which established the almshouse is now beginning with its charity at home, and establishing an almshouse and pauper relations there.

As for the number which this society admits, it is at any rate to be begun with one, the noblest and greatest that we know, and whether the world will ever carry it further, whether, as Chaucer affirms,

> "There be mo sterres in the skie than a pair,"

remains to be proved;—

> "And certaine he is well begone
> Among a thousand that findeth one."

We shall not surrender ourselves heartily to any while we are conscious that another is more deserving of our love. Yet Friendship does not stand for numbers; the Friend does not count his Friends on his fingers; they are not numerable. The more there are included by this bond, if they are indeed included, the rarer and diviner the quality of the love that binds them. I am ready to believe that as private and intimate a relation may exist by which three are embraced, as between two. Indeed we cannot have too many friends; the virtue which we appreciate we to some extent appropriate, so that thus we are made at last more fit for every relation of life. A base Friendship is of a narrowing and exclusive tendency, but a noble one is not exclusive; its very superfluity and dispersed love is the humanity which sweetens society, and sympathizes with foreign nations; for though its foundations are private, it is in effect, a public affair and a public advantage, and the Friend, more than the father of a family, deserves well of the state.

The only danger in Friendship is that it will end. It is a delicate plant though a native. The least unworthiness, even if it be unknown to one's self, vitiates it. Let the Friend know that those faults which he observes in his Friend his own faults attract. There is no rule more invariable than that we are paid for our suspicions by finding what we suspected. By our narrowness and prejudices we say, I will have so much and such of you, my Friend, no more. Perhaps there are none charitable, none disinterested, none wise, noble, and heroic enough, for a true and lasting Friendship.

I sometimes hear my Friends complain finely that I do not appreciate their fineness. I shall not tell them whether I do or not. As if they expected a vote of thanks for every fine thing which they uttered or did. Who knows but it was finely appreciated. It may be that your silence was the finest thing of the two. There are some things which a man never speaks of, which are much finer kept silent about. To the highest communications we only lend a silent ear. Our finest relations are not simply kept silent about, but buried under a positive depth of silence, never to be revealed. It may be that we are not even yet acquainted. In human intercourse the tragedy begins, not when there is misunderstanding about words, but when silence is not understood. Then there can never be an explanation. What avails it that another loves you, if he does not understand you? Such love is a curse. What sort of companions are they who are presuming always that their silence is more expressive than yours? How foolish, and inconsiderate, and unjust, to conduct as if you were the only party aggrieved! Has not your Friend always equal ground of complaint? No doubt my Friends sometimes speak to me in vain, but they do not know what things I hear which they are not aware that they have spoken. I know that I have frequently disappointed them by not giving them words when they expected them, or such as they expected. Whenever I see my Friend I speak to him, but the expector, the man with the ears, is not he. They will complain too that you are hard. O ye that would have the cocoa-nut wrong side outwards, when next I weep I will let you know. They ask for words and deeds, when a true relation is word and deed. If they know not of these things, how can they be informed? We often forbear to confess our feelings, not from pride, but for fear that we could not continue to love the one who required us to give such proof of our affection.

I know a woman who possesses a restless and intelligent mind, interested in her own culture, and earnest to enjoy the highest possible advantages, and I meet her with pleasure as a natural person who not a little provokes me, and I suppose is stimulated in turn by myself. Yet our acquaintance plainly does not attain to that degree of confidence and sentiment which women, which all, in fact, covet. I am glad to help her, as I am helped by her; I like very well to know her with a sort of stranger's privilege, and hesitate to visit her often, like her other Friends. My nature pauses here, I do not well know why. Perhaps she does not make the highest demand on me, a religious demand. Some, with whose prejudices or peculiar bias I have no sympathy, yet inspire me with confidence, and I trust that they confide in me also as a religious heathen at least,–a good Greek. I too have principles as well founded as their own. If this person could conceive that, without wilfulness, I associate with her as far as our destinies are coincident, as far as our Good Geniuses permit, and still value such intercourse, it would be a grateful assurance to me. I feel as if I appeared careless, indifferent, and without principle to her, not expecting more, and yet not content with less. If she could know that I make an infinite demand on myself, as well as on all others, she would see that this true though incomplete intercourse, is infinitely better than a more unreserved but falsely grounded one, without the principle of growth in it. For a companion, I require one who will make an equal demand on me with my own genius. Such a one will always be rightly tolerant. It is suicide and corrupts good manners to welcome any less than this. I value and trust those who love and praise my aspiration rather than my performance. If you would not stop to look at me, but look whither I am looking and further, then my education could not dispense with your company.

> My love must be as free
> As is the eagle's wing,
> Hovering o'er land and sea
> And every thing.
>
> I must not dim my eye
> In thy saloon,
> I must not leave my sky
> And nightly moon.
>
> Be not the fowler's net
> Which stays my flight,
> And craftily is set
> T' allure the sight.
>
> But be the favoring gale
> That bears me on,
> And still doth fill my sail
> When thou art gone.
>
> I cannot leave my sky
> For thy caprice,
> True love would soar as high
> As heaven is.
>
> The eagle would not brook
> Her mate thus won,
> Who trained his eye to look
> Beneath the sun.

Few things are more difficult than to help a Friend in matters which do not require the aid of Friendship, but only a cheap and trivial service, if your Friendship wants the basis of a thorough practical acquaintance. I stand in the friendliest relation, on social and spiritual grounds, to one who does not perceive what practical skill I have, but when he seeks my assistance in such matters, is wholly ignorant of that one with whom he deals; does not use my skill, which in such matters is much greater than his, but only my hands. I know another, who, on the contrary, is remarkable for his discrimination in this respect; who knows how to make use of the talents of others when he does not possess the same; knows when not to look after or oversee, and stops short at his man. It is a rare pleasure to serve him, which all laborers know. I am not a little pained by the other kind of treatment. It is as if, after the friendliest and most ennobling intercourse, your Friend should use you as a hammer and drive a nail with your head, all in good faith; notwithstanding that you are a tolerable carpenter, as well as his good Friend, and would use a hammer cheerfully in his service. This want of perception is a defect which all the virtues of the heart cannot supply.—

The Good how can we trust?
Only the Wise are just.
The Good we use,
The Wise we cannot choose.
These there are none above;
The Good they know and love,
But are not known again
By those of lesser ken.
They do not charm us with their eyes,
But they transfix with their advice;
No partial sympathy they feel
With private woe or private weal,
But with the universe joy and sigh,
Whose knowledge is their sympathy.

Confucius said, "To contract ties of Friendship with any one, is to contract Friendship with his vir tue. There ought not to be any other motive in Friendship." But men wish us to contract Friendship with their vice also. I have a Friend who wishes me to see that to be right which I know to be wrong. But if Friendship is to rob me of my eyes, if it is to darken the day, I will have none of it. It should be expansive and inconceivably liberalizing in its effects. True Friendship can afford true knowledge. It does not depend on darkness and ignorance. A want of discernment cannot be an ingredient in it. If I can see my Friend's virtues more distinctly than another's, his faults too are made more conspicuous by contrast. We have not so good a right to hate any as our Friend. Faults are not the less faults because they are invariably balanced by corresponding virtues, and for a fault there is no excuse, though it may appear greater than it is in many ways. I have never known one who could bear criticism, who could not be flattered, who would not bribe his judge, or was content that the truth should be loved always better than himself.

If two travellers would go their way harmoniously together, the one must take as true and just a view of things as the other, else their path will not be strewn with roses. Yet you can travel profitably and pleasantly even with a blind man, if he practises common courtesy, and when you converse about the scenery will remember that he is blind but that you can see; and you will not forget that his sense of hearing is probably quickened by his want of sight. Otherwise you will not long keep company. A blind man, and a man in whose eyes there was no defect, were walking together, when they came to the edge of a precipice,—"Take care! my friend," said the latter, "here is a steep precipice; go no further this way."—"I know better," said the other, and stepped off.

It is impossible to say all that we think, even to our truest Friend. We may bid him farewell forever sooner than complain, for our complaint is too well grounded to be uttered. There is not so good an understanding between any two, but the exposure by the one of a serious fault in the other will produce a misunderstanding in proportion to its heinousness. The constitutional differences which always exist, and are obstacles to a perfect Friendship, are forever a forbidden theme to the lips of Friends. They advise by their whole behavior. Nothing can reconcile them but love. They are fatally late when they undertake to explain and treat with one another like foes. Who will take an apology for a Friend? They must apologize like dew and frost, which are off again with the sun, and which all men know in their hearts to be beneficent. The necessity itself for explanation,–what explanation will atone for that? True love does not quarrel for slight reasons, such mistakes as mutual acquaintances can explain away, but alas, however slight the apparent cause, only for adequate and fatal and everlasting reasons, which can never be set aside. Its quarrel, if there is any, is ever recurring, notwithstanding the beams of affection which invariably come to gild its tears; as the rainbow, however beautiful and unerring a sign, does not promise fair weather for ever, but only for a season. I have known two or three persons pretty well, and yet I have never known advice to be of use but in trivial and transient matters. One may know what another does not, but the utmost kindness cannot impart what is requisite to make the advice useful. We must accept or refuse one another as we are. I could tame a hyena more easily than my Friend. He is a material which no tool of mine will work. A naked savage will fell an oak with a firebrand, and wear a hatchet out of the rock by friction, but I cannot hew the smallest chip out of the character of my Friend, either to beautify or deform it.

The lover learns at last that there is no person quite transparent and trustworthy, but every one has a devil in him that is capable of any crime in the long run. Yet, as an oriental philosopher has said, "Although Friendship between good men is interrupted, their principles remain unaltered. The stalk of the lotus may be broken, and the fibres remain connected."

Ignorance and bungling with love are better than wisdom and skill without. There may be courtesy, there may be even temper, and wit, and talent, and sparkling conversation, there may be good-will even,—and yet the humanest and divinest faculties pine for exercise. Our life without love is like coke and ashes. Men may be pure as alabaster and Parian Marble, elegant as a Tuscan villa, sublime as Niagara, and yet if there is no milk mingled with the wine at their entertainments, better is the hospitality of Goths and Vandals. My Friend is not of some other race or family of men, but flesh of my flesh, bone of my bone. He is my real brother. I see his nature groping yonder so like mine. We do not live far apart. Have not the fates associated us in many ways? It says, in the Vishnu Purana: "Seven paces together is sufficient for the friendship of the virtuous, but thou and I have dwelt together." Is it of no significance that we have so long partaken of the same loaf, drank at the same fountain, breathed the same air, summer and winter, felt the same heat and cold; that the same fruits have been pleased to refresh us both, and we have never had a thought of different fibre the one from the other!

Nature doth have her dawn each day,
  But mine are far between;
Content, I cry, for sooth to say,
  Mine brightest are I ween.

For when my sun doth deign to rise,
  Though it be her noontide,
Her fairest field in shadow lies,
  Nor can my light abide.

Sometimes I bask me in her day,
  Conversing with my mate,
But if we interchange one ray,
  Forthwith her heats abate.

Through his discourse I climb and see,
  As from some eastern hill,
A brighter morrow rise to me
  Than lieth in her skill.

As 't were two summer days in one,
  Two Sundays come together,
Our rays united make one sun,
  With fairest summer weather.

As surely as the sunset in my latest November shall translate me to the ethereal world, and remind me of the ruddy morning of youth; as surely as the last strain of music which falls on my decaying ear shall make age to be forgotten, or, in short, the manifold influences of nature survive during the term of our natural life, so surely my Friend shall forever be my Friend, and reflect a ray of God to me, and time shall foster and adorn and consecrate our Friendship, no less than the ruins of temples. As I love nature, as I love singing birds, and gleaming stubble, and flowing rivers, and morning and evening, and summer and winter, I love thee my Friend.

But all that can be said of Friendship, is like botany

to flowers. How can the understanding take account of its friendliness?

Even the death of Friends will inspire us as much as their lives. They will leave consolation to the mourners, as the rich leave money to defray the expenses of their funerals, and their memories will be incrusted over with sublime and pleasing thoughts, as monuments of other men are overgrown with moss; for our Friends have no place in the graveyard.

This to our cis-Alpine and cis-Atlantic Friends.

Also this other word of entreaty and advice to the large and respectable nation of Acquaintances, beyond the mountains;—Greeting.

My most serene and irresponsible neighbors, let us see that we have the whole advantage of each other; we will be useful, at least, if not admirable, to one another. I know that the mountains which separate us are high, and covered with perpetual snow, but despair not. Improve the serene winter weather to scale them. If need be, soften the rocks with vinegar. For here lie the verdant plains of Italy ready to receive you. Nor shall I be slow on my side to penetrate to your Provence. Strike then boldly at head or heart or any vital part. Depend upon it the timber is well seasoned and tough, and will bear rough usage; and if it should crack, there is plenty more where it came from. I am no piece of crockery that cannot be jostled against my neighbor without danger of being broken by the collision, and must needs ring false and jarringly to the end of my days, when once I am cracked; but rather one of the old fashioned wooden trenchers, which one while stands at the head of the table, and at another is a milking-stool, and at another a seat for children, and finally goes down to its grave not unadorned with honorable scars, and does not die till it is worn out. Nothing can shock a brave man but dulness. Think how many rebuffs every man has experienced in his day; perhaps has fallen into a horse-pond, eaten fresh-water clams, or worn one shirt for a week without washing. Indeed, you cannot receive a shock unless you have an electric affinity for that which shocks you. Use me, then, for I am useful in my way, and stand as one of many petitioners, from toadstool and henbane up to dahlia and violet, supplicating to be put to my use, if by any means ye may find me serviceable; whether for a medicated drink or bath, as balm and lavender; or for fragrance, as verbena and geranium; or for sight, as cactus; or for thoughts, as pansy.—These humbler, at least, if not those higher uses.

Ah my dear Strangers and Enemies, I would not forget you. I can well afford to welcome you. Let me subscribe myself Yours ever and truly—your much obliged servant. We have nothing to fear from our foes; God keeps a standing army for that service; but we have no ally against our Friends, those ruthless Vandals.

Once more to one and all,

"Friends, Romans, Countrymen, and Lovers."

Let such pure hate still underprop
Our love, that we may be
Each other's conscience,
And have our sympathy
Mainly from thence.

We'll one another treat like gods,
And all the faith we have
In virtue and in truth, bestow
On either, and suspicion leave
To gods below.

Two solitary stars—
Unmeasured systems far
Between us roll,
But by our conscious light we are
Determined to one pole.

What need confound the sphere—
Love can afford to wait,
For it no hour's too late
That witnesseth one duty's end,
Or to another doth beginning lend.

It will subserve no use,
More than the tints of flowers,
Only the independent guest
Frequents its bowers,
Inherits its bequest.

No speech though kind has it,
But kinder silence doles
Unto its mates,
By night consoles,
By day congratulates.

What saith the tongue to tongue?
What heareth ear of ear?
By the decrees of fate
From year to year,
Does it communicate.

Pathless the gulf of feeling yawns—
No trivial bridge of words,
Or arch of boldest span,
Can leap the moat that girds
The sincere man.

No show of bolts and bars
Can keep the foeman out,
Or 'scape his secret mine
Who entered with the doubt
That drew the line.

No warder at the gate
Can let the friendly in,
But, like the sun, o'er all
He will the castle win,
And shine along the wall.

There's nothing in the world I know
That can escape from love,
For every depth it goes below,
And every height above.

It waits as waits the sky,
Until the clouds go by,
Yet shines serenely on
With an eternal day,
Alike when they are gone,
And when they stay.

Implacable is Love,—
Foes may be bought or teazed
From their hostile intent,
But he goes unappeased,
Who is on kindness bent.

Having rowed five or six miles above Amoskeag before sunset, and reached a pleasant part of the river, one of us landed to look for a farm-house, where we might replenish our stores, while the other remained cruising about the stream, and exploring the opposite shores to find a suitable harbor for the night. In the mean while the canal boats began to come round a point in our rear, poling their way along close to the shore, the breeze having quite died away. This time there was no offer of assistance, but one of the boatmen only called out to say, as the truest revenge for having been the losers in the race, that he had seen a wood-duck, which we had scared up, sitting on a tall white-pine, half a mile down stream; and he repeated the assertion several times, and seemed really chagrined at the apparent suspicion with which this information was received. But there sat the summer duck still undisturbed by us.

By and by the other voyageur returned from his inland expedition, bringing one of the natives with him, a little flaxen-headed boy, with some tradition, or small edition, of Robinson Crusoe in his head, who had been charmed by the account of our adventures, and asked his father's leave to join us. He examined, at first from the top of the bank, our boat and furniture, with sparkling eyes, and wished himself already his own man. He was a lively and interesting boy, and we should have been glad to ship him; but Nathan was still his father's boy, and had not come to years of discretion.

We had got a loaf of home-made bread, and musk and water-melons for dessert. For this farmer, a clever and well-disposed man, cultivated a large patch of melons for the Hooksett and Concord markets. He hospitably entertained us the next day, exhibiting his hop-fields and kiln and melon patch, warning us to step over the tight rope which surrounded the latter at a foot from the ground, while he pointed to a little bower at one corner, where it connected with the lock of a gun ranging with the line, and where, as he informed us, he sometimes sat in pleasant nights to defend his premises against thieves. We stepped high over the line, and sympathized with our host's on the whole quite human, if not humane, interest in the success of his experiment. That night especially thieves were to be expected, from rumors in the atmosphere, and the priming was not wet. He was a Methodist man, who had his dwelling between the river and Uncannunuc Mountain; who there belonged, and stayed at home there, and by the encouragement of distant political organizations, and by his own tenacity, held a property in his melons, and continued to plant. We suggested melon seeds of new varieties and fruit of foreign flavor to be added to his stock. We had come away up here among the hills to learn the impartial and unbribable beneficence of Nature. Strawberries and melons grow as well in one man's garden as another's, and the sun lodges as kindly under his hill-side,–when we had imagined that she inclined rather to some few earnest and faithful souls whom we know.

We found a convenient harbor for our boat on the opposite or east shore, still in Hooksett, at the mouth of a small brook which emptied into the Merrimack, where it would be out of the way of any passing boat in the night,–for they commonly hug the shore if bound up stream, either to avoid the current, or touch the bottom with their poles,–and where it would be accessible without stepping on the clayey shore. We set one of our largest melons to cool in the still water among the alders at the mouth of this creek, but when our tent was pitched and ready, and we went to get it, it had floated out into the stream and was no where to be seen. So taking the boat in the twilight, we went in pursuit of this property, and at length, after long straining of the eyes, its green disk was discovered far down the river, gently floating seaward with many twigs and leaves from the mountains that evening, and so perfectly balanced that it had not keeled at all, and no water had run in at the tap which had been taken out to hasten its cooling.

As we sat on the bank eating our supper, the clear light of the western sky fell on the eastern trees and was reflected in the water, and we enjoyed so serene an evening as left nothing to describe. For the most part we think that there are few degrees of sublimity, and that the highest is but little higher than that which we now behold; but we are always deceived. Sublimer visions appear, and the former pale and fade away. We are grateful when we are reminded by interior evidence, of the permanence of universal laws; for our faith is but faintly remembered, indeed, is not a remembered assurance, but a use and enjoyment of knowledge. It is when we do not have to believe, but come into actual contact with Truth, and are related to her in the most direct and intimate way. Waves of serener life pass over us from time to time, like flakes of sunlight over the fields in cloudy weather. In some happier moment, when more sap flows in the withered stalk of our life, Syria and India stretch away from our present as they do in history. All the events which make the annals of the nations are but the shadows of our private experiences. Suddenly and silently the eras which we call history awake and glimmer in us, and *there* is room for Alexander and Hannibal to march and conquer. In other words, the history which we read is only a fainter memory of events which have happened in our own experience. Tradition is a more interrupted and feebler memory.

This world is but canvass to our imaginations. I see men with infinite pains endeavoring to realize to their bodies, what I, with at least equal pains, would realize to my imagination,–its capacities; for certainly there is a life of the mind above the wants of the body and independent of it. Often the body is warmed, but the imagination is torpid; the body is fat, but the imagination is lean and shrunk. But what avails all other wealth if this is wanting? "Imagination is the air of mind," in which it lives and breathes. All things are as I am. Where is the House of Change? The past is only so heroic as we see it. It is the canvass on which our idea of heroism is painted, and so, in one sense, the dim prospectus of our future field. Our circumstances answer to our expectations and the demand of our natures. I have noticed that if a man thinks that he needs a thousand dollars, and cannot be convinced that he does not, he will commonly be found to have them, if he lives and thinks a thousand dollars will be forthcoming, though it be to buy shoe strings with. A thousand mills will be just as slow to come to one who finds it equally hard to convince himself that he needs *them*.

> Men are by birth equal in this, that given
> Themselves and their condition, they are even.

I am astonished at the singular pertinacity and endurance of our lives. The miracle is, that what is *is*, when it is so difficult, if not impossible, for any thing else to be; that we walk on in our particular paths so far, before we fall on death and fate, merely because we must walk in some path; that every man can get a living, and so few can do any more. So much only can I accomplish ere health and strength are gone, and yet this suffices. The bird now sits just out of gunshot. I am never rich in money, and I am never meanly poor. If debts are incurred, why, debts are in the course of events cancelled, as it were by the same law by which they were incurred. I heard that an engagement was entered into between a certain youth and a maiden, and then I heard that it was broken off, but I did not know the reason in either case. We are hedged about, we think, by accident and circumstance, now we creep as in a dream, and now again we run, as if there were a fate in it and all things thwarted or assisted. I cannot change my clothes but when I do, and yet I do change them, and soil the new ones. It is wonderful that this gets done, when some admirable deeds which I could mention, do not get done. Our particular lives seem of such fortune and confident strength and durability as piers of solid rock thrown forward into the tide of circumstance. When every other path would fail, with singular and unerring confidence we advance on our particular course. What risks we run! famine and fire and pestilence, and the thousand forms of a cruel fate,—and yet every man lives till he——dies. How did he manage that? Is there no immediate danger? We wonder superfluously when we hear of a somnambulist walking a plank securely,—we have walked a plank all our lives up to this particular string-piece where we are. My life will wait for nobody, but is being matured still without delay, while I go about the streets and chaffer with this man and that to secure it a living. It is as indifferent and easy meanwhile as a poor man's dog, and making acquaintance with its kind. It will cut its own channel like a mountain stream, and by the longest ridge is not kept from the sea at last. I have found all things thus far, persons and inanimate matter, elements and seasons, strangely adapted to my resources. No matter what imprudent haste in my career; I am permitted to be rash. Gulfs are bridged in a twinkling, as if some unseen baggage train carried pontoons for my convenience, and while from the heights I scan the tempting but unexplored Pacific Ocean of Futurity, the ship is being carried over the mountains piece-meal on the backs of mules and lamas, whose keel shall plow its waves and bear me to the Indies. Day would not dawn if it were not for

THE INWARD MORNING.

Packed in my mind lie all the clothes
  Which outward nature wears,
And in its fashion's hourly change
  It all things else repairs.

In vain I look for change abroad,
And can no difference find,
Till some new ray of peace uncalled
Illumes my inmost mind.

What is it gilds the trees and clouds,
And paints the heavens so gay,
But yonder fast abiding light
With its unchanging ray?

Lo, when the sun streams through the wood,
Upon a winter's morn,
Where'er his silent beams intrude
The murky night is gone.

How could the patient pine have known
The morning breeze would come,
Or humble flowers anticipate
The insect's noonday hum,—

Till the new light with morning cheer
From far streamed through the aisles,
And nimbly told the forest trees
For many stretching miles?

I've heard within my inmost soul
Such cheerful morning news,
In the horizon of my mind
Have seen such orient hues,

As in the twilight of the dawn,
When the first birds awake,
Are heard within some silent wood,
Where they the small twigs break,

Or in the eastern skies are seen,
Before the sun appears,
The harbingers of summer heats
Which from afar he bears.

Whole weeks and months of my summer life slide away in thin volumes like mist and smoke, till at length, some warm morning, perchance, I see a sheet of mist blown down the brook to the swamp, and I float as high above the fields with it. I can recall to mind the stillest summer hours, in which the grasshopper sings over the mulleins, and there is a valor in that time the bare memory of which is armor that can laugh at any blow of fortune. For our lifetime the strains of a harp are heard to swell and die alternately, and death is but "the pause when the blast is recollecting itself."

We lay awake a long while, listening to the murmurs of the brook, in the angle formed by whose bank with the river our tent was pitched, and there was a sort of human interest in its story, which ceases not in freshet or in drought the livelong summer, and the profounder lapse of the river was quite drowned by its din. But the rill, whose

> "Silver sands and pebbles sing
> Eternal ditties with the spring,"

is silenced by the first frosts of winter, while mightier streams, on whose bottom the sun never shines, clogged with sunken rocks and the ruins of forests, from whose surface comes up no murmur, are strangers to the icy fetters which bind fast a thousand contributary rills.

I dreamed this night of an event which had occurred long before. It was a difference with a Friend, which had not ceased to give me pain, though I had no cause to blame myself. But in my dream ideal justice was at length done me for his suspicions, and I received that compensation which I had never obtained in my waking hours. I was unspeakably soothed and rejoiced, even after I awoke, because in dreams we never deceive ourselves, nor are deceived, and this seemed to have the authority of a final judgment.

We bless and curse ourselves. Some dreams are divine, as well as some waking thoughts. Donne sings of one

> "Who dreamt devoutlier than most use to pray."

Dreams are the touchstones of our characters. We are scarcely less afflicted when we remember some unworthiness in our conduct in a dream, than if it had been actual, and the intensity of our grief, which is our atonement, measures inversely the degree by which this is separated from an actual unworthiness. For in dreams we but act a part which must have been learned and rehearsed in our waking hours, and no doubt could discover some waking consent thereto. If this meanness has not its foundation in us, why are we grieved at it? In dreams we see ourselves naked and acting out our real characters, even more clearly than we see others awake. But an unwavering and commanding virtue would compel even its most fantastic and faintest dreams to respect its ever wakeful authority; as we are accustomed to say carelessly, we should never have *dreamed* of such a thing. Our truest life is when we are in dreams awake.

> "And, more to lulle him in his slumber soft,
> A trickling streame from high rock tumbling downe,
> And ever-drizzling raine upon the loft,
> Mixt with a murmuring winde, much like the sowne
> Of swarming bees, did cast him in a swowne.
> No other noyse, nor people's troublous cryes,
> As still are wont t' annoy the walled towne,
> Might there be heard; but careless Quiet lyes,
> Wrapt in eternall silence farre from enemyes."

Thursday.

"He trode the unplanted forest floor, whereon
The all-seeing sun for ages hath not shone,
Where feeds the moose, and walks the surly
bear,
And up the tall mast runs the woodpecker.

* * * * *

Where darkness found him he lay glad at
night;
There the red morning touched him with its
light.

* * * * *

Go where he will, the wise man is at home,
His hearth the earth,—his hall the azure dome;
Where his clear spirit leads him, there's his
road,
By God's own light illumined and foreshowed."

Emerson.

WHEN we awoke this morning, we heard the faint deliberate and ominous sound of rain drops on our cotton roof. The rain had pattered all night, and now the whole country wept, the drops falling in the river, and on the alders, and in the pastures, and instead of any bow in the heavens, there was the trill of the chip-sparrow all the morning. The cheery faith of this little bird atoned for the silence of the whole woodland quire beside. When we first stepped abroad, a flock of sheep, led by their rams, came rushing down a ravine in our rear, with heedless haste and unreserved frisking, as if unobserved by man, from some higher pasture where they had spent the night, to taste the herbage by the river-side; but when their leaders caught sight of our white tent through the mist, struck with sudden astonishment, with their fore feet braced, they sustained the rushing torrent in their rear, and the whole flock stood stock-still, endeavoring to solve the mystery in their sheepish brains. At length, concluding that it boded no mischief to them, they spread themselves out quietly over the field. We learned afterward that we had pitched our tent on the very spot which a few summers before had been occupied by a party of Penobscots. We could see rising before us through the mist a dark conical eminence called Hooksett Pinnacle, a landmark to boatmen, and also Uncannunuc Mountain, broad off on the west side of the river.

This was the limit of our voyage, for a few hours more in the rain would have taken us to the last of the locks, and our boat was too heavy to be dragged around the long and numerous rapids which would occur. On foot, however, we continued up along the bank, feeling our way with a stick through the showery and foggy day, and climbing over the slippery logs in our path with as much pleasure and buoyancy as in brightest sunshine; scenting the fragrance of the pines and the wet clay under our feet, and cheered by the tones of invisible waterfalls; with visions of toadstools, and wandering frogs, and festoons of moss hanging from the spruce trees, and thrushes flitting silent under the leaves; our road still holding together through that wettest of weather, like faith, while we confidently followed its lead. We managed to keep our thoughts dry, however, and only our clothes were wet. It was altogether a cloudy and drizzling day, with occasional brightenings in the mist, when the trill of the tree-sparrow seemed to be ushering in sunny hours.

"Nothing that naturally happens to man, can *hurt* him, earthquakes and thunder storms not excepted," said a man of genius, who at this time lived a few miles further on our road. When compelled by a shower to take shelter under a tree, we may improve that opportunity for a more minute inspection of some of Nature's works. I have stood under a tree in the woods half a day at a time, during a heavy rain in the summer, and yet employed myself happily and profitably there prying with microscopic eye into the crevices of the bark or the leaves or the fungi at my feet. "Riches are the attendants of the miser; and the heavens rain plenteously upon the mountains." I can fancy that it would be a luxury to stand up to one's chin in some retired swamp a whole summer day, scenting the wild honeysuckle and bilberry blows, and lulled by the minstrelsy of gnats and mosquitoes! A day passed in the society of those Greek sages, such as described in the Banquet of Xenophon, would not be comparable with the dry wit of decayed cranberry vines, and the fresh Attic salt of the moss-beds. Say twelve hours of genial and familiar converse with the leopard frog; the sun to rise behind alder and dogwood, and climb buoyantly to his meridian of two hands' breadth, and finally sink to rest behind some bold western hummock! To hear the evening chant of the mosquito from a thousand green chapels, and the bittern begin to boom from some concealed fort like a sunset gun!—Surely one may as profitably be soaked in the juices of a swamp for one day as pick his way dry-shod over sand. Cold and damp,—are they not as rich experience as warmth and dryness?

At present, the drops come trickling down the stubble while we lie drenched on a bed of withered wild oats, by the side of a bushy hill, and the gathering in of the clouds, with the last rush and dying breath of the wind, and then the regular dripping of twigs and leaves the country over, enhance the sense of inward comfort and sociableness. The birds draw closer and are more familiar under the thick foliage, seemingly composing new strains upon their roosts against the sunshine. What were the amusements of the drawing room and the library in comparison, if we had them here? We should still sing as of old,—

My books I'd fain cast off, I cannot read,
'Twixt every page my thoughts go stray at large
Down in the meadow, where is richer feed,
And will not mind to hit their proper targe.

Plutarch was good, and so was Homer too,
Our Shakspeare's life was rich to live again,
What Plutarch read, that was not good nor true,
Nor Shakspeare's books, unless his books were men.

Here while I lie beneath this walnut bough,
What care I for the Greeks or for Troy town,
If juster battles are enacted now
Between the ants upon this hummock's crown?

Bid Homer wait till I the issue learn,
If red or black the gods will favor most,
Or yonder Ajax will the phalanx turn,
Struggling to heave some rock against the host.

Tell Shakspeare to attend some leisure hour,
For now I've business with this drop of dew,
And see you not, the clouds prepare a shower,—
I'll meet him shortly when the sky is blue.

This bed of herd's-grass and wild oats was spread
Last year with nicer skill than monarchs use,
A clover tuft is pillow for my head,
And violets quite overtop my shoes.

And now the cordial clouds have shut all in,
And gently swells the wind to say all's well,
The scattered drops are falling fast and thin,
Some in the pool, some in the flower-bell.

I am well drenched upon my bed of oats;
But see that globe come rolling down its stem,
Now like a lonely planet there it floats,
And now it sinks into my garment's hem.

Drip drip the trees for all the country round,
And richness rare distils from every bough,
The wind alone it is makes every sound,
Shaking down crystals on the leaves below.

For shame the sun will never show himself,
Who could not with his beams e'er melt me so,
My dripping locks—they would become an elf,
Who in a beaded coat does gaily go.

The Pinnacle is a small wooded hill which rises very abruptly to the height of about two hundred feet, near the shore at Hooksett Falls. As Uncannunuc Mountain is perhaps the best point from which to view the valley of the Merrimack, so this hill affords the best view of the river itself. I have sat upon its summit, a precipitous rock only a few rods long, in fairer weather, when the sun was setting and filling the river valley with a flood of light. You can see up and down the Merrimack several miles each way. The broad and straight river, full of light and life, with its sparkling and foaming falls, the islet which divides the stream, the village of Hooksett on the shore almost directly under your feet, so near that you can converse with its inhabitants or throw a stone into its yards, the woodland lake at its western base, and the mountains in the north and north-east, make a scene of rare beauty and completeness, which the traveller should take pains to behold.

We were hospitably entertained in Concord in New Hampshire, which we persisted in calling *New* Concord, as we had been wont, to distinguish it from our native town, from which we had been told that it was named and in part originally settled. This would have been the proper place to conclude our voyage, uniting Concord with Concord by these meandering rivers, but our boat was moored some miles below its port.

The richness of the intervals at Penacook, now Concord in New Hampshire, had been observed by explorers, and according to the historian of Haverhill, in the

"year 1726, considerable progress was made in the settlement, and a road was cut through the wilderness from Haverhill to Penacook. In the fall of 1727, the first family, that of Capt. Ebenezer Eastman, moved into the place. His team was driven by Jacob Shute, who was by birth a Frenchman, and he is said to have been the first person who drove a team through the wilderness. Soon after, says tradition, one Ayer, a lad of 18, drove a team consisting of ten yoke of oxen to Penacook, swam the river, and plowed a portion of the interval. He is supposed to have been the first person who plowed land in that place. After he had completed his work, he started on his return at sunrise, drowned a yoke of oxen while recrossing the river, and arrived at Haverhill about midnight. The crank of the first grist-mill was manufactured in Haverhill, and carried to Penacook on a horse."

But we found that the frontiers were not this way any longer. This generation has come into the world fatally late for some enterprises. Go where we will on the *surface* of things, men have been there before us. We cannot now have the pleasure of erecting the *last* house; that was long ago set up in the suburbs of Astoria city, and our boundaries have literally been run to the South Sea, according to the old patents. But the lives of men, though more extended laterally in their range, are still as shallow as ever. Undoubtedly, as a western orator said, "men generally live over about the same surface; some live long and narrow, and others live broad and short;" but it is all superficial living. A worm is as good a traveller as a grasshopper or a cricket, and a much wiser settler. With all their activity these do not hop away from drought nor forward to summer. We do not avoid evil by fleeing before it, but by rising above or diving below its plane; as the worm escapes drought and frost by boring a few inches deeper. The frontiers are not east or west, north or south, but wherever a man *fronts* a fact, though that fact be his neighbor, there is an unsettled wilderness between him and Canada, between him and the setting sun, or, further still, between him and *it.* Let him build himself a log-house with the bark on where he is, *fronting* IT, and wage there an Old French war for seven or seventy years, with Indians and Rangers, or whatever else may come between him and the reality, and save his scalp if he can.

We now no longer sailed or floated on the river, but trod the unyielding land like pilgrims. Sadi tells who may travel; among others,—"A common mechanic, who can earn a subsistence by the industry of his hand, and shall not have to stake his reputation for every morsel of bread, as philosophers have said."— He may travel who can subsist on the wild fruits and game of the most cultivated country. A man may travel fast enough and earn his living on the road. I have at times been applied to to do work when on a journey; to do tinkering and repair clocks, when I had a knapsack on my back. A man once applied to me to go into a factory, stating conditions and wages, observing that I succeeded in shutting the window of a railroad car in which we were travelling, when the other passengers had failed. "Hast thou not heard of a Sufi, who was hammering some nails into the sole of his sandal; an officer of cavalry took him by the sleeve, saying, come along and shoe my horse." Farmers have asked me to assist them in haying, when I was passing their fields. A man once applied to me to mend his umbrella, taking me for an umbrella mender, because, being on a journey, I carried an umbrella in my hand while the sun shone. Another wished to buy a tin cup of me, observing that I had one strapped to my belt, and a sauce-pan on my back. The cheapest way to travel, and the way to travel the furthest in the shortest distance, is to go afoot, carrying a dipper, a spoon, and a fish-line, some Indian meal, some salt, and some sugar. When you come to a brook or pond, you can catch fish and cook them; or you can boil a hasty-pudding; or you can buy a loaf of bread at a farmer's house for fourpence, moisten it in the next brook that crosses the road, and dip into it your sugar,–this alone will last you a whole day;–or, if you are accustomed to heartier living, you can buy a quart of milk for two cents, crumb your bread or cold pudding into it, and eat it with your own spoon out of your own dish. Any one of these things I mean, not altogether. I have travelled thus some hundreds of miles without taking any meal in a house, sleeping on the ground when convenient, and found it cheaper, and in many respects more profitable, than staying at home. So that some have inquired why it would not be best to travel always. But I never thought of travelling simply as a means of getting a livelihood. A simple woman down in Tyngsboro', at whose house I once stopped to get a draught of water, when I said, recognizing the bucket, that I had stopped there nine years before for the same purpose, asked if I was not a traveller, supposing that I had been travelling ever since, and had now come round again, that travelling was one of the professions, more or less productive, which her husband did not follow. But continued travelling is far from productive. It begins with wearing away the soles of the shoes, and making the feet sore, and ere long it will wear a man clean up, after making his heart sore into the bargain. I have observed that the after-life of those who have travelled much is very pathetic. True and sincere travelling is no pastime, but it is as serious as the grave, or any other part of the human journey, and it requires a long probation to be broken into it. I do not speak of those that travel sitting, the sedentary travellers whose legs hang dangling the while, mere idle symbols of the fact, any more than when we speak of sitting hens we mean those that sit standing, but I mean those to whom travelling is life for the legs, and death too, at last. The traveller must be born again on the road, and earn a passport from the elements, the principal powers that be for him. He shall experience at last that old threat of his mother fulfilled, that he shall be skinned alive. His sores shall gradually deepen themselves that they may heal inwardly, while he gives no rest to the sole of his foot, and at night weariness must be his pillow, that so he may acquire experience against his rainy days.—So was it with us.

Sometimes we lodged at an inn in the woods, where trout-fishers from distant cities had arrived before us, and where, to our astonishment, the settlers dropped in at night-fall to have a chat and hear the news, though there was but one road, and no other house was visible,—as if they had come out of the earth. There we sometimes read old newspapers, who never before read new ones, and in the rustle of their leaves heard the dashing of the surf along the Atlantic shore, instead of the sough of the wind among the pines. But then walking had given us an appetite even for the least palatable and nutritious food.

Some hard and dry book in a dead language, which you have found it impossible to read at home, but for which you have still a lingering regard, is the best to carry with you on a journey. At a country inn, in the barren society of ostlers and travellers, I could undertake the writers of the silver or the brazen age with confidence. Almost the last regular service which I performed in the cause of literature was to read the works of

AULUS PERSIUS FLACCUS.

If you have imagined what a divine work is spread out for the poet, and approach this author too, in the hope of finding the field at length fairly entered on, you will hardly dissent from the words of the prologue,

"Ipse semipaganus
Ad sacra Vatum carmen affero nostrum."

I half pagan
Bring my verses to the shrine of the poets.

Here is none of the interior dignity of Virgil, nor the elegance and vivacity of Horace, nor will any sybil be needed to remind you, that from those older Greek poets there is a sad descent to Persius. You can scarcely distinguish one harmonious sound amid this unmusical bickering with the follies of men.

One sees that music has its place in thought, but hardly as yet in language. When the Muse arrives, we wait for her to remould language, and impart to it her own rhythm. Hitherto the verse groans and labors with its load, and goes not forward blithely, singing by the way. The best ode may be parodied, indeed is itself a parody, and has a poor and trivial sound, like a man stepping on the rounds of a ladder. Homer, and Shakspeare, and Milton, and Marvel and Wordsworth, are but the rustling of leaves and crackling of twigs in the forest, and there is not yet the sound of any bird. The Muse has never lifted up her voice to sing. Most of all, satire will not be sung. A Juvenal or Persius do not marry music to their verse, but are measured fault-finders at best; stand but just outside the faults they condemn, and so are concerned rather about the monster which they have escaped, than the fair prospect before them. Let them live on an age, and they will have travelled out of his shadow and reach, and found other objects to ponder.

As long as there is satire, the poet is, as it were, *particeps criminis*. One sees not but he had best let bad take care of itself, and have to do only with what is beyond suspicion. If you light on the least vestige of truth, and it is the weight of the whole body still which stamps the faintest trace, an eternity will not suffice to extol it, while no evil is so huge, but you grudge to bestow on it a moment of hate. Truth never turns to rebuke falsehood; her own straight-forwardness is the severest correction. Horace would not have written satire so well if he had not been inspired by it, as by a passion, and fondly cherished his vein. In his odes, the love always exceeds the hate, so that the severest satire still sings itself, and the poet is satisfied, though the folly be not corrected.

A sort of necessary order in the development of Genius is, first, Complaint; second, Plaint; third, Love. Complaint, which is the condition of Persius, lies not in the province of poetry. Ere long the enjoyment of a superior good would have changed his disgust into regret. We can never have much sympathy with the complainer; for after searching nature through, we conclude that he must be both plaintiff and defendant too, and so had best come to a settlement without a hearing. He who receives an injury is to some extent an accomplice of the wrong doer.

Perhaps it would be truer to say, that the highest strain of the muse is essentially plaintive. The saint's are still *tears* of joy. Who has ever heard the *Innocent* sing?

But the divinest poem, or the life of a great man, is the severest satire; as impersonal as Nature herself, and like the sighs of her winds in the woods, which convey ever a slight reproof to the hearer. The greater the genius, the keener the edge of the satire.

Hence we have to do only with the rare and fragmentary traits, which least belong to Persius, or shall we say, are the properest utterances of his muse; since that which he says best at any time is what he can best say at all times. The Spectators and Ramblers have not failed to cull some quotable sentences from this garden too, so pleasant is it to meet even the most familiar truth in a new dress, when, if our neighbor had said it, we should have passed it by as hackneyed. Out of these six satires, you may perhaps select some twenty lines, which fit so well as many thoughts, that they will recur to the scholar almost as readily as a natural image; though when translated into familiar language, they lose that insular emphasis, which fitted them for quotation. Such lines as the following, translation cannot render common-place. Contrasting the man of true religion with those who, with jealous privacy, would fain carry on a secret commerce with the gods, he says,–

> "Haud cuivis promptum est, murmurque humilesque
> susurros,
> Tollere de templis; et aperto vivere voto."
>
> It is not easy for every one to take murmurs and low
> Whispers out of the temples, and live with open vow.

To the virtuous man, the universe is the only *sanctum sanctorum*, and the penetralia of the temple are the broad noon of his existence. Why should he betake himself to a subterranean crypt, as if it were the only holy ground in all the world which he had left unprofaned? The obedient soul would only the more discover and familiarize things, and escape more and more into light and air, as having henceforth done with secrecy, so that the universe shall not seem open enough for it. At length, it is neglectful even of that silence which is consistent with true modesty, but by its independence of all confidence in its disclosures, makes that which it imparts so private to the hearer, that it becomes the care of the whole world that modesty be not infringed.

To the man who cherishes a secret in his breast, there is a still greater secret unexplored. Our most indifferent acts may be matter for secrecy, but whatever we do with the utmost truthfulness and integrity, by virtue of its pureness, must be transparent as light.

In the third satire, he asks,

> "Est aliquid quò tendis, et in quod dirigis arcum?
> An passim sequeris corvos, testâve, lutove,
> Securus quò pes ferat, atque ex tempore vivis?"

> Is there any thing to which thou tendest, and
> against which thou directest thy bow?
> Or dost thou pursue crows, at random, with pottery
> or clay,
> Careless whither thy feet bear thee, and live
> *ex tempore*?

The bad sense is always a secondary one. Language does not appear to have justice done it, but is obviously cramped and narrowed in its significance, when any meanness is described. The truest construction is not put upon it. What may readily be fashioned into a rule of wisdom, is here thrown in the teeth of the sluggard, and constitutes the front of his offence. Universally, the innocent man will come forth from the sharpest inquisition and lecturing, the combined din of reproof and commendation, with a faint sound of eulogy in his ears. Our vices always lie in the direction of our virtues, and in their best estate are but plausible imitations of the latter. Falsehood never attains to the dignity of entire falseness, but is only an inferior sort of truth; if it were more thoroughly false, it would incur danger of becoming true.

> "Securus quo pes ferat, atque ex tempore *vivit*,"

is then the motto of a wise man. For first, as the subtle discernment of the language would have taught us, with all his negligence he is still secure; but the sluggard, notwithstanding his heedlessness, is insecure.

The life of a wise man is most of all extemporaneous, for he lives out of an eternity which includes all time. The cunning mind travels farther back than Zoroaster each instant, and comes quite down to the present with its revelation. The utmost thrift and industry of thinking give no man any stock in life; his credit with the inner world is no better, his capital no larger. He must try his fortune again to-day as yesterday. All questions rely on the present for their solution. Time measures nothing but itself. The word that is written may be postponed, but not that on the lip. If this is what the occasion says, let the occasion say it. All the world is forward to prompt him who gets up to live without his creed in his pocket.

In the fifth satire, which is the best, I find,–

> "Stat contrà ratio, et secretam garrit in aurem,
> Ne liceat facere id, quod quis vitiabit agendo."

> Reason opposes, and whispers in the secret ear,
> That it is not lawful to do that which one will spoil
> by doing.

Only they who do not see how any thing might be better done, are forward to try their hand on it. Even the master workman must be encouraged by the reflection, that his awkwardness will be incompetent to do that thing harm, to which his skill may fail to do justice. Here is no apology for neglecting to do many things from a sense of our incapacity,–for what deed does not fall maimed and imperfect from our hands?–but only a warning to bungle less.

The satires of Persius are the farthest possible from inspired; evidently a chosen, not imposed subject. Perhaps I have given him credit for more earnestness than is apparent; but it is certain, that that which alone we can call Persius, which is forever independent and consistent, *was* in earnest, and so sanctions the sober consideration of all. The artist and his work are not to be separated. The most wilfully foolish man cannot stand aloof from his folly, but the deed and the doer together make ever one sober fact. There is but one stage for the peasant and the actor. The buffoon cannot bribe you to laugh always at his grimaces; they shall sculpture themselves in Egyptian granite, to stand heavy as the pyramids on the ground of his character.

Suns rose and set and found us still on the dank forest path which meanders up the Pemigewasset, now more like an otter's or a marten's trail, or where a beaver had dragged his trap, than where the wheels of travel raise a dust; where towns begin to serve as gores, only to hold the earth together. The wild pigeon sat secure above our heads, high on the dead limbs of naval pines, reduced to a robin's size. The very yards of our hostelries inclined upon the skirts of mountains, and, as we passed, we looked up at a steep angle at the stems of maples waving in the clouds.

Far up in the country,—for we would be faithful to our experience,—in Thornton, perhaps, we met a soldier lad in the woods, going to muster in full regimentals, and holding the middle of the road; deep in the forest with shouldered musket and military step, and thoughts of war and glory all to himself. It was a sore trial to the youth, tougher than many a battle, to get by us creditably and with soldierlike bearing. Poor man! He actually shivered like a reed in his thin military pants, and by the time we had got up with him, all the sternness that becomes the soldier had forsaken his face, and he skulked past as if he were driving his father's sheep under a sword-proof helmet. It was too much for him to carry any extra armor then, who could not easily dispose of his natural arms. And for his legs, they were like heavy artillery in boggy places; better to cut the traces and forsake them. His greaves chafed and wrestled one with another for want of other foes. But he did get by and get off with all his munitions, and lived to fight another day; and I do not record this as casting any suspicion on his honor and real bravery in the field.

Wandering on through notches which the streams had made, by the side and over the brows of hoar hills and mountains, across the stumpy, rocky, forested and bepastured country, we at length crossed on prostrate trees over the Amonoosuck, and breathed the free air of Unappropriated Land. Thus, in fair days as well as foul, we had traced up the river to which our native stream is a tributary, until from Merrimack it became the Pemigewasset that leaped by our side, and when we had passed its fountain-head, the Wild Amonoosuck, whose puny channel was crossed at a stride, guiding us toward its distant source among the mountains, and at length, without its guidance, we were enabled to reach the summit of AGIOCOCHOOK.

"Sweet days, so cool, so calm, so bright,
The bridal of the earth and sky,
Sweet dews shall weep thy fall to-night,
For thou must die."

Herbert.

When we returned to Hooksett, a week afterward, the melon man, in whose corn-barn we had hung our tent and buffaloes and other things to dry, was already picking his hops, with many women and children to help him. We bought one watermelon, the largest in his patch, to carry with us for ballast. It was Nathan's, which he might sell if he wished, having been conveyed to him in the green state, and owned daily by his eyes. After due consultation with "Father," the bargain was concluded,–we to buy it at a venture on the vine, green or ripe, our risk, and pay "what the gentlemen pleased." It proved to be ripe; for we had had honest experience in selecting this fruit.

Finding our boat safe in its harbor, under Uncannunuc Mountain, with a fair wind and the current in our favor, we commenced our return voyage at noon, sitting at our ease and conversing, or in silence watching for the last trace of each reach in the river as a bend concealed it from our view. As the season was further advanced, the wind now blew steadily from the north, and with our sail set we could occasionally lie on our oars without loss of time. The lumbermen throwing down wood from the top of the high bank, thirty or forty feet above the water, that it might be sent down stream, paused in their work to watch our retreating sail. By this time, indeed, we were well known to the boatmen, and were hailed as the Revenue Cutter of the stream. As we sailed rapidly down the river, shut in between two mounds of earth, the sound of this timber rolled down the bank enhanced the silence and vastness of the noon, and we fancied that only the primeval echoes were awakened. The vision of a distant scow just heaving in sight round a headland, also increased by contrast the solitude.

Through the din and desultoriness of noon, even in the most oriental city, is seen the fresh and primitive and savage nature, in which Scythians, and Ethiopians, and Indians dwell. What is echo, what are light and shade, day and night, ocean and stars, earthquake and eclipse, there? The works of man are every where swallowed up in the immensity of Nature. The Ægean Sea is but Lake Huron still to the Indian. Also there is all the refinement of civilized life in the woods under a sylvan garb. The wildest scenes have an air of domesticity and homeliness even to the citizen, and when the flicker's cackle is heard in the clearing, he is reminded that civilization has wrought but little change there. Science is welcome to the deepest recesses of the forest, for there too nature obeys the same old civil laws. The little red bug on the stump of a pine, for it the wind shifts and the sun breaks through the clouds. In the wildest nature, there is not only the material of the most cultivated life, and a sort of anticipation of the last result, but a greater refinement already than is ever attained by man. There is papyrus by the river-side, and rushes for light, and the goose only flies overhead, ages before the studious are born or letters invented, and that literature which the former suggest, and even from the first have rudely served, it may be man does not yet use them to express. Nature is prepared to welcome into her scenery the finest work of human art, for she is herself an art so cunning that the artist never appears in his work.

Art is not tame, and Nature is not wild, in the ordinary sense. A perfect work of man's art would also be wild or natural in a good sense. Man tames Nature only that he may at last make her more free even than he found her, though he may never yet have succeeded.

With this propitious breeze, and the help of our oars, we soon reached the Falls of Amoskeag, and the mouth of the Piscataquoag, and recognized, as we swept rapidly by, many a fair bank and islet on which our eyes had rested in the upward passage. Our boat was like that which Chaucer describes in his Dream, in which the knight took his departure from the island,

"To journey for his marriage,
And return with such an host,
That wedded might be least and most. * *
Which barge was as a man's thought,
After his pleasure to him brought,
The queene herself accustomed aye
In the same barge to play,
It needed neither mast ne rother,
I have not heard of such another,
No master for the governance,
Hie sayled by thought and pleasaunce,
Without labor east and west,
All was one, calme or tempest."

So we sailed this afternoon, thinking of the saying of Pythagoras, though we had no peculiar right to remember it,—"It is beautiful when prosperity is present with intellect, and when sailing as it were with a prosperous wind, actions are performed looking to virtue; just as a pilot looks to the motions of the stars." All the world reposes in beauty to him who preserves equipoise in his life, and moves serenely on his path without secret violence; as he who sails down a stream, he has only to steer, keeping his bark in the middle, and carry it round the falls. The ripples curled away in our wake, like ringlets from the head of a child, while we steadily held on our course, and under the bows we watched

"The swaying soft,
Made by the delicate wave parted in front,
As through the gentle element we move
Like shadows gliding through untroubled dreams."

The forms of beauty fall naturally around the path of him who is in the performance of his proper work; as the curled shavings drop from the plane, and borings cluster round the auger. Undulation is the gentlest and most ideal of motions, produced by one fluid falling on another. Rippling is a more graceful flight. From a hill-top you may detect in it the wings of birds endlessly repeated. The two *waving* lines which represent the flight of birds appear to have been copied from the ripple.

The trees made an admirable fence to the landscape, skirting the horizon on every side. The single trees and the groves left standing on the interval, appeared naturally disposed, though the farmer had consulted only his convenience, for he too falls into the scheme of Nature. Art can never match the luxury and superfluity of Nature. In the former all is seen; it cannot afford concealed wealth, and is niggardly in comparison; but Nature, even when she is scant and thin outwardly, satisfies us still by the assurance of a certain generosity at the roots. In swamps, where there is only here and there an evergreen tree amid the quaking moss and cranberry beds, the bareness does not suggest poverty. The single-spruce, which I had hardly noticed in gardens, attracts me in such places, and now first I understand why men try to make them grow about their houses. But though there may be very perfect specimens in front-yard plots, their beauty is for the most part ineffectual there, for there is no such assurance of kindred wealth beneath and around them, to make them show to advantage. As we have said, Nature is a greater and more perfect art, the art of God; though, referred to herself, she is genius, and there is a similarity between her operations and man's art even in the details and trifles.

When the overhanging pine drops into the water, by the sun and water, and the wind rubbing it against the shore, its boughs are worn into fantastic shapes, and white and smooth, as if turned in a lathe. Man's art has wisely imitated those forms into which all matter is most inclined to run, as foliage and fruit. A hammock swung in a grove assumes the exact form of a canoe, broader or narrower, and higher or lower at the ends, as more or fewer persons are in it, and it rolls in the air with the motion of the body, like a canoe in the water. Our art leaves its shavings and its dust about; her art exhibits itself even in the shavings and the dust which we make. She has perfected herself by an eternity of practice. The world is well kept; no rubbish accumulates; the morning air is clear even at this day, and no dust has settled on the grass. Behold how the evening now steals over the fields, the shadows of the trees creeping further and further into the meadow, and ere long the stars will come to bathe in these retired waters. Her undertakings are secure and never fail. If I were awakened from a deep sleep, I should know which side of the meridian the sun might be by the aspect of nature, and by the chirp of the crickets, and yet no painter can paint this difference. The landscape contains a thousand dials which indicate the natural divisions of time, the shadows of a thousand styles point to the hour.—

"Not only o'er the dial's face,
This silent phantom day by day,
With slow, unseen, unceasing pace
Steals moments, months, and years away;
From hoary rock and aged tree,
From proud Palmyra's mouldering walls,
From Teneriffe, towering o'er the sea,
From every blade of grass it falls."

It is almost the only game which the trees play at, this tit-for-tat, now this side in the sun, now that, the drama of the day. In deep ravines under the eastern sides of cliffs, Night forwardly plants her foot even at noonday, and as Day retreats she steps into his trenches, skulking from tree to tree, from fence to fence, until at last she sits in his citadel and draws out her forces into the plain. It may be that the forenoon is brighter than the afternoon, not only because of the greater transparency of its atmosphere, but because we naturally look most into the west, as forward into the day, and so in the forenoon see the sunny side of things, but in the afternoon the shadow of every tree.

The afternoon is now far advanced, and a fresh and leisurely wind is blowing over the river, making long reaches of bright ripples. The river has done its stint, and appears not to flow, but lie at its length reflecting the light, and the haze over the woods is like the inaudible panting, or rather the gentle perspiration of resting nature, rising from a myriad of pores into the attenuated atmosphere.

On the thirty-first day of March, one hundred and forty-two years before this, probably about this time in the afternoon, there were hurriedly paddling down this part of the river, between the pine woods which then fringed these banks, two white women and a boy, who had left an island at the mouth of the Contoocook before daybreak. They were slightly clad for the season, in the English fashion, and handled their paddles unskilfully, but with nervous energy and determination, and at the bottom of their canoe lay the still bleeding scalps of ten of the aborigines. They were Hannah Dustan, and her nurse, Mary Neff, both of Haverhill, eighteen miles from the mouth of this river, and an English boy, named Samuel Lennardson, escaping from captivity among the Indians. On the 15th of March previous, Hannah Dustan had been compelled to rise from childbed, and half-dressed, with one foot bare, accompanied by her nurse, commence an uncertain march, in still inclement weather, through the snow and the wilderness. She had seen her seven elder children flee with their father, but knew not of their fate. She had seen her infant's brains dashed out against an apple-tree, and had left her own and her neighbors' dwellings in ashes. When she reached the wigwam of her captor, situated on an island in the Merrimack, more than twenty miles above where we now are, she had been told that she and her nurse were soon to be taken to a distant Indian settlement, and there made to run the gauntlet naked. The family of this Indian consisted of two men, three women, and seven children, beside an English boy, whom she found a prisoner among them. Having determined to attempt her escape, she instructed the boy to inquire of one of the men, how he should dispatch an enemy in the quickest manner, and take his scalp. "Strike 'em there," said he, placing his finger on his temple, and he also showed him how to take off the scalp. On the morning of the 31st she arose before daybreak, and awoke her nurse and the boy, and taking the Indians' tomahawks, they killed them all in their sleep, excepting one favorite boy, and one squaw who fled wounded with him to the woods. The English boy struck the Indian who had given him the information on the temple, as he had been directed. They then collected all the provision they could find, and took their master's tomahawk and gun, and scuttling all the canoes but one, commenced their flight to Haverhill, distant about sixty miles by the river. But after having proceeded a short distance, fearing that her story would not be believed if she should escape to tell it, they returned to the silent wigwam, and taking off the scalps of the dead, put them into a bag as proofs of what they had done, and then retracing their steps to the shore in the twilight, recommenced their voyage.

Early this morning this deed was performed, and now, perchance, these tired women and this boy, their clothes stained with blood, and their minds racked with alternate resolution and fear, are making a hasty meal of parched corn and moose-meat, while their canoe glides under these pine roots whose stumps are still standing on the bank. They are thinking of the dead whom they have left behind on that solitary isle far up the stream, and of the relentless living warriors who are in pursuit. Every withered leaf which the winter has left seems to know their story, and in its rustling to repeat it and betray them. An Indian lurks behind every rock and pine, and their nerves cannot bear the tapping of a woodpecker. Or they forget their own dangers and their deeds in conjecturing the fate of their kindred, and whether, if they escape the Indians, they shall find the former still alive. They do not stop to cook their meals upon the bank, nor land, except to carry their canoe about the falls. The stolen birch forgets its master and does them good service, and the swollen current bears them swiftly along with little need of the paddle, except to steer and keep them warm by exercise. For ice is floating in the river; the spring is opening; the muskrat and the beaver are driven out of their holes by the flood; deer gaze at them from the bank; a few faint-singing forest birds, perchance, fly across the river to the northernmost shore; the fish-hawk sails and screams overhead, and geese fly over with a startling clangor; but they do not observe these things, or they speedily forget them. They do not smile or chat all day. Sometimes they pass an Indian grave surrounded by its paling on the bank, or the frame of a wigwam, with a few coals left behind, or the withered stalks still rustling in the Indian's solitary cornfield on the interval. The birch stripped of its bark, or the charred stump where a tree has been burned down to be made into a canoe, these are the only traces of man,—a fabulous wild man to us. On either side, the primeval forest stretches away uninterrupted to Canada or to the "South Sea;" to the white man a drear and howling wilderness, but to the Indian a home, adapted to his nature, and cheerful as the smile of the Great Spirit.

While we loiter here this autumn evening, looking for a spot retired enough, where we shall quietly rest to-night, they thus, in that chilly March evening, one hundred and forty-two years before us, with wind and current favoring, have already glided out of sight, not to camp, as we shall, at night, but while two sleep one will manage the canoe, and the swift stream bear them onward to the settlements, it may be, even to old John Lovewell's house on Salmon Brook to-night.

According to the historian, they escaped as by a miracle all roving bands of Indians, and reached their homes in safety, with their trophies, for which the General Court paid them fifty pounds. The family of Hannah Dustan all assembled alive once more, except the infant whose brains were dashed out against the apple-tree, and there have been many who in later times have lived to say that they had eaten of the fruit of that apple-tree.

This seems a long while ago, and yet it happened since Milton wrote his Paradise Lost. But its antiquity is not the less great for that, for we do not regulate our historical time by the English standard, nor did the English by the Roman, nor the Roman by the Greek. "We must look a long way back," says Raleigh, "to find the Romans giving laws to nations, and their consuls bringing kings and princes bound in chains to Rome in triumph; to see men go to Greece for wisdom, or Ophir for gold; when now nothing remains but a poor paper remembrance of their former condition."—And yet, in one sense, not so far back as to find the Penacooks and Pawtuckets using bows and arrows and hatchets of stone, on the banks of the Merrimack. From this September afternoon, and from between these now cultivated shores, those times seemed more remote than the dark ages. On beholding an old picture of Concord, as it appeared but seventy-five years ago, with a fair open prospect and a light on trees and river, as if it were broad noon, I find that I had not thought the sun shone in those days, or that men lived in broad daylight then. Still less do we imagine the sun shining on hill and valley during Philip's war, on the war-path of Church or Philip, or later of Lovewell or Paugus, with serene summer weather, but they must have lived and fought in a dim twilight or night.

The age of the world is great enough for our imaginations, even according to the Mosaic account, without borrowing any years from the geologist. From

Adam and Eve at one leap sheer down to the deluge, and then through the ancient monarchies, through Babylon and Thebes, Brahma and Abraham, to Greece and the Argonauts; whence we might start again with Orpheus and the Trojan war, the Pyramids and the Olympic games, and Homer and Athens, for our stages; and after a breathing space at the building of Rome, continue our journey down through Odin and Christ to——America. It is a wearisome while.–And yet the lives of but sixty old women, such as live under the hill, say of a century each, strung together, are sufficient to reach over the whole ground. Taking hold of hands they would span the interval from Eve to my own mother. A respectable tea-party merely,–whose gossip would be Universal History. The fourth old woman from myself suckled Columbus,–the ninth was nurse to the Norman Conqueror,–the nineteenth was the Virgin Mary, –the twenty-fourth the Cumæan Sibyl,–the thirtieth was at the Trojan war and Helen her name,–the thirty-eighth was Queen Semiramis,–the sixtieth was Eve the mother of mankind. So much for the

—"old woman that lives under the hill,
And if she's not gone she lives there still."

It will not take a very great grand-daughter of hers to be in at the death of Time.

We can never safely exceed the actual facts in our narratives. Of pure invention, such as some suppose, there is no instance. To write a true work of fiction even, is only to take leisure and liberty to describe some things more exactly as they are. A true account of the actual is the rarest poetry, for common sense always takes a hasty and superficial view. Though I am not much acquainted with the works of Goethe, I should say that it was one of his chief excellencies as a writer, that he was satisfied with giving an exact description of things as they appeared to him, and their effect upon him. Most travellers have not self-respect enough to do this simply, and make objects and events stand around them as the centre, but still imagine more favorable positions and relations than the actual ones, and so we get no valuable report from them at all. In his Italian Travels Goethe jogs along at a snail's pace, but always mindful that the earth is beneath and the heavens are above him. His Italy is not merely the fatherland of lazzaroni and virtuosi, and scene of splendid ruins, but a solid turf-clad soil, daily shined on by the sun, and nightly by the moon. Even the few showers are faithfully recorded. He speaks as an unconcerned spectator, whose object is faithfully to describe what he sees, and that, for the most part, in the order in which he sees it. Even his reflections do not interfere with his descriptions. In one place he speaks of himself as giving so glowing and truthful a description of an old tower to the peasants who had gathered around him, that they who had been born and brought up in the neighborhood must needs look over their shoulders, "that," to use his own words, "they might behold with their eyes, what I had praised to their ears"——"and I added nothing, not even the ivy which for centuries had decorated the walls." It would thus be possible for inferior minds to produce invaluable books, if this very moderation were not the evidence of superiority; for the wise are not so much wiser than others as respecters of their own wisdom. Some, poor in spirit, record plaintively only what has happened to them; but others how they have happened to the universe, and the judgment which they have awarded to circumstances. Above all, he possessed a hearty good-will to all men, and never wrote a cross or even careless word. On one occasion the post-boy snivelling "Signor perdonate, quésta è la mia patria," he confesses that "to me poor northerner came something tear-like into the eyes."

Goethe's whole education and life were those of the artist. He lacks the unconsciousness of the poet. In his autobiography he describes accurately the life of the author of Wilhelm Meister. For as there is in that book, mingled with a rare and serene wisdom, a certain pettiness or exaggeration of trifles, wisdom applied to produce a constrained and partial and merely well-bred man,—a magnifying of the theatre till life itself is turned into a stage, for which it is our duty to study our parts well, and conduct with propriety and precision,—so in the autobiography, the fault of his education is, so to speak, its merely artistic completeness. Nature is hindered, though she prevails at last in making an unusually catholic impression on the boy. It is the life of a city boy, whose toys are pictures and works of art, whose wonders are the theatre and kingly processions and crownings. As the youth studied minutely the order and the degrees in the imperial procession, and suffered none of its effect to be lost on him; so the man aimed to secure a rank in society which would satisfy his notion of fitness and respectability. He was defrauded of much which the savage boy enjoys. Indeed he himself has occasion to say in this very autobiography, when at last he escapes into the woods without the gates,—"Thus much is certain, that only the undefinable, wide-expanding feelings of youth and of uncultivated nations are adapted to the sublime, which, whenever it may be excited in us through external objects, since it is either formless, or else moulded into forms which are incomprehensible, must surround us with a grandeur which we find above our reach." He further says of himself,–"I had lived among painters from my childhood, and had accustomed myself to look at objects, as they did, with reference to art." And this was his practice to the last. He was even too *well-bred* to be thoroughly bred. He says that he had had no intercourse with the lowest class of his towns-boys. The child should have the advantage of ignorance as well as of knowledge, and is fortunate if he gets his share of neglect and exposure.–

"The laws of Nature break the rules of Art.

The Man of Genius may at the same time be, indeed is commonly, an Artist, but the two are not to be confounded. The Man of Genius, referred to mankind, is an originator, an inspired or demonic man, who produces a perfect work in obedience to laws yet unexplored. The Artist is he who detects and applies the law from observation of the works of Genius, whether of man or nature. The Artisan is he who merely applies the rules which others have detected. There has been no man of pure Genius; as there has been none wholly destitute of Genius.

Poetry is the mysticism of mankind.

The expressions of the poet cannot be analyzed; his sentence is one word, whose syllables are words. There are indeed no *words* quite worthy to be set to his music. But what matter if we do not hear the words always, if we hear the music?

Much verse fails of being poetry because it was not written exactly at the right crisis, though it may have been inconceivably near to it. It is only by a miracle that poetry is written at all. It is not recoverable thought, but a hue caught from a vaster receding thought.

A poem is one undivided unimpeded expression fallen ripe into literature, and it is undividedly and unimpededly received by those for whom it was matured.

If you can speak what you will never hear,–if you can write what you will never read, you have done rare things.

> The work we choose should be our own,
> God lets alone.

The unconsciousness of man is the consciousness of God.

Deep are the foundations of sincerity. Even stone walls have their foundation below the frost.

What is produced by a free stroke charms us, like the forms of lichens and leaves. There is a certain perfection in accident which we never consciously attain. Draw a blunt quill filled with ink over a sheet of paper, and fold the paper before the ink is dry transversely to this line, and a delicately shaded and regular figure will be produced, in some respects more pleasing than an elaborate drawing.

The talent of composition is very dangerous,–the striking out the heart of life at a blow, as the Indian takes off a scalp. I feel as if my life had grown more outward when I can express it.

On his journey from Brenner to Verona, Goethe writes, "The Tees flows now more gently, and makes in many places broad sands. On the land, near to the water, upon the hill-sides, every thing is so closely planted one to another, that you think they must choke one another,–vineyards, maize, mulberry-trees, apples, pears, quinces and nuts. The dwarf elder throws itself vigorously over the walls. Ivy grows with strong stems up the rocks, and spreads itself wide over them, the lizard glides through the intervals, and every thing that wanders to and fro reminds one of the loveliest pictures of art. The women's tufts of hair bound up, the men's bare breasts and light jackets, the excellent oxen which they drive home from market, the little asses with their loads,–every thing forms a living, animated Heinrich Roos. And now that it is evening, in the mild air a few clouds rest upon the mountains, in the heavens more stand still than move, and immediately after sunset the chirping of crickets begins to grow more loud; then one feels for once at home in the world, and not as concealed or in exile. I am contented as though I had been born and brought up here, and were now returning from a Greenland or whaling voyage. Even the dust of my Fatherland, which is often whirled about the wagon, and which for so long a time I had not seen, is greeted. The clock-and-bell jingling of the crickets is altogether lovely, penetrating, and agreeable. It sounds bravely when roguish boys whistle in emulation of a field of such songstresses. One fancies that they really enhance one another. Also the evening is perfectly mild as the day."

"If one who dwelt in the south and came hither from the south, should hear of my rapture hereupon, he would deem me very childish. Alas! what I here express I have long known while I suffered under an unpropitious heaven, and now may I joyful feel this joy as an exception, which we should enjoy everforth as an eternal necessity of our nature."

Thus we "sayled by thought and pleasaunce," as Chaucer says, and all things seemed with us to flow; the shore itself, and the distant cliffs, were dissolved by the undiluted air. The hardest material seemed to obey the same law with the most fluid, and so indeed in the long run it does. Trees were but rivers of sap and woody fibre, flowing from the atmosphere, and emptying into the earth by their trunks, as their roots flowed upward to the surface. And in the heavens there were rivers of stars, and milky-ways, already beginning to gleam and ripple over our heads. There were rivers of rock on the surface of the earth, and rivers of ore in its bowels, and our thoughts flowed and circulated, and this portion of time was but the current hour. Let us wander where we will, the universe is built round about us, and we are central still. If we look into the heavens they are concave, and if we were to look into a gulf as bottomless, it would be concave also. The sky is curved downward to the earth in the horizon, because we stand on the plain. I draw down its skirts. The stars so low there seem loth to depart, but by a circuitous path to be remembering me, and returning on their steps.

We had already passed by broad daylight the scene of our encampment at Coos Falls, and at length we pitched our camp on the west bank, in the northern part of Merrimack, nearly opposite to the large island on which we had spent the noon in our way up the river.

There we went to bed that summer evening, on a sloping shelf in the bank, a couple of rods from our boat, which was drawn up on the sand, and just behind a thin fringe of oaks which bordered the river; without having disturbed any inhabitants but the spiders in the grass, which came out by the light of our lamp and crawled over our buffaloes. When we looked out from under the tent, the trees were seen dimly through the mist, and a cool dew hung upon the grass, which seemed to rejoice in the night, and with the damp air we inhaled a solid fragrance. Having eaten our supper of hot cocoa and bread and water-melon, we soon grew weary of conversing and writing in our journals, and putting out the lantern which hung from the tent pole, fell asleep.

Unfortunately many things have been omitted which should have been recorded in our journal, for though we made it a rule to set down all our experiences therein, yet such a resolution is very hard to keep, for the important experience rarely allows us to remember such obligations, and so indifferent things get recorded, while that is frequently neglected. It is not easy to write in a journal what interests us at any time, because to write it is not what interests us.

Whenever we awoke in the night, still eking out our dreams with half-awakened thoughts, it was not till after an interval, when the wind breathed harder than usual, flapping the curtains of the tent, and causing its cords to vibrate, that we remembered that we lay on the bank of the Merrimack, and not in our chamber at home. With our heads so low in the grass, we heard the river whirling and sucking, and lapsing downward, kissing the shore as it went, sometimes rippling louder than usual, and again its mighty current making only a slight limpid trickling sound, as if our water-pail had sprung a leak, and the water were flowing into the grass by our side. The wind, rustling the oaks and hazels, impressed us like a wakeful and inconsiderate person up at midnight, moving about and putting things to rights, occasionally stirring up whole drawers full of leaves at a puff. There seemed to be a great haste and preparation throughout Nature, as for a distinguished visitor; all her aisles had to be swept in the night, by a thousand hand-maidens, and a thousand pots to be boiled for the next day's feasting;—such a whispering bustle, as if ten thousand fairies made their fingers fly, silently sewing at the new carpet with which the earth was to be clothed, and the new drapery which was to adorn the trees. And then the wind would lull and die away, and we like it fell asleep again.

Friday.

> "The Boteman strayt
> Held on his course with stayed stedfastnesse,
> Ne ever shroncke, ne ever sought to bayt
> His tryed armes for toylesome wearinesse;
> But with his oares did sweepe the watry
> wildernesse."
>
> *Spenser.*

> "Summer's robe grows
> Dusky, and like an oft-dyed garment shows."
>
> *Donne.*

As we lay awake long before day-break, listening to the rippling of the river and the rustling of the leaves, in suspense whether the wind blew up or down the stream, was favorable or unfavorable to our voyage, we already suspected that there was a change in the weather, from a freshness as of autumn in these sounds. The wind in the woods sounded like an incessant waterfall dashing and roaring amid rocks, and we even felt encouraged by the unusual activity of the elements. He who hears the rippling of rivers in these degenerate days will not utterly despair. That night was the turning point in the season. We had gone to bed in summer, and we awoke in autumn; for summer passes into autumn in some unimaginable point of time, like the turning of a leaf.

We found our boat in the dawn just as we had left it, and as if waiting for us, there on the shore, in autumn, all cool and dripping with dew, and our tracks still fresh in the wet sand around it, the fairies all gone or concealed. Before five o'clock we pushed it into the fog, and leaping in, at one shove were out of sight of the shores, and began to sweep downward with the rushing river, keeping a sharp look-out for rocks. We could see only the yellow gurgling water, and a solid bank of fog on every side forming a small yard around us. We soon passed the mouth of the Souhegan and the village of Merrimack, and as the mist gradually rolled away, and we were relieved from the trouble of watching for rocks, we saw by the flitting clouds, by the first russet tinge on the hills, by the rushing river, the cottages on shore, and the shore itself, so coolly fresh and shining with dew, and later in the day, by the hue of the grape vine, the goldfinch on the willow, the flickers flying in flocks, and when we passed near enough to the shore, as we fancied, by the faces of men, that the Fall had commenced. The cottages looked more snug and comfortable, and their inhabitants were seen only for a moment, and then went quietly in and shut the door, retreating inward to the haunts of summer.

> "And now the cold autumnal dews are seen
>   To cobweb ev'ry green;
> And by the low-shorn rowens doth appear
>   The fast declining year."

We heard the sigh of the first autumnal wind, and even the water had acquired a greyer hue. The sumach, grape, and maple were already changed, and the milkweed had turned to a deep rich yellow. In all woods the leaves were fast ripening for their fall; for their full veins and lively gloss mark the ripe leaf, and not the sered one of the poets; and we knew that the maples, stripped of their leaves among the earliest, would soon stand like a wreath of smoke along the edge of the meadow. Already the cattle were heard to low wildly in the pastures and along the highways, restlessly running to and fro, as if in apprehension of the withering of the grass and of the approach of winter. Our thoughts too began to rustle.

As I pass along the streets of our village of Concord on the day of our annual Cattle-Show, when it usually happens that the leaves of the elms and buttonwoods begin first to strew the ground under the breath of the October wind, the lively spirits in their sap seem to mount as high as any plow-boy's let loose that day; and they lead my thoughts away to the rustling woods, where the trees are preparing for their winter campaign. This autumnal festival, when men are gathered in crowds in the streets as regularly and by as natural a law as the leaves cluster and rustle by the way-side, is naturally associated in my mind with the fall of the year. The low of cattle in the streets sounds like a hoarse symphony or running base to the rustling of the leaves. The wind goes hurrying down the country, gleaning every loose straw that is left in the fields, while every farmer lad too appears to scud before it,—having donned his best pea-jacket and pepper and salt waistcoat, his unbent trousers, outstanding rigging of duck, or kersymere, or corduroy, and his furry hat withal,—to country fairs and cattle-shows, to that Rome among the villages where the treasures of the year are gathered. All the land over they go leaping the fences with their tough idle palms, which have never learned to hang by their sides, amid the low of calves and the bleating of sheep,—Amos, Abner, Elnathan, Elbridge,—

"From steep pine-bearing mountains to the plain."

I love these sons of earth every mother's son of them, with their great hearty hearts rushing tumultuously in herds from spectacle to spectacle, as if fearful lest there should not be time between sun and sun to see them all, and the sun does not wait more than in haying time.

> "Wise nature's darlings, they live in the world
> Perplexing not themselves how it is hurled."

Running hither and thither with appetite for the coarse pastimes of the day, now with boisterous speed at the heels of the inspired negro from whose larynx the melodies of all Congo and Guinea coast have broke loose into our streets; now to see the procession of a hundred yoke of oxen, all as august and grave as Osiris, or the droves of neat cattle and milch cows as unspotted as Isis or Io. Such as had no love for Nature

> "at all,
> Came lovers home from this great festival."

They may bring their fattest cattle and richest fruits to the fair, but they are all eclipsed by the show of men. These are stirring autumn days, when men sweep by in crowds, amid the rustle of leaves, like migrating finches, this is the true harvest of the year, when the air is but the breath of men, and the rustling of leaves is as the trampling of the crowd. We read now-a-days of the ancient festivals, games, and processions of the Greeks and Etruscans, with a little incredulity, or at least with little sympathy; but how natural and irrepressible in every people is some hearty and palpable greeting of Nature. The Corybantes, the Bacchantes, the rude primitive tragedians with their procession and goat-song, and the whole paraphernalia of the Panathenæa, which appear so antiquated and peculiar, have their parallel now. The husbandman is always a better Greek than the scholar is prepared to appreciate, and the old custom still survives, while antiquarians and scholars grow gray in commemorating it. The farmers crowd to the fair today in obedience to the same ancient law, which Solon or Lycurgus did not enact, as naturally as bees swarm and follow their queen.

It is worth the while to see the country's people, how they pour into the town, the sober farmer folk, now all agog, their very shirt and coat collars pointing forward,–collars so broad as if they had put their shirts on wrong end upward, for the fashions always tend to superfluity,–and with an unusual springiness in their gait, jabbering earnestly to one another. The more supple vagabond, too, is sure to appear on the least rumor of such a gathering, and the next day to disappear, and go into his hole like the seventeen-year locust, in an ever shabby coat, though finer than the farmer's best, yet never dressed; come to see the sport, and have a hand in what is going,–to know "what's the row," if there is any; to be where some men are drunk, some horses race, some cockerels fight; anxious to be shaking props under a table, and above all to see the "striped pig." He especially is the creature of the occasion. He empties both his pockets and his character into the stream, and swims in such a day. He dearly loves the social slush. There is no reserve of soberness in him.

I love to see the herd of men feeding heartily on coarse and succulent pleasures, as cattle on the husks and stalks of vegetables. Though there are many crooked and crabbled specimens of humanity among them, run all to thorn and rind, and crowded out of shape by adverse circumstances, like the third chestnut in the burr, so that you wonder to see some heads wear a whole hat, yet fear not that the race will fail or waver in them; like the crabs which grow in hedges, they furnish the stocks of sweet and thrifty fruits still. Thus is nature recruited from age to age, while the fair and palatable varieties die out and have their period. This is that mankind. How cheap must be the material of which so many men are made.

The wind blew steadily down the stream, so that we kept our sails set, and lost not a moment of the forenoon by delays, but from early morning until noon, were continually dropping downward. With our hands on the steering paddle, which was thrust deep into the river, or bending to the oar, which indeed we rarely relinquished, we felt each palpitation in the veins of our steed, and each impulse of the wings which drew us above. The current of our thoughts made as sudden bends as the river, which was continually opening new prospects to the east or south, but we are aware that rivers flow most rapidly and shallowest at these points. The steadfast shores never once turned aside for us, but still trended as they were made; why then should we always turn aside for them?

A man cannot wheedle nor overawe his Genius. It requires to be conciliated by nobler conduct than the world demands or can appreciate. These winged thoughts are like birds, and will not be handled; even hens will not let you touch them like quadrupeds. Nothing was ever so unfamiliar and startling to a man as his own thoughts.

To the rarest genius it is the most expensive to succumb and conform to the ways of the world. Genius is the worst of lumber, if the poet would float upon the breeze of popularity. The bird of paradise is obliged constantly to fly against the wind, lest its gay trappings, pressing close to its body, may impede its free movements.

He is the best sailor who can steer within the fewest points of the wind, and extract a motive power out of the greatest obstacles. Most begin to veer and tack as soon as the wind changes from aft, and as within the tropics it does not blow from all points of the compass, there are some harbors which they can never reach.

The poet is no tender slip of fairy stock, who requires peculiar institutions and edicts for his defence, but the toughest son of earth and of Heaven, and by his greater strength and endurance his fainting companions will recognize the God in him. It is the worshippers of beauty, after all, who have done the real pioneer work of the world.

The poet will prevail to be popular in spite of his faults, and in spite of his beauties too. He will hit the nail on the head, and we shall not know the shape of his hammer. He makes us free of his hearth and heart, which is greater than to offer one the freedom of a city.

Great men, unknown to their generation, have their fame among the great who have preceded them, and all true worldly fame subsides from their high estimate beyond the stars.

Orpheus does not hear the strains which issue from his lyre, but only those which are breathed into it; for the original strain precedes the sound, by as much as the echo follows after; the rest is the perquisite of the rocks and trees and beasts.

When I stand in a library where is all the recorded wit of the world, but none of the recording, a mere accumulated, and not truly cumulative treasure, where immortal works stand side by side with anthologies which did not survive their month, and cobweb and mildew have already spread from these to the binding of those; and happily I am reminded of what poetry is, I perceive that Shakspeare and Milton did not foresee into what company they were to fall. Alas! that so soon the work of a true poet should be swept into such a dust-hole!

The poet will write for his peers alone. He will remember only that he saw truth and beauty from his position, and expect the time when a vision as broad shall overlook the same field as freely.

We are often prompted to speak our thoughts to our neighbors, or the single travellers whom we meet on the road, but poetry is a communication from our home and solitude addressed to all Intelligence. It never whispers in a private ear. Knowing this, we may understand those sonnets said to be addressed to particular persons, or "to a Mistress' Eyebrow." Let none feel flattered by them. For poetry write love, and it will be equally true.

No doubt it is an important difference between men of genius or poets, and men not of genius, that the latter are unable to grasp and confront the thought which visits them. But it is because it is too faint for expression, or even conscious impression. What merely quickens or retards the blood in their veins and fills their afternoons with pleasure they know not whence, conveys a distinct assurance to the finer organization of the poet.

We talk of genius as if it were a mere knack, and the poet could only express what other men conceived. But in comparison with his task, the poet is the least talented of any; the writer of prose has more skill. See what talent the smith has. His material is pliant in his hands. When the poet is most inspired, is stimulated by an *aura* which never even colors the afternoons of common men, then his talent is all gone, and he is no longer a poet. The gods do not grant him any skill more than another. They never put their gifts into his hands, but they encompass and sustain him with their breath.

To say that God has given a man many and great talents, frequently means, that he has brought his heavens down within reach of his hands.

When the poetic frenzy seizes us, we run and scratch with our pen, intent only on worms, calling our mates around us, like the cock, and delighting in the dust we make, but do not detect where the jewel lies, which, perhaps, we have in the mean time cast to a distance, or quite covered up again.

The poet's body even is not fed like other men's, but he sometimes tastes the genuine nectar and ambrosia of the gods, and lives a divine life. By the healthful and invigorating thrills of inspiration his life is preserved to a serene old age.

Some poems are for holidays only. They are polished and sweet, but it is the sweetness of sugar, and not such as toil gives to sour bread. The breath with which the poet utters his verse must be that by which he lives.

Great prose, of equal elevation, commands our respect more than great verse, since it implies a more permanent and level height, a life more pervaded with the grandeur of the thought. The poet often only makes an irruption, like a Parthian, and is off again, shooting while he retreats; but the prose writer has conquered like a Roman, and settled colonies.

The true poem is not that which the public read. There is always a poem not printed on paper, coincident with the production of this, stereotyped in the poet's life. It is *what he has become through his work.* Not how is the idea expressed in stone, or on canvass or paper, is the question, but how far it has obtained form and expression in the life of the artist. His true work will not stand in any prince's gallery.

My life has been the poem I would have writ,
But I could not both live and utter it.

THE POET'S DELAY.

In vain I see the morning rise,
In vain observe the western blaze,
Who idly look to other skies,
Expecting life by other ways.

Amidst such boundless wealth without,
I only still am poor within,
The birds have sung their summer out,
But still my spring does not begin.

Shall I then wait the autumn wind,
Compelled to seek a milder day,
And leave no curious nest behind,
No woods still echoing to my lay?

This raw and gusty day, and the creaking of the oaks and pines on shore, reminded us of more northern climes than Greece, and more wintry seas than the Ægean.

The genuine remains of Ossian, or those ancient poems which bear his name, though of less fame and extent, are, in many respects, of the same stamp with the Iliad itself. He asserts the dignity of the bard no less than Homer, and in his era we hear of no other priest than he. It will not avail to call him a heathen, because he personifies the sun and addresses it; and what if his heroes did "worship the ghosts of their fathers," their thin, airy, and unsubstantial forms? we but worship the ghosts of our fathers in more substantial forms. We cannot but respect the vigorous faith of those heathen, who sternly believed somewhat, and we are inclined to say to the critics, who are offended by their superstitious rites,–Don't interrupt these men's prayers. As if we knew more about human life and a God, than the heathen and ancients. Does English theology contain the recent discoveries?

Ossian reminds us of the most refined and rudest eras, of Homer, Pindar, Isaiah, and the American Indian. In his poetry, as in Homer's, only the simplest and most enduring features of humanity are seen, such essential parts of a man as Stonehenge exhibits of a temple; we see the circles of stone, and the upright shaft alone. The phenomena of life acquire almost an unreal and gigantic size seen through his mists. Like all older and grander poetry, it is distinguished by the few elements in the lives of its heroes. They stand on the heath, between the stars and the earth, shrunk to the bones and sinews. The earth is a boundless plain for their deeds. They lead such a simple, dry, and everlasting life, as hardly needs depart with the flesh, but is transmitted entire from age to age. There are but few objects to distract their sight, and their life is as unincumbered as the course of the stars they gaze at.–

"The wrathful kings, on cairns apart,
Look forward from behind their shields,
And mark the wandering stars,
That brilliant westward move."

It does not cost much for these heroes to live; they do not want much furniture. They are such forms of men only as can be seen afar through the mist, and have no costume nor dialect, but for language there is the tongue itself, and for costume there are always the skins of beasts and the bark of trees to be had. They live out their years by the vigor of their constitutions. They survive storms and the spears of their foes, and perform a few heroic deeds, and then,

> "Mounds will answer questions of them,
> For many future years."

Blind and infirm, they spend the remnant of their days listening to the lays of the bards, and feeling the weapons which laid their enemies low, and when at length they die, by a convulsion of nature, the bard allows us a short and misty glance into futurity, yet as clear, perchance, as their lives had been. When Mac-Roine was slain,

> "His soul departed to his warlike sires,
> To follow misty forms of boars,
> In tempestuous islands bleak."

The hero's cairn is erected, and the bard sings a brief significant strain, which will suffice for epitaph and biography.

> "The weak will find his bow in the dwelling,
> The feeble will attempt to bend it."

Compared with this simple, fibrous life, our civilized history appears the chronicle of debility, of fashion, and the arts of luxury. But the civilized man misses no real refinement in the poetry of the rudest era. It reminds him that civilization does but dress men. It makes shoes, but it does not toughen the soles of the feet. It makes cloth of finer texture, but it does not touch the skin. Inside the civilized man stands the savage still in the place of honor. We are those blue-eyed, yellow-haired Saxons, those slender, dark-haired Normans.

The profession of the bard attracted more respect in those days from the importance attached to fame. It was his province to record the deeds of heroes. When Ossian hears the traditions of inferior bards, he exclaims,–

> "I straightway seize the unfutile tales,
> And send them down in faithful verse."

His philosophy of life is expressed in the opening of the third Duan of Ca-Lodin.

> "Whence have sprung the things that are?
> And whither roll the passing years?
> Where does Time conceal its two heads,
> In dense impenetrable gloom,
> Its surface marked with heroes' deeds alone?
> I view the generations gone;
> The past appears but dim;
> As objects by the moon's faint beams,
> Reflected from a distant lake.
> I see, indeed, the thunderbolts of war,
> But there the unmighty joyless dwell,
> All those who send not down their deeds
> To far, succeeding times."

The ignoble warriors die and are forgotten;

> "Strangers come to build a tower,
> And throw their ashes overhand;
> Some rusted swords appear in dust;
> One, bending forward, says,
> 'The arms belonged to heroes gone;
> We never heard their praise in song.' "

The grandeur of the similes is another feature which characterizes great poetry. Ossian seems to speak a gigantic and universal language. The images and pictures occupy even much space in the landscape, as if they could be seen only from the sides of mountains, and plains with a wide horizon, or across arms of the sea. The machinery is so massive that it cannot be less than natural. Oivana says to the spirit of her father, "Grey-haired Torkil of Torne," seen in the skies,

> "Thou glidest away like receding ships."

So when the hosts of Fingal and Starne approach to battle,

> "With murmurs loud, like rivers far,
> The race of Torne hither moved."

And when compelled to retire,

> —"dragging his spear behind,
> Cudulin sank in the distant wood,
> Like a fire upblazing ere it dies."

Nor did Fingal want a proper audience when he spoke;

> "A thousand orators inclined
> To hear the lay of Fingal."

The threats too would have deterred a man. Vengeance and terror were real. Trenmore threatens the young warrior whom he meets on a foreign strand,

> "Thy mother shall find thee pale on the shore,
> While lessening on the waves she spies
> The sails of him who slew her son."

If Ossian's heroes weep, it is from excess of strength, and not from weakness, a sacrifice or libation of fertile natures, like the perspiration of stone in summer's heat. We hardly know that tears have been shed, and it seems as if weeping were proper only for babes and heroes. Their joy and their sorrow are made of one stuff, like rain and snow, the rainbow and the mist. When Fillan was worsted in fight, and ashamed in the presence of Fingal,

"He strode away forthwith,
And bent in grief above a stream,
His cheeks bedewed with tears.
From time to time the thistles gray
He lopped with his inverted lance."

Crodar, blind and old, receives Ossian, son of Fingal, who comes to aid him in war;–

" 'My eyes have failed,' says he, 'Crodar is blind,
Is thy strength like that of thy fathers?
Stretch, Ossian, thine arm to the hoary-haired.'
I gave my arm to the king.
The aged hero seized my hand;
He heaved a heavy sigh;
Tears flowed incessant down his cheek.
'Strong art thou, son of the mighty,
Though not so dreadful as Morven's prince. * * *
Let my feast be spread in the hall,
Let every sweet-voiced minstrel sing;
Great is he who is within my wall,
Sons of wave-echoing Croma.' "

Even Ossian himself, the hero-bard, pays tribute to the superior strength of his father Fingal.

"How beauteous, mighty man, was thy mind,
Why succeeded Ossian without its strength?"

While we sailed fleetly before the wind, with the river gurgling under our stern, the thoughts of autumn coursed as steadily through our minds, and we observed less what was passing on the shore, than the dateless associations and impressions which the season awakened, anticipating in some measure the progress of the year.—

I hearing get, who had but ears,
  And sight, who had but eyes before,
I moments live, who lived but years,
  And truth discern, who knew but learning's lore.

Sitting with our faces now up stream, we studied the landscape by degrees, as one unrolls a map, rock, tree, house, hill, and meadow, assuming new and varying positions as wind and water shifted the scene, and there was variety enough for our entertainment in the metamorphoses of the simplest objects. Viewed from this side the scenery appeared new to us.

The most familiar sheet of water viewed from a new hill-top, yields a novel and unexpected pleasure. When we have travelled a few miles, we do not recognize the profiles even of the hills which overlook our native village, and perhaps no man is quite familiar with the horizon as seen from the hill nearest to his house, and can recall its outline distinctly when in the valley. We do not commonly know, beyond a short distance, which way the hills range which take in our houses and farms in their sweep. As if our birth had at first sundered things, and we had been thrust up through into nature like a wedge, and not till the wound heals and the scar disappears, do we begin to discover where we are, and that nature is one and continuous every where. It is an important epoch when a man who has always lived on the east side of a mountain, and seen it in the west, travels round and sees it in the east. Yet the universe is a sphere whose center is wherever there is intelligence. The sun is not so central as a man. Upon an isolated hill-top, in an open country, we seem to ourselves to be standing on the boss of an immense shield, the immediate landscape being apparently depressed below the more remote, and rising gradually to the horizon, which is the rim of the shield, villas, steeples, forests, mountains, one above another, till they are swallowed up in the heavens. The most distant mountains appear to rise directly from the shore of that lake in the woods by which we chance to be standing, while from the mountain top, not only this, but a thousand nearer and larger lakes, are equally unobserved.

Seen through this clear atmosphere, the works of the farmer, his plowing and reaping, had a beauty to our eyes which he never saw. How fortunate were we who did not own an acre of these shores, who had not renounced our title to the whole. One who knew how to appropriate the true value of this world would be the poorest man in it. The poor rich man! all he has is what he has bought. What I see is mine. I am a large owner in the Merrimack intervals.–

Men dig and dive but cannot my wealth spend,
Who yet no partial store appropriate,
Who no armed ship into the Indies send,
To rob me of my orient estate.

He is the rich man, and enjoys the fruits of riches, who summer and winter forever can find delight in his own thoughts. Buy a farm! What have I to pay for a farm which a farmer will take?

When I visit again some haunt of my youth, I am glad to find that nature wears so well. The landscape is indeed something real, and solid, and sincere, and I have not put my foot through it yet. There is a pleasant tract on the bank of the Concord, called Conantum, which I have in my mind;–the old deserted farm-house, the desolate pasture with its bleak cliff, the open wood, the river-reach, the green meadow in the midst, and the moss-grown wild-apple orchard,—places where one may have many thoughts and not decide any thing. It is a scene which I can not only remember, as I might a vision, but when I will can bodily revisit, and find it even so, unaccountable, yet unpretending in its pleasant dreariness. When my thoughts are sensible of change, I love to see and sit on rocks which I *have* known, and pry into their moss, and see unchangeableness so established. I not yet gray on rocks forever gray, I no longer green under the evergreens. There is something even in the lapse of time by which time recovers itself.

As we have said, it proved a cool as well as breezy day, and by the time we reached Penichook Brook, we were obliged to sit muffled in our cloaks, while the wind and current carried us along. We bounded swiftly over the rippling surface, far by many cultivated lands and the ends of fences which divided innumerable farms, with hardly a thought for the various lives which they separated; now by long rows of alders or groves of pines or oaks, and now by some homestead where the women and children stood outside to gaze at us, till we had swept out of their sight, and beyond the limit of their longest Saturday ramble. We glided past the mouth of the Nashua, and not long after, of Salmon Brook, without more pause than the wind.—

Salmon Brook,
Penichook,
Ye sweet waters of my brain,
When shall I look,
Or cast the hook,
In your waves again?

Silver eels,
Wooden creels,
These the baits that still allure,
And dragon-fly
That floated by,–
May they still endure?

The shadows chased one another swiftly over wood and meadow, and their alternation harmonized with our mood. We could distinguish the clouds which cast each one, though never so high in the heavens. When a shadow flits across the landscape of the soul, where is the substance? Probably, if we were wise enough, we should see to what virtue we are indebted for any happier moment we enjoy. No doubt we have earned it at some time; for the gifts of Heaven are never quite gratuitous. The constant abrasion and decay of our lives makes the soil of our future growth. The wood which we now mature, when it becomes virgin mould, determines the character of our second growth, whether that be oaks or pines. Every man casts a shadow; not his body only, but his imperfectly mingled spirit; this is his grief; let him turn which way he will, it falls opposite to the sun; short at noon, long at eve. Did you never see it?–But, referred to the sun, it is widest at its base, which is no greater than his own opacity. The divine light is diffused almost entirely around us, and by means of the refraction of light, or else by a certain self-luminousness, or, as some will have it, transparency, if we preserve ourselves untarnished, we are able to enlighten our shaded side. At any rate, our darkest grief has that bronze color of the moon eclipsed. There is no ill which may not be dissipated, like the dark, if you let in a stronger light upon it. Shadows, referred to the source of light, are pyramids whose bases are never greater than those of the substances which cast them, but light is a spherical congeries of pyramids, whose very apexes are the sun itself, and hence the system shines with uninterrupted light. But if the light we use is but a paltry and narrow taper, most objects will cast a shadow wider than themselves.

The places where we had stopped or spent the night in our way up the river, had already acquired a slight historical interest for us; for many upward days' voyaging were unravelled in this rapid downward passage. When one landed to stretch his limbs by walking, he soon found himself falling behind his companion, and was obliged to take advantage of the curves, and ford the brooks and ravines in haste, to recover his ground. Already the banks and the distant meadows wore a sober and deepened tinge, for the September air had shorn them of their summer's pride.—

> "And what 's a life? The flourishing array
> Of the proud summer meadow, which to-day
> Wears her green plush, and is to-morrow hay."

The air was really the "fine element" which the poets describe. It had a finer and sharper grain, seen against the russet pastures and meadows, than before, as if cleansed of the summer's impurities.

Having passed the New Hampshire line and reached the Horseshoe Interval in Tyngsboro', where there is a high and regular second bank, we climbed up this in haste to get a nearer sight of the autumnal flowers, asters, golden-rod, and yarrow, and blue-curls (*Trichostema dichotoma*), humble road-side blossoms, and, lingering still, the harebell and the *rhexia Virginica*. The last, growing in patches of lively pink flowers on the edge of the meadows, had almost too gay an appearance for the rest of the landscape, like a pink ribbon on the bonnet of a Puritan woman.

Asters and golden-rods were the livery which nature wore at present. The latter alone expressed all the ripeness of the season, and shed their mellow lustre over the fields, as if the now declining summer's sun had bequeathed its hues to them. It is the floral solstice a little after mid-summer, when the particles of golden light, the sun-dust, have, as it were, fallen like seeds on the earth, and produced these blossoms. On every hill-side, and in every valley, stood countless asters, coreopses, tansies, golden-rods, and the whole race of yellow flowers, like Brahminical devotees, turning steadily with their luminary from morning till night.

"I see the golden-rod shine bright,
As sun-showers at the birth of day,
A golden plume of yellow light,
That robs the Day-god's splendid ray.

"The aster's violet rays divide
The bank with many stars for me,
And yarrow in blanch tints is dyed,
As moon light floats across the sea.

"I see the emerald woods prepare
To shed their vestiture once more,
And distant elm-trees spot the air
With yellow pictures softly o'er. * *

"No more the water-lily's pride
In milk-white circles swims content,
No more the blue-weed's clusters ride
And mock the heavens' element. * *

"Autumn thy wreath and mine are blent
With the same colors, for to me
A richer sky than all is lent,
While fades my dream-like company.

"Our skies glow purple, but the wind
Sobs chill through green trees and bright grass,
To-day shines fair, and lurk behind
The times that into winter pass.

"So fair we seem, so cold we are,
So fast we hasten to decay,
Yet through our night glows many a star,
That still shall claim its sunny day."

So sang a Concord poet once.

There is a peculiar interest belonging to the still later flowers, which abide with us the approach of winter. There is something witch-like in the appearance of the witch-hazel, which blossoms late in October and in November, with its irregular and angular spray and petals like furies' hair, or small ribbon streamers. Its blossoming, too, at this irregular period, when other shrubs have lost their leaves, as well as blossoms, looks like witches' craft. Certainly it blooms in no garden of man's. There is a whole fairy-land on the hill-side where it grows.

Some have thought that the gales do not at present waft to the voyager the natural and original fragrance of the land, such as the early navigators described, and that the loss of many odoriferous native plants, sweet-scented grasses and medicinal herbs, which formerly sweetened the atmosphere, and rendered it salubrious, by the grazing of cattle and the rooting of swine, is the source of many diseases which now prevail; the earth, say they, having been long subjected to extremely artificial and luxurious modes of cultivation, to gratify the appetite, converted into a stye and hot-bed, where men for profit increase the ordinary decay of nature.

According to the record of an old inhabitant of Tyngsboro', now dead, whose farm we were now gliding past, one of the greatest freshets on this river took place in October, 1785, and its height was marked by a nail driven into an apple-tree behind his house. One of his descendants has shown this to me, and I judged it to be at least seventeen or eighteen feet above the level of the river at the time. According to Barber, the river rose twenty-one feet above the common high-water mark, at Bradford in the year 1818. Before the Lowell and Nashua railroad was built, the engineer made inquiries of the inhabitants along the banks as to how high they had known the river to rise. When he came to this house he was conducted to the apple-tree, and as the nail was not then visible, the lady of the house placed her hand on the trunk where she said that she remembered the nail to have been from her childhood. In the meanwhile the old man put his arm inside the tree, which was hollow, and felt the point of the nail sticking through, and it was exactly opposite to her hand. The spot is now plainly marked by a notch in the bark. But as no one else remembered the river to have risen so high as this, the engineer disregarded this statement, and I learn that there has since been a freshet which rose within nine inches of the rails at Biscuit Brook, and such a freshet as that of 1785 would have covered the railroad two feet deep.

The revolutions of nature tell as fine tales, and make as interesting revelations, on this river's banks, as on the Euphrates or the Nile. This apple-tree, which stands within a few rods of the river, is called "Elisha's apple-tree," from a friendly Indian, who was anciently in the service of Jonathan Tyng, and, with one other man, was killed here by his own race in one of the Indian wars,–the particulars of which affair were told us on the spot. He was buried close by, no one knew exactly where, but in the flood of 1785, so great a weight of water standing over the grave, caused the earth to settle where it had once been disturbed, and when the flood went down, a sunken spot, exactly of the form and size of the grave, revealed its locality; but this was now lost again, and no future flood can detect it; yet, no doubt, Nature will know how to point it out in due time, if it be necessary, by methods yet more searching and unexpected. Thus there is not only the crisis when the spirit ceases to inspire and expand the body, marked by a fresh mound in the churchyard, but there is also a crisis when the body ceases to take up room as such in nature, marked by a fainter depression in the earth.

We sat awhile to rest us here upon the brink of the western bank, surrounded by the glossy leaves of the red variety of the mountain laurel, just above the head of Wicasuck Island, where we could observe some scows which were loading with clay from the opposite shore, and also overlook the grounds of the farmer, of whom I have spoken, who once hospitably entertained us for a night. He had on his pleasant farm, besides an abundance of the beach-plum, or *prunus littoralis*, which grew wild, the Canada plum under cultivation, fine Porter apples, some peaches, and large patches of musk and water melons, which he cultivated for the Lowell market. Elisha's apple-tree, too, bore a native fruit, which was prized by the family. He raised the blood peach, which, as he showed us with satisfaction, was more like the oak in the color of its bark and in the setting of its branches, and was less liable to break down under the weight of the fruit, or the snow, than other varieties. It was of slower growth, and its branches strong and tough. There, also, was his nursery of native apple-trees, thickly set upon the bank, which cost but little care, and which he sold to the neighboring farmers when they were five or six years old. To see a single peach upon its stem makes an impression of paradisiacal fertility and luxury. This reminded us even of an old Roman farm, as described by Varro: "Cæsar Vopiscus Ædilicius, when he pleaded before the Censors, said that the grounds of Rosea were the garden (*sumen* the tid-bit) of Italy, in which a pole being left would not be visible the day after, on account of the growth of the herbage." This soil may not have been remarkably fertile, yet at this distance we thought that this anecdote might be told of the Tyngsboro' farm.

When we passed Wicasuck Island, there was a pleasure boat containing a youth and a maiden on the island brook, which we were pleased to see, since it proved that there were some hereabouts to whom our excursion would not be wholly strange. Before this, a canal-boatman, of whom we made some inquiries respecting Wicasuck Island, and who told us that it was disputed property, supposed that we had a claim upon it, and though we assured him that all this was news to us, and explained, as well as we could, why we had come to see it, he believed not a word of it, and seriously offered us one hundred dollars for our title. The only other small boats which we met with were used to pick up drift-wood. Some of the poorer class along the stream collect, in this way, all the fuel which they require. While one of us landed not far from this island to forage for provisions among the farm-houses whose roofs we saw, for our supply was now exhausted, the other, sitting in the boat, which was moored to the shore, was left alone to his reflections.

If there is nothing new on the earth, still the traveller always has a resource in the skies. They are constantly turning a new page to view. The wind sets the types on this blue ground, and the inquiring may always read a new truth there. There are things there written with such fine and subtil tinctures, paler than the juice of limes, that to the diurnal eye they leave no trace, and only the chemistry of night reveals them. Every man's daylight firmament answers in his mind to the brightness of the vision in his starriest hour.

These continents and hemispheres are soon run over, but an always unexplored and infinite region makes off on every side from the mind, further than to sunset, and we can make no highway or beaten track into it, but the grass immediately springs up in the path, for we travel there chiefly with our wings.

Sometimes we see objects as through a thin haze, in their eternal relations, and they stand like Palenque and the Pyramids, and we wonder who set them up, and for what purpose. If we see the reality in things, of what moment is the superficial and apparent longer? What are the earth and all its interests beside the deep surmise which pierces and scatters them? While I sit here listening to the waves which ripple and break on this shore, I am absolved from all obligation to the past, and the council of nations may reconsider its votes. The grating of a pebble annuls them. Still occasionally in my dreams I remember that rippling water.—

> Oft, as I turn me on my pillow o'er,
> I hear the lapse of waves upon the shore,
> Distinct as if it were at broad noon-day,
> And I were drifting down from Nashua.

With a bending sail we glided rapidly by Tyngsboro' and Chelmsford, each holding in one hand half of a tart country apple-pie which we had purchased to celebrate our return, and in the other a fragment of the newspaper in which it was wrapped, devouring these with divided relish, and learning the news which had transpired since we sailed. The river here opened into a broad and straight reach of great length, which we bounded merrily over before a smacking breeze, with a devil-may-care look in our faces, and our boat a white bone in its mouth, and a speed which greatly astonished some scow boatmen whom we met. The wind in the horizon rolled like a flood over valley and plain, and every tree bent to the blast, and the mountains like school-boys turned their cheeks to it. They were great and current motions, the flowing sail, the running stream, the waving tree, the roving wind. The north wind stepped readily into the harness which we had provided, and pulled us along with good will. Sometimes we sailed as gently and steadily as the clouds overhead, watching the receding shores and the motions of our sail; the play of its pulse so like our own lives, so thin and yet so full of life, so noiseless when it labored hardest, so noisy and impatient when least effective; now bending to some generous impulse of the breeze, and then fluttering and flapping with a kind of human suspense. It was the scale on which the varying temperature of distant atmospheres was graduated, and it was some attraction for us that the breeze it played with had been out of doors so long. Thus we sailed, not being able to fly, but as next best, making a long furrow in the fields of the Merrimack toward our home, with our wings spread, but never lifting our heel from the watery trench; gracefully plowing homeward with our brisk and willing team, wind and stream, pulling together, the former yet a wild steer, yoked to his more sedate fellow. It was very near flying, as when the duck rushes through the water with an impulse of her wings, throwing the spray about her, before she can rise. How we had stuck fast if drawn up but a few feet on the shore!

When we reached the great bend just above Middlesex, where the river runs east thirty-five miles to the sea, we at length lost the aid of this propitious wind, though we contrived to make one long and judicious tack carry us nearly to the locks of the canal. We were here locked through at noon by our old friend, the lover of the higher mathematics, who seemed glad to see us safe back again through so many locks; but we did not stop to consider any of his problems, though we could cheerfully have spent a whole autumn in this way another time, and never have asked what his religion was. It is so rare to meet with a man outdoors who cherishes a worthy thought in his mind, which is independent of the labor of his hands. Behind every man's busy-ness there should be a level of undisturbed serenity and industry, as within the reef encircling a coral isle there is always an expanse of still water, where the depositions are going on which will finally raise it above the surface.

The eye which can appreciate the naked and absolute beauty of a scientific truth is far more rare than that which is attracted by a moral one. Few detect the morality in the former, or the science in the latter. Aristotle defined art to be Λόγος τοῦ ἔργου ἄνευ ὕλης, *the principle of the work without the wood*; but most men prefer to have some of the wood along with the principle; they demand that the truth be clothed in flesh and blood and the warm colors of life. They prefer the partial statement because it fits and measures them and their commodities best. But science still exists every where as the sealer of weights and measures at least.

We have heard much about the poetry of mathematics, but very little of it has yet been sung. The ancients had a juster notion of their poetic value than we. The most distinct and beautiful statement of any truth must take at last the mathematical form. We might so simplify the rules of moral philosophy, as well as of arithmetic, that one formula would express them both. All the moral laws are readily translated into natural philosophy, for often we have only to restore the primitive meaning of the words by which they are expressed, or to attend to their literal instead of their metaphorical sense. They are already *supernatural* philosophy. The whole body of what is now called moral or ethical truth existed in the golden age as abstract science. Or, if we prefer, we may say that the laws of Nature are the purest morality. The Tree of Knowledge is a Tree of Knowledge of good and evil. He is not a true man of science who does not bring some sympathy to his studies, and expect to learn something by behavior as well as by application. It is childish to rest in the discovery of mere coincidences, or of partial and extraneous laws. The study of geometry is a petty and idle exercise of the mind, if it is applied to no larger system than the starry one. Mathematics should be mixed not only with physics but with ethics, *that* is *mixed* mathematics. The fact which interests us most is the life of the naturalist. The purest science is still biographical. Nothing will dignify and elevate science while it is sundered so wholly from the moral life of its devotee, and he professes another religion than it teaches, and worships at a foreign shrine. Anciently the faith of a philosopher was identical with his system, or, in other words, his view of the universe.

My friends mistake when they communicate facts to me with so much pains. Their presence, even their exaggerations and loose statements, are equally good facts for me. I have no respect for facts even except when I would use them, and for the most part I am independent of those which I hear, and can afford to be inaccurate, or, in other words, to substitute more present and pressing facts in their place.

The poet uses the results of science and philosophy, and generalizes their widest deductions.

The process of discovery is very simple. An unwearied and systematic application of known laws to nature, causes the unknown to reveal themselves. Almost any *mode* of observation will be successful at last, for what is most wanted is method. Only let something be determined and fixed around which observation may rally. How many new relations a foot-rule alone will reveal, and to how many things still this has not been applied! What wonderful discoveries have been, and may still be, made, with a plumb-line, a level, a surveyor's compass, a thermometer, or a barometer! Where there is an observatory and a telescope, we expect that any eyes will see new worlds at once. I should say that the most prominent scientific men of our country, and perhaps of this age, are either serving the arts and not pure science, or are performing faithful but quite subordinate labors in particular departments. They make no steady and systematic approaches to the central fact. A discovery is made, and at once the attention of all observers is distracted to that, and it draws many analogous discoveries in its train; as if their work were not already laid out for them, but they had been lying on their oars. There is wanting constant and accurate observation with enough of theory to direct and discipline it.

But above all, there is wanting genius. Our books of science, as they improve in accuracy, are in danger of losing the freshness and vigor and readiness to appreciate the real laws of Nature, which is a marked merit in the oft-times false theories of the ancients. I am attracted by the slight pride and satisfaction, the emphatic and even exaggerated style in which some of the older naturalists speak of the operations of Nature, though they are better qualified to appreciate than to discriminate the facts. Their assertions are not without value when disproved. If they are not facts, they are suggestions for Nature herself to act upon. "The Greeks," says Gesner, "had a common proverb (Λαγος καθευδον) a sleeping hare, for a dissembler or counterfeit; because the hare sees when she sleeps; for this is an admirable and rare work of Nature, that all the residue of her bodily parts take their rest, but the eye standeth continually sentinel."

Observation is so wide awake, and facts are being so rapidly added to the sum of human experience, that it appears as if the theorizer would always be in arrears, and were doomed forever to arrive at imperfect conclusions; but the power to perceive a law is equally rare in all ages of the world, and depends but little on the number of facts observed. The senses of the savage will furnish him with facts enough to set him up as a philosopher. The ancients can still speak to us with authority, even on the themes of geology and chemistry, though these studies are thought to have had their birth in modern times. Much is said about the progress of science in these centuries. I should say that the useful results of science had accumulated, but that there had been no accumulation of knowledge, strictly speaking, for posterity; for knowledge is to be acquired only by a corresponding experience. How can we *know* what we are *told* merely? Each man can interpret another's experience only by his own. We read that Newton discovered the law of gravitation, but how many who have heard of his famous discovery have recognized the same truth that he did? It may be not one. The revelation which was then made to him has not been superseded by the revelation made to any successor.—

> We see the *planet* fall,
> And that is all.

In a review of Sir James Clark Ross' Antarctic Voyage of Discovery, there is a passage which shows how far a body of men are commonly impressed by an object of sublimity, and which is also a good instance of the step from the sublime to the ridiculous. After describing the discovery of the Antarctic Continent, at first seen a hundred miles distant over fields of ice,—stupendous ranges of mountains from seven and eight to twelve and fourteen thousand feet high, covered with eternal snow and ice, in solitary and inaccessible grandeur, at one time the weather being beautifully clear, and the sun shining on the icy landscape; a continent whose islands only are accessible, and these exhibited "not the smallest trace of vegetation," only in a few places the rocks protruding through their icy covering, to convince the beholder that land formed the nucleus, and that it was not an iceberg;—the practical British reviewer proceeds thus, sticking to his last, "On the 22d of January, afternoon, the Expedition made the latitude of 74° 20′, and by 7^{h}

P. M., having ground (ground! where did they get ground?) to believe that they were then in a higher southern latitude than had been attained by that enterprising seaman, the late Captain James Weddel, and therefore higher than all their predecessors, an extra allowance of grog was issued to the crews as a reward for their perseverance."

Let not us sailors of late centuries take upon ourselves any airs on account of our Newtons and our Cuviers. We deserve an extra allowance of grog only.

We endeavored in vain to persuade the wind to blow through the long corridor of the canal, which is here cut straight through the woods, and were obliged to resort to our old expedient of drawing by a cord. When we reached the Concord, we were forced to row once more in good earnest, with neither wind nor current in our favor, but by this time the rawness of the day had disappeared, and we experienced the warmth of a summer afternoon. This change in the weather was favorable to our contemplative mood, and disposed us to dream yet deeper at our oars, while we floated in imagination further down the stream of time, as we had floated down the stream of the Merrimack, to poets of a milder period than had engaged us in the morning. Chelmsford and Billerica appeared like old English towns, compared with Merrimack and Nashua, and many generations of civil poets might have lived and sung here.

What a contrast between the stern and desolate poetry of Ossian, and that of Chaucer, and even of Shakspeare and Milton, much more of Dryden, and

Pope, and Gray. Our summer of English poetry, like the Greek and Latin before it, seems well advanced toward its fall, and laden with the fruit and foliage of the season, with bright autumnal tints, but soon the winter will scatter its myriad clustering and shading leaves, and leave only a few desolate and fibrous boughs to sustain the snow and rime, and creak in the blasts of ages. We cannot escape the impression that the Muse has stooped a little in her flight, when we come to the literature of civilized eras. Now first we hear of various ages and styles of poetry; it is pastoral, and lyric, and narrative, and didactic; but the poetry of runic monuments is of one style, and for every age. The bard has in a great measure lost the dignity and sacredness of his office. Formerly he was called a *seer*, but now it is thought that one man sees as much as another. He has no longer the bardic rage, and only conceives the deed, which he formerly stood ready to perform. Hosts of warriors earnest for battle could not mistake nor dispense with the ancient bard. His lays were heard in the pauses of the fight. There was no danger of his being overlooked by his contemporaries. But now the hero and the bard are of different professions. When we come to the pleasant English verse, the storms have all cleared away, and it will never thunder and lighten more. The poet has come within doors, and exchanged the forest and crag for the fireside, the hut of the Gael, and Stonehenge with its circles of stones, for the house of the Englishman. No hero stands at the door prepared to break forth into song or heroic action, but a homely Englishman, who cultivates the art of poetry. We see the comfortable fireside, and hear the crackling fagots in all the verse.

Notwithstanding the broad humanity of Chaucer,

and the many social and domestic comforts which we meet with in his verse, we have to narrow our vision somewhat to consider him, as if he occupied less space in the landscape, and did not stretch over hill and valley as Ossian does. Yet, seen from the side of posterity, as the father of English poetry, preceded by a long silence or confusion in history, unenlivened by any strain of pure melody, we easily come to reverence him. Passing over the earlier continental poets, since we are bound to the pleasant archipelago of English poetry, Chaucer's is the first name after that misty weather in which Ossian lived, which can detain us long. Indeed, though he represents so different a culture and society, he may be regarded as in many respects the Homer of the English poets. Perhaps he is the youthfullest of them all. We return to him as to the purest well, the fountain furthest removed from the highway of desultory life. He is so natural and cheerful, compared with later poets, that we might almost regard him as a personification of spring. To the faithful reader his muse has even given an aspect to his times, and when he is fresh from perusing him, they seem related to the golden age. It is still the poetry of youth and life, rather than of thought; and though the moral vein is obvious and constant, it has not yet banished the sun and daylight from his verse. The loftiest strains of the muse are, for the most part, sublimely plaintive, and not a carol as free as nature's. The content which the sun shines to celebrate from morning to evening, is unsung. The muse solaces herself, and is not ravished but consoled. There is a catastrophe implied, and a tragic element in all our verse, and less of the lark and morning dews, than of the nightingale and evening shades. But in Homer and Chaucer there is more of the innocence and serenity of youth, than in the more modern and moral poets. The Iliad is not Sabbath but morning reading, and men cling to this old song, because they still have moments of unbaptized and uncommitted life, which give them an appetite for more. To the innocent there are neither cherubim nor angels. At rare intervals we rise above the necessity of virtue into an unchangeable morning light, in which we have only to live right on and breathe the ambrosial air. The Iliad represents no creed nor opinion, and we read it with a rare sense of freedom and irresponsibility, as if we trod on native ground, and were autochthones of the soil.

Chaucer had eminently the habits of a literary man and a scholar. There were never any times so stirring that there were not to be found some sedentary still. He was surrounded by the din of arms. The battles of Hallidon Hill and Neville's Cross, and the still more memorable battles of Cressy and Poictiers, were fought in his youth; but these did not concern our poet much, Wickliffe and his reform much more. He regarded himself always as one privileged to sit and converse with books. He helped to establish the literary class. His character as one of the fathers of the English language, would alone make his works important, even those which have little poetical merit. He was as simple as Wordsworth in preferring his homely but vigorous Saxon tongue, when it was neglected by the court, and had not yet attained to the dignity of a literature, and rendered a similar service to his country to that which Dante rendered to Italy. If Greek sufficeth for Greek, and Arabic for Arabian, and Hebrew for Jew, and Latin for Latin, then English shall suffice for him, for any of these will serve to teach truth "right as divers pathes leaden divers folke the right waye to Rome." In the Testament of Love he writes, "Let then clerkes enditen in Latin, for they have the propertie of science, and the knowinge in that facultie, and lette Frenchmen in their Frenche also enditen their queinte termes, for it is kyndely to their mouthes, and let us shewe our fantasies in soche wordes as we lerneden of our dames tonge."

He will know how to appreciate Chaucer best, who has come down to him the natural way, through the meagre pastures of Saxon and ante-Chaucerian poetry; and yet, so human and wise he appears after such diet, that we are liable to misjudge him still. In the Saxon poetry extant, in the earliest English, and the contemporary Scottish poetry, there is less to remind the reader of the rudeness and vigor of youth, than of the feebleness of a declining age. It is for the most part translation or imitation merely, with only an occasional and slight tinge of poetry, oftentimes the falsehood and exaggeration of fable, without its imagination to redeem it, and we look in vain to find antiquity restored, humanized, and made blithe again by some natural sympathy between it and the present. But Chaucer is fresh and modern still, and no dust settles on his true passages. It lightens along the line, and we are reminded that flowers have bloomed, and birds sung, and hearts beaten, in England. Before the earnest gaze of the reader, the rust and moss of time gradually drop off, and the original green life is revealed. He was a homely and domestic man, and did breathe quite as modern men do.

There is no wisdom that can take place of humanity, and we find *that* in Chaucer. We can expand at last in his breadth, and we think that we could have been that man's acquaintance. He was worthy to be a citizen of England, while Petrarch and Boccacio lived in Italy, and Tell and Tamerlane in Switzerland and in Asia, and Bruce in Scotland, and Wickliffe, and Gower, and Edward the Third, and John of Gaunt, and the Black Prince, were his own countrymen as well as contemporaries; all stout and stirring names. The fame of Roger Bacon came down from the preceding century, and the name of Dante still possessed the influence of a living presence. On the whole, Chaucer impresses us as greater than his reputation, and not a little like Homer and Shakspeare, for he would have held up his head in their company. Among early English poets he is the landlord and host, and has the authority of such. The affectionate mention which succeeding early poets make of him, coupling him with Homer and Virgil, is to be taken into the account in estimating his character and influence. King James and Dunbar of Scotland speak of him with more love and reverence than any modern author of his predecessors of the last century. The same childlike relation is without a parallel now. For the most part we read him without criticism, for he does not plead his own cause, but speaks for his readers, and has that greatness of trust and reliance which compels popularity. He confides in the reader, and speaks privily with him, keeping nothing back. And in return the reader has great confidence in him, that he tells no lies, and reads his story with indulgence, as if it were the circumlocution of a child, but often discovers afterwards that he has spoken with more directness and economy of words than a sage. He is never heartless,

> "For first the thing is thought within the hart,
> Er any word out from the mouth astart."

And so new was all his theme in those days, that he did not have to invent, but only to tell.

We admire Chaucer for his sturdy English wit. The easy height he speaks from in his Prologue to the Canterbury Tales, as if he were equal to any of the company there assembled, is as good as any particular excellence in it. But though it is full of good sense and humanity, it is not transcendent poetry. For picturesque description of persons it is, perhaps, without a parallel in English poetry; yet it is essentially humorous, as the loftiest genius never is. Humor, however broad and genial, takes a narrower view than enthusiasm. To his own finer vein he added all the common wit and wisdom of his time, and every where in his works his remarkable knowledge of the world, and nice perception of character, his rare common sense and proverbial wisdom, are apparent. His genius does not soar like Milton's, but is genial and familiar. It shows great tenderness and delicacy, but not the heroic sentiment. It is only a greater portion of humanity with all its weakness. He is not heroic, as Raleigh, nor pious, as Herbert, nor philosophical, as Shakspeare, but he is the child of the English muse, that child which is the father of the man. The charm of his poetry consists often only in an exceeding naturalness, perfect sincerity, with the behavior of a child rather than of a man.

Gentleness and delicacy of character are every where apparent in his verse. The simplest and humblest words come readily to his lips. No one can read the Prioress' tale, understanding the spirit in which it was written, and in which the child sings *O alma redemptoris mater*, or the account of the departure of Constance with her child upon the sea, in the Man of Lawe's tale, without feeling the native innocence and refinement of the author. Nor can we be mistaken respecting the essential purity of his character, disregarding the apology of the manners of the age. A simple pathos and feminine gentleness, which Wordsworth only occasionally approaches, but does not equal, are peculiar to him. We are tempted to say that his genius was feminine, not masculine. It was such a feminineness, however, as is rarest to find in woman, though not the appreciation of it; perhaps it is not to be found at all in woman, but is only the feminine in man.

Such pure, and genuine, and childlike love of Nature is hardly to be found in any poet.

Chaucer's remarkably trustful and affectionate character appears in his familiar, yet innocent and reverent, manner of speaking of his God. He comes into his thought without any false reverence, and with no more parade than the zephyr to his ear. If Nature is our mother, then God is our father. There is less love and simple practical trust in Shakspeare and Milton. How rarely in our English tongue do we find expressed any affection for God. Certainly, there is no sentiment so rare as the love of God. Herbert almost alone expresses it, "Ah, my dear God!" Our poet uses similar words with propriety, and whenever he sees a beautiful person, or other object, prides himself on the "maistry" of his God. He even recommends Dido to be his bride,—

—"if that God that heaven and yearth made,
Would have a love for beauty and goodnesse,
And womanhede, trouth, and semeliness."

But in justification of our praise, we must refer to his works themselves; to the Prologue to the Canterbury Tales, the account of Gentilesse, the Flower and the Leaf, the stories of Griselda, Virginia, Ariadne, and Blanche the Dutchesse, and much more of less distinguished merit. There are many poets of more taste and better manners, who knew how to leave out their dulness, but such negative genius cannot detain us long; we shall return to Chaucer still with love. Some natures which are really rude and ill developed, have yet a higher standard of perfection than others which are refined and well balanced. Even the clown has taste, whose dictates, though he disregards them, are higher and purer than those which the artist obeys. If we have to wander through many dull and prosaic passages in Chaucer, we have at least the satisfaction of knowing that it is not an artificial dulness, but too easily matched by many passages in life. We confess that we feel a disposition commonly to concentrate sweets, and accumulate pleasures, but the poet may be presumed always to speak as a traveller, who leads us through a varied scenery, from one eminence to another, and it is, perhaps, more pleasing, after all, to meet with a fine thought in its natural setting. Surely fate has enshrined it in these circumstances for some end. Nature strews her nuts and flowers broadcast, and never collects them into heaps. This was the soil it grew in, and this the hour it bloomed in; if sun, wind and rain came here to cherish and expand the flower, shall not we come here to pluck it?

A true poem is distinguished not so much by a felicitous expression, or any thought it suggests, as by the atmosphere which surrounds it. Most have beauty of outline merely, and are striking as the form and bearing of a stranger, but true verses come toward us indistinctly, as the very breath of all friendliness, and envelope us in their spirit and fragrance. Much of our poetry has the very best manners, but no character. It is only an unusual precision and elasticity of speech, as if its author had taken, not an intoxicating draught, but an electuary. It has the distinct outline of sculpture, and chronicles an early hour. Under the influence of passion all men speak thus distinctly, but wrath is not always divine.

There are two classes of men called poets. The one cultivates life, the other art,—one seeks food for nutriment, the other for flavor; one satisfies hunger, the other gratifies the palate. There are two kinds of writing, both great and rare; one that of genius, or the inspired, the other of intellect and taste, in the intervals of inspiration. The former is above criticism, always correct, giving the law to criticism. It vibrates and pulsates with life forever. It is sacred, and to be read with reverence, as the works of nature are studied. There are few instances of a sustained style of this kind; perhaps every man has spoken words, but the speaker is then careless of the record. Such a style removes us out of personal relations with its author, we do not take his words on our lips, but his sense into our hearts. It is the stream of inspiration, which bubbles out, now here, now there, now in this man, now in that. It matters not through what ice-crystals it is seen, now a fountain, now the ocean stream running under ground. It is in Shakspeare, Alpheus, in Burns, Arethuse; but ever the same.—The other is self-possessed and wise. It is reverent of genius, and greedy of inspiration. It is conscious in the highest and the least degree. It consists with the most perfect command of the faculties. It dwells in a repose as of the desert, and objects are as distinct in it as oases or palms in the horizon of sand. The train of thought moves with subdued and measured step, like a caravan. But the pen is only an instrument in its hand, and not instinct with life, like a longer arm. It leaves a thin varnish or glaze over all its work. The works of Goethe furnish remarkable instances of the latter.

There is no just and serene criticism as yet. Nothing is considered simply as it lies in the lap of eternal beauty, but our thoughts, as well as our bodies, must be dressed after the latest fashions. Our taste is too delicate and particular. It says nay to the poet's work, but never yea to his hope. It invites him to adorn his deformities, and not to cast them off by expansion, as the tree its bark. We are a people who live in a bright light, in houses of pearl and porcelain, and drink only light wines, whose teeth are easily set on edge by the least natural sour. If we had been consulted, the backbone of the earth would have been made, not of granite, but of Bristol spar. A modern author would have died in infancy in a ruder age. But the poet is something more than a scald, "a smoother and polisher of language;" he is a Cincinnatus in literature, and occupies no west end of the world. Like the sun, he will indifferently select his rhymes, and with a liberal taste weave into his verse the planet and the stubble.

In these old books the stucco has long since crumbled away, and we read what was sculptured in the granite. They are rude and massive in their proportions, rather than smooth and delicate in their finish. The workers in stone polish only their chimney ornaments, but their pyramids are roughly done. There is a soberness in a rough aspect, as of unhewn granite, which addresses a depth in us, but a polished surface hits only the ball of the eye. The true finish is the work of time and the use to which a thing is put. The elements are still polishing the pyramids. Art may varnish and gild, but it can do no more. A work of genius is rough-hewn from the first, because it anticipates the lapse of time, and has an ingrained polish, which still appears when fragments are broken off, an essential quality of its substance. Its beauty is at the same time its strength, and it breaks with a lustre.

The great poem must have the stamp of greatness as well as its essence. The reader easily goes within the shallowest contemporary poetry, and informs it with all the life and promise of the day, as the pilgrim goes within the temple, and hears the faintest strains of the worshippers; but it will have to speak to posterity, traversing these deserts, through the ruins of its outmost walls, by the grandeur and beauty of its proportions.

But here on the stream of the Concord, where we have all the while been bodily, Nature, who is superior to all styles and ages, is now, with pensive face, composing her poem Autumn, with which no work of man will bear to be compared.

In summer we live out of doors, and have only impulses and feelings, which are all for action, and must wait commonly for the stillness and longer nights of autumn and winter before any thought will subside. We are sensible that behind the rustling leaves, and the stacks of grain, and the bare clusters of the grape, there is the field of a wholly new life, which no man has lived; that even this earth was made for more mysterious and nobler inhabitants than men and women. In the hues of October sunsets, we see the portals to other mansions than those which we occupy, not far off geographically.—

"There is a place beyond that flaming hill,
From whence the stars their thin appearance shed,
A place beyond all place, where never ill,
Nor impure thought was ever harbored."

Sometimes a mortal feels in himself Nature, not his Father but his Mother stirs within him, and he becomes immortal with her immortality. From time to time she claims kindredship with us, and some globule from her veins steals up into our own.

I am the autumnal sun,
With autumn gales my race is run;
When will the hazel put forth its flowers,
Or the grape ripen under my bowers?
When will the harvest or the hunter's moon,
Turn my midnight into mid-noon?
I am all sere and yellow,
And to my core mellow.
The mast is dropping within my woods,
The winter is lurking within my moods,
And the rustling of the withered leaf
Is the constant music of my grief.

To an unskilful rhymer the Muse thus spoke in prose:

The moon no longer reflects the day, but rises to her absolute rule, and the husbandman and hunter acknowledge her for their mistress. Asters and goldenrods reign along the way, and the life-ever-lasting withers not. The fields are reaped and shorn of their pride, but an inward verdure still crowns them. The thistle scatters its down on the pool, and yellow leaves clothe the vine, and naught disturbs the serious life of men. But behind the sheaves, and under the sod, there lurks a ripe fruit, which the reapers have not gathered, the true harvest of the year, which it bears for ever, annually watering and maturing it, and man never severs the stalk which bears this palatable fruit.

Men nowhere, east or west, live yet a *natural* life, round which the vine clings, and which the elm willingly shadows. Man would desecrate it by his touch, and so the beauty of the world remains veiled to him. He needs not only to be spiritualized, but *naturalized*, on the soil of earth. Who shall conceive what kind of roof the heavens might extend over him, what seasons minister to him, and what employment dignify his life! Only the convalescent raise the veil of nature. An immortality in his life would confer immortality on his abode. The winds should be his breath, the seasons his moods, and he should impart of his serenity to Nature herself. But such as we know him he is ephemeral like the scenery which surrounds him, and does not aspire to an enduring existence. When we come down into the distant village, visible from the mountain top, the nobler inhabitants with whom we peopled it have departed, and left only vermin in its desolate streets. It is the imagination of poets which puts those brave speeches into the mouths of their heroes. They may feign that Cato's last words were

"The earth, the air, and seas I know, and all
The joys and horrors of their peace and wars;
And now will view the Gods' state and the stars,"

but such are not the thoughts nor the destiny of common men. What is this heaven which they expect, if it is no better than they expect? Are they prepared for a better than they can now imagine? Where is the heaven of him who dies on a stage, in a theatre? Here or nowhere is our heaven.—

> "Although we see celestial bodies move
> Above the earth, the earth we till and love."

We can conceive of nothing more fair than something which we have experienced. "The remembrance of youth is a sigh." We linger in manhood to tell the dreams of our childhood, and they are half forgotten ere we have learned the language. We have need to be earth-born as well as heaven-born, γηγενεὶς, as was said of the Titans of old, or in a better sense than they. There have been heroes for whom this world seemed expressly prepared, as if creation had at last succeeded; whose daily life was the stuff of which our dreams are made, and whose presence enhanced the beauty and ampleness of Nature herself. Where they walked,

> "Largior hic campos æther et lumine vestit
> Purpureo: Solemque suum, sua sidera nôrunt."

"Here a more copious air invests the fields, and clothes with purple light; and they know their own sun and their own stars." We love to hear some men speak, though we hear not what they say; the very air they breathe is rich and perfumed, and the sound of their voices falls on the ear like the rustling of leaves or the crackling of the fire. They stand many deep. They have the heavens for their abettors, as those who have never stood from under them, and they look at the stars with an answering ray. Their eyes are like glow-worms, and their motions graceful and flowing, as if a place were already found for them, like rivers flowing through valleys. The distinctions of morality, of right and wrong, sense and nonsense, are petty, and have lost their significance, beside these pure primeval natures. When I consider the clouds stretched in stupendous masses across the sky, frowning with darkness, or glowing with downy light, or gilded with the rays of the setting sun, like the battlements of a city in the heavens, their grandeur appears thrown away on the meanness of my employment; the drapery is altogether too rich for such poor acting. I am hardly worthy to be a suburban dweller outside those walls.

> "Unless above himself he can
> Erect himself, how poor a thing is man!"

With our music we would fain challenge transiently another and finer sort of intercourse than our daily toil permits. The strains come back to us amended in the echo, as when a friend reads our verse. Why have they so painted the fruits, and freighted them with such fragrance, as to satisfy a more than animal appetite?

> "I asked the schoolman, his advice was free,
> But scored me out too intricate a way."

These things imply, perchance, that we live on the verge of another and purer realm, from which these odors and sounds are wafted over to us. The borders of our plot are set with flowers, whose seeds were blown from more Elysian fields adjacent. They are the pot-herbs of the gods. Some fairer fruits and sweeter fragrances wafted over to us, betray another realm's vicinity. There, too, does Echo dwell, and there is the abutment of the rainbow's arch.

> A finer race and finer fed
> Feast and revel o'er our head,
> And we titmen are only able
> To catch the fragments from their table.

Theirs is the fragrance of the fruits,
While we consume the pulp and roots.
What are the moments that we stand
Astonished on the Olympian land!

We need pray for no higher heaven than the pure senses can furnish, a *purely* sensuous life. Our present senses are but the rudiments of what they are destined to become. We are comparatively deaf and dumb and blind, and without smell or taste or feeling. Every generation makes the discovery, that its divine vigor has been dissipated, and each sense and faculty misapplied and debauched. The ears were made, not for such trivial uses as men are wont to suppose, but to hear celestial sounds. The eyes were not made for such grovelling uses as they are now put to and worn out by, but to behold beauty now invisible. May we not *see* God? Are we to be put off and amused in this life, as it were with a mere allegory? Is not Nature, rightly read, that of which she is commonly taken to be the symbol merely? When the common man looks into the sky, which he has not so much profaned, he thinks it less gross than the earth, and with reverence speaks of "the Heavens," but the seer will in the same sense speak of "the Earths," and his Father who is in them. "Did not he that made that which is *within*, make that which is *without* also?" What is it, then, to educate but to develope these divine germs called the senses? for individuals and states to deal magnanimously with the rising generation, leading it not into temptation,–not teach the eye to squint, nor attune the ear to profanity? But where is the instructed teacher? Where are the *normal* schools?

A Hindoo sage said, "As a dancer having exhibited herself to the spectator, desists from the dance, so does Nature desist, having manifested herself to soul——. Nothing, in my opinion, is more gentle than Nature; once aware of having been seen, she does not again expose herself to the gaze of soul."

It is easier to discover another such a new world as Columbus did, than to go within one fold of this which we appear to know so well; the land is lost sight of, the compass varies, and mankind mutiny; and still history accumulates like rubbish before the portals of nature. But there is only necessary a moment's sanity and sound senses, to teach us that there is a nature behind the ordinary, in which we have only some vague preëmption right and western reserve as yet. We live on the outskirts of that region. Carved wood, and floating boughs, and sunset skies, are all that we know of it. We are not to be imposed on by the longest spell of weather. Let us not, my friends, be wheedled and cheated into good behavior to earn the salt of our eternal porridge, whoever they are that attempt it. Let us wait a little, and not purchase any clearing here, trusting that richer bottoms will soon be put up. It is but thin soil where we stand; I have felt my roots in a richer ere this. I have seen a bunch of violets in a glass vase, tied loosely with a straw, which reminded me of myself.—

I am a parcel of vain strivings tied
By a chance bond together,
Dangling this way and that, their links
Were made so loose and wide,
Methinks,
For milder weather.

A bunch of violets without their roots,
And sorrel intermixed,
Encircled by a wisp of straw
Once coiled about their shoots,
The law
By which I'm fixed.

A nosegay which Time clutched from out
Those fair Elysian fields,
With weeds and broken stems, in haste,
Doth make the rabble rout
That waste
The day he yields.

And here I bloom for a short hour unseen,
Drinking my juices up,
With no root in the land
To keep my branches green,
But stand
In a bare cup.

Some tender buds were left upon my stem
In mimicry of life,
But ah! the children will not know,
Till time has withered them,
The woe
With which they're rife.

But now I see I was not plucked for naught,
And after in life's vase
Of glass set while I might survive,
But by a kind hand brought
Alive
To a strange place.

That stock thus thinned will soon redeem its hours,
And by another year,
Such as God knows, with freer air,
More fruits and fairer flowers
Will bear,
While I droop here.

This world has many rings, like Saturn, and we live now on the outmost of them all. None can say deliberately that he inhabits the same sphere, or is contemporary with, the flower which his hands have plucked, and though his feet may seem to crush it, inconceivable spaces and ages separate them, and perchance there is no danger that he will hurt it. What after all do the botanists know? Our lives should go between the lichen and the bark. The eye may see for the hand, but not for the mind. We are still being born, and have as yet but a dim vision of sea and land, sun, moon and stars, and shall not see clearly till after nine days at least. That is a pathetic inquiry among travellers and geographers after the site of ancient Troy. It is not near where they think it is. When a thing is decayed and gone, how indistinct must be the place it occupied!

The anecdotes of modern astronomy affect me in the same way as do those faint revelations of the Real which are vouchsafed to men from time to time, or rather from eternity to eternity. When I remember the history of that faint light in our firmament, which we call Venus, which ancient men regarded, and which most modern men still regard, as a bright spark attached to a hollow sphere revolving about our earth, but which we have discovered to be *another world* in itself,–how Copernicus, reasoning long and patiently about the matter, predicted confidently concerning it, before yet the telescope had been invented, that if ever men came to see it more clearly than they did then, they would discover that it had phases like our moon, and that within a century after his death the telescope was invented, and that prediction verified, by Galileo,–I am not without hope that we may, even here and now, obtain some accurate information concerning that OTHER WORLD which the instinct of mankind has so long predicted. Indeed, all that we call science, as well as all that we call poetry, is a particle of such information, accurate as far as it goes, though it be but to the confines of the truth. If we can reason so accurately, and with such wonderful confirmation of our reasoning, respecting so-called material objects and events infinitely removed beyond the range of our natural vision, so that the mind hesitates to trust its calculations even when they are confirmed by observation, why may not our speculations penetrate as far into the immaterial starry system, of which the former is but the outward and visible type? Surely, we are provided with senses as well fitted to penetrate the spaces of the real, the substantial, the eternal, as these outward are to penetrate the material universe. Veias, Menu, Zoroaster, Socrates, Christ, Shakspeare, Swedenborg,–these are some of our astronomers.

There are perturbations in our orbits produced by the influence of outlying spheres, and no astronomer has ever yet calculated the elements of that undiscovered world which produces them. I perceive in the common train of my thoughts a natural and uninterrupted sequence, each implying the next, or, if interruption occurs it is occasioned by a new object being presented to my *senses*. But a steep, and sudden, and by these means unaccountable transition, is that from a comparatively narrow and partial, what is called common sense view of things, to an infinitely expanded and liberating one, from seeing things as men describe them, to seeing them as men cannot describe them. This implies a sense which is not common, but rare in the wisest man's experience; which is sensible or sentient of more than common.

In what inclosures does the astronomer loiter! His skies are shoal, and imagination, like a thirsty traveller, pants to be through their desert. The roving mind impatiently bursts the fetters of astronomical orbits, like cobwebs in a corner of its universe, and launches itself to where distance fails to follow, and law, such as science has discovered, grows weak and weary. The mind knows a distance and a space of which all those sums combined do not make a unit of measure,–the interval between that which *appears*, and that which *is*. I know that there are many stars, I know that they are far enough off, bright enough, steady enough in their orbits,–but what are they all worth? They are more waste land in the West,–star territory,–to be made Slave States, perchance, if we colonize them. I have interest but for six feet of star, and that interest is transient. Then farewell to all ye bodies, such as I have known ye.

Every man, if he is wise, will stand on such bottom as will sustain him, and if one gravitates downward more strongly than another, he will not venture on those meads where the latter walks securely, but rather leave the cranberries which grow there unraked by himself. Perchance, some spring a higher freshet will float them within his reach, though they may be watery and frost-bitten by that time. Such shrivelled berries I have seen in many a poor man's garret, aye, in many a church bin and state coffer, and with a little water and heat they swell again to their original size and fairness, and added sugar enough, stead mankind for sauce to this world's dish.

What is called common sense is excellent in its department, and as invaluable as the virtue of conformity in the army and navy,–for there must be subordination,–but uncommon sense, that sense which is common only to the wisest, is as much more excellent as it is more rare. Some aspire to excellence in the subordinate department, and may God speed them. What Fuller says of masters of colleges is universally applicable, that "a little alloy of dulness in a master of a college makes him fitter to manage secular affairs."

> "He that wants faith, and apprehends a grief
> Because he wants it, hath a true belief;
> And he that grieves because his grief's so small,
> Has a true grief, and the best Faith of all."

Or be encouraged by this other poet's strain.

> "By them went Fido marshal of the field:
> Weak was his mother when she gave him day;
> And he at first a sick and weakly child,
> As e'er with tears welcomed the sunny ray;
> Yet when more years afford more growth and might,
> A champion stout he was, and puissant knight,
> As ever came in field, or shone in armor bright.

> "Mountains he flings in seas with mighty hand;
> Stops and turns back the sun's impetuous course;
> Nature breaks Nature's laws at his command;
> No force of Hell or Heaven withstands his force;
> Events to come yet many ages hence,
> He present makes, by wondrous prescience;
> Proving the senses blind by being blind to sense."

"Yesterday, at dawn," says Hafiz, "God delivered me from all worldly affliction; and amidst the gloom of night presented me with the water of immortality."

In the life of Sadi by Dowlat Shah, occurs this sentence. "The eagle of the immaterial soul of Shaikh Sadi shook from his plumage the dust of his body."

Thus thoughtfully we were rowing homeward to find some autumnal work to do, and help on the revolution of the seasons. Perhaps Nature would condescend to make use of us even without our knowledge, as when we help to scatter her seeds in our walks, and carry burrs and cockles on our clothes from field to field.

All things are current found
On earthly ground,
Spirits and elements
Have their descents.

Night and day, year on year,
High and low, far and near,
These are our own aspects,
These are our own regrets.

Ye gods of the shore,
Who abide evermore,
I see your far headland,
Stretching on either hand;

I hear the sweet evening sounds
From your undecaying grounds;
Cheat me no more with time,
Take me to your clime.

As it grew later in the afternoon, and we rowed leisurely up the gentle stream, shut in between fragrant and blooming banks, where we had first pitched our tent, and drew nearer to the fields where our lives had passed, we seemed to detect the hues of our native sky in the south-west horizon. The sun was just setting behind the edge of a wooded hill, so rich a sunset as would never have ended but for some reason unknown to men, and to be marked with brighter colors than ordinary in the scroll of time. Though the shadows of the hills were beginning to steal over the stream, the whole river valley undulated with mild light, purer and more memorable than the noon. For so day bids farewell even to solitary vales uninhabited by man. Two herons, *Ardea herodias*, with their long and slender limbs relieved against the sky, were seen travelling high over our heads,—their lofty and silent flight, as they were wending their way at evening, surely not to alight in any marsh on the earth's surface, but, perchance, on the other side of our atmosphere, a symbol for the ages to study, whether impressed upon the sky, or sculptured amid the hieroglyphics of Egypt. Bound to some northern meadow, they held on their stately, stationary flight, like the storks in the picture, and disappeared at length behind the clouds. Dense flocks of blackbirds were winging their way along the river's course, as if on a short evening pilgrimage to some shrine of theirs, or to celebrate so fair a sunset.

"Therefore, as doth the pilgrim, whom the night
 Hastes darkly to imprison on his way,
Think on thy home, my soul, and think aright
 Of what's yet left thee of life's wasting day:
  Thy sun posts westward, passed is thy morn,
  And twice it is not given thee to be born."

The sun-setting presumed all men at leisure, and in a contemplative mood; but the farmer's boy only whistled the more thoughtfully as he drove his cows home from pasture, and the teamster refrained from cracking his whip, and guided his team with a subdued voice. The last vestiges of daylight at length disappeared, and as we rowed silently along with our backs toward home through the darkness, only a few stars being visible, we had little to say, but sat absorbed in thought, or in silence listened to the monotonous sound of our oars, a sort of rudimental music, suitable for the ear of Night and the acoustics of her dimly lighted halls;

"Pulsæ referunt ad sidera valles,"

and the valleys echoed the sound to the stars.

As we looked up in silence to those distant lights, we were reminded that it was a rare imagination which first taught that the stars are worlds, and had conferred a great benefit on mankind. It is recorded in the Chronicle of Bernaldez, that in Columbus's first voyage the natives "pointed towards the heavens, making signs that they believed that there was all power and holiness." We have reason to be grateful for celestial phenomena, for they chiefly answer to the ideal in man. The stars are distant and unobtrusive, but bright and enduring as our fairest and most memorable experiences. "Let the immortal depth of your soul lead you, but earnestly extend your eyes upwards."

As the truest society approaches always nearer to solitude, so the most excellent speech finally falls into Silence. Silence is audible to all men, at all times, and in all places. She is when we hear inwardly, sound when we hear outwardly. Creation has not displaced her, but is her visible frame-work and foil. All sounds are her servants and purveyors, proclaiming not only that their mistress is, but is a rare mistress, and earnestly to be sought after. They are so far akin to Silence, that they are but bubbles on her surface, which straightway burst, an evidence of the strength and prolificness of the under-current; a faint utterance of Silence, and then only agreeable to our auditory nerves when they contrast themselves with and relieve the former. In proportion as they do this, and are heighteners and intensifiers of the Silence, they are harmony and purest melody.

Silence is the universal refuge, the sequel to all dull discourses and all foolish acts, a balm to our every chagrin, as welcome after satiety as after disappointment; that back ground which the painter may not daub, be he master or bungler, and which, however awkward a figure we may have made in the foreground, remains ever our inviolable asylum, where no indignity can assail, no personality disturb us.

The orator puts off his individuality, and is then most eloquent when most silent. He listens while he speaks, and is a hearer along with his audience. Who has not hearkened to Her infinite din? She is Truth's speaking trumpet, the sole oracle, the true Delphi and Dodona, which kings and courtiers would do well to consult, nor will they be baulked by an ambiguous answer. For through Her all revelations have been made, and just in proportion as men have consulted her oracle within, they have obtained a clear insight, and their age has been marked as an enlightened one. But as often as they have gone gadding abroad to a strange Delphi and her mad priestess, their age has been dark and leaden. Such were garrulous and noisy eras, which no longer yield any sound, but the Grecian or silent and melodious era, is ever sounding and resounding in the ears of men.

A good book is the plectrum with which our else silent lyres are struck. We not unfrequently refer the interest which belongs to our own unwritten sequel, to the written and comparatively lifeless body of the work. Of all books this sequel is the most indispensable part. It should be the author's aim to say once and emphatically, "He said," "ἔφη," "ἔ." This is the most the book maker can attain to. If he make his volume a mole whereon the waves of Silence may break, it is well.

It were vain for me to endeavor to interpret the Silence. She cannot be done into English. For six thousand years men have translated her with what fidelity belonged to each, and still she is little better than a sealed book. A man may run on confidently for a time, thinking he has her under his thumb, and shall one day exhaust her, but he too must at last be silent, and men remark only how brave a beginning he made; for when he at length dives into her, so vast is the disproportion of the told to the untold, that the former will seem but the bubble on the surface where he disappeared. Nevertheless, we will go on, like those Chinese cliff swallows, feathering our nests with the froth, which may one day be bread of life to such as dwell by the seashore.

We had made about fifty miles this day with sail and oar, and now, far in the evening, our boat was grating against the bulrushes of its native port, and its keel recognized the Concord mud, where some semblance of its outline was still preserved in the flattened flags which had scarce yet erected themselves since our departure; and we leaped gladly on shore, drawing it up, and fastening it to the wild apple-tree, whose stem still bore the mark which its chain had worn in the chafing of the spring freshets.

THE END.

Index

Editorial Appendix

Notes on Illustrations

Henry D. Thoreau — following page 422

Thoreau lived at the Emersons' home and worked for his room and board in 1841-1843 and 1847-1848; during the latter period he completed *A Week on the Concord and Merrimack Rivers.* Edward Emerson made this drawing from memory, to portray Thoreau as he appeared in his early thirties. Emerson intended to use the drawing in his memoir, *Henry Thoreau as Remembered by a Young Friend* (1917), but later changed his plans.—Concord Free Public Library.

John Thoreau, Jr.

Thoreau's elder brother, fellow teacher at the Concord Academy, and companion on the original Concord-and-Merrimack excursion in 1839. His sudden and agonizing death from lockjaw in 1842 inspired Thoreau to write *A Week* as a memorial to their voyage. This painting, attributed to Sophia Thoreau, is of an unknown date; it probably depicts John near the time of his death.—Concord Antiquarian Society.

Second manuscript draft of *A Week*

Thoreau wrote two drafts of *A Week*, the first in 1845 at Walden Pond, and the second in 1847-1848. Part of the second draft probably became his printer's setting copy, since surviving draft fragments are mostly rejected or heavily revised portions of text. This leaf from the second draft shows Thoreau's revisions of a passage from the chapter "Wednesday," where he discusses the changing population of Manchester, New Hampshire. For an analysis of this crux, see Textual Note 245.30.—Henry E. Huntington Library.

Page proof for *A Week* (page 396)

The surviving page proof of *A Week*, containing several stages of Thoreau's correction and revision, is copy-text for the Princeton Edition. This page contains (1) the printer's ink correction of an inverted hyphen, (2) Thoreau's pencil correction of a lowercase letter, and (3) Thoreau's pencil correction of spacing, with a request for "dash" and "3 more white lines." The printer made all three changes, but in adding a rule and more vertical space, he dropped three lines of printed text from the 1849 edition (see right). All the corrections are pre-1849, and Thoreau's note, "I must have indicated that more space was wanted here" probably alludes to instructions in the printer's setting copy, now lost. Elsewhere, the page proof has post-1849 corrections; some were restored in the 1868 edition.—Henry E. Huntington Library.

First edition of *A Week* (page 396)

In copies that Thoreau gave away—and, after 1853, that he personally sold—he made a few corrections, including the three lines missing from page 396. Note the two variants from page proof, a comma added after "winter" and "the field" changed to "a field." These slight changes are probably Thoreau's errors of memory, not distinct revisions; hence they are not accepted as emendations of the copy-text. This page is from Thoreau's memorial copy of *A Week*, containing a lock of John Thoreau's hair; Sophia read to Henry from this copy on the morning of his death, May 12, 1862.—Robert H. Taylor Collection, Princeton, New Jersey.

Thoreau's map of Concord and Merrimack Rivers

Probably drawn or traced not long after their voyage, this map depicts the Thoreau brothers' entire trip from Concord, Massachusetts ("Con") to Mount Washington in New Hampshire, and return; August 31 to September 12, 1839. The triangles mark overnight stays on both the north- and south-bound legs of this journey; the original scale is one-eighth of an inch to the mile. Thoreau apparently did not wish to include a map in either the first or second edition of *A Week*; he did use a map in *Walden*, derived from his personal survey drawings.—Clifton Waller Barrett Collection, University of Virginia Library.

Henry D. Thoreau, by Edward Emerson.

John Thoreau, Jr., attributed to Sophia Thoreau.

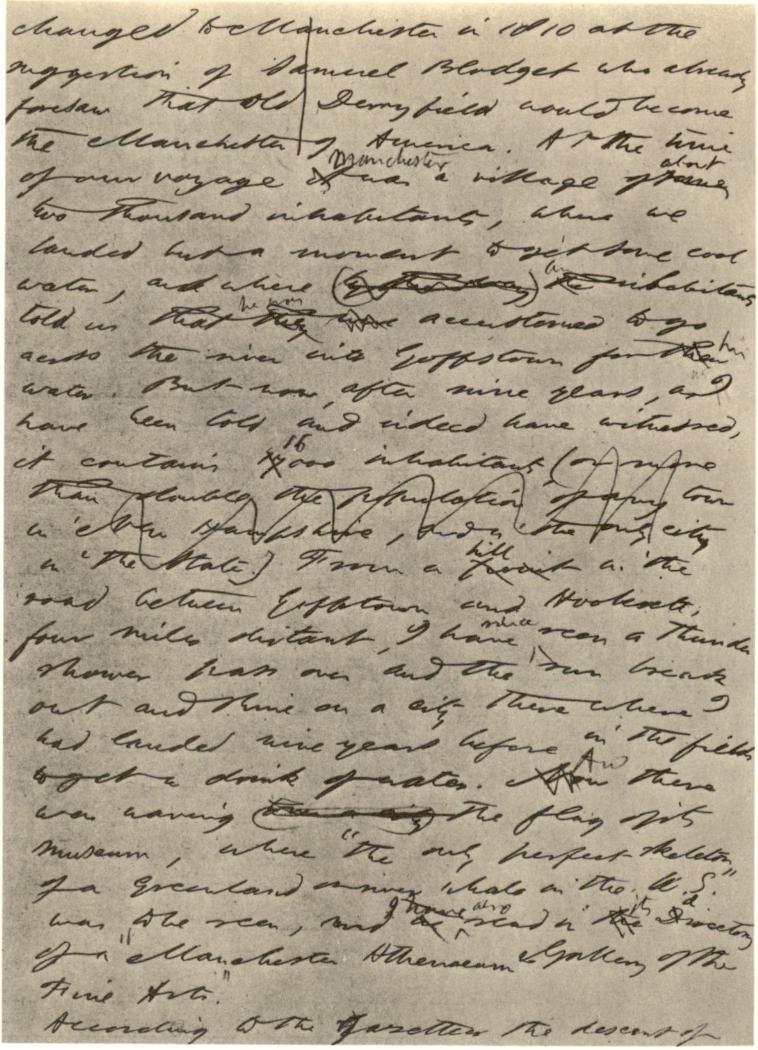
changed to Manchester in 1810 at the suggestion of Samuel Blodget who already foresaw that old Derryfield would become the Manchester of America. At the time of our voyage Manchester was a village of about two thousand inhabitants, where we landed but a moment to get some cool water, and where an inhabitant told us that he was accustomed to go across the river into Goffstown for his water. But now, after nine years, as I have been told and indeed have witnessed, it contains 16000 inhabitants. From a hill on the road between Goffstown and Hooksett, four miles distant, I have since seen a thunder shower pass over and the sun break out and shine on a city there where I had landed nine years before in the fields to get a drink of water. And there was waving the flag of its museum, where "the only perfect skeleton of a Greenland river whale in the U. S." was to be seen, and I have also read in its Directory of a "Manchester Athenaeum & Gallery of the Fine Arts."
According to the Gazetteer the descent of

Second manuscript draft, 1847-1849, from "Wednesday."

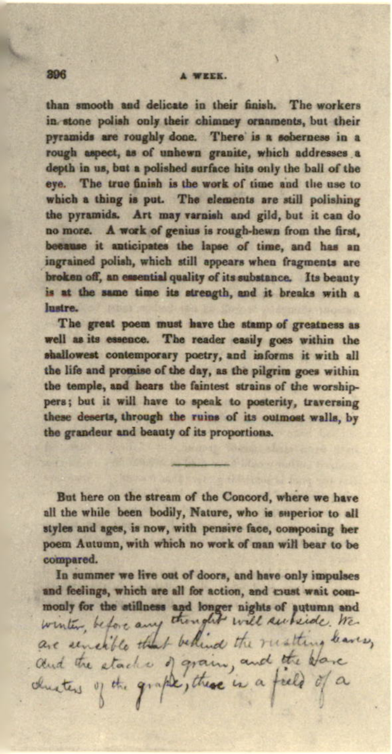

396 A WEEK.

than smooth and delicate in their finish. The workers in stone polish only their chimney ornaments, but their pyramids are roughly done. There is a soberness in a rough aspect, as of unhewn granite, which addresses a depth in us, but a polished surface hits only the ball of the eye. The true finish is the work of time and the use to which a thing is put. The elements are still polishing the pyramids. Art may varnish and gild, but it can do no more. A work of genius is rough-hewn from the first, because it anticipates the lapse of time, and has an ingrained polish, which still appears when fragments are broken off, an essential quality of its substance. Its beauty is at the same time its strength, and it breaks with a lustre.

The great poem must have the stamp of greatness as well as its essence. The reader easily goes within the shallowest contemporary poetry, and informs it with all the life and promise of the day, as the pilgrim goes within the temple, and hears the faintest strains of the worshippers; but it will have to speak to posterity, traversing these deserts, through the ruins of its outmost walls, by the grandeur and beauty of its proportions.

But here on the stream of the Concord, where we have all the while been bodily, Nature, who is superior to all styles and ages, is now, with pensive face, composing her poem Autumn, with which no work of man will bear to be compared.

In summer we live out of doors, and have only impulses and feelings, which are all for action, and must wait commonly for the stillness and longer nights of autumn and winter, before any thought will subside. We are sensible that behind the rustling leaves, and the stacks of grain, and the bare clusters of the grape, there is a field of a

Page proof, March-April 1849, with corrections.

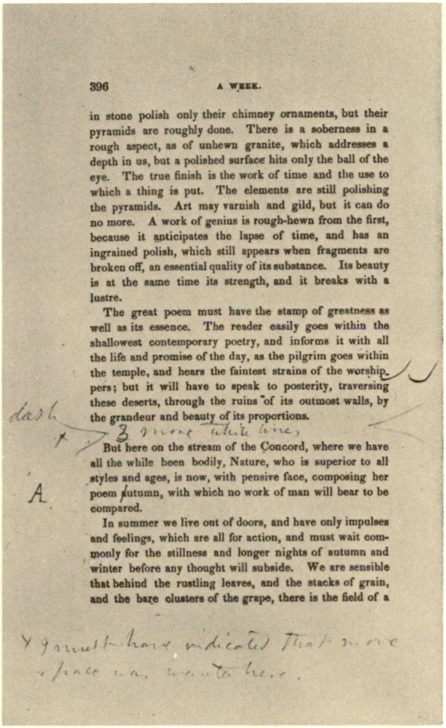

396 A WEEK.

in stone polish only their chimney ornaments, but their pyramids are roughly done. There is a soberness in a rough aspect, as of unhewn granite, which addresses a depth in us, but a polished surface hits only the ball of the eye. The true finish is the work of time and the use to which a thing is put. The elements are still polishing the pyramids. Art may varnish and gild, but it can do no more. A work of genius is rough-hewn from the first, because it anticipates the lapse of time, and has an ingrained polish, which still appears when fragments are broken off, an essential quality of its substance. Its beauty is at the same time its strength, and it breaks with a lustre.

The great poem must have the stamp of greatness as well as its essence. The reader easily goes within the shallowest contemporary poetry, and informs it with all the life and promise of the day, as the pilgrim goes within the temple, and hears the faintest strains of the worshippers; but it will have to speak to posterity, traversing these deserts, through the ruins of its outmost walls, by the grandeur and beauty of its proportions.

dash

X 3 more white lines

But here on the stream of the Concord, where we have all the while been bodily, Nature, who is superior to all styles and ages, is now, with pensive face, composing her poem Autumn, with which no work of man will bear to be compared.

A

In summer we live out of doors, and have only impulses and feelings, which are all for action, and must wait commonly for the stillness and longer nights of autumn and winter before any thought will subside. We are sensible that behind the rustling leaves, and the stacks of grain, and the bare clusters of the grape, there is the field of a

X I must have indicated that more space was wanted here.

First edition, May 1849, with corrections.

Map of original journey, ca. 1839, by Henry Thoreau.

Acknowledgments

FOR permission to refer to, copy, and publish manuscript material, as particularized in the Editorial Appendix, the editors are indebted to the Huntington Library, San Marino, California; Houghton Library, Harvard University; Henry W. and Albert A. Berg Collection, the New York Public Library; Astor, Lenox and Tilden Foundations; Pierpont Morgan Library, New York; Albert E. Lownes Thoreau Collection, Brown University Library; Abernethy Library of American Literature, Middlebury College; The Carl and Lily Pforzheimer Foundation, Inc., New York; Robert H. Taylor Collection, Princeton, New Jersey; and to Mr. W. Stephen Thomas, Rochester, New York.

Generous contributions of assistance, expertise, and good will were made by John C. Broderick, Herbert F. Cahoon, Mary Fenn, Malcolm Ferguson, Walter Harding, Alan Jutzi, Jennifer Lehmann, Albert Lownes, Kevin MacDonnell, Lee C. Mitchell, Joseph J. Moldenhauer, Marcia Moss, Marcus McCorisson, Robert Sattlemeyer, Claude Simpson, Lola Szladits, and James Thorpe; and also the Reference, Microfilm, and Special Collections departments of the Firestone Library, Princeton University.

The following members of the Textual Center staff worked on the volume: William Brennan, Verlyn Klinkenborg, Veronica Makowsky, Randy Nelson, Elizabeth Roemer, Nancy Simmons, Kevin Van Anglen. Carolyn Kappes typed the printer's copy of the Editorial Appendix and assisted the editors at every stage of preparing copy for the Press.

Material assistance was generously provided by

Princeton University, the University of Texas, Columbia University, and the National Endowment for the Humanities through the Modern Language Association and the Center for Editions of American Authors.

Editorial Contributions

Carl F. Hovde prepared text and editorial apparatus for *A Week on the Concord and Merrimack Rivers*, which were reviewed and verified by William L. Howarth, Elizabeth Hall Witherell, and Joseph J. Moldenhauer in consultation with Mr. Hovde. Linck C. Johnson wrote the Historical Introduction and Mr. Hovde the Textual Introduction, which were reviewed and verified by the same personnel in consultation with the authors. Thomas Blanding reviewed the Historical Introduction. Paul O. Williams supplied the Index. William L. Howarth and Elizabeth Hall Witherell supervised production of the volume and made such decisions as were required.

List of Abbreviations

A Week	Henry D. Thoreau, *A Week on the Concord and Merrimack Rivers*. See 49 and 68, below.
ATQ	*American Transcendental Quarterly*, Journal of New England Writers, Drawer 1080, Hartford, Conn.
Chalmers	*The Works of the English Poets, From Chaucer to Cowper*; . . . ed. Alexander Chalmers (London: C. Whittingham, 1810), 12 vols. Cited by volume and page numbers.
Channing	*The Collected Poems of William Ellery Channing the Younger, 1817-1901*, ed. Walter Harding (Gainesville: Scholar's Facsimiles & Reprints, 1967).
Corr.	*The Correspondence of Henry David Thoreau*, ed. Walter Harding and Carl Bode (New York: New York University Press, 1958).
CMHS	Collections of the Massachusetts Historical Society (Boston: [various publishers], 1806-date). Cited by volume and page numbers.
CPB	T's Commonplace Book at NN.
CRS	"Concord River" and "Saturday," first draft manuscript at NN. See *LMHDT*, Items D2b and D3a.
CS	*The Concord Saunterer*, The Thoreau Lyceum, Concord, Mass.
CSmH	Henry E. Huntington Library, San Marino, Ca. See also HM.
Days	Walter Harding, *The Days of Henry Thoreau* (New York: Knopf, 1965).
Dial	*The Dial: A Magazine for Literature, Philosophy, and Religion*, 4 vols. I: (Boston: Weeks, Jordan and Company, 1841); II: (Bos-

ton: E. P. Peabody, 1842); III: (Boston: E. P. Peabody, 1843); IV: (Boston: James Munroe and Company, 1844). Cited by volume and page numbers.

Early Essays — Henry D. Thoreau, *Early Essays and Miscellanies*, ed. Joseph J. Moldenhauer (Princeton: Princeton University Press, 1975).

ELH — End-of-Line Hyphenation in PE.

ESQ — *The Emerson Society Quarterly*, The Emerson Society, Hartford, Conn.

FD — Linck C. Johnson, "'A Natural Harvest': The Writing of *A Week on the Concord and Merrimack Rivers*, with the Text of the First Draft," Ph.D. dissertation, Princeton University, 1974.

HI — Historical Introduction in PE.

HM — Huntington Manuscript; manuscripts at CSmH. For HM 943, 956, 13182, 13194, 13195, 13201, see the index of *LMHDT*.

Hovde — Carl F. Hovde, "The Writing of Henry D. Thoreau's *A Week on the Concord and Merrimack Rivers*: A Study of Textual Materials and Techniques," Ph.D. dissertation, Princeton University, 1956.

ICarbS — Morris Library, Southern Illinois University, Carbondale, Ill.

J — Thoreau's Journal. An edited text is in *W*, vols. 7-20; also issued as *The Journal of Henry David Thoreau* (Boston: Houghton Mifflin Co., 1906), 14 vols. Cited by arabic volume and page numbers. PE text is in progress; see PJ.

JMN — *The Journals and Miscellaneous Notebooks of Ralph Waldo Emerson*, ed. William H. Gilman, *et al.* (Cambridge: Harvard University Press, 1960-date).

Johnson — *Johnson's English Dictionary*, as Improved by Todd, and Abridged by Chalmers, with Walker's Pronouncing Dictionary . . . (Philadelphia: Griffith & Simon, 1844).

LB — Thoreau's Long Book, a manuscript Journal volume (1842-1846) designated MA 1303 at the Pierpont Morgan Library, New York. PE text to appear in PJ 2, *Journal*; a partial text is in J 1, pp. 438-487.

Lett. — *The Letters of Ralph Waldo Emerson*, ed. Ralph Rusk (New York: Columbia University Press, 1939), 6 vols. Cited by volume and page numbers.

LMHDT — William L. Howarth, *The Literary Manuscripts of Henry David Thoreau*, No. 3 in Calendars of American Literary Manuscripts (Columbus: Ohio State University Press, 1974). Cited by item numbers, sections A-G.

Loeb — An edition from The Loeb Classical Library, as cited.

MA — Manuscripts at the Pierpont Morgan Library, New York. For MA 594, a commonplace book, and MA 608, a volume of Journal transcriptions, see the index to *LMHDT* and PJ 1.

MCo — Concord Free Public Library, Concord, Mass.

MH — Houghton Library, Harvard University, Cambridge, Mass. Unless otherwise noted, refers to miscellaneous manuscripts designated bMS Am 278.5, Folder 15.

MS — Manuscript

NjP — Firestone Library, Princeton University, Princeton, N.J.

NN — The New York Public Library, New York, N.Y. Unless otherwise noted, refers to manuscripts in the Berg Collection of English and American Literature.

P	Proof as printed (uncorrected) for the 1849 edition. Rare Book 110229 at CSmH.
PE	Princeton Edition, *The Writings of Henry D. Thoreau* (Princeton: Princeton University Press, 1971-date). Refers to the present edition of *A Week on the Concord and Merrimack Rivers.*
PJ	Princeton edition of Thoreau's Journal, in progress.
PJ 1	*Journal, 1837-1844*; ten manuscript volumes in page proof (in press).
Pms	Autograph correction or revision on P; pre-1849 (or presumably pre-1849).
Pms+	Made by the printer.
Pms++	Made by the printer or T.
Pms(1) or (2)	Stages of correction or revision in same passage.
Pms-a	Autograph correction or revision on P; post-1849.
RLF	H. H. Furness, ed., *Records of a Lifelong Friendship, 1807-1882, Ralph Waldo Emerson and William Henry Furness* (Boston: Houghton Mifflin Co., 1910).
RPB	John Hay Library, Brown University, Providence, R.I. Refers to manuscripts in Albert E. Lownes Thoreau Collection, as well as university holdings.
Shakspeare	*The Plays of William Shakspeare* (London: T. Longman, *et al.*, 1783), 15 vols. Cited by title of play, with act, scene, and line numbers.
Shanley	J. Lyndon Shanley, *The Making of Walden* (Chicago: University of Chicago Press, 1957).
T	Henry David Thoreau
TI	Textual Introduction in PE.

TLN — *Thoreau's Literary Notebook in the Library of Congress.* Facsimile Text edited by Kenneth Walter Cameron (Hartford: Transcendental Books, 1964).

TN — Textual Notes in PE.

TSB — *The Thoreau Society Bulletin*, State University College, Geneseo, N.Y.

TV — Table of Variants in PE.

VtMiM — The Julian W. Abernethy Collection of American Literature, Starr Library, Middlebury College, Middlebury, Vt.

W — *The Writings of Henry David Thoreau* (Boston: Houghton Mifflin Co., 1906), 20 vols. Cited by volume and page numbers. See also J.

Walden — Henry D. Thoreau, *Walden*, ed. J. Lyndon Shanley (Princeton: Princeton University Press, 1971).

Walker — *Critical Pronouncing Dictionary and Expositor of the English Language* . . . by John Walker. First Pocket Edition (Hartford: Silas Andrus, 1823).

Webster — *An American Dictionary of the English Language*; . . . by Noah Webster, LL.D. . . . Revised and Enlarged by Chauncey A. Goodrich (Philadelphia: J. B. Lippencott [*sic*], 1856).

WST — Thoreau manuscripts owned by W. Stephen Thomas, Rochester, N.Y. For descriptions, see FD and the index to *LMHDT*.

49 — Henry D. Thoreau, *A Week on the Concord and Merrimack Rivers* (Boston: James Munroe and Company, 1849).

68 — Henry D. Thoreau, *A Week on the Concord and Merrimack Rivers*, new and rev. ed. (Boston: Ticknor and Fields, 1868).

Historical Introduction

On August 31, 1839, Henry Thoreau and his elder brother John closed their schoolhouse in Concord, Massachusetts, and began a two-week boating and walking trip into New Hampshire. Their destination was the White Mountains, but the goals of Thoreau's life were less clearly defined. Twenty-two years old and a recent graduate of Harvard College, he was seeking a vocation consonant with his interests and independence. The literary life (on whose "privileges and pleasures" he had expounded at Harvard) attracted him increasingly. Earlier in 1839 Emerson informed Margaret Fuller that "Henry Thoreau has broke out into good poetry & better prose" (*Lett.*, II, p. 182),[1] but there was no outlet for the writings Thoreau had accumulated in his Journal since October 1837. He therefore probably had no plan to write a book about the brothers' summer trip when they left Concord.

Shortly after their return to Concord the *Dial* was founded, and with Emerson's blessing Thoreau undertook a literary career. He started to expand his brief excursion notes into an essay in 1840, but soon turned to projects that promised swifter recognition: poems, essays, and translations for the *Dial*. His plans for a book emerged only after John's death in 1842; he jotted short passages in Journal volumes he kept between 1842 and 1844. In 1845 he moved to Walden Pond, "to transact some private business with the fewest obstacles," as he retrospectively declared in *Walden* (pp. 19-20). That business was—or at least conspicuously involved—the composition of an extended nar-

[1] For abbreviations, see pp. 427-431.

rative about the 1839 journey. At the pond Thoreau wrote a first draft in 1845 and a second draft in 1847. Unable to find a publisher in 1847, he continued to revise and expand his manuscript until 1849. Then, at Emerson's urging, Thoreau published *A Week on the Concord and Merrimack Rivers* at his own expense.

Although the first edition was a financial failure, Thoreau did not lose faith in *A Week*. In later years he sold or distributed many copies, and he also revised the text before his death in 1862. Through the efforts of his friends, a "New and Revised Edition" was finally published in 1868. The book enjoyed somewhat better sales, even if readers continued to deride the heterodoxy and apparent formlessness of *A Week*. Yet its reputation has endured, and in recent years critics have begun to recognize that this story of a river excursion also depicts the spiritual and artistic growth of its author.

"Memoirs of a Tour" 1839-1840

"Some village friends stood upon a promontory lower down the stream to wave us a last farewell," Thoreau recalls in *A Week*, "but we, having already performed these shore rites, with excusable reserve, as befits those who are embarked on unusual enterprises, who behold but speak not, silently glided past the firm lands of Concord" (16.27-32).[2] Thoreau's mock-heroic description of the brothers' departure reflects his awareness that, on a literal level, *A Week* is anything but an epic. Indeed, if the notes he later recopied in his Journal are an indication, the actual trip

2 Unless otherwise specified, quotations in the Editorial Appendix are from the PE text of *A Week*, punctuated according to immediate context.

was even less eventful than his book suggests. On Saturday, August 31, he jotted down his impressions of the Billerica night, and the next day, while sitting on the bank of the Middlesex Canal, he added a brief description of Concord River between Ball's Hill and Billerica. Thereafter, he tersely recorded each day's progress up the Merrimack. Their river voyage ended Wednesday night a few miles below Hooksett, New Hampshire. On Thursday they walked ten miles to Concord, New Hampshire, where they boarded a stage for Plymouth on Friday. "The scenery commences on Sanbornton square," Thoreau noted that evening, "whence the White Mountains are first visible" (PJ 1, p. 136).[3] They devoted the next four days to hiking and mountain climbing. But while he carefully recorded the dimensions of the Stone Flume at Lincoln, Thoreau had less to say about climbing Agiocochook, or Mount Washington: "'Sept 10th ascended the mountain and rode to Conway'" (PJ 1, p. 137). Returning to Concord, New Hampshire, on Wednesday, the brothers reached their boat the next morning and, with wind and current in their favor, arrived at Concord, Massachusetts, by Friday night, September 13.

In contrast to Thoreau, Emerson quickly inferred a significance in the brothers' journey. Following his

[3] In J these notes are printed as entries for August 31-September 13, 1839. However, in the manuscript Journal (MA 1302:2), the notes appear under the date "June 21st 1840." T wrote "copied from pencil" above the notes and put them in quotation marks to set them off from interpolated comments and the following entry. Sometime in 1841 he transcribed the surviving contents of his early Journal volumes into three smaller volumes, so it is not possible to determine when he first transcribed his notes "copied from pencil." Thus the Journal entries for 1839 through the fall of 1841 quoted below are transcripts, while his notes "copied from pencil" are apparently transcripts of transcripts.

own trip to the White Mountains, which had yielded for him "few striking experiences," Emerson returned to Concord on the evening of September 2, 1839, too late to observe the Thoreaus' departure (*JMN*, VII, pp. 234-235). He wrote enthusiastic letters to Margaret Fuller about his own journey (*Lett.*, II, pp. 220-222), but privately expressed dissatisfaction: "How tedious is the perpetual self preservation of the traveller. . . . Not a blessed moment does he forget himself & yielding to the new world of facts that environ him, utter without memory that which they say" (*JMN*, VII, pp. 235-236). On September 14, one day after the Thoreaus returned to Concord, Emerson implicitly compared their trip with his own:

> Now here are my wise young neighbors who instead of getting like the wordmen into a railroad-car where they have not even the activity of holding the reins, have got into a boat which they have built with their own hands [,] with sails which they have contrived to serve as a tent by night, & gone up the river Merrimack to live by their wits on the fish of the stream & the berries of the wood. My worthy neighbor Dr B[artlett]. expressed a true parental instinct when he desired to send his boy with them to learn something. (*JMN*, VII, p. 238)

Emerson's thoughts anticipated several important themes in *A Week*. Contrasting their trip to ordinary forms of travel and education, he stressed the brothers' freedom, self-reliance, and harmony with nature. Unlike the "wordmen," his derisive term for those who knew nothing except what they were taught in classrooms, the Thoreaus had gone to school in nature and learned her secrets. By yielding themselves to a "new world of facts," they succeeded where he had failed.

Emerson probably did not suggest that Thoreau

write an account of that journey, but in other ways he definitely encouraged Thoreau's development as a writer. A few days after the brothers returned to Concord, Emerson helped establish the *Dial*, which he viewed as an ideal opportunity for his young friend. "My Henry Thoreau will be a great poet for such a company," he prophesied, "& one of these days for all companies" (*Lett.*, II, p. 225). He at once began urging Thoreau to contribute and Margaret Fuller, the editor, to accept Thoreau's submissions. In November she agreed to print his poem, "Sympathy," and after Emerson read Thoreau's "fine critique on Persius" in March 1840 he proclaimed it also "well worthy" of the *Dial* (*Lett.*, II, p. 259).

Encouraged by the acceptance of "Aulus Persius Flaccus," Thoreau began to consider other essay topics. He probably drafted the following list of projected lectures or essays with the *Dial* in mind:

Love.
Sound & Silence
Horace
Greek Poetry
The Brave man
Memoirs of a Tour–A Chit-chat with Nature.
Music
Hindoo Scripture.[4]

The fact that Thoreau later included these subjects and "Aulus Persius Flaccus" in *A Week* indicates how fully the book recapitulates his early career, and how strongly Emerson influenced him. Except for "Memoirs of a Tour–A Chit-chat with Nature," a banal title

[4] "Index rerum" (HM 945), p. 19 [recto]. This list is undated, but T probably wrote it in early 1840. The handwriting is characteristic of his early period, and all the topics are in his Journal of 1837-1840. "Hindoo Scripture," in a different ink, may be a somewhat later addition.

that probably refers to the river excursion, Thoreau's topics resemble Emerson's lectures between 1835 and 1840, including a series on English Literature, "Love," "Heroism," "Art," and "Religion." But "Memoirs of a Tour" suggests that Thoreau was also influenced by travel books like Henry Brackenridge's *Journal of a Voyage up the River Missouri* (1815), Thomas L. McKenney's *Sketches of a Tour to the Lakes* (1827), and Ross Cox's *Adventures on the Columbia River* (1832), all of which he read at Harvard, as well as Goethe's *Italienische Reise*, which he discussed in the early Journal and later in *A Week*.[5] Goethe's "object is faithfully to describe what he sees. . . . (It is this trait which is chiefly to be prized in the book)," he noted, "–even the reflections of the author do not interfere with his descriptions" (PJ 1, p. 16).

Thoreau began to reconstruct his own "tour" in the Journal for June 1840. He first wrote an extended description of the brothers' equipment and preparations. Using nature's "fertile idleness" as an analogy for their holiday, he stressed the idyllic aspects of the voyage: "Gradually the village murmur subsides–as when one falls into a placid dream . . . or as silently as fresh thoughts awaken us to new morning or evening light" (PJ 1, p. 125). On June 15 he "stood by the river to-day considering the forms of the elms reflected in the water" (PJ 1, p. 127), and the next day he recalled: "The river down which we glided for that long afternoon was like a clear drop of dew with the heavens and the landscape reflected in it" (PJ 1,

[5] T's withdrawals from the Harvard College Library are listed in Kenneth W. Cameron, *Emerson the Essayist* (Raleigh, N.C.: Thistle Press, 1945), II, pp. 191-208. For a discussion of parallels between *A Week* and Brackenridge's account, see John Aldrich Christie, *Thoreau as World Traveller* (New York: Columbia University Press, 1965), pp. 251-252.

p. 128). Similarly, he recorded the "faint bugle notes" (PJ 1, p. 132) heard on June 19, and then he wrote the following paragraphs:

> I shall not soon forget the sounds which lulled me when falling asleep on the banks of the Merrimack.
>
> Far into night I hear some tyro beating a drum incessantly with a view to some country muster, and am thrilled by an infinite sweetness as of a music which the breeze drew from the sinews of war. (PJ 1, p. 132)

By mid-June, perhaps sensing that he did not have sufficient material to complete "Memoirs of a Tour," Thoreau also drafted passages for an essay called "The Service," portions of which he had written as "A Chapter on Bravery" in December 1839. Except for the rather incongruous word "lulled," his June 19 entry resembles the martial spirit of "The Service," the first of many projects that delayed completion of his literary excursion. Margaret Fuller rejected "The Service" because in reading it she never once felt in the "stream of thought," and continually heard "the grating of tools on the mosaic" (*Corr.*, p. 42). The only portions of the essay published during Thoreau's lifetime, in fact, were passages he later revised for *A Week*.

"Merrimack & Musketaquid" 1841-1842

Early in June 1841, after boating with Thoreau along the Concord River, Emerson wrote in his journal:

> Then the good river-god has taken the form of my valiant Henry Thoreau here & introduced me to the riches of his shadowy starlit [,] moonlit stream, a lovely new world lying as close & yet as unknown to this vulgar trite one of streets & shops as death to life or poetry to prose. Through one field only we went to the boat &

> then left all time, all science, all history behind us and entered into Nature with one stroke of a paddle. Take care, good friend! I said, as I looked west into the sunset overhead & underneath, & he with his face toward me rowed towards it,—take care; you know not what you do, dipping your wooden oar into this enchanted liquid, painted with all reds & purples & yellows which glows under & behind you. (*JMN*, VII, p. 454)

Emerson's excited discovery of this "new world"—and his genial warning—may have been on Thoreau's mind when he indexed the Journal volumes later that summer and drew up another list of potential writing projects:

> Merrimack & Musketaquid
> Sound and Silence
> Bravery.
> Concord.
> Friendship.
> Books & style.
> Seeing
> Obligation.
> Dying
> Devil.
> Journal.[6]

While similar to his 1840 list of topics, this one contains some important substitutions and additions. Most significantly, Thoreau changed "Memoirs of a Tour—A Chit-chat with Nature" to "Merrimack & Musketaquid," and moved it to the top of his list. His account in the Journal for September 4, 1841, of another projected work, "a poem to be called 'Concord,'" suggests that he wished to add a new dimension to his descriptive writings:

> For argument I should have the River—the Woods—

[6] "Index rerum" (HM 945), front endpaper [verso]. This list was probably written at about the same time as the penciled index.

> the Ponds—the Hills—the Fields—the Swamps and Meadows—the Streets and Buildings—and the Villagers. Then Morning—Noon—and Evening—Spring Summer—Autumn and Winter—Night—Indian Summer—and the Mountains in the Horizon. (PJ 1, p. 330).

Thoreau's growing interest in the varied phenomena of Concord apparently prompted a corresponding change in his projected story of the river voyage. In contrast to "Memoirs of a Tour—A Chit-chat with Nature," in which "Nature" is a personified abstraction, "Merrimack & Musketaquid" is sharply focused. These two streams, one dead and stagnant, as its old Indian name "Musketaquid," or "Grass-ground River," suggests, the other alive and flowing, offered Thoreau all he needed for "argument"—the drama of human life and history, the changing seasons, and the amplitude of natural forms. Thus, while he continued to plan Transcendental essays like "Friendship" and "Bravery," by the summer of 1841 Thoreau had begun to tailor his writing to fit new and more specific interests.

After several restive months at the Emersons', in September Thoreau made plans to build a hut at Flint's Pond in the neighboring town of Lincoln, where he might put his literary house in order. That fall he spent a few months editing and transcribing the surviving portions of his three Journal volumes from 1837-1841 into five transcript volumes called "Gleanings Or What Time Has Not Reaped Of My Journal." Apparently he was confident they would yield a final harvest of essays, including "Merrimack & Musketaquid."[7]

[7] For a discussion of T's plans at this time to write a book of essays, see Thomas Blanding, "Apollo Serving King Admetus: Thoreau Bargains for a Farm and a Book in 1841," an unpublished lecture on deposit at the Thoreau Lyceum, Concord, Mass.

In October Emerson gave Margaret Fuller a penciled draft of what seems to have been an autobiographical fragment by Thoreau. On the 18th she acknowledged receipt to its author:

> The pencilled paper Mr E. put into my hands. I have taken the liberty to copy it You expressed one day my own opinion that the moment such a crisis is passed we may speak of it. There is no need of artificial delicacy, of secrecy, it keeps its own secret; it cannot be made false. Thus you will not be sorry that I have seen the paper. Will you not send me some other records of the good week. (*Corr.*, p. 57)

Her closing words "good week" appear to be a direct reference to Thoreau's nascent book about the river journey, and Allen Hovey has suggested that "the 'pencilled paper' . . . held the rough sketch of the book's underlying theme."[8] Little evidence, however, supports this speculation. The "crisis" was probably occasioned by his lapsed romance with Ellen Sewall a year earlier, and the "records of the good week" might well refer to a different document, possibly to passages Thoreau had drafted in his 1840 Journal and then recopied in one of his transcript volumes. In either case, Fuller's letter suggests that the project was uppermost in his mind that fall. But circumstances again blocked its completion, for he was denied permission to build a hut at Flint's Pond and so postponed his plan to begin drafting essays.

Perhaps more than any other single event, John Thoreau, Jr.'s death from lockjaw on January 11, 1842, determined the themes and action of *A Week*. "[Henry] says John is not lost but nearer to him than

[8] Allen Beecher Hovey, *The Hidden Thoreau* (Beirut, Lebanon: Catholic Press, 1966), p. 56. For another view, see Henry Seidel Canby, *Thoreau* (Boston: Houghton Mifflin Co., 1939), p. 123.

ever," Lidian Emerson approvingly wrote her sister Lucy Jackson Brown a week later, "for he knows him better than he ever did before and to know a friend better brings him nearer."[9] Yet Thoreau's Journal entries in February and March record a desperate attempt to assuage his grief, and in a March letter to Emerson, who had lost his son, Waldo, two weeks after John died, Thoreau strikingly prefigured his later description of autumn flowers and foliage in *A Week*. Insisting that for flowers or grasses "the law of their death is the law of new life" (*Corr.*, p. 64), he concluded:

> So it is with the human plant. We are partial and selfish when we lament the death of the individual, unless our plaint be a paean to the departed soul, and a sigh as the wind sighs over the fields, which no shrub interprets into its private grief.
>
> One might as well go mourning for every sere leaf—but the more innocent and wiser soul will snuff a fragrance in the gales of autumn, and congratulate Nature upon her health. (*Corr.*, p. 65)

This letter helps to explain why Thoreau depicted autumnal phenomena in *A Week*, which ostensibly describes a late summer voyage. That book is Thoreau's "paean to the departed soul," whose loss—described in the opening elegiac hymn, "Where'er thou sail'st who sailed with me,"—is dramatically resolved in a meditation on the autumnal landscape in the last chapter. Thus, while he did not begin the first draft of *A Week* until 1845, by 1842 he had established a form, theme, and line of action. Over the next two years he developed these by writing a series of preliminary "excursions," prototypes for the book that was to come.

[9] Quoted in Joel Myerson, "More Apropos of John Thoreau," *American Literature*, 45 (March 1973), 106.

Early Excursions 1842-1844

In late March 1842 Thoreau's literary career received a boost when Emerson assumed editorship of the *Dial*. Though Margaret Fuller had resigned, Emerson kept her informed of the journal's prospects. On April 10 he wrote her: "I read a little lately in the 'Scientific Surveys' of Massachusetts . . . and this day I have, as I hope, set Henry Thoreau on the good track of giving an account of them in the Dial, explaining to him the felicity of the subject for him as it admits of the narrative of all his woodcraft boatcraft & fishcraft" (*Lett.*, III, p. 47).

"Natural History of Massachusetts," which appeared in the July number of the *Dial*, was far from what Emerson expected, but his suggestion was important. Thoreau roughly followed the divisions of the State *Reports*, and traced representative species of each phylum or group through a full year. He thus managed to unify a series of seemingly random and casual observations of nature by ordering them according to the seasons in which they occurred. Readers may still hear "the grating of tools on the mosaic," especially in the awkward transitions from natural description to philosophical speculation, but the essay represents an early step toward the seasonal patterns of *A Week* and *Walden*.

Although Emerson was disappointed by Thoreau's essay (*Lett.*, III, p. 75), Nathaniel Hawthorne, who moved into the Old Manse in July, was favorably impressed. Thoreau "is a good writer," he noted in his journal, "at least, he has written one good article, a rambling disquisition on Natural History in the last Dial, . . . so true, minute, and literal in observation, yet giving the spirit as well as letter of what he sees, even as a lake reflects its wooded banks, showing every leaf, yet giving the wild beauty of the whole scene."[10] His analogy is revealing, for that afternoon Thoreau had taken him boating on Concord River. Hawthorne quickly agreed to buy Thoreau's boat, the Musketaquid, which the brothers had sailed on their river journey, and he rechristened it Pond Lily. More significantly, Hawthorne also acquired Thoreau's view of the river's emblematic character, which he soon began to describe in strikingly similar terms.[11]

During the summer and fall of 1842 Thoreau revised and expanded the notes he had taken during a trip to Mount Wachusett in July. The manuscripts of "A Walk to Wachusett," published in the *Boston Miscellany of Literature* for January 1843, demonstrate that he never intended to write a simple travel essay. In one version Thoreau flatly stated that "though a 'Journey of a Day,' we meant that it should be a 'Picture of Human Life.' "[12] He also heavily revised his description of sunset from the mountain top, which originally read:

> And then the same tragedy was repeated on the west side as far as the Connecticut and Green Mountains—and the rays of the sun fell on us two alone of all New England men. And we had only to rise a little higher that the sun might never set to us.[13]

[10] Nathaniel Hawthorne, *The American Notebooks*, ed. Claude M. Simpson (The Centenary Edition, Columbus: Ohio State University Press, 1972), p. 355.

[11] Cf. PJ 1, pp. 127-128 (J 1, p. 140); and Hawthorne's *American Notebooks*, pp. 360-361 (September 18, 1842). T later used this material in *A Week* (45.30-46.1); Hawthorne used his description in "The Old Manse" in *Mosses from an Old Manse* (1846).

[12] MH, Folder 10.

[13] From an unpublished draft of the essay in a notebook at NN, identified as "Nature Album, May and June 1842" in the Appendix to PJ 1.

Changing "tragedy" to "scene," and deleting the imaginary ascent, Thoreau subdued the emotional intensity of his original description. The elegiac tone of the first version may betray a continuing effort to come to terms with his brother's death, since they had also ascended a mountain on their 1839 journey. In the fall of 1842 Thoreau drafted passages for a projected essay or book about the river voyage, including a description of the Merrimack that subtly suggests his nostalgia:

> In many parts the merrimack is as fresh and natural as ever– In many parts of its course the shore and surrounding scenery exhibit only the revolutions of nature– The pine stands up erect on its brink–and the alders and willows fringe its edge–and only the beaver and the redman are wanting to complete the picture. (PJ 1, p. 445).

About this time he also began to transcribe entries related to the river trip from his earlier Journal into a large manuscript volume which in annotations to his personal copy of the *Dial* he called "long book" (hereafter Long Book).[14] He seems to have worked on the river excursion only at odd moments, sketching a book and anticipating a time when he would have the leisure to compose a full draft. Despite Leo Marx's contention that the excursion was Thoreau's "one satisfactory structural pattern,"[15] in 1842 and 1843 he continued to develop a variety of themes and forms, creating dissimilar works that influenced the ultimate shape of *A Week*.

Between April and December 1842, planning "an article, Lyceum lecture, or small book on subjects of

14 Thoreau's copy of the *Dial* is at ICarbS.

15 Leo Marx, "Thoreau's Excursions," *Yale Review*, 51 (Spring 1962), 367.

central importance to him,"[16] Thoreau transcribed Journal entries on two topics he had included on his lists of projected essays–"Hindoo Scripture" and "Books & style." Emerson was probably aware of the project, for he asked Thoreau to edit selections from *The Laws of Menu*, which were printed along with his translation of *Prometheus Bound* in the January 1843 number of the *Dial*. Although his notebook had many entries on Hindu scripture, Thoreau excerpted only a small portion for "Dark Ages," a short essay on ancient history, which, as acting editor, he included in the April 1843 *Dial* and later added to *A Week*. In February he delivered a lecture on Sir Walter Raleigh, which combined Thoreau's interests in history and in literary style, and he thought enough of the lecture to revise it for the *Dial*.[17] But the *Dial* ceased publication before "Sir Walter Raleigh" could appear. It thus joined "The Service" and his essay on the Hindu scripture as unpublished materials available for *A Week*, where Hindu sages, heroes of Greek tragedy, a Renaissance writer-explorer, and a host of other figures would eventually appear as images of the ideal nineteenth-century hero.

Thoreau's decision to go to Staten Island to tutor the son of William Emerson early in 1843 launched his most serious attempt to become a self-supporting

16 Kenneth Cameron, *Transcendental Climate*, 3 vols. (Hartford: Transcendental Books, 1963), III, p. 901. This volume contains a facsimile and transcript of the notebook, MA 608, identified as "Transcripts, 1840-1842" in PJ 1.

17 Walter Harding, "A Check List of Thoreau's Lectures," *Bulletin of the New York Public Library*, 52 (February 1948), 79, and the "Textual Note" to "Sir Walter Raleigh" in *Early Essays*, p. 391. Unless otherwise noted, Harding's article is used to date T's lectures.

writer. In New York Thoreau renewed his acquaintance with Horace Greeley, who later acted as an agent for his works. But, although he sold "The Landlord" and "Paradise (to be) Regained" to the *Democratic Review*, he found that few other periodicals paid for contributions. He next tried the book publishers. "Some propose to me to do what an honest man cannot—" he wrote his mother: "Among others I conversed with Harpers . . . but they say that they are making fifty thousand dollars annually, and their motto is to let well alone" (*Corr.*, p. 135).

While in New York, his thoughts often turned to Concord. In May he sent his sister Helen a copy of his poem "Brother where dost thou dwell?" in which he seeks John's presence among familiar scenes: "Dost thou still haunt the brink / Of yonder river's tide?" (*Corr.*, p. 109). To Emerson he described the river as his most vivid memory of Concord: "Yet will my thoughts revert to those dear hills and that *river* which so fills up the world to the brim, worthy to be named with Mincius and Alpheus still drinking its meadows while I am far away" (*Corr.*, p. 123). Thus, when Emerson requested a contribution for the *Dial*, Thoreau responded with a Concord excursion, "A Winter Walk." In it, he adumbrated the central image of *A Week*:

> We see the fields and forests from a new and wilder side, for the river flows in the rear of the towns, and the fields and gardens come down to it with a sort of unpretension and frankness, as they do not front upon the highway. It is the outside and edge of the earth. . . . It is a beautiful illustration of the law of obedience, the flow of a river; the path for a sick man, a highway down which an acorn cup may float secure with its freight. Its slight occasional falls, whose precipices would not diversify the landscape, are celebrated by

> mist and spray, and attract the traveller from far and near. From the remote interior its current conducts him like a skilful leach, by broad and easy steps descending into the plain, or by one gentle inclined plane, to the sea. Thus by an early and constant yielding to the inequalities of the ground, it secures itself the easiest passage.[18]

Thoreau emphasized an idyllic rather than heroic side of river travel in order to develop his theme of "the law of obedience." But at the end of his essay, he hinted that obedience to nature's laws may lead to conflicts with social laws: "Let a brave devout man spend the year in the woods of Maine or Labrador, and see if the Hebrew scriptures speak adequately to his condition and experience, from the setting in of winter to the breaking up of the ice."[19] Implicitly, such a life demanded a new testament, which he hoped to write. He had not gone to Labrador, but he had seen the White Mountains of New Hampshire. Thus, on October 15, 1843, he wrote in the Journal:

> We had resolved to travel to those White mountains—whither the old colonists went in search of the great carbuncles—the Crystal hills which one John Field an Irish man had visited—as Winthrop says. . . .
>
> Why should we take the reader who may be gentle and tender, through this rude tract—where the ways are steep and the views none of the best for such as are tenderly bred— Rude men and rough paths would he have to encounter—and many a cool blast over the mountain side. (PJ 1, p. 478).

Thoreau described a similar contrast "between the stern and desolate poetry of Ossian and that of Chaucer and the early English bards" (PJ 1, p. 487),

[18] From Thoreau's MS copy for the *Dial* printer, quoted by permission of The Carl H. Pforzheimer Library.

[19] *Ibid.*

when he lectured on "The Ancient Poets" at the Concord Lyceum on November 29. Later he included a revised version in *A Week*, where Ossian is an emblem of endurance, a counterpart to other signs of vitality Thoreau finds in man and nature. Although his attempt to establish himself in the New York literary world ended in failure, by the time Thoreau left William Emerson's household and returned to Concord in December 1843, he had amassed materials that would help to shape *A Week*.

"Excursion on Concord and Merrimack Rivers" 1844-1846

After Christmas, Thoreau went to work in his father's pencil factory. He had swiftly revised his lecture on "The Ancient Poets" for the January 1844 *Dial*, where it appeared as "Homer. Ossian. Chaucer." along with his translations of Pindar. But the April number, which included more Pindar and the essay "Herald of Freedom," was the last, and Thoreau was left with no ready outlet for his writings. Ironically, the collapse of the *Dial* proved as influential as its inception, for now he was virtually forced to turn to a long and sustained project.

During the winter of 1843-1844, Thoreau had little contact with Emerson, then working on *Essays: Second Series*. Emerson was apparently disappointed by Thoreau's New York venture, for earlier he had written: "Ellery says, that Writers never do any thing: they are passive observers. . . . H will never be a writer[;] he is active as a shoemaker" (*JMN*, IX, p. 45).[20] Channing, whose first book, *Poems*, was published in April 1843, had at least temporarily re-

[20] Emerson later indexed this passage under "H.D.T."

placed Thoreau as Emerson's hope for a Transcendental bard. Ellery "puts all poets & especially all prophets far far in the background," Emerson exclaimed in a letter to Margaret Fuller shortly after Thoreau returned from New York (*Lett.*, III, p. 230).

Margaret Fuller was also busy during the winter of 1843-1844. She informed Emerson in November: "Some leaves are written of my record of the West out of which I hope to make a little book. . . . I shall bring in with brief criticisms of books read there, a kind of letter box, where I shall put a part of one of S. Ward's letters, one of Ellery's and apropos to that July moon under which I received it, a letter containing Triformis" (*Lett.*, III, p. 220n.). She completed *Summer on the Lakes* in May 1844. Emerson, who arranged for its publication, called it "a very good & entertaining book" (*Lett.*, III, p. 255), and Thoreau, who had talked to her about the trip when she visited at William Emerson's in 1843, no doubt read the book shortly after it was published early in the summer of 1844. Perry Miller believes Thoreau "received from *Summer* much of the impetus for his similar compilation, *A Week on the Concord and Merrimack Rivers*."[21] *Summer on the Lakes* may, indeed, have suggested how he might expand his river excursion by inserting seemingly unrelated materials, including extracts from books, literary criticism, and poems.

Thoreau was soon free to begin work on a book about the brothers' journey. In September Emerson purchased Wyman field on the shore of Walden Pond, thus adding "an absurdity or two to my usual ones," as he told his brother William (*Lett.*, III, p. 262). His purchase offered Thoreau a long-awaited opportunity

[21] Perry Miller, ed., *Margaret Fuller, American Romantic* (Garden City, N.Y.: Anchor Books, 1963), p. 116.

to live by a pond. In anticipation of this move, Thoreau continued to gather and organize materials for *A Week.* He revised and copied relevant Journal entries into Long Book, and drafted original passages of narration and description, including a lengthy account of his summer 1844 trip to the Berkshires.

Previously Thoreau had written Journal entries specifically for *A Week*; by the fall of 1844 he had begun to incorporate unrelated entries, ranging from November 3, 1837 (PJ 1, p. 10), up to the spring of 1844 (PJ 1, p. 497). For example, on June 30, 1840, he had written in the Journal: "I sailed from Fair Haven last evening as gently and steadily as the clouds sail through the atmosphere. The wind came blowing blithely from the South west fields, and stepped into the folds of our sail like a winged horse—pulling with a strong and steady impulse" (PJ 1, p. 145). In Long Book, by changing "I" to "we," and the "wind blowing blithely from the South west fields" to the "north wind," Thoreau transformed this mild day on the Concord to a brisk day on the Merrimack below Chelmsford (LB). Moreover, in 1840 he had used the "pulse" of the sail as a happy example of the correspondence between man and nature; in 1844, more than two years after John's death, Thoreau stressed the frailty and suspense of human life. Thus while formerly he was "blown on by God's breath" (PJ 1, p. 145), now the brothers remained "always at the mercy of the breeze" (LB).

Thoreau initially planned eight chapters, one for each day the brothers spent on the rivers, including two Thursdays, September 5 and 12, but he clearly did not intend to write a literal account of their excursion. After inscribing an epigraph to his brother on the first page of Long Book, he copied entries from the Journal on friendship, Indian relics, summer and autumn flowers, and the fish of Concord River. He also copied and drafted poetry and passages on writers, the Concord cattle show, and his summer trip to the Berkshires in 1844. From these transcriptions Thoreau drafted a lecture on "Concord River," which included most of the entries on fish. He delivered "Concord River" at the Concord Lyceum on March 25, 1845, then copied more poems and drafted original passages on silence and a concluding paragraph for the voyage in Long Book. He probably considered his preparations complete, for he then numbered each entry according to its designated chapter in the first draft of *A Week*.[22]

That summer, replying to Evert Duyckinck's request for the names of prospective young contributors to Wiley & Putnam's new series of "American Books," Hawthorne stated:

> As for Thoreau, there is one chance in a thousand that he might write a most excellent and readable book; but I should be sorry to take the responsibility, either towards you or him, of stirring him up to write anything. . . . The only way, however, in which he could ever approach the popular mind, would be by writing a book of simple observation of nature, somewhat in the vein of White's *History of Selborne*. (*Days*, pp. 243-244)[23]

22 T listed the chapters on pages 27-[28] of Long Book, and numbered passages in the notebook 1-8 in pencil. In the first draft he identified these eight chapters by day and/or date, i.e. "Sat[urday], Aug[ust] 31st, 1839." In the first draft, the introductory section on Concord River was untitled. Hereafter, chapters in the first draft are cited by T's final chapter titles, i.e. "Concord River," "Saturday," etc.

23 Wiley & Putnam's series, "The Library of American

In fact, Thoreau had already moved into his house at Walden Pond, where he began a first draft of *A Week.* This project proved to be far more than a "book of simple observation of nature." The first draft contains detailed descriptions of nature, but also extended digressions. Thoreau devoted half of "Saturday" to a description of the fish in Concord River, particularly those which were abundant "until the dam and afterward the canal at Billerica, and the factories at Lowell put an end to their migrations hitherward" (FD, 20). In "Sunday" he defended the vigor and freedom of the Indian's forest life, and, defining his own aspirations as a writer, called for a literature that would reflect the more primeval aspects of nature. Similarly, his discussion of the ancient and exalted wisdom of Hindu scripture in "Monday" was an attempt to discover an analogue to his own spiritual aspirations. Seeking to locate in personal experience values like those he had found in history and literature, in "Tuesday" Thoreau first described a moment of illumination atop Saddleback Mountain, and then added an account of his 1844 trip to the Berkshires, where he had met Rice, a man who exemplified, if to an exaggerated and somewhat comic degree, the virtues of a primitive life.

Thoreau's discussion of friendship in the first draft of "Wednesday" gathered together these various strands, for it described the most natural and elevating bond between men—"a fragmentary and godlike

---

Books," commenced with a collection of Poe's *Tales* and another of his poems in 1845, and later included Margaret Fuller's *Papers on Literature and Art* (1846), Hawthorne's *Mosses from an Old Manse* (1846), and Melville's *Typee* (1846). See Perry Miller, *The Raven and the Whale* (New York: Harcourt, Brace, & World, 1956), *passim.*

intercourse of ancient date still kept up at intervals" (FD, 126). Although Thoreau did not mention his brother by name, the discourse on friendship commemorated John Thoreau. In the last paragraph of "Friday," Thoreau sounded a note of triumphant innocence and expectancy as the brothers leap "gladly on shore" and fasten their boat to a "little apple tree whose stem still bore the mark which its chain had worn—in the chafing of the spring freshet" (FD, 165). Having made his own escape to Walden Pond, Thoreau depicted their excursion as a discovery of the wildness that survives in literature, man, and nature.

Thoreau appears to have anticipated writing an account of his life in the woods from the moment he arrived at the pond, but *A Week* was his first priority. He apparently completed the first draft in the fall of 1845, and he began to revise it sometime after writing a lecture on Thomas Carlyle, delivered before the Concord Lyceum on February 4, 1846. Most of his changes that spring expanded the draft manuscript. Having included two leaves from the 1842 essay on Hindu scripture in the first draft, he next quarried other unpublished writings for additional brief passages. For example, while he later gleaned "Sir Walter Raleigh" for the discussion of literary style in "Monday" (Hovde, 145-146), at first he adopted only a few passages about Raleigh's *History of the World*. These he inserted into a description of useful books in "Sunday," where they complement Thoreau's own narrative ideals: "For the most part an author only *writes* history, treating it as a dead subject, but Raleigh tells it like a fresh story."[24] He selected passages from "The Service" with similar care, and added them to

24 MH, Folder 19. T's notes on the verso of the leaf indicate its projected location in his first draft of *A Week*.

a discussion of music at the end of "Monday."[25] He thus constructed a plausible chain of associations: drum–sounds–music–harmony–natural laws–heroism. Indeed, since heroism is a strong theme in *A Week*, his depiction of the brothers' response to the drummer near Nashua seems more appropriate than it had been in the setting provided by "The Service."[26]

By midsummer 1846, Thoreau had completed his revisions and read portions of the first draft to friends. One of these auditors was Emerson, who immediately pressed for publication. On July 16 Emerson wrote Charles King Newcomb: "In a short time, if Wiley & Putnam smile, you shall have Henry Thoreau's 'Excursion on Concord & Merrimack rivers,' a seven days' voyage in as many chapters, pastoral as Isaak Walton, spicy as flagroot, broad & deep as Menu" (*Lett.*, III, p. 338). His comment suggests that Thoreau had decided to combine his two Thursday chapters, September 5th and 12th, perhaps in an effort to enhance the unity of his account, provisionally entitled "Excursion on Concord and Merrimack Rivers." But Thoreau may not have planned to publish the "Excursion" so soon, since at the time he was busy revising his Carlyle lecture, which he sent to Horace Greeley in August. Probably he had read to Emerson directly from the untidy, heavily revised first draft of the "Excursion," from which he would have to prepare fair copy for submission to a publisher. Moreover, he had recently drafted several long passages on Hindu scripture in the Journal, and he

[25] He copied these passages on two leaves at MH, Folder 4, D.

[26] Cf. Perry Miller, *Consciousness in Concord: The Text of Thoreau's Hitherto "Lost Journal" (1840-41) and Commentary* (Boston: Houghton Mifflin Co., 1958), pp. 142-143.

apparently planned other substantial additions before preparing a final copy (NN).

In his first draft Thoreau had devoted only three brief paragraphs to the days he and John had spent in the White Mountains. But in late August he drafted a seven-page account of the brothers' walking tour to link the two recently combined "Thursday" chapters. Appropriately, he made a transition between river and mountains by alluding to the sources of the Merrimack: "It was already water of Squam and Newfound lake and Winnipiseogee, and White mountain snow dissolved on which we were floating" (NN). The White Mountains had been hospitable, and his Journal account contains leisurely reminiscences of the rude inns and villages the brothers had visited. Soon he encountered Mount Katahdin in Maine, however, which proved neither hospitable nor sympathetic to man. Thoreau was fascinated by this home of "Chaos and Old Night"[27] and when he returned to Concord in late September he devoted 170 pages of Journal to his experiences in Maine. The dark vision glimpsed on Katahdin did not suit his thematic purpose in the "Excursion," but when Thoreau resumed work on it in the late fall of 1846 he apparently decided not to domesticate his account of the White Mountains. In the final version of *A Week* Agiocochook, while less terrifying than Katahdin, is equally remote and mysterious.

A Week *and* Walden *1847-1849*

During the winter of 1846-1847 Thoreau worked

27 Henry D. Thoreau, *The Maine Woods*, ed. Joseph J. Moldenhauer (Princeton: Princeton University Press, 1972), p. 70. T's theme of "Necessity and Fate" emerged more strongly in drafts of "Ktaadn, and the Maine Woods," published in 1848.

on drafts of both *A Week* and *Walden.* In February Horace Greeley invited him to follow up the Carlyle essay with similar articles on Emerson, Hawthorne, and others: "in a year or two, if you take care not to write faster than you think, you will have the material of a volume worth publishing" (*Corr.*, p. 174). But Thoreau declined, hoping to publish another book even sooner. He had already completed part of a first draft of *Walden*, which he read as "A History of Myself" before the Concord Lyceum on February 10, and he was at work on a second and presumably final draft of *A Week.* Thus on February 27, announcing the publication of "Thomas Carlyle and His Works" in *Graham's Magazine*, Emerson wrote Carlyle: "You are yet to read a good American book made by this Thoreau, & which is shortly to be printed, he says."[28]

Two weeks later Emerson informed Evert Duyckinck of Wiley & Putnam that Thoreau had "just completed a book of extraordinary merit" entitled "An Excursion on the Concord & Merrimack Rivers," and about as long as Dickens' *Pictures of Italy.* If that estimate is accurate, the second draft had expanded to roughly seventy thousand words, or nearly twice its first draft length. As Thoreau's agent, Emerson recognized that the narrative was "a very slender thread for such big beads & ingots as are strung on it," so he stressed to Duyckinck the value of Thoreau's other material: "It will be . . . attractive to *lovers of nature* . . . to scholars for its excellent literature, & to all thoughtful persons for its originality & profoundness. . . . It is really a book of the results of the studies of years" (*Lett.*, III, p. 384). Bronson Alcott, to whom Thoreau read a portion of the manuscript on March 16, was even more enthusiastic:

[28] *The Correspondence of Emerson and Carlyle*, ed. Joseph Slater (New York: Columbia University Press, 1964), p. 415.

"This evening I pass with Thoreau at his hermitage on Walden, and he reads me some passages from his MS volume which he is preparing to print some day entitled 'A Week on the Concord and Merrimac Rivers.' . . . It is a Virgil and Gilbert White and Yankee settler all, singing his prose-poems with remembrance of his reading and experiences in the woods and road-paths by way of episode and variety—a portraying of a dreamland lying wild and yet unvisited here in New England, and still remote from everybody but the bold dreamer himself. . . .

". . . It preserves to us whatever of the wild and mystic remains to us along our brooksides and rivers. . . .

"It has the merit, moreover, that somehow, despite all presumptions to the contrary, the sod and sap and fibre and flavour of New England have found at last a clear relation to the literature of other and classic lands, and we drink off here the quintessence also of literature the coolest and freshest. Egypt, India, Greece, England, flow from the poet's hand as he scoops the waters for us from the rivers. . . .

"Poems are here also, vigorous and rugged enough to defy Quarles or Donne. . . . Criticism, too, we have, of the like radical quality and toughness. Homer, Hesiod, Æschylus, and Chaucer have got some one to look into their merit now, and modernize and make them indigenous and home-felt once in Concord."[29]

While only fragments of the second draft of *A Week* have survived, Alcott's description helps account for its growth during the winter of 1846-1847. Thoreau had found useful material in his Journal of the early days at Walden, including a passage on flowers "whose seeds were blown from more elysian fields," and entries on memory, history, and fables (MA

[29] Bronson Alcott, *The Journals of Bronson Alcott*, ed. Odell Shepard (Boston: Little, Brown, 1938), pp. 213-214. Since Alcott copied this passage into his diary in 1849, after he read the published version of *A Week*, he may have revised accordingly. Thus it is not clear whether or not T had settled on a final title for the book by March 1847.

1302:8). But Alcott's reference to "the literature of other and classic lands" suggests that Thoreau may have inserted revised copies of articles he had published in the *Dial*, such as "Dark Ages," and "Homer. Ossian. Chaucer." His own copies of the *Dial* bear numerous corrections and revisions of these works, mostly destined for incorporation into the text of *A Week*.[30] Alcott also noted that Thoreau planned to print *A Week* "some day." This suggests that Thoreau may not have authorized Emerson to approach Duyckinck, who promptly announced in the *Literary World*: "Henry D. Thoreau, Esq., whose elaborate paper on Carlyle, now publishing in Graham's Magazine, is attracting considerable attention, has also completed a new work of which report speaks highly. It will probably be soon given to the public."[31] In fact, at least three weeks after Emerson described the manuscript to Duyckinck as "quite ready" (*Lett.*, III, p. 384), Thoreau began drafting the Hannah Dustan story, a major addition to "Thursday," and he continued to revise his manuscript during the spring of 1847.[32]

"I should not have delayed sending you my manuscript so long," Thoreau wrote Duyckinck on May 28, 1847, "if I had not known that delay would be no inconvenience to you, and advantage to the sender" (*Corr.*, p. 181). But Thoreau's delay had been

[30] T's alterations in the volumes, now at ICarbS, reflect three stages of work: immediately succeeding *Dial* publication, preceding 49, and preceding 68. See *Early Essays*, pp. 384, 386.

[31] *Literary World*, March 27, 1847. Quoted in Miller, *The Raven and the Whale*, p. 192.

[32] On a Journal leaf from the 1847 "New Book" (HM 924), T noted: "heard a hyla Ap. 6th pond ice melted Ap 8th 1847." A line across the page separates this entry from the beginning of the Hannah Dustan story.

costly, since by May Duyckinck had been dismissed as editor of the *Literary World* and had lost influence with Wiley & Putnam, the major backers of that journal.[33] Thoreau asked for a prompt answer, noting that he planned a long journey. He was referring either to a government survey in Michigan he hoped to join, or obliquely to the writing of *Walden*. Then on June 14 he again wrote Duyckinck, telling him that he would wait two weeks for an answer, and asking him to return the manuscript for further corrections.[34] After resubmitting it to Duyckinck on July 3, Thoreau waited impatiently for a decision. On July 27 he sent an inquiry (*Corr.*, p. 184), and must have received a negative answer shortly thereafter, for on August 6 Emerson approached his friend, William Henry Furness:

> I write because Henry D. Thoreau has a book to print. Henry D. Thoreau is a great man in Concord, a man of original genius & character, who knows Greek, & knows Indian also,—not the language quite as well as John Eliot—but the history monuments & genius of the Sachems, being a pretty good Sachem himself, master of all woodcraft, & an intimate associate of the birds, beasts, & fishes, of this region. I could tell you many a good story of his forest life.—He has written what he calls "A week on the Concord and Merrimack Rivers," which is an account of an excursion made by himself & his brother (in a boat which he built) some time ago, from Concord, Mass., down the Concord river & up the Merrimack, to Concord, N. H.—I think it a book of wonderful merit, which is to go far & last long. It will re-

33 For a discussion of the circumstances surrounding Duyckinck's dismissal, which Perry Miller describes as "the major crisis of his career," see *The Raven and the Whale*, pp. 186-202, 209.

34 Walter Harding has discovered that this letter, dated January 14, 1847, in *Corr.*, p. 173, actually dates from June 1847.

> mind you of Izaak Walton, and, if it have not all his sweetness, it is rich, as he is not, in profound thought.—Thoreau sent the manuscript lately to Duyckinck . . . who examined it, & "gave a favorable opinion of it to W[iley]. & P[utnam]." They have however declined to publish it. And I have promised Thoreau that I would inquire a little in N. Y. & Philadelphia before we begin to set our own types. Would Mr. Hart, or Mr. Kay like to see such a manuscript? It will make a book as big as my First Series of Essays. They shall have it on half profits or on any reasonable terms. Thoreau is mainly bent on having it printed in a cheap form for a large circulation. (*RLF*, pp. 60-61, *brackets supplied*)

If this estimate is accurate, Thoreau's second draft had expanded from seventy to roughly ninety thousand words since Emerson had approached Duyckinck five months earlier. But to Furness Emerson stressed Thoreau's native qualities rather than his scholarship. Although Thoreau had changed the title from "An Excursion on the Concord and Merrimack Rivers" to "A Week on the Concord and Merrimack Rivers," possibly to stress its formal shape and de-emphasize the travel motif, Emerson described it primarily as a travel book. Interestingly, he reported that Thoreau hoped to publish *A Week* in a cheap format, possibly even by printing the book himself.[35] Furness, however, replied that while he would apply to Mr. Hart he was "doubtful of success" (*RLF*, p. 63). Unable to find a publisher, Thoreau probably did not seriously consider taking the risk alone.

Emerson wrote Margaret Fuller on August 29 that

[35] When Emerson was seeking a publisher for *Summer on the Lakes*, he wrote Margaret Fuller: "Henry Thoreau has been showing me triumphantly how much cheaper & every way wiser it would be to publish the book ourselves . . . but such heroisms are not for me this spring" (*Lett.*, III, p. 250; April 26, 1844).

Thoreau was "on the point of concluding the contract" for *A Week* (*Lett.*, III, p. 413), but in fact the manuscript was still making the rounds of other publishers when Thoreau left Walden Pond on September 6 to move in with Emerson's family. On September 19 Furness wrote that he had talked to Hart about Thoreau's book, but that Hart was not interested. "He is run down, he says, with applications to print" (*RLF*, p. 66). Ten days later Emerson's brother, also acting as Thoreau's agent, wrote that he was waiting for an answer from Harpers, but apparently none came before Emerson sailed for England on October 5. Finally, on November 14, Thoreau wrote Emerson in London:

> I suppose you will like to hear of my book, though I have nothing worth writing about it. Indeed, for the last month or two I have forgotten it, but shall certainly remember it again. Wiley & Putnam, Monroe, the Harpers, and Crosby & Nichols have all declined printing it with the least risk to themselves; but Wiley & Putnam will print it in their series, and any of them, anywhere, at *my* risk. If I liked the book well enough, I should not delay; but for the present I am indifferent. I believe this is, after all, the course you advised,—to let it lie. (*Corr.*, p. 191)

Thoreau's indifference may have been defensive, for delay was certainly not the course Emerson advised. "I am not of opinion that your book should be delayed a month," he replied. "I should print it at once, nor do I think that you would incur any risk in doing so that you cannot well afford" (*Corr.*, p. 195). Thoreau's reply has not survived, but on December 27, writing about other matters, he told James Munroe and Company: "I may as well inform you that I do not intend to print *my book* anywhere immediately" (*Corr.*, p. 198).

He was not exaggerating when he told Emerson he

had not looked at *A Week* for "a month or two." During the fall and winter of 1847 he was writing lectures on "Ktaadn" and "The Relation of the Individual to the State," which he read before the Concord Lyceum early in 1848. Emerson continued to exert pressures on him to publish *A Week*, however, and on March 8, 1848, Thoreau wrote James Elliot Cabot:

> My book, fortunately, did not find a publisher ready to undertake it, and you can imagine the effect of delay on an author's estimate of his own work. However, I like it well enough to mend it, and shall look at it again directly when I have dispatched other things. (*Corr.*, p. 210)

Thus, after sending a revised version of "Ktaadn" to Horace Greeley at the end of March, Thoreau again turned to *A Week*. He apparently did not plan to make major revisions, however, for on April 16 Alcott wrote Charles Lane that "Thoreau has a Book nearly off his hands."[36] But on May 19, declining a request for copy, Thoreau wrote Greeley: "My book is swelling again under my hands, but as soon as I have leisure I shall see to those shorter articles" (*Corr.*, p. 225).

A Week was indeed "swelling" throughout 1848. As early as January 12 Thoreau told Emerson that he had written "what will do for a lecture on Friendship" (*Corr.*, p. 204), an expanded version of part of the first draft version of "Wednesday." He read it to Alcott, who pronounced it "superior to anything" he had ever heard.[37] Thoreau added the longer version to the second draft. Similarly, in March H.G.O. Blake, a teacher from Worcester who was two years ahead of

[36] *The Letters of A. Bronson Alcott*, ed. Richard L. Herrnstadt (Ames: Iowa State University Press, 1969), p. 137.

[37] Quoted in F. B. Sanborn, *Henry D. Thoreau* (Boston: Houghton, Mifflin and Co., 1882), p. 304.

Thoreau at Harvard, reread Thoreau's article on Persius in the July 1840 *Dial* and wrote that he found in it "pure depth and solidity of thought" (*Corr.*, p. 214). Thoreau replied that he had not read the article in years and "had to look at that page again, to learn what was the tenor of my thoughts then" (*Corr.*, p. 214). But he was apparently also pleased with the early effort, for he later inserted a corrected version of "Aulus Persius Flaccus" in "Thursday."

Thoreau's work on "The Relation of the Individual to the State," an account of his arrest in the summer of 1846 for refusing to pay a poll tax, may have inspired more thoughts on religion, "one of the dead institutions" (NN). Earlier he tried to avoid polemics in *A Week*, but as late as 1847 or 1848 he added a critique of orthodox Christianity to "Sunday." It is noteworthy that Thoreau begins this critique just as the brothers are entering the Merrimack and moving against its current, for their progress seems to symbolize his own growing resistance to the prevailing social and religious currents of his native New England. After a walking tour through southern New Hampshire in the summer of 1848, he added to "Sunday" a story about a minister who had accosted him because "I was bending my steps to a mountain-top on the Sabbath, instead of a church, when I would have gone further than he to hear a true word spoken on that or any day" (75.38-76.1).[38]

As he expanded the second draft, Thoreau excised or revised incongruities and redundancies, including an account in "Thursday" of the brothers' astonish-

[38] During the trip T bought a copy of Charles T. Fox's *History of the Old Township of Dunstable*, which provided useful points about local history and geography for *A Week*. See *Days*, pp. 233-234.

ment at meeting an organ grinder from New York seeking work "away up here in New Hampshire." After describing the man's helpless condition, Thoreau concluded: "It is the sum of all wisdom not to do desperate things. The great mass of mankind lead lives of quiet desperation. What is called resignation is confirmed desperation– From the desperate city you go into the desperate country and have to console yourself with the bravery of minks and muskrats." Thoreau apparently felt that the organ grinder's desperate journey "to the Gulf of St. Lawrence, where he would probably jump in," contrasted too strongly with the brothers' successful journey to "Unappropriated Land," so he deleted the whole account, leaving only Sadi's more general statement about men who may travel (304.24-28). Later, he shifted the story's locale and added his thoughts on "quiet desperation" to *Walden* (8.7-11; Shanley, pp. 52-53).

Thoreau also canceled descriptions of fishing and hunting, references to his own illness, and a defense of mercy killing (cf. Hovde, 213ff.). Most significantly, he rejected a meditation on death that originally appeared before the description of autumn flowers in "Friday." In Perry Miller's view, similar revisions of a passage on the old Nashua cemetery reveal that death as a subject "became too much for him, he could not master it."[39]

But by omitting these early references to illness and death, Thoreau had not evaded the subject; instead, he suspended its resolution until the autumnal landscape appears in "Friday," at a place and time more appropriate to the form and philosophy of *A Week*. And in "Friday," an explicit meditation on death was obvious and redundant, for Thoreau had

[39] Miller, *Consciousness in Concord*, p. 68; MH.

already created an imaginary landscape answering in each particular to man's condition—a landscape poised between fruition and decay, yet offering signs of endurance and intimations of rebirth.

When Emerson returned to Concord in late July, he apparently found Thoreau preparing not one but two books for publication. Confident that he had *A Week* well in hand, Thoreau had begun to revise *Walden* with an eye to both lectures and early book publication.[40] Emerson was silent about *Walden*, but he seems to have been displeased with at least one of Thoreau's additions to *A Week*, a critique of the *Bhagavat-Geeta* added to the discussion of Hindu scripture in "Monday." Objecting that books should be "thankfully received in their first impression & not examined & surveyed by theodolite & chain, as if they were part of the railroad," Emerson concluded: "I owed,—my friend & I,—owed a magnificent day to the Bhagavat Geeta. . . . Let us not now go back & apply a minute criticism to it, but cherish the venerable oracle" (*JMN*, x, p. 360).

In contrast to his apparent dissatisfaction with portions of *A Week*, Emerson was delighted with "Ktaadn, and the Maine Woods," which was published serially in the *Union Magazine* from July through November 1848. Reading "Ktaadn," Emerson exclaimed: "We have not had since ten years a pamphlet which I have saved to bind! and here at last is Bushnell's; and now, Henry Thoreau's Ascent of Katahdin" (*JMN*, xi, p. 20). Greeley, who had placed the essay, was equally enthusiastic in an introduction to some extracts published in the *New York Daily Tribune*. Privately, he

[40] For a detailed discussion of T's revisions of *Walden* during 1848 and 1849, see Shanley, pp. 27-30 and 34-91 *passim*.

again urged Thoreau to write shorter articles. "You must write to the magazines to let the public know who and what you are," he wrote Thoreau on October 28, "Ten years hence will do for publishing books" (*Corr.*, p. 232).

Thoreau ignored Greeley's advice, yet the publication of James Russell Lowell's *A Fable for Critics* on October 31 probably spurred him to seek wider recognition. In the poem, Lowell had satirized Thoreau and Channing as imitators of Emerson:

> "There comes ———, for instance; to see him's rare sport,
> Tread in Emerson's tracks with legs painfully short;
> How he jumps, how he strains, and gets red in the face,
> To keep step with the mystagogue's natural pace!
> He follows as close as a stick to a rocket,
> His fingers exploring the prophet's each pocket.
> Fie, for shame, brother bard; with good fruit of your own,
> Can't you let neighbor Emerson's orchards alone?
> Besides, 'tis no use, you'll not find e'en a core,–
> ——— has picked up all the windfalls before."[41]

As Channing's biographer has noted, Lowell paired them "so efficiently that later critics cannot decide which man stretched his short legs to walk in Emerson's footsteps, and which picked over Emerson's discarded apples."[42] The charge was not a new one, but in late 1848, as he was completing two distinctly original books, it must have been particularly galling to Thoreau.

[41] James Russell Lowell, *A Fable for Critics* (New York: G. P. Putnam, 1848), p. 30.

[42] Frederick T. McGill, Jr., *Channing of Concord* (New Brunswick, N.J.: Rutgers University Press, 1956), p. 111.

Although he had finished the second draft by summer's end, in the fall and winter Thoreau drafted entries in his Journal on reformers, great men, the East, Greece, and Rome, which entered the pages of *A Week.* He also continued to revise *Walden.* The first version of *Walden* was only slightly longer than the first draft of *A Week*, and Thoreau did not expand it significantly in 1848. Instead, he worked on improving its style, with the hope of seeing it published soon after *A Week.* He wrote a second version of *Walden*, revised it, and wrote a third version "so close upon [version] II that they almost seem one piece" (Shanley, p. 28). By February 1849, having completed *A Week*, and preparing to make a fair copy of *Walden*, he was again ready to approach publishers.

He first sent *A Week* to Ticknor & Company, apparently with an advance inquiry about *Walden.* On February 8 they proposed to publish *Walden*, offering ten per cent of the retail price as his profit (*Corr.*, p. 236). *A Week* did not fare as well; on the 16th they agreed to publish it only at his expense, after a down payment of $450 (*Corr.*, pp. 237-238). Thoreau refused both offers, either because *A Week* was in more finished form, or because he believed it should precede *Walden.* He next sent *A Week* to James Munroe and Company, who offered to let him pay costs out of expected sales, as long as he guaranteed full reimbursement to the publisher. *Walden* was to follow publication of *A Week.* Thoreau agreed to those terms, despite his Aunt Maria's warnings. She thought parts of *A Week* were blasphemous and darkly prophesied it would not sell enough copies to pay the publishing costs (*Days*, p. 246). His literary friends were more encouraging. Hawthorne wrote, "Mr. Alcott delighted my wife and me . . . by announcing that you had a book in press. I rejoice at it, and nothing doubt of such success as will be worth having."[43]

In his rush to complete two books, Thoreau apparently had not made a fair copy of the revised second draft of *A Week*. By March 16, as he wrote his cousin George Thatcher, he was receiving proof sheets from the printers and too busy to take a lecture engagement in Bangor, Maine (*Corr.*, p. 240). Within a week he reported again to Thatcher, saying the book "is likely to turn out much larger than I expected" (*Corr.*, p. 241). The pace increased; when Elizabeth Peabody requested a copy of his essay "Resistance to Civil Government" for her first volume of *Aesthetic Papers*, he apologized, "I have so much writing to do at present, with the printers in the rear of me, that I have almost no time left, . . . " (*Corr.*, p. 242). That remark suggests that he may have been drafting or revising later portions of text even as earlier sections were being typeset.

The printer had difficulty reading the manuscript, forcing Thoreau to make nearly a thousand corrections before returning the proof sheets on April 30, but the printer subsequently ignored many of these corrections. Added to his concern for his elder sister, Helen, who was dying of tuberculosis, these complications probably dampened the excitement he must have felt when he went to Boston to pick up his author's copies on May 26. Finally, on May 30, 1849, nearly ten years after the excursion it ostensibly describes, *A Week on the Concord and Merrimack Rivers* was published. The book appeared less than two weeks before Helen Thoreau died on June 14.

[43] Nathaniel Hawthorne, Letter to Thoreau, February 19, 1849. MS at the Morgan Library, New York. Cf. *Corr.*, p. 238.

"I Had a Friend, I Wrote a Book" 1849-1862

On May 26, 1849, Bronson Alcott noted in his diary: "Today comes Henry Thoreau to town and gives me a copy of his book, just published by James Munroe & Co., entitled 'A Week on Concord and Merrimac Rivers' . . . An American book, worthy to stand beside Emerson's Essays on my shelves."[44] Thoreau's first book, however, was not destined to stand soon on many other shelves. Four years later, he wrote in the Journal:

> For a year or two past, my *publisher*, falsely so called, has been writing from time to time to ask what disposition should be made of the copies of "A Week on the Concord and Merrimack Rivers" still on hand, and at last suggesting that he had use for the room they occupied in his cellar. So I had them all sent to me here, and they have arrived to-day by express, filling the man's wagon,–706 copies out of an edition of 1000 which I bought of Munroe four years ago, and have been ever since paying for, and have not quite paid for yet. The wares are sent to me at last, and I have an opportunity to examine my purchase. They are something more substantial than fame, as my back knows, which has borne them up two flights of stairs to a place similar to that to which they trace their origin. Of the remaining two hundred and ninety and odd, seventy-five were given away, the rest sold. I have now a library of nearly nine hundred volumes, over seven hundred of which I wrote myself. (J 5, p. 459)

In retrospect, reasons for the failure of *A Week* seem apparent. The first book by a virtually unknown author, it was published with no fanfare by Munroe, which had little stake in its success. As Brooks Atkinson asserted, it was "one of the strangest books that ever looked a bewildered public in the eye. . . . a catch-

[44] *The Journals of Bronson Alcott*, p. 209.

all of lovely outdoor facts, thoughtful essays, local lore, translations of classical verse and club-footed poetry."[45] Nonetheless, *A Week* attracted fairly wide notice at home and abroad, and while contemporary reviewers were occasionally offended, they were not "bewildered" by *A Week.*

Predictably, the first published review appeared in Greeley's *New York Tribune* on June 13, 1849, less than two weeks after publication. This anonymous review, occupying nearly two full columns on the front page, was mixed; it praised Thoreau's observations of nature and his "scholastic treasures" (while pointing out that the latter were "a little too ostentatiously displayed"), but objected: "His philosophy, which is the Pantheistic egotism vaguely characterized as Transcendental, does *not* delight us. It seems second hand, imitative, often exaggerated—a bad specimen of a dubious and dangerous school." Challenging Thoreau's "misplaced Pantheistic attack on the Christian faith," the reviewer asked him to "reconsider his too rashly expressed notions," and offered space in the *Tribune* for a reply.[46]

Thoreau, who suspected his adversary was Greeley, did not respond publicly,[47] but the *Tribune* review

45 [Brooks Atkinson], "River Centennial," *New York Times* (August 31, 1939), 18.

46 Anon., "H. D. Thoreau's Book," *New York Tribune* (June 13, 1849); reprinted in *TSB*, 27 (April 1949), [1-3].

47 Nearly three years later, he noted in the Journal: "Horace Greeley found some fault with me to the world because I presumed to speak of the New Testament using my own words and thoughts, and challenged me to a controversy. The one thought that I had was that it would give me real pleasure to know that he loved it as sincerely and enlightenedly as I did; but I felt that he did not care so much about it as I" (J 3, p. 257). However, most critics have attributed the review to George Ripley, who joined the *Tribune* in May 1849.

stirred some controversy on the subject of "Pantheism." Another newspaper commended the book as *"a prophylactic* of the California fever" and "a healthy and harmless stimulant to those who are removed from the circle of infection." While the writer could not applaud Thoreau's religious philosophy, he noted that the "peculiar speculations" could easily be skipped, and replied to the *Tribune* review: "We should no more fear the 'dangerous tendencies of this book' to propagate Pantheism than that the image of the Goddess of Liberty on our coin, would tend to revive her Pagan worship."[48] The *New Hampshire Patriot*, a Concord magazine that deemed *A Week* "a remarkable volume," and noted "on closing the book we find ourselves in love with the author, satisfied with ourselves and at peace with the world," cautiously concluded: "We do not by any means endorse the author's Pantheism, but will let it stand or fall for itself."[49] Evert Duyckinck, who had regained editorship of the *Literary World* in 1848, was less tolerant in a two-page review printed on September 22. After praising Thoreau's love of nature and of good books, Duyckinck noted:

> when this writer, so just, observant, and considerate, approaches what civilized men are accustomed to hold the most sacred of all, he can express himself in a flippant style which he would disdain to employ towards a muscle or a tadpole. . . . We are not so rash or uninformed in the ways of the world as to presume to give counsel to a transcendentalist, so we offer no

[48] Anon., Review of *A Week on the Concord and Merrimack Rivers* [unidentified newspaper, 1849?]; rpt. *TSB*, 130 (Winter 1975), 8.

[49] Anon., Review of *A Week on the Concord and Merrimack Rivers, The New Hampshire Patriot & State Gazette*, New Series, 3 (July 26, 1849), 2.

> advice; but we may remark as a curious matter of speculation to be solved in the future—the probability or improbability of Mr. Thoreau's ever approaching nearer to the common sense or common wisdom of mankind.[50]

Most critics agreed that *A Week* had been influenced by Emerson, but many praised Thoreau's originality. "The numerous admirers of Carlyle and Emerson will read this book with a relish; for Mr. T. writes in their vein and to some extent in their dialect," one reviewer remarked, "yet he is not a servile imitator . . . having his own sphere in which to move, and his own mission to consummate."[51] *Holden's Dollar Magazine*, which called *A Week* "a rare work in American literature," went even further. While "some people have compared it with Emerson's essays," it noted, "in style and habits of thought they are quite unlike, and we think that Mr. Thoreau may be safely judged, in reference to his own merits, without comparing his name with Emerson's."[52] Ironically, however, the editor of *Godey's Lady's Book* was convinced that John Greenleaf Whittier had written *A Week*: "Mr. Whittier touches all his themes with the true poet's wand; all show forms of beauty and gleams of light that . . . make the cold and rugged landscape

[50] [Evert Duyckinck], "Thoreau's Travels" [Review of *A Week on the Concord and Merrimack Rivers*], *The Literary World*, 138 (September 22, 1849), 245, 247. Duyckinck is identified as the author of this review by Perry Miller, *The Raven and the Whale*, p. 262.

[51] Anon., Review of *A Week on the Concord and Merrimack Rivers* [unidentified newspaper, 1849?]; quoted in *Days*, p. 251.

[52] [Charles Frederick Briggs], "Deferred Books" [Review of *A Week on the Concord and Merrimack Rivers*], *Holden's Dollar Magazine*, 4 (July 1849), 448. Briggs is identified as the author of this review by Perry Miller, *The Raven and the Whale*, p. 263.

appear soft and charming. It is just the book to read in the idleness of summer, when wishing to enjoy the pleasures of journeying, without the inconvenience which the actual packing up and going off in hot steamboats and dusty cars occasions."[53]

In October 1849 reviews of *A Week* began to appear in England, where a few copies were imported by John Chapman, Ltd. Although less concerned with Thoreau's religious views than their American counterparts, English reviewers were divided about the merits of his formal digressions. Sophia Dobson Collet, writing for the London *People's Review*, believed Thoreau's "occasional digressions" were "not unworthy to stand beside [the essays] of Emerson himself."[54] In contrast, the *Athenaeum* dismissed them as "the vagrant thoughts and fancies to which a man of education and reading habits may give himself up in 'hours of idleness,' " and concluded: "The manner is that of the worst offshoots of Carlyle and Emerson: all Mr. Thoreau's best things are spoilt in the utterance. If he would trust in his own genius, he has that to say which might command a larger audience. But imitations of an imitation! The world is too old and the prophets are too many for such things to have a chance of a public hearing in these days."[55] *A Week*

53 [Sarah Joseph Hale], Review of *A Week on the Concord and Merrimack Rivers*, *Godey's Lady's Book*, 39 (September 1849); rpt. *TSB*, 29 (October 1949), [3-4]. This issue of *TSB* also reprints a review from the *Pictorial National Library*, which briefly described *A Week* and noted that T's "primitive habits of living" had "attracted some attention in the vicinity of Concord."

54 Sophia Dobson Collet, Review of *A Week on the Concord and Merrimack Rivers*, *People's Review*, undated clipping in Bronson Alcott's Autobiographical Collections, MH; quoted in *Days*, p. 252.

55 Anon., Review of *A Week on the Concord and Merrimack*

received far more favorable notice from the *Westminster Review*, which called it an "exceedingly pleasant narrative":

> The author is evidently one who has read much, and thought much,—a keen observer and lover of nature, and one whom we could gladly journey with, amid the scenery described in this volume. Notwithstanding occasional attempts at fine writing, and some rather long-winded disquisitions upon religion, literature, and other matters,—sometimes naturally arising from the incidents of the voyage, sometimes lugged in apparently without rhyme or reason,—the book is an agreeable book, and all the irrelevant matter may be skipped by those who don't like it, while such as prefer this kind of reading to the narrative portions, may revel in it to their heart's content; and so may each class of readers find something to suit them in these pages.[56]

James Russell Lowell, whose review of *A Week* appeared in the *Massachusetts Quarterly Review* for December 1849, offered the most balanced evaluation on either side of the Atlantic, praising Thoreau's digressions on books and friendship, denigrating those on Eastern scripture, Anacreon, and Persius. The book convinced him that Thoreau's was a distinctive talent, especially in his treatment of nature. "One would say this was the work of some bream Homer," he exclaimed: "Melville's pictures of life in Typee have no attraction beside it." He even urged Thoreau to write a report on the ichthyology of Massachusetts. For Lowell, the "great charm" of *A Week* was its spontaneity: "The door of the portfolio-cage has been left

Rivers, Athenaeum (October 27, 1849); rpt. *TSB*, 29 (October 1949), [3]. *Hours of Idleness* was the title of one of Byron's first books, a collection of lyrics published in 1807.

56 Anon., Review of *A Week on the Concord and Merrimack Rivers, Westminster Review*, 52 (January 1850), 309-310; rpt. *TSB*, 59 (Spring 1957), [2-3].

open, and the thoughts have flown out of themselves." This comment anticipated his principal critique of the book's structure. Noting it "professes to be the journal of a week on Concord and Merrimack Rivers," he appropriated Thoreau's metaphor of the river journey to demonstrate the apparent irrelevance of his digressions:

> We come upon them like snags, jolting us headforemost out of our places as we are rowing placidly up stream or drifting down. Mr. Thoreau becomes so absorbed in these discussions, that he seems, as it were, to *catch a crab*, and disappears uncomfortably from his seat at the bow-oar. We could forgive them all, . . . we could welcome them all, were they put by themselves at the end of the book. But as it is, they are out of proportion and out of place, and mar our Merrimacking dreadfully. We were bid to a river-party, not to be preached at.[57]

Despite all this attention, *A Week* did not sell, and its failure brought Thoreau's relationship with Emerson to a crisis. Since 1846 Emerson had put increasing pressure on Thoreau to complete and publish *A Week*. He was confident that Thoreau would produce an important book, without financial risk, but by 1849, even before publication of *A Week*, his enthusiasm had diminished. On May 22 he wrote friends in England that he had "nothing very good to tell you of the people here, no books, no poets, no artists." As an afterthought, he added: "I ought to say, however, that my friend Thoreau is shortly to print a book . . . which, I think, will win the best readers abroad & at home" (*Lett.*, IV, p. 145). And when Theodore Parker asked Emerson to review *A Week* for the *Massachusetts Quarterly Review*, he declined, noting he was

[57] James Russell Lowell, Review of *A Week on the Concord and Merrimack Rivers*, *Massachusetts Quarterly Review*, 3 (December 1849), 40-51; rpt. *TSB*, 35 (April 1951), [1-3].

"of the same clan & parish" (*Lett.*, IV, p. 151). While Emerson helped Thoreau send out seventy-five copies to potential reviewers and to various British and American literary figures, the initial responses were not encouraging. Carlyle, for example, to whom Emerson had boasted about Thoreau for nearly ten years, wrote in August: "I got Thoreau's Book; and meant well to read it, but have not yet succeeded, tho' it went with me thro' all Ireland: tell him so, please. Too Jean-Paulish, I found it hitherto."[58] Since Emerson had once complained that he grew "weary & nervous" reading Richter's *Wahrheit aus Jean Paul's Leben* because of its "perpetual emphasis perpetual superlative" (*Lett.*, III, p. 92), he could hardly have viewed Carlyle's comment as flattering to Thoreau, and it possibly confirmed his own reservations about *A Week*.

By September 1849 Thoreau knew that *A Week* would never sell enough copies to pay publication costs. Apparently reacting to a conversation with Emerson, Thoreau wrote in the Journal:

> We never have the benefit of our friend's criticism, and none is so severe & scorching–until he is estranged from us. . . .
>
> The fruit of partiality is enmity.
>
> I had a friend, I wrote a book, I asked my friend's criticism, I never got but praise for what was good in it;–my friend became estranged from me and then I got blame for all that was bad, & so I got at last the criticism which I wanted. (HM 13182)

Given Thoreau's exalted ideal of friendship and Emerson's high expectations for his disciple, this

[58] *The Correspondence of Emerson and Carlyle*, p. 457. A month later Carlyle described *A Week* as "a very fantastic yet not quite worthless Book" in a letter to Jane Carlyle. *Ibid.*, p. 457n. For a brief summary of other private responses, see *Days*, pp. 252-253.

breach between them was probably inevitable, yet it is ironic that the issue was publication of a book dedicated to a long-dead friend. "W[e] lose our friends when they cease to be friends, not when they die," Thoreau wrote in his Journal early in 1850: "Death is no separation compared with that which takes place when we cease to have confidence in one with whom we have walked in confidence" (HM 13182). By October the two men were meeting "with malice prepense," as Emerson noted in his journal (*JMN*, XI, p. 283), and, while they continued to be close acquaintances, they never quite regained their confidence in one another.

After 1850, Thoreau continued to write and publish, but his hopes for a literary career were altered. Increasingly, he wrote for himself or for an idealized audience in his Journal, where he noted on June 29, 1851:

> I thought that one peculiarity of my "Week" was its *hypæthral* character, to use an epithet applied to those Egyptian temples which are open to the heavens above, *under the ether*. I thought that it had little of the atmosphere of the house about it, but might wholly have been written, as in fact it was to a considerable extent, out-of-doors. It was only at a late period in writing it, as it happened, that I used any phrases implying that I lived in a house or led a *domestic* life. I trust it does not smell [so much] of the study and library, even of the poet's attic, as of the fields and woods; that it is a hypæthral or unroofed book, lying open under the ether and permeated by it, open to all weathers, not easy to be kept on a shelf. (J 2, pp. 274-275)

Two years after the publication of *A Week*, Thoreau could refer to it with remarkable detachment, yet still with the hope that it might prove a success. He attempted to pay off his debt to Munroe by lecturing, which, he wrote Blake early in 1853, "has not offered to pay for that book which I printed," and by surveying, which he punningly referred to as "weeks which are bought at the rate I have named" (*Corr.*, p. 295). The book cost him $290. Even after the unsold copies were returned in October 1853, he continued to revise it with an eye toward a new edition.

After the failure of *A Week*, Munroe refused to publish *Walden*. By 1854, Munroe had gone out of business, and a new firm, Ticknor & Fields of Boston, agreed to publish Thoreau's second book, and it appeared in August. *Walden* received wider notice than *A Week*, and few of the reviewers noted Thoreau's previous volume. He must have been gratified by a review in the *National Anti-Slavery Standard*, which discussed both books at length: "These books spring from a depth of thought which will not suffer them to be put by, and are written in a spirit in striking contrast with that which is uppermost in our time and country. . . . The life exhibited in them teaches us, much more impressively than any number of sermons could, that this Western activity of which we are so proud, these material improvements, this commercial enterprise, this rapid accumulation of wealth, even our external, associated philanthropic action, are vastly very easily overrated." Noting with surprise that the books had not received "more adequate notice," the reviewer singled out for special praise "Solitude," "Where I Lived, and What I Lived For," and "Higher Laws" in *Walden*, and the essay on Friendship in *A Week*, which he called the most noble discourse on the subject "in the whole course of literature, ancient and modern."[59]

[59] Anon., Review of *Walden; or, Life in the Woods*, *National Anti-Slavery Standard* (December 16, 1854), 3; rpt. *TSB*, 38

Thoreau was also pleased when Edwin Morton, a Harvard undergraduate, devoted the bulk of an article on "Thoreau and his Books" to *A Week.* "His book is an artistic and beautiful performance," Morton noted, "more so, I think, than 'Walden.' This refers to the form merely, not to the matter, a good deal of which is surprisingly true and beautiful, though not without much that is open to just criticism." Morton objected to Thoreau's emphasis on Hindu scripture, "when we have as good or better of our own," but he was enthusiatic about passages like the description of daybreak on Saddleback Mountain, "hardly less sublime than anything which has been said to Mount Blanc." Thoreau's true "mission," he concluded, was to be a "priest and poet of Nature" rather than a critic of society.[60]

Hoping to make *A Week* available and thus to recoup at least part of his financial loss, Thoreau sent twelve copies on consignment to Ticknor & Fields on October 18, 1854, and inquired about the possibility of reissuing the copies he had received from Munroe.[61] On April 30, 1855, he wrote again: "Is it not time to republish 'A Week on the Concord & Merrimack Rivers'? You said you would notify me when it was; but I am afraid that it will soon be too late for

---

(Winter 1952), [2]. In a letter to Blake, T asked: "Did you see the notice of Walden in the last Anti-Slavery Standard? You will not be surprised if I tell you that it reminded me of you" (*Corr.*, p. 358).

60 Edwin Morton, "Thoreau and his Books," *Harvard Magazine* (January 1855); rpt. *Pertaining to Thoreau*, ed. Samuel Arthur Jones (Detroit: Edwin B. Hill, 1901), pp. 51-72. To express his appreciation, T left a copy of *A Week* with F. B. Sanborn, Morton's Harvard roommate, as a gift to Morton. See F. B. Sanborn, *Henry D. Thoreau*, p. 196.

61 J 7, p. 8; Francis H. Allen, comp., *A Bibliography of Henry David Thoreau* (Boston: Houghton Mifflin Co., 1908), p. 4.

this season" (*Corr.*, p. 375). Despite the greater success of *Walden*, which sold 738 copies out of an edition of 2,000 copies during the first year,[62] Ticknor & Fields declined to reissue *A Week*. Thoreau thus remained his own agent, selling the book for $1.25 to a few admirers who were interested enough to write to him directly. "The 'Week' had so poor a publisher that it is quite uncertain whether you will find it in any shop," he wrote Calvin Greene. "I am not sure but authors must turn booksellers themselves" (*Corr.*, p. 406).

As interest in *Walden* ebbed, Thoreau's chances of finding any publisher to reissue *A Week* grew remote. By 1859 *Walden* was also out of print. Yet he apparently continued to revise *A Week* intermittently during this period, when he was also hired to undertake a study of Concord River during the summer of 1859—twenty years after the river excursion and ten years since publication of *A Week*. "Henry T. occupies himself with the history of the river," Emerson wrote Elizabeth Hoar, "measures it, weighs it, and strains it through a colander to all eternity."[63] Thoreau verified the comments he had made in "Concord River" about the effect of the dams on the haying lands, but his report aroused such controversy that he approvingly quoted testimony that the river was "dammed at both ends and cursed in the middle" (J 13, p. 149).

In February 1862, James T. Fields, editor of the *Atlantic Monthly* and partner in the firm of Ticknor & Fields, proposed a new edition of *Walden*. Thoreau quickly agreed, mentioning that he still had 146

[62] Walter Harding, "The First Year's Sales of Thoreau's *Walden*," *TSB*, 117 (Fall 1971), 3.

[63] Ralph Waldo Emerson, Letter to Elizabeth Hoar, August 3, 1859. MS at NNPM. Quoted in *Days*, p. 411.

bound and 450 unbound copies of *A Week* on hand (*Corr.*, p. 637). The publisher apparently ignored this hint, but Thoreau persisted. "You have made me no offer for The 'Week,'" he wrote on April 2: "Do not suppose that I rate it too high, I shall be glad to dispose of it; & it will be advantage to advertize it with Walden" (*Corr.*, p. 645). Eventually, Fields agreed to reissue *A Week* and to pay Thoreau forty cents per copy.

Thoreau knew by that time that he would not live to see a new edition of *A Week*, but, even after Fields came to Concord on April 12 to purchase the unsold copies, he asked Ellery Channing to correct an error in the text. Shortly before he died, Thoreau called Edmund Hosmer to his bedside and gave him a copy of *A Week*. Inscribed "Henry D. Thoreau/Concord," it contained a lock of hair attached below the verse "Where'er thou sail'st who sailed with me," and identified as "From a lock of John Thoreau's hair." On the morning of May 6, Thoreau asked Sophia to read aloud from the last chapter of *A Week*. When she read the sentence, "We glided past the mouth of the Nashua, and not long after, of Salmon Brook, without more pause than the wind" (351.27-29), he reportedly said: "*Now comes good Sailing.*" He died a few moments later.[64]

[64] Calvin Greene and Ellery Channing jotted this account of the deathbed scene in their copies of *A Week*, now at NjP, VtMiM, and NN. Greene attributed the story to Sophia, whom he visited after T's death. Channing's annotated copy of *A Week* confirms Greene's story and describes the correction T requested. In *Memories of Concord* (Boston: Four Seas, 1926), p. 106, Mary Hosmer Brown describes a copy of *A Week* which he gave to her grandfather. This copy, clearly T's own, is now in the Robert H. Taylor Collection, Princeton, New Jersey. See Thomas Blanding, "A Last Word from Thoreau," CS, 11 (Winter 1970), 16, and Thomas Woodson, "Another

"Mr. Thoreau's Friends" 1862-1880

In the May 1862 issue of the *Atlantic Monthly*, Ticknor & Fields announced publication of "New Editions" of *A Week* and *Walden*.[65] Only their title pages were new, however; neither text contained corrections or revisions. *Walden* was reprinted from plates of the 1854 edition and the 450 unbound copies of *A Week* Fields had purchased from Thoreau were bound with the new title page. The 145 bound copies Fields also bought were either scrapped, or sold in their original Munroe bindings in order to minimize costs.[66] When the new publishers bound the 1849 sheets, they neglected to remove the back leaf, which announced that *Walden* would soon be published.

With the active encouragement of Fields and the devoted labors of Sophia Thoreau, Channing, and Emerson, Thoreau's uncollected and unpublished writings soon reached print.[67] "Walking," the first of seven essays printed in the *Atlantic Monthly* between 1862 and 1864, appeared in June, with an announcement that others would follow "in their proper seasons." Between 1863 and 1866 Ticknor & Fields pub-

---

Word on Thoreau's Last 'Good Sailing,'" *CS*, 12 (Spring 1977), 17.

[65] All quotations from Ticknor & Fields's advertisements for *A Week* are from Raymond Borst, "Thoreau Advertisements from the *Atlantic Monthly*," *TSB*, 129 (Fall 1974), 4-6.

[66] Ticknor & Fields listed only the cost of printing 500 new title pages and binding 450 copies of *A Week*. See Walter Harding, "The Early Printing Records of Thoreau's Books," *ATQ*, 11 (Summer 1971), 56. Information about the printing records of T's books between 1862 and 1880 is from this source, 44-59.

[67] For some of the information on the posthumous editing, publication, and reception of Thoreau's writings during the 1860s and 1870s, I am indebted to research compiled by Thomas Blanding.

lished five new volumes of Thoreau's writings: *Excursions*, 1863; *The Maine Woods*, 1864; *Cape Cod*, 1865; *Letters to Various Persons*, 1865; and *A Yankee in Canada, with Anti-Slavery and Reform Papers*, 1866. Except for *Letters*, which Emerson edited, Sophia Thoreau and Channing prepared these volumes for the press. As the *New York Times* remarked, "Mr. Thoreau's friends are doing good service to his memory and to American literature by the collection and preservation of his remains."[68]

Thoreau's friends had also not forgotten his hopes for a new and revised edition of *A Week*. As early as July 17, 1863, Channing wrote Marston Watson, one of Thoreau's Plymouth friends: "Mr. Thoreau's last book [*Excursions*] is now through the press, hardly any original matter. Am looking at his corrected copy of the Week, with a view to a new ed."[69] Evidently Thoreau had incorporated corrections from the proof sheets and made further revisions in a copy of *A Week* that has not survived. Channing probably completed work on this text by November, when he began writing "Henry D. Thoreau" for the Boston *Commonwealth*. He sent the marked copy to Fields, but the publisher was understandably reluctant to print a revised edition of *A Week* until his supply of the 1862 edition was exhausted.

In their advertisements for Thoreau's writings after 1862, Ticknor & Fields emphasized his talent as a nature writer. *A Week*, they proclaimed, "will be welcomed by the many admirers of Mr. Thoreau, and by all lovers of out-door life and sport." Most critics

68 Anon., Review of *Cape Cod*, *New York Times* (May 2, 1865), 2.

69 Kenneth Walter Cameron, "Thoreau and Emerson in Channing's Letters to the Watsons," *ESQ*, 14 (1959), 80.

shared the publisher's estimate of Thoreau; often, however, they noted differences between *A Week* and his other volumes. The *New York Times* praised *The Maine Woods* by implicitly contrasting it to *A Week*: "There is nothing about 'Boodh' in it. 'Brama' and 'Vishnu' are alike unnoticed. In short, it is clear of Thoreau's most objectionable peculiarities, and abounds with striking descriptions of scenery, acute observations, such as a genuine field-naturalist delights to make, and fine thoughts evolved in the mind of the writer from communion with the forest and the wilderness, yet free from man's intrusion."[70] Similarly, a reviewer for the *Circular*, a newsletter of the Oneida Community, found "little [in *Walden*] to offend a just and enlightened reverence," but objected to Thoreau's discussion of the New Testament in *A Week*. He also reprimanded Thoreau for his "glorification of Hindoo philosophy," noting: "When he escapes from it and turns to his own woods, and streams, and sky, he becomes original and suggestive. That old world philosophy does not suit the new, western nature."[71] Even Thomas Wentworth Higginson, one of Thoreau's warmest admirers, regretted that he "spent [so] much mental force in fighting shadows," the Church and the State, and asserted that, unlike *Walden* and *The Maine Woods*, "the 'Week' has no unity but that of the chronological epoch it covers,—a week which is probably the most comprehensive on record, ranging from the Bhagvat-Geetha to the 'good time coming.' "[72]

[70] Anon., Review of *The Maine Woods, New York Times* (June 6, 1864), 2.

[71] Quoted in "Thoreau at the Oneida Community," *TSB*, 115 (Spring 1971), 4.

[72] Thomas Wentworth Higginson, Review of *The Maine Woods, The Atlantic Monthly*, 14 (September 1864), 386-387.

But *A Week* gained supporters as well as detractors. In late 1865 Emerson told Charles J. Woodbury it was Thoreau's "noblest work, pervaded with delightful ideas,"[73] and that summer John Weiss published a strong defense of Thoreau's religious views in the *Christian Examiner.* Weiss, a Unitarian minister and one of Thoreau's classmates at Harvard, called him the most religious writer of the period, comparable to Jonathan Edwards. Illustrating Thoreau's "personal consciousness of God," Weiss cited passages from *A Week*: "It is in the interest of holiness that he speaks slightingly of Scripture and its holy men. . . . He catches up this Buddha for a chance defence against the conventional Christ of Democrats, slaveholders, sharpers in trade and in society, literal theologians, and over-pious laymen." Yet he also stressed Thoreau's coldness and the "severe ideal" of his essay on friendship in *A Week*, thus deflecting attention from Thoreau's writings to his life and personal character.[74]

Thoreau's friends believed publication of *Letters to Various Persons* in 1865 would firmly establish his reputation; instead, this volume raised serious questions about his personality and beliefs. The *New York Times* called the *Letters* "hard and barren" and concluded that Thoreau's "cold and selfish isolation from human cares and interests" offered no solution to the problems of the age.[75] The *Boston Review*, which had earlier criticized *Excursions* and *Cape Cod* for their unorthodox religious views, thought the only redeeming feature of the volume was the fact that "the spirit-

[73] Charles J. Woodbury, *Talks with Ralph Waldo Emerson* (New York: Baker & Taylor, 1890), p. 90.

[74] Reverend John Weiss, "Thoreau," *Christian Examiner* (July 1865); rpt. in *Pertaining to Thoreau*, pp. 141, 147.

[75] Anon., Review of *Letters to Various Persons*, *New York Times* (July 31, 1865), 5.

ualists get some sharp and hard hits which atone for a good deal of Concord transcendentalism, materialism, and Hindu-mania,"[76] while James Russell Lowell, who may have been biased by a previous quarrel with Thoreau, elaborated upon his deficiencies as a man and writer in an ostensible review of the *Letters*. Ignoring *A Week*, portions of which he had warmly praised fifteen years earlier, Lowell described Thoreau as cynical about man and sickly sentimental about nature: "His whole life was a search for the doctor."[77] These and similar attacks on *A Yankee in Canada, with Anti-Slavery and Reform Papers* the next year did little to increase the sales of *A Week*, an even more controversial book.

Early in 1865 James T. Fields inquired in his Memorandum Book: "How many 'Concord River' by Thoreau have we on hand?" Not many copies could have remained, but even so the 1862 edition was probably not exhausted until the summer of 1866, when Ticknor & Fields failed to list *A Week* in an advertisement for Thoreau's "Works" in the *Atlantic Monthly*. Perhaps because of the poor reception and slow sales of *Letters* and *A Yankee in Canada*, the publisher did not hasten production of a new text. In the company of Longfellow's translation of Dante and Hawthorne's *American Notebooks*, *A Week* was included in Fields's lists of "Books in Preparation" in October 1866 and January 1867,[78] but the "New and Revised

[76] Quoted in John C. Broderick, "Reviews of Thoreau's Posthumous Books," *University of Texas Studies in English*, 34 (1955), 333.

[77] James Russell Lowell, Review of *Letters to Various Persons*, *North American Review*, 101 (October 1865), 604. For an account of the Thoreau-Lowell dispute, see *The Maine Woods*, pp. 361-362.

[78] Memorandum and Account Book in the James T. Fields Collection, CSmH: Uncatalogued Papers, Box 7, Packet 27.

Edition" was not published until December 1867, when 1,300 copies were made available at two dollars each.

Ticknor & Fields tried to insure the success of this new edition, declaring in the February 1868 *Atlantic Advertiser and Miscellany* that the book, "which has been out of print some time, supplies a decided want." They also reprinted portions of a review from the *Philadelphia North American* that praised Thoreau's "fine appreciation of natural scenery." But the reviewer acknowledged that "the essence of the work consists . . . far more in the detached essays upon thought, religion, art, nature, and a thousand other topics that occupy most of the space" and warned that Thoreau "sometimes challenges orthodox thought abruptly." Such comments were not likely to attract many readers to *A Week*; in September Ticknor & Fields's advertisement in the *Atlantic Monthly* quoted a more positive review from the *Independent*: "If any would steal into the regions of perpetual summer, let him take the proffered hand of Thoreau, and by the side of a slender New England river walk with the sages and poets of all ages. He cannot help but learn, and cannot choose but admire."

Franklin B. Sanborn, editor of the *Commonwealth* and a fervent admirer of Thoreau's writings, interpreted the new edition of *A Week* as a sign that there was still "a taste and a demand" for a book that had been "unsaleable" twenty years earlier. Sanborn was not surprised, for he believed no "modern" book was "more likely to live and pass into the hands of posterity." Describing the brothers' trip as the "occasion" for Thoreau's moralizing, learning, wit, and poetry, he concluded: "To the hearty admirers of Henry Thoreau his first book will always seem his best. It had in it the morning freshness of his genius, and was spiced, like the morning breeze, with fragrance from a thousand gardens of wisdom and song."[79]

Despite Sanborn's proselytizing and Ticknor & Fields's efforts, *A Week* was not widely reviewed, and it continued to sell sluggishly. The 1868 edition of 1,300 copies lasted five years, and publication of Bronson Alcott's *Concord Days* in 1872 and Ellery Channing's *Thoreau, the Poet-Naturalist* a year later apparently spurred little interest in *A Week*, for 150 copies reprinted in 1873 satisfied public demand until 1878, when another 146 copies were printed. These sold more briskly, many of them probably to visitors at the newly founded Concord School of Philosophy, and an additional 175 copies were printed in 1880. But the total copies of *A Week* printed between 1862 and 1880, including 595 copies of the 1849 edition, amounted to only 2,366. Compared to Twain's *The Innocents Abroad*, which sold one hundred thousand copies in 1869-1871, *A Week* created barely a ripple.[80] All of Thoreau's other volumes sold better than *A Week* during this period, including the less noteworthy *Letters* and *A Yankee in Canada*, and his reputation continued to rest upon the firm foundation of *Walden* and the attractive qualities of *Excursions*, *The Maine Woods*, and *Cape Cod*.

The Recognition of A Week *1880-1977*

In 1880 Thomas Wentworth Higginson confidently

[79] [Franklin B. Sanborn], Review of *A Week on the Concord and Merrimack Rivers*, *The Commonwealth*, 6 (December 21, 1867), 16. Sanborn's review also included Ellery Channing's identification of some of T's quotations in *A Week*, which "alone would give perpetuity to the book that contained them."

[80] James D. Hart, *The Popular Book* (New York: Oxford University Press, 1950), p. 147.

affirmed to the reading public that Thoreau's literary fame was secure. "Indeed, it has already survived two of the greatest dangers that can beset reputation," Higginson noted, "—a brilliant satirist for a critic, and an injudicious friend for a biographer."[81] However, if Lowell's review of Thoreau's *Letters*, reprinted in *My Study Windows* (1871), and Channing's *Thoreau, the Poet-Naturalist* (1873) did not destroy his reputation, they did supply ammunition for many later reviews. To most of his critics, Thoreau was at once a "Nihilist" who "repudiated the idea of owing any obedience to the State, any reverence to the Church, or any duty to society,"[82] yet also "the parent of the out-of-door school of writers represented by John Burroughs, Frank Bolles, Bradford Torrey, Olive Thorne Miller, Maurice Thompson, and many others."[83] Consequently, *A Week*, which to many readers exemplified nihilism rather than nature, appealed very little during the 1880s and 1890s.

John Burroughs himself denied any similarities between Thoreau's writings and his own, noting that Thoreau's aims were "mainly ethical," while his were "entirely artistic."[84] As if to dramatize their differences, in 1881 Burroughs published "Pepacton: A Summer Voyage," an account of a trip on the east branch of the Delaware River. Unlike *A Week*, which Burroughs later described as "a record of other and

[81] Thomas Wentworth Higginson, *Short Studies of American Authors* (Boston: Lee and Shepard, 1880), p. 22. Higginson also quoted a then unpublished Journal passage describing the return of unsold copies of *A Week* in 1853, pp. 27, 30-31.

[82] Francis H. Underwood, *The Builders of American Literature* (Boston: Lee and Shepard, 1893), p. 214.

[83] Fred Lewis Pattee, *A History of American Literature* (New York: Silver, Burdett, 1896), p. 227.

[84] From a letter to Charles E. Benton, 1879; see Clara Barrus, *The Life and Letters of John Burroughs*, 2 vols. (Boston: Houghton Mifflin, 1925), I, p. 212.

much longer voyages upon other and less tangible rivers than those named in the title,"[85] "Pepacton" is tangibility itself. According to a recent biographer, Burroughs, like Thoreau, sought to convey "the author's sense of wonder in familiar surroundings," but Burroughs was more successful, for he wrote without "fanfare or didacticism." Burroughs' contemporaries apparently agreed, for the volume containing "Pepacton" sold well and was even adopted for use in Chicago by a teacher who thought students would benefit from "the tonic of a quiet literature rather than the stimulant of a stormy or dramatic one."[86]

If *A Week* was little read or appreciated in America, it received even less attention in England. In *Thoreau: His Life and Aims* (1877), A. H. Japp had quoted from and briefly summarized *A Week*, which he valued for its "picturesque description" and "wise reflections." "Nor is it devoid of scientific interest," Japp continued, "though, as yet, he [Thoreau] seems more inclined to muse and to make holiday than to do serious work."[87] Two years later Robert Louis Stevenson, who thought Thoreau's writings became increasingly prosaic after *Walden*, praised the passages in *A Week* describing the fish of Concord River as "remarkable for a vivid truth of impression and a happy suitability of language, not frequently surpassed." But Stevenson also cited the friendship essay as an example of Thoreau's "cold, distant personality," and although he later retracted his most severe

[85] John Burroughs, "Henry D. Thoreau," *Century Magazine* (July 1882); rpt. *Indoor Studies* (Boston: Houghton Mifflin, 1889), p. 2.

[86] Perry D. Westbrook, *John Burroughs* (New York: Twayne, 1974), pp. 61, 74.

[87] H. A. Page [Alexander Hay Japp], *Thoreau: His Life and Aims* (Boston: James R. Osgood, 1877), pp. 18-19.

criticisms, his essay strongly affected Thoreau's reputation in the late nineteenth century.[88]

The growing fame of *Walden* and the success of H.G.O. Blake's four volumes of selections from the *Journal*, published by Houghton Mifflin between 1881 and 1892, created some demand for Thoreau's other writings. Even his admirers, however, remained apologetic about *A Week*. In a prefatory note to the first English edition, pirated by Walter Scott Ltd. in 1889, Will H. Dircks attributed the form of *A Week* to Thoreau's "incapacity for system" and lack of a "formulated system of ideas," calling it "an instance of the extension of the transcendental arrogance of the individual to all that individual's performances."[89] Henry S. Salt, whose biography of Thoreau appeared a year later, was equally critical of the book's structure, but noted that its "very lack of cohesion and entire disregard of method contribute to enhance the effect of its poetical mysticism and brilliant descriptive power, while several of the discourses introduced into it—notably those on Friendship and Religion—are written in Thoreau's most admirable and telling style."[90] Horace Scudder's introduction to *A Week* in Houghton Mifflin's ten-volume New Riverside Edition of Thoreau's *Writings* (1894) was less complimentary. Some years earlier, Scudder had disparaged *A Week*, remarking that *Walden* and *Cape Cod* were likely to remain Thoreau's "most finished and agree-

[88] Robert Louis Stevenson, "Henry David Thoreau: His Character and Opinions," *Cornhill Magazine*, 41 (June 1880), 665, 667. The retraction appears in *Familiar Studies of Men and Books* (London: Chatto and Windus, 1882), pp. xix-xxiii.

[89] Will H. Dirck, "Preface" to *A Week* (London: Walter Scott, [1889]), p. xv.

[90] H. S. Salt, *The Life of Henry David Thoreau* (London: Richard Bentley & Son, 1890), p. 141.

able books."[91] His introduction was consistent with this preference, for he called it "Thoreau's commonplace book as well as journal" and approvingly quoted James Russell Lowell's censure of its formlessness. While the New Riverside Edition of the *Writings* sold well, these remarks hardly encouraged prospective readers of *A Week*.[92]

In 1900 Nathan H. Dole claimed that *A Week* had become "one of the classics of out-of-door literature,"[93] and other signs also indicated that it was slowly gaining recognition, though not always on terms flattering to Thoreau. Brander Matthews attributed the initial failure of *A Week* to Thoreau's "frank egotism,"[94] while Leon H. Vincent explained "the indifference of the author's contemporaries to a very original work" by suggesting they were discouraged by Thoreau's "hobbling verse" and the book's "stiff, almost self-conscious air."[95] Horace Scudder's introduction to *A Week* was reprinted in the twenty-volume Walden Edition of Thoreau's *Writings* (1906), but Bradford Torrey's editing of the *Journal* produced a series of thoughtful essays on Thoreau. In one, Torrey suggested that most of Thoreau's posthumous books were "narratives of travel," but *A Week* and *Walden* were

91 Horace Elisha Scudder, ed. *American Prose* (Boston: Houghton Mifflin, 1882), p. 301.

92 *The Writings of Henry David Thoreau*, 10 vols. (Boston: Houghton Mifflin & Co., 1894), I, p. x.

93 Nathan H. Dole, "Introduction" to *A Week* (New York: Thomas Y. Crowell, 1900), p. xxiv.

94 Brander Matthews, *An Introduction to the Study of American Literature* (New York: American Book Company, 1896), p. 187.

95 Leon H. Vincent, *American Literary Masters* (Boston: Houghton Mifflin, 1906), p. 329.

of a higher caliber, "studies in high and plain living,—practical philosophy, spiritual economy, the right use of society and solitude, books and nature."[96]

Most critics in the early twentieth century continued to stress the formlessness of *A Week*. William P. Trent called the book delightful, but noted that "while a joy to some readers, [it] is not well enough constructed to rival *Walden* in popular favor."[97] Like many English readers, Archibald MacMechan attributed the form of *A Week* to Thoreau's "American contempt for tradition," and suggested if Thoreau "had undergone Stevenson's rigid self-imposed discipline in the writer's craft, he might have made *A Week* as complete a little masterpiece as *An Inland Voyage*."[98] Others made even stranger comparisons. Odell Shepard thought *A Week* had no more unity than Dante's *Divina Commedia*, and, despite its lack of "intelligible form," he considered it the best of Thoreau's books. "It is less contentious and is written with more youthful gusto than *Walden*," he asserted, and "has more continuity than *Excursions* . . . or any of the books which have been made out of his journals."[99] Vernon L. Parrington agreed that *Walden* lacked "the exuberant beauty" of *A Week*, "its noble talk and scathing criticism," but he considered *Walden*

96 Bradford Torrey, *Friends on the Shelf* (Boston: Houghton Mifflin, 1906), p. 103.

97 William P. Trent, *A History of American Literature* (London: William Heinemann, 1903), p. 342.

98 *The Cambridge History of American Literature*, ed. W. P. Trent, *et al.*, 3 vols. (New York: G. P. Putnam's Sons, 1917-21), II, pp. 9-10.

99 *A Week*, ed. Odell Shepard (New York: Scribners, 1921), pp. xxv-xxvi.

the greater work because it was more unified in its philosophy.[100] Suggesting that *A Week* was Thoreau's only book that failed to give "some form to the free developments of the main theme," Brooks Atkinson called it "a gloriously elaborated, incoherent chronicle of a boating trip."[101]

In an anthology of Thoreau's writings published in 1937, Henry Seidel Canby "relieved" *A Week* of its "irrelevant essays, put in because the then youthful Thoreau had them on hand, and wished to make a kind of collected works of his first published book." While Canby considered two of these "irrelevant essays," "Friendship" and "The Christian Fable," important enough to include in another part of the anthology,[102] he felt that omitting them from *A Week* strengthened its narrative line, and he reiterated this view in a biography of Thoreau published two years later. It is an "American masterpiece," he wrote, but an "overstuffed masterpiece."[103] Thus a century after the brothers' voyage, most critics still agreed with James Russell Lowell's 1849 review of *A Week*, and Atkinson borrowed some of its imagery to commemorate the centennial of the voyage: "Although Henry could navigate the Concord and Merrimac Rivers without striking the rocks that rose above the late Summer current, he could scarcely find his way through the idealisms that filled his Yankee head." If

[100] Vernon L. Parrington, *Main Currents in American Thought*, 3 vols. (New York: Harcourt, Brace, 1927-30), II, p. 406.

[101] Brooks Atkinson, *Henry Thoreau: The Cosmic Yankee* (New York: Knopf, 1927), pp. 76, 19.

[102] *The Works of Thoreau*, ed. Henry S. Canby (Boston: Houghton Mifflin, 1937), p. v.

[103] Henry S. Canby, *Thoreau* (Boston: Houghton Mifflin, 1939), pp. 274-275.

it were not for *Walden*, he concluded, *A Week* would rest forever in the "limbo of books that no one reads."[104]

Departing from this mainstream of criticism, F. O. Matthiessen noted important similarities in the growth of *A Week* and *Walden*. This organic process, he contended, helped Thoreau "to transform his week's boat trip with his brother from a private to a symbolical event, since the record was bathed in memory for a decade . . . before it found its final shape in words."[105] Joseph Wood Krutch acknowledged Matthiessen's opinion, but regretted Thoreau's choice of a subject for his first book. Although the method of *Walden* was similar, Krutch thought "the scheme which works astonishingly well in the later book hardly works at all in the earlier one."[106]

By mid-century, an increasing recognition of Thoreau's artistry in *Walden* encouraged new readers to examine his achievement in *A Week*. Carl Hovde, the first scholar since F. B. Sanborn to study the manuscripts in detail, concluded that Thoreau had deliberately selected and revised his materials for *A Week*: "The book is not the arbitrary collection of descriptions, *pensées*, and quotations which it has often been considered, but is, despite its shortcomings, a unified work of art which was carefully wrought" (Hovde, 1). Sherman Paul extended Matthiessen's claims, arguing that *A Week* was "deliberately organic" in form. "It was unified on both literal and spiritual levels . . . a bold attempt to create a new form, to adventure

104 [Brooks Atkinson], "River Centennial," *New York Times* (August 31, 1939), 18.

105 F. O. Matthiessen, *American Renaissance* (New York: Oxford University Press, 1941), p. 167.

106 Joseph Wood Krutch, *Henry David Thoreau* (New York: William Sloane, 1948), p. 95.

beyond the safe beaten paths of literature."[107] Others remained unconvinced. In an otherwise laudatory review of Paul's study, Walter Harding criticized the chapter on *A Week* as "symbol-chasing" that threatened to make "the book a greater one than it is."[108]

In recent years, critics have dropped some of the traditional objections and have sought to uncover narrative and symbolic patterns in *A Week.* Alan Beecher Hovey suggests that Thoreau deliberately wrote a book his contemporaries could not understand, an allegory of his own artistic and spiritual development.[109] William B. Stein finds a movement towards spiritual enlightenment of the sort celebrated in Eastern mysticism,[110] while Joseph J. Moldenhauer and J. J. Boies call attention to the circle as a controlling metaphor in *A Week.*[111] Others describe the form as an outgrowth of Thoreau's Transcendentalism. Lawrence Buell, for example, argues that it was Thoreau's most ambitious work, exceeded in intellectual achievement only by Theodore Parker's *A Discourse of Matters Pertaining to Religion*: "For it attempts nothing less than to encompass the whole of Thoreau's intellectual and spiritual development, in-

[107] Sherman Paul, *The Shores of America: Thoreau's Inward Exploration* (Urbana: University of Illinois Press, 1958), p. 210.

[108] Walter Harding, Review of *The Shores of America*, *TSB*, 66 (Winter 1959), [3].

[109] Alan Beecher Hovey, *The Hidden Thoreau* (Beirut, Lebanon: Catholic Press, 1966), pp. 53-87.

[110] William B. Stein, "Thoreau's First Book: A Spoor of Yoga," *ESQ*, 41 (1965), 3-25 and "Thoreau's *A Week* and *Om* Cosmography," *ATQ*, 11 (1971), 15-37.

[111] Joseph J. Moldenhauer, "Images of Circularity in Thoreau's Prose," *Texas Studies in Literature and Language*, Vol. 1, No. 2 (Summer 1959), 245-263; J. J. Boies, "Circular Imagery in Thoreau's *A Week*," *College English*, 26 (February 1965), 350-355.

deed to take in the whole cultural history of mankind." While he acknowledges that this was a "quixotic task," Buell suggests that it puts *A Week* "in the same category with those other great American failures, from Melville to Dreiser to Williams, which together make up so much of what is interesting in our literary history."[112]

The most recent critics take an even more congratulatory view. Robert Sayre calls *A Week* "the second or third most famous literary river trip in America, after *Huckleberry Finn* and *Life on the Mississippi*." For Sayre, the story's order unfolds through its allusions to Indian life and culture, creating "a condensed history, in an inferential, poetic form, of Indian-European relations in America. . . ."[113] Stressing other patterns in Thoreau's first book—the movement from Concord and back again, the ascent and descent of mountains, the cycles of the day, the week, and the seasons—Frederick Garber concludes, "the design of the *Week* is unsurpassed in Thoreau's work for the complex counterpoint of its components."[114]

Although *A Week* has reappeared in reprints and new editions at least every fifteen or twenty years since it was published in 1849, it has usually proven to be a stumbling block, even to Thoreau's admirers. While no one can predict the future growth of the

[112] Lawrence Buell, *Literary Transcendentalism* (Ithaca: Cornell University Press, 1973), p. 207. See also James McIntosh, *Thoreau as Romantic Naturalist* (Ithaca: Cornell University Press, 1974) and William J. Wolf, *Thoreau: Mystic, Prophet, Ecologist* (Philadelphia: Pilgrim Press, 1974).

[113] Robert F. Sayre, *Thoreau and the American Indians* (Princeton: Princeton University Press, 1977), pp. 28-29.

[114] Frederick Garber, *Thoreau's Redemptive Imagination* (New York: New York University Press, 1977), p. 193.

book's reputation, recent critics have begun to make its meanings available to us, and it seems to be gaining long overdue recognition for its place in American literature. In "The Poet's Delay," Thoreau asked:

Shall I then wait the autumn wind,
Compelled to seek a milder day,
And leave no curious nest behind,
No woods still echoing to my lay?
(343.20-23)

His "curious nest" may well be *A Week*, for in its penultimate paragraph Thoreau expresses his hope that, like "those Chinese cliff swallows," he has feathered the nest with "froth" that will prove to be "bread of life to such as dwell by the seashore" (393.17-20).

Textual Introduction

A WEEK draws upon notes, Journal passages, and periodical publications by Thoreau, dating from 1837 to 1849. His printer's copy for the book (now lost), although it probably included some printed pages, was chiefly a heavily revised manuscript, which led to a number of printer's errors on the proof. Thoreau corrected the errors and made some substantive revisions on the proof, but not all of his changes entered the 1849 printing. He apparently continued to correct and revise the book after publication, entering some revisions on the original proofs, and some on another, unidentified, form of the text: perhaps a duplicate set of proofs, a bound copy of the 1849 edition, or a set of unbound sheets that came into his possession in 1853. One of these later forms apparently served as printer's copy for the posthumous 1868 edition, which includes revisions otherwise impossible to account for: proof changes that the printer neglected in 1849, returns to pre-1849 versions that exist only in the Journal and early drafts, and stylistic changes that are clearly authorial.

RELEVANT VERSIONS OF TEXT

As the Historical Introduction reveals, Thoreau's writing and revising of *A Week* extended over many years. He produced several working versions, in manuscript and print, that are relevant to the task of establishing a critical text. These papers have been cited and described already; therefore, a brief account of them here, in genetic order, will suffice.

Journal, Commonplace Books, Notes

Various Journal entries, extracts in commonplace books, and notes preceded Thoreau's composition of *A Week*; later he revised these materials and added them to his drafts. The earliest Journal entries he used for this purpose were dated November 1837, and the latest entries came from the spring of 1849, just prior to publication of the first edition. While he was working on *A Week*, he sometimes removed entries for physical transfer to his working drafts of *A Week*, where he recopied and revised them further. However, many of the entries used in *A Week* remain in the fourteen manuscript volumes of Journal for these years. The same is true for the four commonplace books Thoreau kept between 1836 and 1850; there he recorded lengthy quotations from his reading in philosophy, literature, history, ethnology, and natural history. He obviously consulted these volumes when later composing *A Week*, for many of his quotations in the book derive from these fuller extracts. Several loose sheafs of "reading notes" also survive from the same period, with copies of passages–Francis Quarles, Hindu scripture, Scottish ballads–directly related to *A Week*. Like the Journal entries and commonplace books, these early versions of source material provide useful glosses on readings in the later text. The exact sources themselves, when they can be identified and obtained, may also illuminate various textual problems, though they have no textual authority. Thoreau was not a mechanical quoter or translator; often he saw fit to reshape sources according to his own literary needs. Hence, an editor must examine available scholarship on Thoreau's reading habits, consulting the proper authorities and editions when necessary.[1]

Early Writings

Beyond these materials, many of Thoreau's early writings are available, in both manuscript and printed form, which he later revised and adapted for *A Week*.[2] These poems, lectures, and essays are important, as they may provide readings that correct or clarify ambiguities in later versions. Many of the poems in *A Week* survive in early manuscript drafts, and eleven were published in the *Dial* between July 1840 and April 1843. Thoreau's early prose writings are even more significant, for eventually he added to *A Week* revised segments of a number of separate works. He adapted passages from works unpublished in his lifetime, including two essays, "The Service" and "Sir Walter Raleigh." As for his published essays or translations, *A Week* includes revised versions of "Aulus Persius Flaccus," "A Walk to Wachusett," "The Laws of Menu," "Anacreon," "Dark Ages," "Homer. Ossian. Chaucer.," and "Pindar." With one exception ("A Walk to Wachusett," published in

[1] *LMHDT*, pp. 365-367, has a table of cross-references between the Journal and *A Week*; see also section F, "Notes and Notebooks," pp. 289-293, for descriptions of the commonplace books and reading notes, 1836-1850. The Thoreau Edition Textual Center at NjP maintains an index of more than 2,000 titles T is known to have read, quoted, or otherwise consulted. The Center compiled the index from various works by Walter Harding, Kenneth Cameron, Arthur Christie, John Christy, and others, and from numerous rare book catalogues. The Center also maintains a collection of 800 volumes that duplicate editions owned or consulted by T.

[2] For a general discussion of the problems see Raymond Adams, "The Bibliographical History of Thoreau's *A Week on the Concord and Merrimack Rivers*," *The Papers of the Bibliographical Society of America*, 43 (1949), 39-47.

the *Boston Miscellany* in January 1843), all of these pieces first appeared in the *Dial* between July 1840 and April 1844. Moreover, Thoreau owned a full set of the *Dial* in which he entered revisions that anticipate later draft versions of *A Week* or readings of the printed proof sheets. All of these materials are clearly relevant to the task of establishing a critical text.[3]

Manuscript Draft

A considerable amount of manuscript draft for *A Week* has survived, though none of it is printer's copy. All but a little of the first draft survives: 107 leaves written in 1845-1846, which yield important evidence about Thoreau's persistent themes and design for his book. Thoreau wrote a second draft in 1847, which he revised and expanded during 1847-1849. Most of the surviving second-draft manuscripts are rejected or heavily revised portions of text, a circumstance suggesting that the remainder of the draft, now lost, formed part of the text Thoreau sent to his printer. The manuscript leaves of these two drafts are widely scattered among public repositories and private owners, but recent scholarship and inexpensive methods of duplication have made these materials available to the interested scholar.[4]

Printer's Copy

The manuscript sent to Munroe in 1849 is lost, and few references to it exist other than some notes ap-

[3] See Francis H. Allen, *A Bibliography of Henry David Thoreau* (Boston: Houghton Mifflin Co., 1908), pp. 64-79, for titles and dates of T's early published poems and essays. T's corrected set of *Dial* is now in the Special Collections Division, ICarbS.

[4] For a descriptive census of the manuscripts, see *LMHDT*, pp. 186-209. A reconstruction and full history of the first draft are in FD.

pearing on the extant proof. At proof p. 45 Thoreau asked the printer to arrange some lines of poetry, "as in the MS." Since many of the sheets were probably revised in Thoreau's handwriting, the printer's copy may have been difficult to read. These conditions may be deduced from Thoreau's corrections on the proof, where the printer has misread elements that are frequently ambiguous in other Thoreau manuscripts: paragraph indentations, capital letters, dashes, commas, and certain similarly formed letters (s/r, e/c, a/u). A clear and completely recopied manuscript would have required much time and paper; it also would have interrupted Thoreau's work on *Walden* and his essays. If such a fair copy ever existed, no evidence for it has survived.

Another condition of the printer's copy can be deduced from the proof sheets: generally, fewer printer's errors appear in passages derived from "Aulus Persius Flaccus," "Anacreon," "Dark Ages," and "Homer. Ossian. Chaucer."—all in print by January 1844—than elsewhere in the proof. For these sections the printer apparently read copy more legible than Thoreau's usual holograph. The manuscript probably contained printed texts of those works, and of other published essays and poems, now revised for use in *A Week*. Thoreau owned one complete set of the *Dial* (see footnote 3), which bears his corrections and revisions, many directed toward the text of *A Week*. But those are incomplete or tentative revisions; the final versions were probably made on excised pages of another set and then added to the printer's copy. Thoreau seems to have followed this habit in later years, for printed texts of his essays are often missing from his personal copies of the magazines.[5]

[5] T's personal copies of magazines other than the *Dial*—all

None of these conjectures about the form of printer's copy can be positively confirmed, however, for it has not survived. Apparently Munroe did not return it to Thoreau; some corrections on the proof sheets suggest he had no manuscript copy for his reference.

As his letter to Elizabeth Peabody suggests (HI, p. 470), Thoreau apparently submitted his manuscript to the printer in sections. Two penciled printer's notes in the proof also verify this conjecture: on p. 277, "We are all out of Copy please send soon as convenient," signed "Printer."; and on p. 289, "Have not Rec'd any Copy. Monday Morning." The notes appear on the first rectos of successive signatures (24 and 25), indicating the printer at times sent proof to Thoreau in single signatures.

Proof Sheets

The earliest printed version of *A Week* is the page proof for the first edition, set by Thurston, Torrey and Company for the publisher, James Munroe and Company. That page proof is now in the collection of the Huntington Library in San Marino, California, identified as Rare Book 110229. The pages, cut and untrimmed, vary between 12 and 13.5 cm. in width and between 20.5 and 21.5 cm. in length. The proof title page bears the correct 1849 date of publication; on p. [2] the copyright submission is dated 1848, which was changed to 1849 in the first edition. The proof consists of thirty-five unsewn and unbound twelve-page signatures, numbered consecutively on the first recto of each signature; the number is repeated with an asterisk on the third recto. The first "1" does not

---

with his texts missing—are at VtMiM, MCo, ICarbS, and in the private collection of Mrs. Edmund Fenn, Concord, Massachusetts.

appear, figure "3" was missing on p. 25 but corrected by an unidentified hand, and the third recto of signature 35, the last page of text, lacks a signature mark. The text ends on p. 413, and is followed on p. [415] by an advertisement stating that *Walden* or *Life in the Woods* "will soon be published."

Thoreau returned proof in sections, as indicated by his note on p. 85: "in 2nd line page 79 if not too late instead of prop*o*gate prop*a*gate." Page 85 is the first recto of signature 8; he had already corrected and returned signature 7. But how did he know exactly where the error appeared? Perhaps he held a second set of proof in Concord for his reference; that set, however, has not come to light, despite persistent searches by scholars.

The proof contains three different levels of correction, two of them pre-publication and the third post-publication. First, Munroe's employees (hereafter called "the printer" even though several individuals were involved) went through the text and directed numerous marginal queries to Thoreau. Mostly the printer marked technical errors for his own subsequent correction: matters of registration, spacing, type font, reversed letters, and gross typographical errors in punctuation and spelling. Second, Thoreau responded to some of these queries and also attended to the sense of his text: corrections and revisions of wording, punctuation as a matter of style in addition to correctness, and the relation between text and blank space, or "white lines," as he called it. Third, Thoreau made a number of important changes after 1849, discussed below (TI, pp. 515-519).

Positively identifying a writer is difficult when only corrections are involved, but usually the printer's marks and Thoreau's can be distinguished by their medium. The printer almost always used ink, and a pen that commonly left bold, black strokes; Thoreau mostly used a pencil. However, there are two exceptions to Thoreau's usual practice, one relatively simple and the other more complex. The staightforward case occurs in signature 5 (pp. 49-60): Thoreau first made corrections in pencil and then wrote over them in ink. The more difficult case occurs in signatures 1 and 2, where all the corrections but one are in ink. Some, including notes on type size and placement on pp. 7, 15, and 17, are recognizable as Thoreau's hand. Others are brief and the hand is not so clearly Thoreau's, but the nature of these alterations strongly suggests his involvement. For example, on p. 19, uncorrected proof reads: "and no doubt many russet-clad children," which is corrected in ink to "and it may be that many russet-clad children." This appears in the 1849 text as "and it may be many russet-clad children," probably shortened because the full correction would have forced the printer to reset several lines. The ink alteration in proof must be Thoreau's: it does not merely correct a compositor's misreading of manuscript—there is no obvious error—it takes an author's prerogative of revising directly on the proofs. If the printer had made such a change on his own, Thoreau would probably have canceled it.

Moreover, two ink queries point to Thoreau's involvement: one questions the spelling of a Philadelphia publisher's name on p. [1], and on p. [2] another queries the dating of a copyright application with the "District Court of the District of Massachusetts." These are matters requiring a publisher's services; hence Thoreau probably addressed the queries to Munroe, the only party who could easily respond.

While a printer might have made these queries, the weight of evidence here is on Thoreau's side.

Finally, a note from the printer on proof page [1] tends to verify that Thoreau alone made the proof corrections in signatures 1 and 2. That note, in faint pencil, reads as follows (doubtful readings in angle brackets):[6]

> Not having received ⟨sets of⟩ proof from you, we now send these.—There ⟨are⟩ a number of Queries and errors in ⟨those sent⟩ which are not marked on these. Of course, you will please be the ⟨more⟩ particular in finding these.

On p. 3 another pencil note appears—perhaps related to the note above: "⟨We⟩ probably omited [*sic*] to write the word proof on the wrapper.—" The note suggests that Munroe shipped Thoreau a first set of signatures 1 and 2, containing the printer's initial corrections and queries. Thoreau apparently did not think he was obliged to return this set, perhaps because it was not identified as proof. Munroe then sent a second set, unmarked by the printer, and asked Thoreau to correct it, presumably by reading against the first set. Only the second set of proof for signatures 1 and 2 survives, as part of Rare Book 110229 at the Huntington Library; Thoreau probably never returned the first set to Munroe. These circumstances explain why printer's marks, common in most of the text beyond p. 24, do not appear in signatures 1 and 2. In his second set Thoreau simply wrote the necessary changes in ink.

[6] The pencil text has been worn by friction or possibly erased. The present editor's reading was aided by special photography, through the courtesy of Mr. Alan Jutzi and others at CSmH.

Given the difficulty of Thoreau's hand, his printer made numerous errors when setting type from manuscript; but on the whole his work is impressive. Yet his treatment of changes the author requested in proof seems slipshod, especially since Thoreau was paying for publication. Technical errors in typesetting were usually rectified, many of Thoreau's substantive and accidental changes were entered, but in several instances the printer ignored Thoreau's corrections altogether—perhaps because they would have forced him to reset several lines of type. In "Tuesday," for example, a phrase on proof pp. 195-196 first read "a school-boy's theme, such as youths write and after burn." Thoreau changed "after" to "afterward" but his correction did not enter the 1849 edition. Perhaps the printer simply overlooked this change, but probably he ignored it rather than reset—and repage—type. In the "russet-clad children" passage cited above, the printer emended to a shorter form, again apparently to avoid resetting. Simple carelessness seems to have caused other errors, including one affecting the largest amount of text (see TN 377.23-26).

Thoreau was an inveterate reviser; thus, a fair number of his alterations are not mere corrections but substantive revisions of the text. Such changes on page proof rarely please publishers, but in this case Thoreau was bearing all expenses himself. He did not hesitate to add, omit, sharpen, or adjust the tone, nor to rearrange rhythms as he saw fit. In "Sunday," for instance, the uncorrected proof says of Society Islanders: "Among them a man could make himself a god out of a piece of wood, which would frighten him out of his wits in a few minutes." This sentence misplaced his emphasis, so he changed its order to let the man "make himself a god out of a piece of wood, in a few minutes, which would frighten him out of his wits" (see TV *65.33-34). In his desire for precision he often chose carefully between analogous terms: "Occasionally" became "From time to time" (see TV 27.34) or "sometimes" (53.34); "seemed" became "appeared" (212.15). For shades of meaning he alternated lower-case and capital letters: "Nature" was altered to "nature" in one passage (339.6), while "nature" became "Nature" at another (364.13); "Spring" changed to "spring" (368.20), while "autumn" gave way to "Autumn" (377.18). Other changes simply correct mistakes: in "Tuesday" the original text has canal boats taking "three or four days each way between Concord and Charleston," which Thoreau corrects to "2 or 3 days" (see TV 210.13). All of these revisions are deliberate; sometimes he revised phrases twice before they were satisfactory (see TV 97.23).

During revision he continued to work for a concise and rhythmically graceful style. He might eliminate extra words, as when "is often perceived" became "is perceived" (142.23), or recast sentences to close them more firmly (see TV 254.3, 341.9). Even at this late stage he added or omitted long phrases. In "Sunday" he sharpened a complaint about people who desert the "frontier territories" of truth and justice, adding they do so "for fear of far more insignificant foes" than Indians (112.15-16). He also canceled a characterization of the Sabbath: "and deeper silence than ordinary brooded over the earth, and we fancied that the morning was the eve of a celestial day" (see TV 46.2-4). None of these changes signifies a distinct change of intent; they merely verify his understandable concern for the merits of this first book-length publication.

1849 Edition

Little information survives about the printing and publishing of the first edition. To date, searches at important libraries[7] have failed to locate the records of Munroe and Company. Surviving correspondence documents some of the understandings between Thoreau and Munroe (see HI, p. 469), but the following details are still unknown: the cost to Munroe compared with Thoreau's expenses; the size of the press run, which may have varied from the 1,000 reported by Thoreau; the reason why a mere 550 bound copies would appear in three distinct cloth colors and two different binding stamps;[8] the day of publication; and the record of sales from 1849 to 1853, when Munroe returned unsold copies to Thoreau.

A bibliographical description of the 1849 edition is as follows:[9]

> Front endpapers, flyleaf, [1]2-34^{6} 35^{4} = 208 leaves, signed $* on 3r in [1] —34; pp. [1-7] 8-14 [15-17] 18-44 [45-47] 48-120 [121-123] 124-185 [186-189] 190-246 [247-249] 250-311 [312-315] 316-350 [351-353] 354-413 [414-416]; Back flyleaf, endpapers.

A Week was through the press by May 26, 1849. Thoreau's letter to H.G.O. Blake, August 10, 1849, states that he left in Munroe's shop an addressed

[7] The libraries include major Thoreau collections at CSmH, NN, MH, plus the Boston Public Library, the Massachusetts Historical Society, the American Antiquarian Society, and the Morgan Library.

[8] In a letter to Walter Harding dated February 10, 1947, Albert E. Lownes listed the variations as (1) smooth, light brown cloth; the sides stamped with an elaborate foliage decoration; (2) pebbled, dark brown cloth, similarly stamped; (3) smooth black cloth; the sides undecorated, except for a simple lined border.

[9] Copy described is the Edmund Hosmer copy in the Robert H. Taylor Collection, Princeton, New Jersey.

copy "to be sent to you immediately, on the twenty-sixth of May, before a copy had been sold" (*Corr.*, p. 246).

The printer had incorporated many of the proof corrections, whether made by Thoreau or by himself, but he is probably responsible for several instances of apparently unauthorized changes from authorial forms.[10] Moreover, more than two dozen substantive changes marked by Thoreau on proofs do not appear in the 1849 edition.[11] These changes are in the "Pms" category, which includes revisions known to have been made for the 1849 text because they appear there, and revisions for which a later time cannot be established conclusively. Most involve only a letter, some a single word; these as well as a group of changes in accidentals marked on proofs but not appearing in 1849[12] seem to be printer's errors. As discussed below (TI, pp. 515-518) Thoreau wrote revisions on the proof after 1849, but he probably would not have entered minor changes for a later edition on any marked proofs of the earlier edition, since those changes would be hard to distinguish.

In some copies of the first edition Thoreau wrote corrections of three major errors.[13] The total number

10 See TV 17.4, 67.6, 94.12, 116.23, 158.17-18.

11 See TV 26.21, 35.28, 40.10, 49.15, 51.23-24, 51.24, 52.35-53.1, 53.4, 53.28, 74.15-16, 103.23, *116.7, 124.27, *132.27, *134.2, 160.27, 168.19, 168.29, 182.31-32, 183.8, 184.23, 185.30, *245.30, *377.23-26, 387.10.

12 See TV 11.34, 18.14, 36.17, 36.18, 45.29, 50.5, 50.13, *65.33-34, 70.17, 78.33, 79.8, 81.9, 103.12, 116.26, 129.31, 129.33-130.1, 130.3, 132.33, 134.2, 155.9, 188.23-24, 192.28, 213.14, 300.29, 335.3, 336.6, 381.18, 388.23, 393.2.

13 Machine collations verify that no variants were introduced during the press run of 1,000 copies. Three copies of the 1849 edition were collated on a Lindstrand Comparator at

of these copies is uncertain; they consisted of presentation copies he distributed in 1849 and approximately 100 copies he sold or gave away between 1853 and 1862. He probably saw far more than these three mistakes, but did not undertake to set them right. He changed "work" to "wash" (116.7), "experience" to "expediency" (134.2), and he wrote in three lines of text missing at the bottom of page 396: "winter before any thought will subside. We are sensible that behind the rustling leaves, and the stacks of grain, and the bare clusters of the grape, there is the field of a" (377.23-26).

In two of these cases Thoreau's corrections on the proof confirm the proper readings. The mistakes on pp. 120 and 139 were simple misreadings of his original manuscript; either the printer ignored Thoreau's proof corrections or Thoreau made them after 1849. The third error, on p. 396, occurred because Thoreau wanted more space between a paragraph on "The great poem" and the next paragraph, which returns to the river journey—"But here on the stream of the Concord, . . ." In the line space that was already there, he asked for a "dash" and "3 more white lines"—that is, a rule and three blank lines. These three corrections in first edition copies are the only ones known to be made by Thoreau.[14] Possibly he made other holograph corrections—corrections not recorded in the proof, nor in examined copies of the first edition, nor in extant letters and comments to friends—which

---

the Thoreau Edition Textual Center, NjP. Two copies are in Special Collections, NjP (Ex 3960.6.396.14, copies 1 and 2); one is the Edmund Hosmer copy in the Robert H. Taylor Collection, Princeton, New Jersey.

14 The Edmund Hosmer copy is unusual in having all three corrections in T's hand; it also contains a lock of hair, identified in a note as John Thoreau, Jr.'s. See HI, p. 483.

might support editorial emendation of the proof, but no evidence for them has yet appeared.[15]

Post-1849 Revisions of Proof

Thoreau wrote a group of major revisions on the page proof sometime after the first edition appeared in 1849. The proof sheets are complicated in an interesting way by this third level of holograph corrections, which is later than both the printer's initial markings and Thoreau's subsequent revisions for the 1849 printing. Clearly Thoreau was looking ahead to eventual publication of a second edition. Exactly when he made these changes is uncertain; he may have entered them over several years, beginning soon after publication of the 1849 text, or in a concentrated period sometime between 1849 and his death in 1862 (see below, TI, p. 523). Whatever their exact date, the corrections must represent a stage of textual development between the 1849 version and the second edition of 1868, for some of them appear in

15 See Albert E. Lownes, "Some Statistics About Thoreau's Week," *TSB*, 66 (Winter 1959), 1-2, for information about his census of copies of the first edition. In a letter to Walter Harding, March 30, 1964, Lownes listed 41 copies of the 1849 printing, indicating which of the three corrections each contains. Another census has been undertaken by Kevin MacDonnell, Special Collections, University of Houston Library; in a letter to the Textual Center, November 4, 1977, he reported having accounted for 73 copies of 1849 and 6 copies of the 1862 reissue of the 1849 sheets.

Several important copies, like those of Daniel Ricketson (Brown University), Mary Russell Watson (SUNY at Binghamton), W. E. Channing (NN), and Calvin Greene (NjP), contain other manuscript notes and corrections, but none is clearly by Thoreau or at his request. Sophia Thoreau's copy is described by its last known owner as bearing corrections and notes by both Thoreau and his sister, but unfortunately its present location is unknown. See Paul Lemperly, *Among My Books* (Cleveland: Rowfant Club, 1929), pp. 38-39.

both proof and 1868, but not in 1849. In the Table of Variants, these revisions are designated "Pms-a."

Several examples will demonstrate the kinds of post-1849 revisions Thoreau made. The uncorrected proof for "Sunday" originally stated that Jehovah is "not so much of a gentleman, not so gracious and catholic, . . ." Thoreau first revised this to "not so much of a gentleman, in the true sense, not so gracious and catholic, . . ." Then he revised a second time to "not so much of a gentleman among gods,, [*sic*] not so gracious and catholic,"–the version that appeared in 1849, except with a comma after "gentleman" and the double comma corrected. The 1868 reading goes back to the original version in the uncorrected proof, however, which no editor or printer could have obtained from the first edition (see TV 65.1).[16]

In "Tuesday" Thoreau writes about the life of the canal-boatmen. The first edition reports "they make two or three trips from Merrimack to Lowell and back, about twenty-five miles each way, in a week, according to wind and weather." This 1849 version is exactly that of the uncorrected proof; but the proof contains a later autograph revision that enters the 1868 text: "They make two or three trips in a week, according to wind and weather, from Merrimack to Lowell and back, about twenty-five miles each way" (213.35-214.2).

A similar change appears in "Wednesday," where

[16] Other examples of 68 readings directly related to uncorrected proof are TV 46.2-4, 74.15-16, 168.19, 168.29, and 183.8. TV *116.7, *134.2, *377.23-26 are also examples of pre-1849 forms not occurring in 1849 but present in 1868; since T corrected these three errors by hand in some copies of 1849, he may have remembered them without recourse to proof.

Thoreau reports that Manchester, New Hampshire, had about two thousand inhabitants at the time of the 1839 voyage. The corrected proof and the 1849 text go on to read: "But now, after nine years, as I have been told and indeed have witnessed, it contains sixteen thousand inhabitants." Yet the proof also has a later alteration: "But now, as I have been told, and indeed have witnessed, it contains fifteen thousand inhabitants." He probably wrote the first version in 1848, nine years after his visit to Manchester. His later elimination of a chronological reference suggests a time well beyond 1848, and the change from "sixteen" to "fifteen" suggests current information, a trend continued when the figure became "fourteen" thousand in the 1868 text (see TN 245.30).

In his post-1849 proof revisions Thoreau corrected few errors; mostly he revised for greater accuracy and brevity. He made his largest deletion in "Sunday," canceling several negative sentences within a positive discussion of religious faith (see TV *66.29-30). A point about graveyards in "Monday" he clarified by dropping some words, here bracketed: "When the stone is a slight one, [and stands upright, pointing to the skies,] it does not oppress the spirits of the traveller to meditate by it;" (169.20-21). Other brief phrases he sharpened by omission: "The housekeeper says, I never had any new crockery [in my life] but I began to break the old" (260.8-10; *brackets supplied*). Throughout, he added information for clarity: "We camped . . . on the confines of Nashville" became "We camped . . . on the confines of what is now Nashville" (171.13-15). These post-1849 revisions cluster in "Sunday" through "Wednesday," possibly reflecting Thoreau's desire to improve the book's leisurely and meditative center, which early readers had strongly criticized. The more vigorous chapters that open and close his narrative have very few post-1849 revisions.

Other Post-1849 Revisions

One might naturally ask why Thoreau, wishing to continue revising *A Week* after its publication, went back to the cluttered proof sheets when he could have begun with an unmarked copy of the 1849 text. Certainly, the proof version had fewer uncorrected errors, and it also contained his latest revisions. Yet the more heavily corrected proof pages must have been difficult to read, and the great bulk of their changes had already entered the 1849 version. In any event, though he made some post-1849 revisions on the first edition proof, it did not serve as printer's copy, for many changes in the second edition do not appear on the proof sheets at all. By the same token, some changes on the proof anticipate 1868 wording, but only as "drafts"; they were further revised elsewhere before reaching final form (see TV 170.30-31). But where? Apparently he did not turn to a set of unbound sheets, for his letter of February 24, 1862, to Ticknor and Fields declares that he never opened the wrapped packages of sheets (*Corr.*, p. 637), and the Ticknor and Fields Cost Books record the purchase of all 450 unbound copies.[17]

Thoreau quite probably continued his revision on a bound copy of the 1849 edition. After May 1849, he always had copies on hand for presentation and sale;

[17] MH, MS Am 1185.6, Vol. 5 (June 1867-April 1870), 255. A selected transcription and explanation of these records, 1862-1880, appears in Walter Harding, "The Early Printing Records of Thoreau's Books," *ATQ*, 11 (Summer 1971), 44-59.

after October 1853, when Munroe returned the unsold balance, Thoreau's home became a virtual warehouse for his book. Of course, some other document may have suited his needs, but the evidence for its existence is negligible. Duplicate first-edition proof sheets were printed for some signatures (1 and 2, at least; see above, TI, p. 509), so Thoreau may have possessed a second unmarked set. This set might have been easier to handle than a bound copy, but it would have been more difficult to use for revising: it would have neither the earlier corrections, like a clean 1849 copy, nor a record of needed type changes, like the marked 1849 proof. Whatever document Thoreau used, he must have compared it with the marked 1849 proof, for the 1868 text adopts two kinds of readings from that source: post-1849 revisions entered on the proof and pre-1849 corrections ignored or missed by the printer.

1862 Reissue

A complete textual history of *A Week* must account for the 1862 reissue by Ticknor and Fields of the 1849 sheets (see HI, p. 484). On October 28, 1853, according to his Journal, Thoreau received from Munroe 706 unsold copies of the first edition, a delivery that prompted his well-known reflections on authorship (see HI, p. 471).[18] On April 30, 1855, he wrote to a publisher, almost certainly Ticknor and Fields, trying unsuccessfully to get the book reissued (see HI, pp. 481-482). Finally, by February 24, 1862, he had secured a publisher's interest. His letter to Tick-

[18] Thoreau's count in the Journal entry is 706 copies, but a note from Munroe that preceded shipment gave the total as 700, 250 bound and 450 in sheets, and Thoreau later informed Ticknor and Fields "I found by count the number of bound volumes to be correct" (*Corr.*, p. 637).

nor and Fields on that date reports a current count of 596 volumes on hand, 146 bound and 450 in sheets (*Corr.*, p. 637). What survives of a letter from Ticknor and Fields dated April 6, 1862, suggests that negotiations had been completed for their purchase of the remainder (*Corr.*, p. 646). Apparently Thoreau kept one bound copy, for Ticknor and Fields's Cost Books record the purchase of 595 copies, 145 bound and 450 in sheets; Thoreau received forty cents per copy, or $238.00. A payment is listed for the printing of 500 title pages. Later that year the firm bound these sheets with the new title page, bearing its own imprint. In every respect—except title page and copyright notice—the contents of this 1862 reissue exactly match the 1849 edition, including its advertisement for *Walden*, "soon to be published."[19]

Thoreau's promotion of the 1862 reissue poses some interesting questions: Why did he urge publication of the corrupt and incomplete 1849 text, when he had spent so much time correcting and revising a new one? In April 1862 he knew he was dying; might not the public regard this issue as a "deathbed edition," expressing his final intentions? One answer is that he may have had no choice. Ticknor and Fields showed no appetite for a new edition in 1862; when contact-

[19] Machine collations verify that the 1862 and 1849 texts are identical, with no evidence of corrections or reset type. Two copies of each text were collated, 1849 against 1862; one pair on a Hinman Collator at the American Antiquarian Society, Worcester, Massachusetts; the other on a Lindstrand Comparator at the Thoreau Edition Textual Center, NjP. The respective call numbers or owners are (Worcester collation): 1849—No. 95361 at MCo; 1862—Amos Cotting copy, American Antiquarian Society; (Princeton collation): 1849—Edmund Hosmer copy, Robert H. Taylor Collection, Princeton, New Jersey; 1862—Malcolm Ferguson Collection, Concord, Massachusetts.

ing Thoreau about his essays and *Walden*, the firm did not mention *A Week*, probably because the first edition had never sold well. Another answer is that Thoreau's own thrift would not permit him to leave in his attic study almost 600 unsold books, supplanted by a new edition. His apparent decision was to sell off the old edition first, withholding the second edition until needed. This plan was not impractical, since a new and revised text might sustain interest in *A Week* even after his death. Moreover, his family would benefit from the arrangement; with existing stock now sold and a new edition later, the book might at last recover its early loss and earn some measure of profit.

1868 "New and Revised" Edition

No evidence of a contract for the revised second edition has survived, but apparently Ticknor and Fields took an option to publish at a suitable time—presumably after the 1862 reissue was exhausted. Exactly what served as printer's copy for the second edition is also unknown, for only two cryptic references to it have come to light. The first is in a letter from Ellery Channing to Marston Watson, dated July 17, 1863: "Mr. Thoreau's last book [*Excursions*] is now through the press, hardly any original matter. Am looking at his corrected copy of the Week, with a view to a new ed." (see HI, footnote 69). The second reference appears in James T. Fields's business diary. An entry for the winter of 1864-1865 queries: "How many Concord River by Thoreau have we on hand?" He was alluding to the 1862 reissue, but probably with the second edition in mind. By October 1866, Fields could list books scheduled for publication in 1867, including "Thoreau's Week on Concord River (copy in the safe)." The title later appears with reference to books in preparation by January 1867.

Fields's "copy in the safe" must refer to the setting copy for the second edition, and his term "copy" probably means this version was printed, for in similar entries he uses "MSS" to describe an author's holograph manuscript.[20] The book was printed, corrected, and copyrighted by November 19, 1867. During production the firm paid for thirty-one hours of proof correction. That number is low, considering the one hundred hours devoted to *The Maine Woods* (1864), and the sixty hours spent on *Letters to Various Persons* (1865). These figures strongly suggest that the 1868 text of *A Week* was set from printed copy. One thousand three hundred copies were printed with the date 1868, and three later reprintings came from the same plates: one hundred fifty copies in the fall of 1873; one hundred seventy-five in the spring of 1880; and an undetermined number in 1883. The firm records no expenses for plate correction after 1868, and the reprintings themselves contain no variants other than title page dates.[21]

[20] Memorandum and Account Book in the James T. Fields Collection, CSmH: Uncatalogued Papers, Box 7, Packet 27. The pages are unnumbered.

[21] Ticknor and Fields Cost Books, *op. cit.*, Vol. 5 (June 1867-April 1870), 255; Vol. 7 (September 1872-October 1875), 72; Vol. 11 (January-August 1880), 74; a Cost Book entry for 1883 has not been found, but see *infra.* Machine collations verify that, aside from normal plate wear, no changes to the 1868 text occurred in any of its subsequent printings. At a point where 68 reads ["So], for example 80 reads ['So] (*brackets supplied*), but the latter results from worn type and is not a true single quotation mark. Three copies of the 1868 text were collated on a Lindstrand Comparator at the Thoreau Edition Textual Center, NjP. The call numbers or owners are: F72.C575 at the Library of Congress; 3960.6.396.13 at NjP; Malcolm Ferguson Collection, Concord, Massachusetts.

A peculiar feature of the second edition is its historical anonymity. That Thoreau prepared its text seems clear, yet evidence supporting that assumption is largely internal. The only positive reference to his work on a new edition is in Channing's 1863 letter to Marston Watson, cited above. No other allusions—either to plans for a second edition or to completion of the task—are known to exist in Thoreau's Journal, letters, notes, or notebooks; or in extant letters, journals, and diaries of his close friends and editors—Sophia Thoreau, Ralph Waldo Emerson, Amos Bronson Alcott, William Ellery Channing.

Correspondence not extant could probably answer many questions. This editor's surmise is that Thoreau's work on the second edition, begun on the first edition proof after 1849, was concluded in a fresh copy not long before his death, when he was also busily working on other literary materials. A likely date for the final revisions would lie between July 1861 and February 1862. Prior to his trip to Minnesota in May 1861, he concentrated on "Wild Fruits" and "The Dispersion of Seeds," and worked on the latter again after his return to Concord in July. From February to April 1862 he was working on the *Atlantic* essays, and from April to May on *The Maine Woods*. But Thoreau's silence in this period about *A Week* is so complete as to be surprising, and it emphasizes the need for caution when assessing the authority of the 1868 edition.

Under careful scrutiny, the 1868 text stands up well as an authorial version. Thoreau worked on his marked proof sheets after 1849, probably thinking of

---

One copy of the 1883 reprinting (NjP, 3960.6.396) was also collated on the Lindstrand Comparator against the NjP copy of 1868.

a new edition (see TI, pp. 515-518). In forty-three instances a reading first printed in 1868 is anticipated by an autograph proof change, either pre- or post-1849. Though autograph evidence is lacking for the other 153 substantive changes from 1849 in 1868 that are accepted in PE, the 1868 text is clearly, though indirectly, descended from the marked proof for 1849. Some 1868 readings exist only in early manuscript versions of *A Week.* In the section on friendship in "Wednesday," for example, the 1868 text adds two sections absent from proof and 1849, but found on a draft page written ca. 1847: "Yet reserve is the freedom and abandonment of lovers. It is the reserve of what is hostile or indifferent in their natures, to give place to what is kindred and harmonious" (273.30-33). In the same early version are two lines of poetry, which appear in 1868 but not in the 1849 proof (see 175.5-6).[22] No one but Thoreau could or would return to his manuscripts and marked proof to supply revisions for a second edition.

Like Thoreau's revisions on the marked proof, most of the 1868 variants–changes in pronouns, verbs, and the arrangement of phrases–lead to greater clarity and economy of expression. In the 1849 text, a description of a densely wooded island concludes: "Not long after one or two more occurred." In 1868 "occurred" gives way to "were passed," a more precise phrase (243.15). Thoreau's wariness of "occasionally," so conspicuous in the 1849 corrections, survived in 1868, where "occasionally and" changes to "rarely or" (86.7). The 1868 text also corrects certain matters of fact, as when the principal quarry for "Chelms-

[22] See TN 66.16, 86.7, 94.20, 273.30-33 for other examples of early MS versions of 1868 readings.

ford granite" became "Westford" (110.22). Instead of "moss," American rocks are covered with "lichens" (250.25), and the "double-spruce" becomes a "single-spruce" (318.24).

Most of the 1868 revisions are improvements, but few shorten Thoreau's longest published narrative. The longest omission is of a single complete sentence. In the 1849 text, a paragraph about Eastern religions concludes with two sentences: "But they who are unconcerned about the consequences of their actions, are not therefore unconcerned about their actions.– Yet we know not where we should look for a loftier speculative faith." The 1868 text drops the second sentence, perhaps because its compliment has a touch of condescension (see TV 141.7-8).

The most notable 1868 changes are additions to the text. About half consist of single words and brief phrases; the rest are longer phrases, sentences, and in one case a long paragraph. Besides polishing language, the additions work in new ideas, reflections, plus more than a dozen quotations at appropriate points. Several of these additions and changes reflect Thoreau's experiences and reading habits after 1849,[23] supporting the authority of 1868 variants.

Discussing worshippers, Thoreau asked in the 1849 edition: "What is this heaven which they expect, if it is no better than they expect? Are they prepared for a better than they can now imagine? Here or nowhere is our heaven.–" The 1868 text adds a sentence after the second one: "Where is the heaven of him who dies on a stage, in a theatre?" (379.31-380.1). The 1868 version of "Thursday" includes a possible reference to Thoreau's own ill health. To the 1849

[23] See TN 21.10, 29.14-16, 195.26-27, 318.24, 390.2.

passage reading "those to whom travelling is life for the legs," the later text adds, "and death too, at last" (306.23).

Parts of the 1868 text differ markedly from 1849, often in the same sections Thoreau heavily revised before 1849, as his surviving manuscripts verify. The essay on friendship in "Wednesday," for example, was changed substantially for 1868. Almost two dozen changes appear in this section alone, the additions totaling almost one full page of text. In the section on music in "Monday," for which several heavily revised manuscript fragments survive, Thoreau added two sentences, two lines of original verse, and a quotation from an Eastern poet (175.2-11). The longest single addition in 1868 is a paragraph containing quotations from Edward Johnson's *Wonder-Working Providence of Sion's Saviour in New England 1628-1651* (10.17-11.17). The passage describes seventeenth-century Concord and environs, stressing the similarities of past and present time. Thoreau first read Johnson while studying New England history in early 1855, as background for his revision of *Cape Cod.*

In his early manuscripts Thoreau often modified or deleted critical comments about people or institutions, but a reverse of this tendency appears in 1868, with an added critique of clergymen, another subject he worked at length in the manuscripts. An 1849 paragraph about churches ends: "Certainly, such temples as these shall ere long cease to deform the landscape." The 1868 text has an additional illustration drawn from a trip he made to Cape Cod in June 1850:

> There are few things more disheartening and disgusting than when you are walking the streets of a strange village on the Sabbath, to hear a preacher shouting like a

> boatswain in a gale of wind, and thus harshly profaning the quiet atmosphere of the day. You fancy him to have taken off his coat, as when men are about to do hot and dirty work. (76.15-22)

Another version of this passage appears in *Cape Cod*:

> The next summer, as I sat on a hill there one sultry Sunday afternoon, the meeting-house windows being open, my meditations were interrupted by the noise of a preacher who shouted like a boatswain, profaning the quiet atmosphere, and who, I fancied, must have taken off his coat. Few things could have been more disgusting or disheartening. (*W* 4:253)

A final important instance of addition in 1868 is the presence of a fourth motto before the text of "Concord River." The new motto, an expansion of lines that appeared in 1849 (110.14), consists of four lines from Ovid's *Metamorphoses*, with Thoreau's translation.

> Fluminaque obliquis cinxit declivia ripis;
> Quæ, diversa locis, partim sorbentur ab ipsa;
> In mare perveniunt partim, campoque recepta
> Liberioris aquæ, pro ripis litora pulsant.
> *Ovid*, Met. I. 39.

> He confined the rivers within their sloping banks,
> Which in different places are part absorbed by the earth,
> Part reach the sea, and being received within the plain
> Of its freer waters, beat the shore for banks. (4.1-9)

Mottoes generally establish an initial theme and tone: this addition is much less personal than the ones carried over from 1849. Those three are by Thoreau; the addition by another poet conveys greater distance and formality. The new lines invoke a spiritual world, and a creative, shaping god, whose identity in Ovid is equivocal. The lines continue Thoreau's river theme, but they focus attention less on the physical voyage of the protagonist than on the imaginative voyage of a creative artist, who "confined the rivers within their sloping banks."

Each of these illustrated revisions for the 1868 edition seems demonstrably authorial. Taken as a whole, they reflect Thoreau's effort to fulfill his design for *A Week*, confided to the Journal: "it is a hypæthral or unroofed book, lying open under the ether and permeated by it, open to all weathers, not easy to be kept on a shelf" (J 2, p. 275; June 29, 1851). The edition printed in 1868 may have remained open to all weathers, but it was not open to further revision. No subsequent text of *A Week* bears the mark of Thoreau's authority.

CHOICE OF COPY-TEXT

The text of this edition has been prepared in accord with the principles and procedures of modern textual criticism.[24] The copy-text for *A Week* must be the proof sheets for the first edition and their three levels of holograph correction, as described above (TI, pp. 506-511). Corrected proof is the surviving text closest to Thoreau's lost printer's copy; thus the proof acci-

[24] A development in which W. W. Greg, Fredson Bowers, and others have been influential. See the *Statement of Editorial Principles and Procedures: A Working Manual for Editing Nineteenth-Century American Texts*, rev. ed. prepared by the Center for Editions of American Authors (New York: Modern Language Association, 1972) and *The Center for Scholarly Editions: An Introductory Statement*, prepared by the Center for Scholarly Editions (New York: Modern Language Association, April 1977). These booklets contain selected bibliographies of works in textual theory and practice. Other PE volumes also contain discussions of editorial rationale; see particularly that by Joseph J. Moldenhauer, ed. *The Maine Woods* (1972), pp. 385-389 *et passim*.

dentals[25] have more authority than those of the first edition. Of crucial importance is the fact that Thoreau himself corrected this proof, going over it with great care. While he was not always consistent in his corrections, abundant evidence in the proof establishes his intentions and normal practices. No other extant version of *A Week* received from him this amount or this kind of attention.

The chief problem with choosing proof as copy-text is that it contains three levels of correction: the printer's and Thoreau's before the first edition; and Thoreau's after 1849, made with a second edition in mind. Most of the printer's marks concern the technical appearance of type—wrong type font, inverted letters, improper spacing, irregular lines, etc.; these corrections are not substantive, and Thoreau did not usually respond to them except to note irregularities the printer overlooked. But the printer also concerned himself with substantive matters, often writing query marks in the margins and underlining the element in question. In most instances Thoreau responded to these queries by making an appropriate correction; if the query was irrelevant or inappropriate, Thoreau ignored or canceled it. Now and then the printer made a textual correction—changing an obvious misspelling, or an assumed error in punctuation. If Thoreau altered or canceled one of these corrections, this edition follows his marking; if he allowed a printer's change to stand, this edition concurs, presuming Thoreau's careful scrutiny. These unaltered pre-1849 correc-

[25] Features of the text that do not affect discursive meaning are called accidentals. These are usually matters of punctuation, spelling, capitalization, etc. Substantives are features that do affect discursive meaning: these may also be matters of punctuation, etc., but are usually words.

tions are identified in the apparatus as the printer's—or as of doubtful origin, if the handwriting is ambiguous.

Both Thoreau's pre- and post-1849 revisions on the proof are admitted to the text, because both are in his hand and plainly represent his intention. When reasons exist for questioning or rejecting an autograph proof change, a Textual Note explains the doubt or the emendation.

For a different reason in each case, none of the other relevant versions of *A Week* can serve as copy-text. The surviving manuscripts are early versions, and they are fragmentary. Passages from Journal and commonplace books, earliest and most fragmentary, obviously cannot qualify as copy-text. As for surviving drafts, the fact of their survival means Thoreau had already revised their contents, or deleted them from his printer's copy before it was sent to Munroe and subsequently lost. These drafts (ca. 1847-1848) contain few sustained blocks of text; a good many four-page and some eight-page units survive, but larger ones are rare.[26] While these early versions cannot serve as copy-text, they are valuable for research into textual problems; when a crux occurs, an early version can often support editorial decisions.

The printed poems, translations, and essays Thoreau revised for *A Week* are also too early to serve as copy-text; moreover, they are separate literary works. Nonetheless, the early forms may help to resolve questions about later readings, even if they precede Thoreau's intentions when he prepared *A Week* for print.

The 1849 edition itself cannot be copy-text because it stands farther from the manuscript printer's copy

26 The first draft, written ca. 1845-1847, is more intact; see FD.

than does Thoreau's corrected proof. Numerous changes from the proof first appear in 1849; presumably the printer made them directly on the standing type after the proofs had left Thoreau's hand. Since we have no evidence that Thoreau saw or approved these changes before publication, the Princeton edition generally rejects them as non-authorial. The first edition does, of course, have authority in some situations. When a copy-text crux arises from an error in the printing process, the first edition offers parallel evidence because it was printed from the same type as the proof. For example, on p. 226 of the proof an area was poorly inked, but the obscured readings are legible in the 1849 text (see TV 216.20-23). Tables and Textual Notes indicate the few instances where copy-text has been emended to 1849 readings. Some copies of the first edition contain holograph corrections, but as indicated above (TI, pp. 513-514), only three corrections of this kind are unequivocally by Thoreau. The first two also appear in the copy-text as his holograph corrections, and the third became necessary when the printer dropped three lines of type from the proof before publication.

Copies of the first edition that were re-issued in 1862, with new title and copyright pages, have no greater authority than the first edition itself, and therefore cannot be copy-text.

The 1868 edition has textual authority, but cannot be copy-text. Neither its printer's copy nor corrected proof has survived. The proof, even if extant, would have no authorial weight because Thoreau did not correct it. Printer's copy, though of great textual importance, could not be copy-text unless Thoreau had clearly given meticulous attention to the accidentals—an unusual step for any author to take when revising a work. Accidentals in the 1868 text thus have no authority except where they are the only evidence available—that is, when they occur in a new passage, presumably added by the author.

The importance of the 1868 edition lies in its substantive differences from the first. If Thoreau made these changes, then the 1868 substantives represent his latest intention, and they should enter a critical text. This logic would not apply if great differences existed between the two versions—differences so large as to constitute two works of distinct conception and achievement, like the first and last editions of *Leaves of Grass* that Whitman supervised. But the editions of *A Week* do not differ on this scale. Between them stand over 150 authorial substantive variants, almost entirely matters of phrasing, polish, and modest addition, which refine the execution but do not change the work's basic design or character.

How reliable are the 1868 substantives? More than two dozen derive from authorial readings that did not appear in 1849. For example, a sentence in the 1849 edition appeared thus: "The stillness was intense and almost conscious, as if it were a natural Sabbath. The air. . . ." In proof the sentence was longer, but Thoreau canceled two phrases, here enclosed in brackets: "The stillness was intense and almost conscious, as if it were a natural Sabbath, [and deeper silence than ordinary brooded over the earth, and we fancied that the morning was the eve of a celestial day.] The air. . . ." The latter half of this cancellation reappears in 1868: "The stillness . . . Sabbath, and we fancied that the morning was the evening of a celestial day." (see TV 46.2-4). In this case and others like it, the 1868 reading is demonstrably Thoreau's; it therefore is accepted. Other 1868 readings are supported by pre-copy-text versions. The present editor, and members of the Textual Center staff, have thoroughly searched early manuscript and printed materials for pre-copy-text versions that might support new readings from 1868, as well as for information on other matters.

Of course, every 1868 variant must be examined carefully. If an 1868 reading that varies from 1849 also appears in copy-text, the change is undoubtedly authorial (see TV 187.21); if it exists in a pre-copy-text manuscript, the variant is most certainly Thoreau's (see TN 273.30-33). If an 1868 reading is derived from but not identical to a copy-text form that did not appear in 1849, the 1868 reading has authority because Thoreau revised the copy-text (see TV 170.30-31). If the 1868 reading has no predecessors, but indicates familiarity with context, with Thoreau's sources, or with his characteristic language, images, and rhetorical devices, the reading has an acceptable degree of authority (see TN 29.14-16).

Yet skepticism is in order if an 1868 change is minor, isolated, and does not correct or improve the text. Changes of that sort may be only printers' errors or unauthorized corrections (see TV 186.11). Smaller and less significant changes are more likely to be non-authorial. Deletions both small and large are suspect, for typesetters are more likely to omit words than to add them. Finally, a large number of 1868 changes in spelling, punctuation, or paragraphing must be rejected because they are Ticknor and Fields's house styling and demonstrably contrary to Thoreau's usual practices—as in the consistent change from "Shakspeare" to "Shakespeare" throughout 1868.

EDITORIAL DECISIONS

Setting Copy

The editor and staff members at the Thoreau Edition Textual Center created a setting copy for this edition by marking an enlarged photocopy of the 1849 edition to correspond to the copy-text accidentals. Next, they emended the setting copy to incorporate substantive changes in copy-text, as reported in the Table of Emendations. Their emendation decisions derived from multiple collations of the copy-text, plus the 1849 and 1868 editions. Finally, they read the setting copy against the original copy-text, simultaneously checking the tables of Variants and Emendations for accuracy.[27]

Variants

All variants were examined and recorded in this process, but the Table of Variants in this edition lists only substantive variants. Accidental variants are not recorded in the Table, for they have no meaningful effect, but merely alter the typographical appearance of punctuation, spelling, or word-division. Many of the 1868 accidentals are clearly "house style" and thus have no textual authority. The following changes between copy-text/1868 illustrate the effect of house styling: Shakspeare/Shakespeare; nature/Nature; plow/

[27] Photographic enlargement was made of a copy at NN (*KL c.2). The original proof sheets of 1849 are at CSmH (Rare Book 110229). The editor performed six sight collations using setting copy: three against another copy of 1849 at NN (*KL c.1), and three against the editor's personal copy of 1868. He recorded all substantive and accidental variants among copy-text, 1849, and 1868 versions on a master table. Staff members of the Thoreau Edition Textual Center performed two sight collations of the setting copy against a microfilm of copy-text and NjP copies of 1849 and 1868 (3960.6.396.14; 3960.6.396.13), to verify this record. The same personnel, using the same materials, proofread the typescript apparatus twice. Machine collations of multiple copies of the 1849, 1862, and 1868 editions were also performed, as described above (see footnotes 13, 21).

plough; river/River; oriental/Oriental; occidental/Occidental; Capt./Captain; western/Western; eastern/Eastern; Tyngsboro'/Tyngsborough; gazetteer/Gazetteer; friends/Friends; farther/further; and further/farther. Two other stylistic changes occur between copy-text and 68: 68 adds a question mark to each rhetorical question, and an "s" to each plural possessive, e.g. Prioress'/Prioress's. A full listing of these variants is deposited with other relevant materials at the Thoreau Edition Textual Center, Firestone Library, Princeton University.

A second group of unrecorded accidental variants includes proof corrections of typographical anomalies: broken type, inverted type, wrong font type, improper vertical or horizontal alignment of type, inked spaces, and corrections of running titles, page numbers, signature numbers, and end-of-line hyphens for non-compound words. The printer corrected most of these, but Thoreau marked a few others. The variants cannot be easily recorded, and the editor believes no useful purpose would be served by publishing descriptions. Thus the Princeton Edition accepts all corrections of these anomalies; no record of variants appears on the Table nor on the list deposited at the Textual Center. Any unusual or important corrections are discussed in Textual Notes.

A third group of unrecorded accidental variants includes the printer's and Thoreau's queries—"Qy" or "?" in margins—and proof corrections of vertical or horizontal spacing. Again, the variants cannot be easily recorded or described; hence, significant cases are discussed in the Textual Notes. Thoreau gave careful attention to the spacing of his copy on the page. His corrections are of two kinds: horizontal indentations and vertical spaces involving both prose and poetry.

To signify a major shift in thought or narrative action, he typically used a paragraph indentation and one to four blank or "white lines." His concern for this feature caused the major omission of three lines of type, as discussed above (TI, p. 514), and he made similar space corrections on other proof pages.[28]

Thoreau corrected poetry indentations by placing line margins precisely. In one example, on p. 101 he quotes Francis Quarles:

"Merchants, arise,
And mingle conscience with your merchandise."

The short line was originally set above "conscience" but he moved it farther right. He made frequent corrections of this kind on proof pages.[29]

Thoreau asked for a "dash" or rule in the text at 303.4 (see TN 289.15), 367.30 (see TN 348.26), and 396.32 (see TN 377.23-26); but he did not correct the rules appearing under chapter titles. The proof has no rules under chapter titles for "Concord River," "Saturday," "Tuesday," and "Friday." He made no corrections, yet in 1849 only "Concord River" still lacks a rule, and there a quotation appears between title and text. Since Thoreau apparently left the matter to his printer, this edition omits the 1849 chapter rules and substitutes spaces for other rules, such as those used to separate prose and poetry texts. See "Design," below (TI, pp. 542-543).

Emendations

Except for recorded emendations, the editor has followed copy-text throughout. Emending has been

28 See TN 214.24-25, 307.20.

29 See TN 43.1-7, 46.31-35, 99.31, 110.14, 203.28, 297.33.

held to a conservative limit; thus the text often has unemended peculiarities, which are not errors but idiosyncracies in Thoreau's style. His uncorrected spelling, pointing, and phrasing are followed exactly, since later variants cannot supersede these readings, and the text is understandable despite certain inconsistencies. Different spellings of the same words are allowed to stand: "Pasaconway" (81.9) and "Passaconaway" (252.18-19, 254.4). His apparently erratic use of "further" and "farther" is not regularized. In the early manuscript versions he commonly wrote "further" instead of "farther": "further" is also dominant in the proof, but "farthest" occurs at 329.16 (312.28) and at 156.10-11 (150.32) the reading is "farthest . . . farthest", as in an early manuscript version (MH). In fact, in Thoreau's day the two words were often used interchangeably.

Thoreau attended to capitalization in the proof, often changing lower-case or upper-case forms with special effects in mind. Yet while he altered "Sudbury river" to "Sudbury River" (5.29) and "Assabeth river" to "Assabeth River" at (5.31), he left similar forms unrevised: see "Concord river" at 12.2, and also 30.12, 211.21, 246.26-27. Word-division is also variable: "sugar-maples" (202.23) is like "white-maples" (216.1) and "red-maple" (251.13-14); but "sugar maple" also occurs (99.1). These variations are common in Thoreau's manuscripts, even in multiple uses of the same term. Consequently, the inconsistent copy-text readings are not emended.

Inconsistent punctuation resulting from autograph corrections is also followed, except in the case of transposition when the unemended passage makes no sense (see TN 65.33-34). When marking proof Thoreau often inserted punctuation marks with a caret, especially for quotation marks and apostrophes. His autograph caret points were sometimes placed improperly in proof, but silently corrected in the 1849 edition. For example, where the proof reads [therein.] Thoreau corrected to read [therein".], yet the 1849 text reads [therein."] (112.12, *brackets supplied*). Because its rationale is to preserve copy-text accidentals, this edition follows Thoreau's autograph correction. Often the 1849 "corrections" are in fact erroneous: Thoreau altered "Tyngsboro' " to "Tyngsboro'," in proof, but 1849 reads "Tyngsboro,' " (119.14); moreover, copy-text accidentals are demonstrably more consistent with the author's usual practices.

Whenever the copy-text is misleading, incomplete, or otherwise ambiguous, however, the editor has emended according to established principles. Some emendations in this edition were anticipated by editions appearing after 1868, but those cases do not authorize present emendations. Emendations are of two kinds, substantive and accidental, and they have been drawn from three sources: the 1849 text, the 1868 text, and the present editor's authority. Each of these categories has sub-categories, according to the nature and chronology of available variants.

Substantives emended from 1849 are of two kinds. First, though most variants in 1849 are superseded by copy-text readings, some provide necessary emendations of the copy-text. For example, errors appear in proof because of Thoreau's incomplete corrections. In one place, he wanted to revise the spelling of "ploughing" to "plowing," but his correction, if followed literally, reads "plouwing." The printer set "plowing" in 1849; hence that text provides an emendation of the copy-text (8.20).

Second, some uncorrected errors in proof were

caught in 1849, apparently by the printer as he perfected type. For example, in proof a line of poetry read "Lo, when the sun streams patient through the wood,"; "patient" is an error: the word properly belongs four lines below. The error is not marked for correction, yet the printer did correct it, possibly referring to his setting copy for guidance. Thus proof and 1849 vary, and the 1849 reading is accepted as an emendation (295.9).

Substantives emended from 1868 are of five kinds. First, 1868 readings are accepted when they complete passages that are partially or imperfectly revised in copy-text. See the discussion of changing population figures for Manchester, N.H., above (TI, pp. 516-517).

Second are those 1868 readings corroborated or anticipated by authorial versions other than copy-text. For example, two lines of poetry in 1868 are not in proof or 1849, but they exist in a manuscript draft, ca. 1847, though in a different context (see TN 175.5-6).

Third are those 1868 readings significant enough to suggest authorial intent (see above, TI, p. 533), even when other documentary evidence is lacking. In one instance, proof reads "the contemplations of those Indian sages have influenced the intellectual development of mankind. . . ." The 1868 reading is even stronger: "the contemplations of those Indian sages have influenced, and still influence, the intellectual development of mankind . . ." (143.12-14). This revision seems authorial: it agrees with Thoreau's high estimate of Eastern thought, and it hardly seems a change that might arise from a printer or editor.

Fourth is a group of minor revisions or deletions that significantly clarify or improve the text. At 270.27-28, for instance, an 1868 reading is accepted:

the sexes "are most commonly and surely the complements of each other" rather than "of one another," as in proof and 1849. The change is small but presumably authorial, because it augments Thoreau's original sense. But the 1868 text also has many "improvements" of dubious authority; all variants of that sort were rejected. For example, on p. 257 both proof and 1849 read "By what a delicate and far-fetched contribution every island is made!" but in 1868 "far-fetched" becomes "far-stretched," thus eliminating a *double entendre* (see TV *243.26). Thoreau was not likely to have dropped the pun, and a small change of this sort, affecting three letters, could be merely a printer's error in 1868.

Fifth, a few 1868 readings correct for the first time positive errors in the copy-text. These corrections are adopted for clarity, rather than on a claim of authorial origin. On p. 98, for example, 1868 translates the Homeric Greek as "sped us," correcting both the printed proof "speed as" and Thoreau's autograph revision "sped as," an illogical reading reproduced in 1849 (see TN 94.20).

Substantives emended by the editor are of two kinds. First, he emends if an obvious error in proof was uncorrected in both 1849 and 1868, and evidence from early manuscripts is unavailable. At 104.30 "sentences" must be plural to agree with the verb "have," but in proof, 1849, and 1868 it was singular.

Second, while the policy of this edition is not to "improve" Thoreau, the editor has emended some copy-text readings that are less obviously errors. In one instance, he has corrected Thoreau's reading of Homer, where the English is wrong (see TN 92.29). Thoreau's quotations and translations often depart from their sources, but this edition emends only if the variants introduce errors of fact or interpretation (see

TN 10.33). Often, misquotations are Thoreau's deliberate revisions of sources; to emend would restrict his poetic license. Whenever possible, the editor has consulted Thoreau's original sources, in their known or probable editions, to see if emendations are necessary. For many quotations appearing only in 1868, the editor has established authority either by citing the quotation's appearance in Thoreau's notebooks (CPB, *TLN*), or by comparing it to his known sources. Some of Thoreau's significant departures from sources, here unemended, are discussed in Textual Notes.

Another basis for emendation is W. E. Channing's copy of *A Week*, at 298.24. A textual note explains this emendation fully.

Accidentals emended from 1849 are errors not corrected on proof, but apparently caught by the printer and corrected to readings consistent with Thoreau's intentions or usual practices. On p. 102 a sentence in proof ends with a comma; in 1849 a period replaces the comma (see Emendations 98.26). Presumably, Thoreau accepted the 1849 correction.

Accidentals emended from 1868 are of two kinds. First, 1868 corrects a number of positive errors in proof or 1849. At 87.33 the misspelled "Virgiania" of proof and 1849 is emended to 1868 "Virginia"; and at 161.23 the transposed letters of "Loevwell's" in proof and 1849 are emended to 1868 "Lovewell's."

Second, when substantive variants first appearing in 1868 are adopted as emendations, their accidentals are adopted as well. Thus, the 1868 additions of botanical names are accepted in their capitalized forms, because the copy-text usage is too inconsistent to justify emending (see TV 20.18-19, *195.26-27).

Accidentals emended by the editor are not numerous. He emends an obvious error in proof if it was not corrected in either 1849 or 1868. At 196.10 the reading "*sciurus*" is supplied, because of the incorrect "*striurus*" in proof and 1849, and "*Scriurus*" in 1868.

Finally, the editor has consistently emended one set of copy-text accidentals and listed them on the "End-of-Line Hyphenation" table in this edition. When compound words are hyphenated at the ends of printed lines in copy-text, they must be closed or hyphenated in accordance with Thoreau's normal practice. However, his "normal practice" in word-division was inconsistent. Since the hyphens are copy-text accidentals, variants in 1849 or 1868 cannot support emendations, but pre-copy-text variants can. Hence, the editor has drawn his emendations from the same or similar words appearing (1) elsewhere in the copy-text; (2) in early manuscript or printed versions of the passage; (3) in printed sources for the passage, if any; and (4) in Thoreau's lexicons.

Given this evidence, the editor has deleted or retained hyphens, producing compounds like "rail-road" or "railroad."[30] He has excluded place names (Londonderry), and compounds formed with prefixes or suffixes (inhospitable), unless evidence suggests that hyphenated forms are possible. Words that coincidentally resemble compounds (season, mushroom) are also excluded. The table has two sections, A and B; the first lists end-line compounds appearing in copy-text and the second lists those produced by typesetting in this edition.

Design

Unaffected by emendation policies is the treatment

[30] Evidence of Thoreau's use of a third form, e.g., "rail road," has no bearing on the emendation, since that form is not resolvable without emending twice, to delete the hyphen and retain a space.

of certain non-textual design features in this edition: front matter, including title page, copyright notice, and Table of Contents; chapter titles and half-titles; initial words in chapters; running titles, page numbers, and signature numbers; the size and style of typography, spacing, indentations, or margins; and back matter, including Index and Editorial Appendix. Page and line numbers of the text were determined by the series format adopted for THE WRITINGS OF HENRY D. THOREAU. In the tables that follow, *literal* page and line numbers appear. The line scale printed on the dust jacket and endpapers of this volume provides an accurate count for all pages with ordinary spacing and typography; for any pages with smaller type or unusual spacing, a literal line-count applies.

In accord with guidelines established by the Center for Editions of American Authors, this volume has been examined in printer's copy by an independent textual expert, Professor Don L. Cook of Indiana University, and has been proofread at least five times by three different individuals, including the editor and Editor-in-Chief, in galley and page proof.

Textual Notes

THE Textual Notes chiefly explain decisions to emend, or not to emend, that vary from general principles described in the Textual Introduction. The Notes also cite earlier versions and sources that bear on an editorial decision. Sources are identified as "probable" when the title is in question; when the edition is uncertain, the most likely one is cited. Variations in the order of phrases or accidentals are noted only when they affect a decision. Finally, the Notes describe unusual features in the proof sheets—Thoreau's notes to the printer, and query or question marks referring to lines of type. All quotations are literal; contextual punctuation therefore appears *outside* the quotation marks.

The version cited is copy-text unless otherwise identified, e.g., as 49, 68, or PE. For abbreviations used, see the List of Abbreviations, pp. 427-431.

In a few cases, one note describes all instances of the same Alteration (see TN 5.16). Only the first example appears on the Table of Variants; successors are listed in the Textual Note.

title: T asked for "A WEEK" "one size larger"; 49 reads "A WEEK". T queried publisher's name, "BLACKISTON", but 49 is unchanged. Copyright "1848" in P queried but uncorrected; 49 reads "1849". See TI, p. 508, on these query marks.

3.4 Brother—.: After verses, unidentified hand wrote "⟨We⟩ probably omited [*sic*] to write the word proof on the wrapper,—". Note may refer to set of proof previously sent to T in Concord. See TI, p. 509. See also TN 74.29.

5.16 River: "river" in P; altered in Pms here and at 5.17, 5.29, 5.31, 9.17, 9.35, 34.9, 36.30, and 43.9. T's practice was inconsistent (cf. 12.2 and 30.12). 49 follows Pms correction except at 5.29 and 5.31.

6.12 Bridge: "bridge" in P; a Pms alteration also made at 22.24 and 34.27. 49 follows Pms.

10.33 5 and 20: PE; as in T's source, Edward Johnson, *A History of New England, or Wonder-Working Providence of Sion's Saviour, in New England* (London, 1654), p. 84. P, 49, and 68 "5 to 20" is emended as T's copying error. See also TN 60.6, 303.28.

15.1 "Come,: In proof, preceded by a half-title and T's note, asking for type "one size larger—more open and a little higher up". 49 follows, and adds a rule between title and quotation that PE omits (see TI, p. 536).

15.2 These . . . delicates: Also in *TLN*, p. 250; and T's source, Francis Quarles, *Emblems, Divine and Moral.* (Chiswick, 1825), p. 222. 68 "Those . . . delicacies" is an error.

15.3 *Christ's Invitation*: 68; in *TLN*, p. 250, T wrote "Christ's invitation to the soul" to identify these lines. They appeared by error on proof pages 15 and 17; T requested small italics for title and author on p. 15 and canceled the repetition on p. 17.

15.4 AT length: In proof, preceded by T's note, "Title one size larger—and more open". 49 follows, and adds a rule below title.

19.14-17 On Ponkawtasset . . . day.: 68; Francis Allen (in *A Bibliography of Henry David Thoreau* [Boston: Houghton Mifflin Co., 1908], p. 169) criticized 68 changes as "no improvement", but two can be explained. First, 68 "Billericay" rhymes, while P "Billerica", pronounced "Bill-rík-a", does not (see 50.6 for another instance of "Billericay" in a passage added in 68). Second, the "poet" William Ellery Channing had a more secure reputation in the 1850's, which could explain why his "fine ray" "Doth often shine" in 68 instead of "faintly" shining as in Pms and 49.

20.4-5 pickerel from . . . pads, or a bream from her nest, and: Also in three earlier versions (PJ 1, p. 126; LB; CRS). 68 omissions are probably non-authorial.

20.21 large white balls: Also in two earlier versions (LB; CRS). 68 omission is probably non-authorial.

21.10 tansy, . . . prime.: 68; P reads "now in its

prime" and an early version (LB) reads "Tansy in its prime". T's close observation of succession of flowers, after 1850, possibly yielded more precise information about when tansy blooms. See also TV 21.9.

29.14-16 Old Josselyn . . . Partridge.: 68; T withdrew John Josselyn's *New Englands rarities discovered: in birds, beasts, fishes, serpents, and plants of that country* . . . (London, 1672) from the Harvard College Library, January 14, 1851 (Kenneth Cameron, *Emerson the Essayist*, 2 vols. [Raleigh: The Thistle Press, 1945], II, p. 195). See also TV 31.5-6.

35.22 not so settled: Cross in margin and line under "s" of "so"; "s" in P looks misaligned, but may be wrong font. Unidentified hand, possibly printer's, notes "s. cap." beside "x". 49 corrects.

35.25 independent on: Also in an earlier version (CRS). In proof, printer queried; T affirmed P reading by canceling query mark and underlining "on". Cf. *Walden*, TN 183.33.

37.5 Nature: "nature" in P; a Pms alteration also made at 113.34 and 364.13. 49 follows Pms. Cf. TN 210.19; TV 35.34.

37.28 phil-*anthropy*: In Pms T corrected P "*philan-/thropy*" by canceling "*phil*" and noting in margin: "phil-(upright with hyphen)". Cf. "phil-*anthropic*" in *Walden*, 212.33.

43.1-7 "The river . . . again.": In P lines were set flush at left margin; T directed, "Arrange these lines thus, as in the MS." and illustrated with the first few words of each line. The requested arrangement slopes left, lines 1 and 4 indented flush, and lines 3 and 5 flush left, as in his source, William Ellery Channing, "Boat Song" in *Dial*, I (October 1840), 223. 49 follows Pms.

46.13-14 holiday: 68; P and 49 "holyday" may be an error; an earlier version (HM 13195) reads "holidays".

46.31-35 "Sweet . . . purity.": In P lines had alternating indentation; T directed, "arrange the above thus" and illustrated with the first word of each line. The requested arrangement slopes left, lines 1 and 4 indented flush. It varies slightly from T's source, W. E. Channing, "Boat Song" in *Dial*, I (October 1840), 223, where lines 3 and 5 are flush left (see TN 43.1-7). 49 follows only part of T's direction, setting lines 2 and 3 flush rather than sloping. E. Allison notes a variant between 49 and Channing's *Poems* (1843), but that text was not T's source. See *TSB*, 121 (Fall 1972), 8.

57.20 Firste: 49; printer altered P "First" to "Firste", then canceled alteration. Printer may have checked setting copy to restore "Firste"; three earlier versions (LB; *TLN*, p. 242; HM 13195) and T's source, John Gower, *Confessio Amantis*, bk. 4, lines 2427-2432, in Chalmers, II, p. 113b, read "Firste".

60.5 Muhammedans: Printer underlined and wrote "See above" in margin, referring to his query of "Mahometans" at 59.33. T changed neither; his source for 60.5, Joseph Wolff, *Narrative of a Mission to Bokhara*, 2 vols. (London, 1845), I, p. 90, reads "Muhammedans".

60.6 Hodeyda: PE; as in T's source, Wolff, *Narrative of a Mission to Bokhara* (see TN 60.5). P, 49, and 68 "Hodyeda" is an error. See also TN 10.33, 303.28.

65.33-34 wood, in . . . wits.: PE; in rearranging phrases, T neglected to change punctuation. 49 and 68 have comma after "minutes" but lack comma after "wood" (not canceled in Pms).

66.16 seventh: 68; also in an earlier version (PJ I, p. 32); "sixth" in P, 49, and another earlier version (MH) is incorrect, since context indicates six days have passed.

66.29-30 him? One: 68; Pms-a is identical in substantives, but T neglected to cancel dash after "him?" which leads into next sentence in P, Pms, and 49 (see TV).

67.34 "God . . . Khu.": 68; CPB and T's source, Rammohun Roy, *Translation of Several Principal Books, Passages, and Texts of the Veds* (London, 1832), p. 12, read "God is the letter ku as well as khu."

68.28-29 "Spectators . . . tragedies.": 68; as in *TLN*, p. 330, and T's source, a poem prefaced to Chalmers's selection of Francis Beaumont, VI, p. 180b.

71.9-12 Pythagoras . . . literature.: 68; as in *TLN*, p. 33. T's source, Jamblichus of Chalchis, *Life of Pythagoras*, trans. Thomas Taylor (London, 1818), p. 196, attributes quotation to Sextus the Pythagorean.

74.29 propagate: In proof on page 85, first recto of signature 8, T wrote "in 2nd line page 79 if not too late instead of propogate propagate." 49 follows; T made correction from memory, a note, or on a duplicate set of proof held for reference. See also TN 3.4.

76.15-22 There are . . . work.: 68; another version of this passage appears in *Cape Cod* (see TI, pp. 526-527).

80.33-82.15 "being . . . away.": The small type in P, 49, and 68 is retained. This passage and one at 254.13-255.19 consist of quotations linked by T's own language, a combination usually appearing in regular type. In these two cases, T apparently thought the quoted material too long for that treatment. Cf. TN 221.15-17.

86.7 rarely or: 68; "occasionally and" in P and 49. An earlier version (MH) reads: "which is but partially if ever overflown at present." Both 68 and MH suggest an event less common than P does; apparently time confirmed T's earlier opinion that the Merrimack would rarely overflow.

90.27 or: Also in three earlier versions (PJ 1, p. 14; LB; HM 13195); 68 omission is probably non-authorial.

92.29 midday meal: PE; "morning meal" in P, 49, 68, and an earlier version (PJ 1, p. 57). Yet T's probable source, *The Iliad of Homer*, bk. 11, line 86, ed. C. C. Felton (Boston, 1834), p. 160, reads *δεῖπνον*, referring in Homer's dialect to principal meal of the day, usually served in early afternoon. Felton glosses line 84 (92.24-25 in PE) to mean "The day increased till noon." (p. 433); in this context "morning meal" is incorrect. T apparently erred in translating and never corrected. PE emends with "midday" to maintain two-syllable rhythm in line.

94.12 lifesome.—: Also in an earlier version (PJ 1, p. 57). T marked an "X" beneath "s" and again in margin to indicate misalignment; he also inserted a dash after "lifesome". 49 and 68 "lifelike" is probably non-authorial.

94.20 sped us: 68; also in an earlier version (PJ 1, p. 57). T altered P "speed" to "sped", but apparently overlooked "as", hence 49 reads "sped as". His probable source, *Iliad*, bk. 11, lines 725-726, p. 175, reads

ἔνθεν ρανσυδιη σὺν τεύχεσι θωρηχθέντες,
ἔνδιοι ικόμεσθ' ἱερὸν ῥόον 'Αλφειοῖο.

or "Thence with all speed, arrayed in our armor, we

came at midday to the sacred stream of Alpheius." T's is a free rendering, but 49 "sped as" is incorrect.

97.21 "Merchants, arise,: T directed these words, centered in P, to be set "over merchandise"; 49 follows.

99.31 "ask . . . light,: T directed "ask", set over "perpetual" in P, to be set "over 'the' "; 49 follows.

102.3 Though . . . well,: T noted "This line begins a ¶ ⟨*underlined*⟩ in larger type not verse", correcting P arrangement of it as first of four reduced lines of poetry, with "Though" set over "in"; 49 follows.

104.30 sentences: PE; "sentence" in P, 49, and 68 creates subject-verb disagreement. One earlier version (HM 943) reads "sentences".

107.1-3 "speaking . . . god.": 68; as in *TLN*, p. 42, and T's source, Heinrich Ritter, *The History of Ancient Philosophy*, trans. Alexander Morrison, 4 vols. (London, 1838-1846), I, p. 233.

109.29-30 first. . . . We: Aware of typesetting problems caused by his cancellation of a sentence (see TV 109.10-11), T here noted "no matter if this space is increased"; in 49 three blank lines appear.

110.14 "campoque recepta: T directed "put this over pulsant", correcting P where it appears above "o" of "Liberioris"; 49 follows.

110.22 Westford: 68; "Chelmsford" in P and 49. In T's probable reference, John Hayward, *The New England Gazetteer*, 6th ed. (Concord, N.H., 1839), both towns are identified as sources of "Chelmsford granite". Chelmsford entry reads: "Chelmsford abounds in limestone and granite; considerable of the latter is transported to Boston by the Middlesex canal, which passes through the town." Westford entry reads: "Quantities of fine granite, commonly called 'Chelmsford granite,' are found here, quarried and transported." During his post-49 revisions of *A Week*, T may have decided to identify this type of granite with Westford.

113.13 Island Brook: Capitals are underlined with a marginal question mark, but no change appeared until 68 "island brook". PE does not emend, since context suggests T intended a proper name.

115.26 made. A: Deleted passage is circled, canceled with a wavy line, and marked "omit" in margin.

116.7 wash: Pms and 68; "work" in P and 49. T

made this correction in his own copy of 49 (see TI, p. 514), as well as in other copies he sold or gave away. See also TN 134.2, 377.23-26.

116.28 prevail.: T directed "Make this ¶ terminate somewhere short of the end of the line." He may have anticipated typesetting problems after deleting a sentence (see TV 115.26). In 49 "pre-/vail." ends the paragraph.

117.5-6 "The hye . . . mynde.": 68; as in *TLN*, p. 114, and T's source, Joseph Ritson, ed., *Robin Hood*, 2 vols., 2nd ed. (London, 1832), I, p. 5.

117.8-11 "His shoote . . . slaine.": 68; as in *TLN*, p. 117, and Ritson, I, p. 118. A fragmentary and largely rejected earlier version of "Monday" (RPB) contains these lines, but reads "met" in line 3.

117.18-19 seaward, . . . oak: A marginal question mark beside this line may refer to "early rising"; space between these words is underlined.

117.23-30 "All courageous . . . gone.": 68; *TLN*, p. 112, and T's source, James Sibbald, *Chronicles of Scottish Poetry*, 4 vols. (Edinburgh, 1802), IV, p. lxii, read "curageous" in line 1, "breist" in line 3, and "thair" in line 4. 68 "foue" is emended as a printer's error to Sibbald and *TLN* "fone".

120.13 Chaplin: Printer underlined and entered marginal query mark; T canceled latter.

121.8 halls: T altered P "walls"; one possible source, Charles J. Fox, *History of the Old Township of Dunstable* (Nashua, N.H., 1846), p. 130, reads "walls", but another, Samuel Penhallow, *The History of the Wars of New-England* (Boston, 1726), p. 135, reads "halls".

123.17 the high banks: An earlier version (HM 956) reads "the steep banks". 68 "the banks" is probably non-authorial.

129.11 best tell: Also in two earlier versions (PJ 1, p. 349; MH). 68 "tell best" is probably non-authorial.

130.17 his way: As in T's probable source, "The Lordling Peasant" in Thomas Evans, ed. *Old Ballads* (London, 1810), IV, p. 136. 68 "the way" is probably non-authorial.

131.28 jailer: Printer altered P "jailer" to "jailor", which appears in 49, but T's later pencil correction cancels marginal "o" and enters "stet?".

132.27 West: "west" in P and 49; altered in Pms

here and at 132.32, 165.17. 49 follows Pms only at 165.17.

134.2 expediency: Pms and 68; "experience" in P and 49. See also TN 116.7, 377.23-26. T made this correction in his own copy of 49 (see TI, p. 514) as well as in other copies he sold or gave away.

135.1-2 Antigone . . . asks,: T's interpolation, but in P set as part of quotation. Pms marginal note points to line and directs printer to set in "common type with more space around it."; 49 follows.

135.16 body.: In proof, followed by T's note "if convenient increase this space", to separate Greek and Hindu materials. 49 follows.

138.1 Brahmans: Marginal query mark refers to second "a", underlined in Pms+. T corrected "Brahmin" to "Brahman" at 136.34 and 140.18. "Brahman" is consistent spelling of T's source, *Bhagvat-Geeta*, trans. Charles Wilkins (London, 1785); *OED* notes "Brahmin" and "Brahman" were popular and scholarly forms, respectively, in nineteenth century.

138.22 tracks: Also in T's source, Warren Hastings, Introductory Letter "To Nathaniel Smith, Esq." in *Bhagvat-Geeta*, p. 9; 68 "tracts" is an error.

143.25 seems: Printer underlined and entered marginal question mark.

144.19 into: Also in an earlier version (HM 956); 68 "in" is probably non-authorial.

149.12 indifferently: "indiffer-/ently" in P was canceled in pencil, another word written in margin; both cancellation and penciled word (now illegible) were erased.

154.3 leaves that: Also in two earlier versions (LB; HM 956); 68 "leaves which" is probably non-authorial.

154.29 that: Also in an earlier version (MA 608); 68 "which" is probably non-authorial.

155.9 Alwákidi's: PE; T's source, Simon Ockley's *The History of the Saracens* (London, 1718), reads "Alwákidi" (p. xxi). Plural possessive in P, 49, and 68 is incorrect. Emendations at 155.10 and 155.12 are also based on Ockley (pp. xxi-xxii); T miscopied these names in an earlier version (PJ 1, p. 416) and they appeared incorrectly in his essay "Dark Ages" in *Dial*, 3 (April 1843), 527. See also *Early Essays*, p. 384.

163.37 nought: Printer underlined "ou" and entered marginal query mark. He may have noted T's inconsistent spelling; cf. "Nought" at 22.18 and "naught" at 378.31.

166.10 gristly: Printer underlined "tly" and entered marginal question mark. Since T did not alter, PE accepts. 68 "grisly" is probably non-authorial.

171.15 of what . . . Nashville, by: Phrase "what is now", first printed in 68, interlined in Pms-a above line 9; "ville" in left margin. At some point printer underlined and queried P "Nashua". Probable sequence of variants: P "of Nashua by"; Pms and 49 "of Nashville, by"; Pms-a and 68 "of what is now Nashville, by".

171.18 stretched . . . tamed: A marginal question mark may refer to P "over head"; close-up marks appear between the words.

173.1-3 Far . . . bank/of . . . drum: Lines were set too close together and T careted in vertical space mark. 49 follows.

175.5-6 Therefore . . . sweep.: 68; two earlier versions (*TLN*, p. 63; MH) are closer to T's source, Felicia Hemans, "The Voice of Music" in *The Poetical Works of Mrs. Hemans*, 2 vols. (Philadelphia, 1832), I, p. 52: "Therefore a current of sadness deep, / Through the stream of thy triumphs is heard to sweep." *TLN* (titled "To Music") and MH (in quotation marks) read "streams" and "triumph".

175.7-11 The Indian . . . existence.": 68; CPB and T's source, Calidas, *Sacontalà; or, The Fatal Ring*, trans. Sir William Jones in *The Works of Sir William Jones*, 13 vols. (London, 1807), IX, p. 465, vary in the first few phrases: "Perhaps the sadness of men, otherwise happy, on seeing beautiful forms and listening to sweet melody, arises. . . ."

181.16 Hugunots: Corrected from P "Hugenots". Same spelling change occurs at 181.22 and 181.28; 49 follows Pms.

186.12 thought: Printer underlined "ht" and entered marginal query mark.

189.33 wrack: Printer underlined "rack" and entered marginal query mark.

195.26-27 (*Tamias Lysteri*, Aud.): 68; "Aud." designates T's probable reference, Audubon and Bachman,

Viviparous Quadrupeds of North America, 3 vols. (New York, 1846-1853), I, p. 65.

196.2 beside: 68 "besides" could be authorial, but three of T's lexicons (Walker, Johnson, Webster) list both forms and T's usage throughout P is inconsistent (cf. "beside" at 27.9; "besides" at 28.1), providing no basis for emending.

196.10 *sciurus*: PE; emended to agree with preceding correct form in P (195.26). P and 49 read "*striurus*"; 68 was changed to still incorrect "*Scriurus*".

197.12-15 In the New . . . preserved.": 68; quotation in T's source, John W. Barber, *Historical Collections . . . of Every Town in Massachusetts* (Worcester, 1841), p. 432. T cites the "New Hampshire Historical Collections for 1815"; Barber cites *CMHS* for 1815. The sentence actually appears in *CMHS* for 1816.

197.27-29 a small . . . taken.: 68; variants are in T's source, Barber's *Historical Collections*, p. 432. As at 197.12-15, Barber is quoting *CMHS* for 1816.

198.2 louring: Printer underlined "our" and entered marginal query mark; cf. "lowering" in 68.

198.6 to go work: 68 "to go to work" could be authorial, but the longer infinitive diminishes the blunt impact of phrase in P.

201.8-9 man, . . . not: A marginal question mark beside this line may refer to "a while"; space between these words is underlined.

203.28 "in a . . . glade,: T directed this line, set over "mountains" in P, to be set "over environed"; 49 is four letter spaces short of request.

204.8 and inquired: Also in an earlier version (HM 956); 68 "and I inquired" is probably non-authorial, since pronoun is clear from context.

210.19 nature: "Nature" in P; altered in Pms here and at 217.3, 217.14, 247.18, 256.13, 328.21, 339.6, and 350.29. 49 follows Pms.

214.24-25 thoughts. The: In proof, followed by T's note, asking for extra space to signify end of section on canal boats: "liberal . . . thoughts" is last line on p. 224 and "The . . . from" is first line on p. 225, making break hard to distinguish; T requested space on both proof pages. Neither 49 nor 68 follows.

221.15-17 Signed . . . names.: T's description, not quotation, of the signatures as they appear in his source, Jeremy Belknap, *The History of New-Hampshire*, 2nd ed., 3 vols. (Boston, 1813), I, p. 346. Small type found in P, 49, and 68 is retained. Cf. TN 80.33-82.15.

225.22 ANACREON.: T directed title to be set "one size larger". In P a rule separated title and quotation; in response to printer's "Qy dash", T deleted rule.

225.23 but: Also in an earlier version (*Dial*, 3 [April 1843], 484); 68 "for" is probably non-authorial. P accurately translates T's source, *The Greek Anthology*, Book VII, Epigram 25 (attributed to Simonides), line 9: ἀλλ' ἔτ ἐκεῖνον, or "but still that". T's edition is unknown, but see Loeb, ed. W. R. Paton, II, p. 18.

227.15 These: An unidentified hand near "Perhaps these" in P reads "Less lead", but no change appears in 49.

243.26 far-fetched: 68 "far-stretched" loses word-play and is probably non-authorial.

245.19 These: Printer underlined "ese" and entered marginal query mark; T canceled latter.

245.30 fourteen: 68; an earlier version (HM 13195, see Illustrations) first read "17000", which T altered to "16000", figure appearing in P and 49. This reductive trend continues with Pms "fifteen thousand" and 68 "fourteen thousand". United States census reports list 13,932 in 1850.

251.32 more: Printer underlined and entered marginal query mark; T canceled latter.

252.23-28 "that . . . miracles.": As in T's "Indian book 1" (MA 596), and his probable source, Thomas Hutchinson, *The History of the Colony of Massachusetts Bay*, 2 vols. (London, 1765), I, p. 474, excepting the last four words, which are new in 68. Perhaps T intended them as a summary of material about Indian powwows, which follows the quoted passage in Hutchinson.

258.13 one-winged: Printer underlined "one", and "s" of "birds" (258.13), entering a marginal query mark at each line, to call attention to apparent disagreement in number. T canceled query marks and clarified situation by hyphenating "one winged".

260.14 Virtue's: 68; Virtues' in P and 49. Earlier

versions read "Virtue's" (PJ 1, p. 76; *Dial*, 1 [July 1840], 71); context requires the singular possessive.

263.16 Friend: "friend" in P; altered in Pms here and from P "friends" or "friendship" to "Friends" or "Friendship" at 265.32, 266.27, 274.28, 279.13, and 286.3. 49 follows Pms. T's practice in this matter was inconsistent.

263.31-32 who . . . columns: Last line on proof p. 277, first recto of signature 22, after which printer wrote "We are all out of Copy / please send soon as convenient / Printer." Cf. TN 276.30.

264.13-18 Mencius . . . all.": 68; T's translation, also in CPB, of Confucius et Mencius, *Les Quatres Livres de Philosophie Morale et Politique de la Chine*, trans. M. G. Pauthier (Paris, 1841), p. 394. Series of periods does not indicate ellipsis, but marks paragraph break in original.

264.24-25 on that . . . faintly,: In proof, printer underlined "on that" and entered marginal query mark; T canceled latter.

267.5-6 "He that . . . doe.": 68; as in CPB and T's source, Thomas Park, ed., *Heliconia*, 3 vols. (London, 1815), II, "The Phoenix Nest," p. 7.

273.14 know of: Also in an earlier version (MH). 68 "know" is probably non-authorial; P "know of" preserves colloquial tone of passage.

273.30-33 Yet reserve . . . harmonious.: 68; also in an earlier version (MH).

276.30 remains . . . proved;—: Last line in proof p. 289, first recto of signature 25, after which printer wrote "Have not Rec'd any Copy. / Monday Morning". Cf. TN 263.31-32.

280.31 Few . . . than: 68; in Pms, T wrote an underlined "¶" and a mark indicating line should be moved left; P spacing is retained in 49. It is slightly larger than other paragraph indentations.

284.28-30 "Seven . . . together.": 68; as in CPB and T's source, *The Vishnu Purana*, trans. H. H. Wilson (London, 1840), p. 112.

289.15 Who . . . bent.: T asked for "more space" and "dash" after poem; 49 provides a rule and extra space.

293.16 any: 68 "anything" is probably non-authorial, styled to parallel "any thing" at 293.12.

296.6 blast: Also in an earlier version (PJ 1, p. 350); T's probable source, Thomas Gray, *Poems of Mr. Gray, to Which are Added Memoirs of His Life and Writings*, 4 vols., ed. William Mason (New York, 1778), IV, p. 60; and a fragmentary college essay (*Early Essays*, 76.16) read "gust".

297.33 Wrapt . . . enemyes.": T directed: "The last line a little More to the left." and illustrated by writing "Wr" to left of "Wrapt"; 49 follows.

298.24 chip-sparrow: PE; from W. E. Channing's copy of 49, now in NN, where Channing marked "tree-sparrow" and wrote " 'chip-sparrow.' H. wished to have this corrected April 23, '62." (see Thomas Woodson, "Another Word on Thoreau's Last 'Good Sailing,' " *CS*, 12 [Spring 1977], 17). Before then, T probably had changed P and 49 "tree-sparrow" to 68 "hair bird" in the text from which 68 was set; in J he used both "chip-sparrow" (J 4, p. 10), "hair bird" (J 5, p. 302), and "chip-birds" (J 11, p. 197). A later authority, Henry Minot's *The Land-Birds and Game-Birds of New England* (Boston, 1877), p. 210, notes that "hair-bird" and "chipping sparrow" are variant names for same species. Channing's story is repeated by F. B. Sanborn, *The Personality of Thoreau* (Boston: Roberts Brothers, 1902), p. 70, who relates that "thirteen days before his death" T asked Channing to correct a mistake in *A Week*.

298.26 quire: Also in two earlier versions (LB; HM 13195). Printer underlined and entered marginal query mark; T canceled latter. 68 "choir" is probably non-authorial.

300.1-2 brightenings . . . seemed: A marginal question mark beside this line may refer to "tree-sparrow"; "tree" is underlined. See TN 298.24.

300.14 leaves or: Also in an earlier version (PJ 1, p. 56). 68 "leaves of" is an error, since fungi have no leaves.

303.28 grist-mill: PE; as in T's source, Benjamin L. Mirick, *The History of Haverhill, Massachusetts* (Haverhill, 1832), p. 146. P, 49, and 68 "saw-mill" is considered an error of fact. See also TN 10.33, 60.6.

307.20 AULUS . . . FLACCUS.: T entered carets above and below this line on both sides and directed "More blanc [*sic*] space around these words."; 49 follows.

308.5-6 as . . . for: A marginal question mark beside this line may refer to "Muse"; "M" is underlined.

313.7 of . . . character.: T asked for a "dash" to close section on Persius; 49 provides a rule.

314.19 Wild: Printer underlined "W" and entered marginal query mark; T canceled latter.

314.24 days: In P, 49, and 68 and an early commonplace book (MA 594); "day" in T's source, George Herbert, "Vertue." T probably used Thomas Campbell, *Specimens of the British Poets*, 7 vols. (London, 1819), III, p. 81. He never corrected "days", and in this context may be alluding to "days" of *A Week.*

318.24 single-spruce: 68; "double-spruce" in P and 49. "Single" and "double" are common names for white and black spruce, respectively. In J 9, p. 378, T noted that he had previously misidentified both species as black, or double, spruce. Though context does not confirm one reading as correct, PE accepts 68 as authorial.

320.20 of pores: Printer underlined "of p" and entered marginal query mark; T canceled latter.

329.30-330.35 "The Tees . . . nature.": Printer asked if long quotation from Goethe should be set in "sm. Type", but no change occurred in 49.

334.4 tryed: As in *TLN*, p. 268; T's source, Spenser, *The Faerie Queene*, bk. 2, canto 12, stanza 29 (probably in Chalmers, III, p. 141a), reads "tyred." Since "tryed" does not alter the sense, PE does not emend.

336.18 base: Also in 49 and two earlier versions (LB). 68 "bass" is probably non-authorial; while less archaic, it loses word-play of "base".

344.7 and we are: 68 "and are" disrupts parallelism with first clause and is probably non-authorial.

344.8 rites: Printer underlined and entered marginal query mark; T canceled latter.

347.4 Oivana: Printer underlined "iva" and entered marginal query mark; T canceled latter.

348.26 strength?": T asked for "dash", entered one here, and at bottom of page directed "Make 2 white lines more here." indicating extra space after dash with two carets. 49 has a rule, but no additional space.

351.22 lives: Printer underlined and entered marginal query mark; T canceled latter.

354.14-355.4 "I . . . day.": T directed first line of each stanza, set flush with second in P, to be set "over the 3[d] line"; 49 follows.

355.7 with us the: Printer underlined "the" and entered marginal query mark; T canceled latter.

356.5-7 According . . . 1818.: 68; T also quotes Barber's *Historical Collections* (Worcester, 1841) in W, IV, p. 222 (*Cape Cod*).

358.20 supposed: Also in an earlier version (MH), where "supposed that" was altered from "and asked if". 68 "suspected" is probably non-authorial.

363.34 distracted: Printer underlined and entered marginal query mark; T canceled latter.

370.19-20 oftentimes . . . without: A marginal question mark beside this line may refer to "oftentimes", which is underlined.

377.23-26 winter . . . the field of a: P and 68; lacking in 49. T asked for "dash" and "3 more white lines" below dash; at bottom of this proof page he later wrote, "I must have indicated that more space was wanted here." To give more space, printer dropped three lines at bottom of page. T entered this passage, with minor variants, in his own copy of 49 as well as in other copies he sold or gave away. Though the Hosmer copy addition is authorial, it varies only in reading "winter," and "a field"; PE does not emend. See also TN 116.7, 134.2.

387.9 more: Printer underlined "o" and entered marginal query mark; T canceled latter.

388.1 alloy: "allay" in *TLN*, p. 343, and in T's source, Thomas Fuller, cited in Charles Lamb's "Specimens from the Writings of Fuller" in *The Prose Works of Charles Lamb*, 3 vols. (London, 1838), I, p. 171. The two words differ in meaning, but since no error of fact is apparent, PE does not emend.

390.2 Two herons, *Ardea herodias*: 68; change recognizes distinction between *ardea herodias*, Great Blue Heron, and *ardea cærula*, Blue Heron. Latter species, according to T's probable reference, Alexander Wilson, *American Ornithology* (New York, 1852), p. 535, "in the Northern States . . . [is] found chiefly in the neighborhood of the ocean."

Table of Variants

THE Table reports all substantive differences, and all accidental differences that affect meaning, among relevant forms of *A Week*. For abbreviations used, see the List of Abbreviations, pp. 427-431.

The PE reading appears before a bracket, followed by its source, and then by rejected substantive variants. A version not listed agrees in substantives with PE. Thus, "260.9 crockery but] Pms-a; crockery in my life but P 49 68" means that "crockery but" appears only in Pms-a, from which PE has adopted it.

Changes in spelling, capitalization, italics, foreign language spelling or diacritics, and paragraphing that have substantive effect are reported. The tilde ~ means a word is identical with PE; the caret ‸ means a mark of punctuation is missing. Pointed brackets ⟨ ⟩ indicate a conjectural reading or editorial comment. A virgule / marks an end-of-line in type.

Only selected accidental changes in punctuation, word-division, or typographical format appear on this table; positive errors in spelling or punctuation appearing solely in 68 are not reported. For details, see TI, pp. 534-536. Where PE adopts 68 substantives, the 68 accidentals are normally adopted unless other MS evidence is available. Entries marked with an asterisk * are discussed in TN. Some TNs discuss consistent groups of variants, reported on the TV only once (see TV and TN 5.16).

3.10 lands, new] 68; lands and new P; lands new Pms 49

3.12 And many dangers were] Pms; And there were many dangers P

	4.1-9	Fluminaque . . . banks.] 68; *lacking* P 49
*	5.16	River] Pms; river P
	5.21	Great Meadows] Pms; great meadows P
	5.23	historian] Pms-a; Historian Pms 49
*	6.12	Bridge] Pms; bridge P
	6.28-29	cut-grass] Pms; pipe-grass P
	7.7	Nine-Acre-Corner] Pms; Nine-acre-corner P
	7.19	swimming] Pms; running P
	7.30	aground on] 49; aground on on P
	7.31	Island] Pms; island P
	7.33	Coast] Pms; coast P
	8.19	clearing] Pms; cleaning P
	8.20	plowing] 49; ploughing P 68
	8.32	in the oaks] Pms; in oaks P
	9.21	Revolution] Pms; revolution P
	9.24	eighth] Pms; eight P
	9.31	sudden] Pms; rudder P
	10.17-11.17	Let us here read . . . towns to winter."] 68; *lacking* P 49
*	10.33	5 and 20] PE; 5 to 20 68
	11.34	sea;–"] Pms; ~;^" P; ~;"– 49
	12.1	and] Pms; And P
	12.2	river] P; River 49
	12.13	Mountains . . . Moon] Pms; mountains . . . moon P
	12.15	Pharaohs] Pms; Pharao P
	13.6	trees, that] P; ~^~ 68
*	15.2	These . . . delicates] P; Those . . . delicacies 68
*	15.3	*Christ's Invitation*] 68; *Invitation* P 49
*	15.4	AT length] Pms; *in* P *preceded by* "Come, come, my lovely fair, and let us try/These rural delicates."/ *Invitation to the Soul.* QUARLES.
	15.19	curtseyed] P; courtesied 68
	15.23	long, by] P; ~^~ 49 68
	16.15	best. These] Pms; ~. ¶ ~ P

	17.4	it may be that many] Pms; no doubt many P; it may be many 49 68
	17.6	rail, though wholly] Pms; rail, wholly P
	17.22	Time] Pms; time P
	17.24	an historical] P; a historical 49 68
	18.2	heart] Pms; hearts P
	18.3	Province] Pms; province P
	18.14	That day, are long since gone] Pms; Are long since dead and gone P; That day are long since gone 49 68
	19.5	Mosses . . . Manse] Pms; mosses . . . manse P
*	19.14-17	On Ponkawtasset . . . day.] 68; *in* P: On Ponkawtasset, since we took our way / Down this fair stream toward neighboring Billerica, / . . . / Doth twinkle oft . . . day. *in* Pms 49: On Ponkawtasset, since, with such delay, / Down this still stream we took our meadowy way, / . . . / Doth faintly shine . . . day.
	19.26	pal'd] Pms; paled P
*	20.4-5	pickerel from . . . pads, or a bream from her nest, and] P; pickerel or a bream from . . . pads, and 68
	20.18-19	(*Salix Purshiana*)] 68; *lacking* P 49
*	20.21	large white balls] P; large balls 68
	20.21	small] 68; *lacking* P 49
	20.24	in front of] 68; in the midst of P 49
	20.34	*eupatorium*] Pms; *cupatorium* P
	21.5	purple Gerardia, the] 68; *lacking* P 49
	21.9	still] 68; *lacking* P 49
*	21.10	past] 68; in P 49
	21.35	go] Pms; wend P
	22.5	Ann's] Pms; Anne's P
	24.1	stands in] Pms; stands on P
	24.8	–"renning] Pms; ‸"Renning P
	24.9	honor] Pms; Honor P

	24.10	discovery in] Pms; discovery on P
	24.29	fish,] P; ~; 68
	25.9	bibles] P; Bibles 68
	26.12	on] Pms; upon P
	26.21	Fresh Water] Pms; fresh-water P 49
	26.21	Sun Fish] P; Sun-Fish 68
	26.21-22	*vulgaris*] Pms; *Vulgaris* P
	26.23	Fresh Water] Pms; fresh-water P Fresh-Water 68
	26.23	Sun Fish] P; Sun-Fish 68
	27.34	From time to time] 49; Occasionally P; from time to time Pms
	28.5	bream] Pms+; Bream P
	29.8	clear] Pms; thick P
*	29.14-16	Old Josselyn . . . Partridge.] 68; *lacking* P 49
	29.18	*Leuciscus*] Pms; *Leneiscus* P
	29.29	older, or with] Pms; older, with P
	29.31	swim in] Pms; swim on P
	30.2	never] Pms; ever P
	30.5	eddy, a] Pms; eddy, and a P
	30.9	mine] Pms; mire P
	30.13	Aboljacknagesic] Pms; Aboljacknagesac P
	30.15	Ktaadn] Pms; Katahdin P
	30.17	*Leuciscus argenteus*] Pms; *Leneiscus Argenteus* P
	30.20-21	named. The Shiner] Pms; ~. *no* ¶ ~ ~ P
	30.21	*Leuciscus crysoleucas*] Pms; *Leneiscus Crysoleucas* P
	31.2	heats. A slighter] Pms; ~. ¶ ~ ~ P
	31.3	shiner] Pms; Shiner P
	31.3-4	ponds. The Pickerel] Pms; ~. *no* ¶ ~ ~ P
	31.4	*reticulatus*] Pms; *Reticulatus* P
	31.5-6	which Josselyn . . . Wolf,] 68; *lacking* P 49
	31.25	*Pimelodus nebulosus*] Pms; *Pinelodus Nebulosus* P

32.9-10	*Catostomi Bostonienses* and *tuberculati*] Pms; *Catostome Bostoniensis* and *Tuberculatus* P
32.17	red chivin] Pms; Red Chivin P
32.20	baits] Pms; bait P
32.22	these] Pms+; the P
32.24	*Muræna Bostoniensis*] Pms; *Muraena Bostonensis* P
32.25	of eel] 68; *lacking* P 49
32.33	Stone-Sucker] Pms; stone-sucker P
33.10	bottoms] Pms; bottom P
33.16	the river] Pms; this river P
34.2	and the fry] Pms; and fry P
34.16	even] Pms; ever P
34.28	captain] Pms; Captain P
34.32	except] Pms; but P
34.32	maneuvres] Pms; manouvres P; manœuvres 49
34.33	that] Pms; this P
35.7	know of] P; know 68
35.9	4.] Pms; ∼., P; ∼, 68
35.12	Account Current] Pms; account current P
35.24	shad] Pms+; had P
35.26-27	is the] 68; was the P; was this 49
35.28	this same] Pms; the same P 49
35.30	after] 49; often P; afterfte Pms
35.33	Great Mower] Pms; great mower P
35.34	Nature's] Pms; nature's P
36.15	lands] Pms; land P
36.16	bold adopts . . . views,] Pms; boldly 'dopts . . . views‸ P
36.17	checquer;] Pms; checquers, P; ∼, 49 68
36.18	Cæsar"–] Pms; Casar⟨,⟩"? P; Casar?" Pms+; ∼;"– 49; ∼";– 68
36.19	As if] Pms; ¶ As if P; as if 68
37.3	Corporation] Pms; corporation P
* 37.5	Nature] Pms; nature P
37.18	Shad] Pms; shad P

37.19	mouth] Pms; mouths P
* 37.28	phil-*anthropy*] Pms; *philan-/thropy* P
38.6	mayest] P; mayst 68
38.23	attraction] Pms; attractions P
38.23	heavens] Pms; heaven P
38.31	wishfully] Pms; wistfully P
38.33	Time] Pms+; time P
39.1-2	Ball's Hill . . . Bridge] Pms(2); Balls' hill . . . Bridge P; Balls' hill . . . bridge Pms+ (1)
39.10	cut-grass] Pms; cut grass P 68
39.10	teem with life] Pms; teem life P
39.23	draught] P; draft 68
40.10	we] 68; he P 49
40.10	tent] Pms; tents P 49
40.16-17	Ostia. That] Pms(2); Ostia. It was the harbor of Carthage, and we the Phænician traders who had founded a city on the hill-side. That P; *in* Pms+(1) a *of* æ *cancelled,* œ *written in margin*
40.30	At intervals we were] Pms; We were occasionally P
41.21-22	hounding] Pms; bounding P
41.30	had] P; would 68
43.6	should] Pms; would P
43.12	*Sieur de Monts. Relations of the Jesuits,* 1604.] Pms; *Relations of the Jesuits,* 1604. *Sieur de Monts.* P
43.15	subtiler] Pms; subtler P
43.23	Saint] Pms; saint P
44.5	Fox Island] Pms+; Fox island P
44.9	Ball's] Pms; Balls' P
44.12	sometimes] Pms; occasional P
44.26	mikania, *mikania*] Pms; Mikania, *Mikania* P
44.29-30	water willow, *salix Purshiana*] Pms(2); Water willow, *salix Purshiana* P; Water Willow, *Salix purshiana* Pms(1)
44.33	on] Pms; upon P
45.15	in] Pms; on P
45.24	Sends] Pms; Lends P

45.29	arms,"–] Pms; ∼."‸ P; ∼,–" 49
45.30	And] Pms; ¶ ∼ P
45.30	sung] Pms; sang P
46.2-4	Sabbath, and we fancied . . . the evening of . . . day. The air] 68; Sabbath, and deeper silence than ordinary brooded over the earth, and we fancied that the morning was the eve of a celestial day. The air P; Sabbath. The air Pms 49
46.8	checkered] Pms; chequered P
* 46.13-14	holiday] 68; holyday P 49
47.1	At] Pms; ¶ ∼ P
47.8	gnarled] Pms; guarded P
47.34	thy] Pms; the P
48.9	boat,] P; ∼‸ 49 68
48.18	unfathomable. Wherever] Pms; unfathomable‸ wherever P
48.20	noticed] P; notice 68
48.25	opaque reflect] Pms; opaque, in one sense, reflect P
49.8	and that] Pms; and how P
49.9	beautiful as the fairest works of art or nature] Pms; beautiful as a Tuscan villa P
49.15	sabbath] Pms; Sabbath P 49
49.16	out on] Pms; out upon P
49.30	bridges] Pms; bridge P
50.4	monuments,] P; ∼,– 49 68
50.5	Billerica, (Villa-rica?) now] Pms; Billerica, ‸Villarica?‸ now P; Billerica, (Villarica?) now 49 68
50.5-7	dotage, named . . . Shawshine. I] 68; dotage. I P 49
50.13	that,–aye,] Pms; ∼,‸∼, P; ∼,‸∼,– 49; that,–ay, 68
50.34	tolleth] Pms; tollest P
50.35	soon] Pms; noon P
51.13	History] Pms; ¶ ∼ P
51.23-24	Reverend Pastor] Pms; reverend pastor P 49
51.24	Society] Pms; society P 49

51.35	bound,–."] Pms; bound, ‸ &c." P
52.7	Hill:" it] Pms; Hill." It P; Hill."–It 68
52.20	plot. He] 68; plot. And thus he plants a town. He P 49
52.30	catnip] Pms; catsup P
52.32-33	And . . . town.] 68; *lacking* P 49
52.35-53.1	Red Man] Pms; red man P 49
53.2	Massachusetts'] Pms; ~‸ P 68
53.4	Red] Pms; red P 49
53.27	Angle-land] Pms; Angleland P
53.28	Red Men] Pms; red men P 49
53.34	sometimes] Pms; occasionally P
54.9	amenities] Pms; curiosities P
54.13	visions,] P; vision; 68
54.28	are] Pms; is P
55.5	We] Pms; ¶ ~ P
55.19-20	from time to time] Pms; occasionally P
55.20-21	nature.] Pms; ~! P
56.11	former's] Pms; farmer's P
56.17	There] Pms; ¶ ~ P
57.2	Election-bird] Pms; election birds P
57.7-8	Still less . . . strong wilderness tints] Pms-a; But I have not yet seen such bright and far-fetched tints P; still less . . . strong & wild tints Pms; Still less . . . strong and wild tints 49; Still less . . . strong and wilderness tints 68
57.19	Iadahel] Pms; Idahel P
* 57.20	Firste] Pms^{+}(1); First P Pms^{+}(2)
58.11	island] Pms; Island P
58.29	son of] Pms; son of the P
59.1	men; the] Pms; men; and the P 68
59.3	Sphinx] Pms; Sphynx P 49
59.6	Sibyls] Pms^{+}; Sybils P
59.24	from west] 68; from to west P 49
* 60.5	Muhammedans] P; Mahometans 49 68
60.6	Sanaa] Pms; Sannaa P
60.17	he who can write] Pms; he that can unite P
60.32	Argonauts] Pms; Argonatus P

	61.16	the history] P; the the history 49
	61.23	but its scenery is the more] Pms; but the scenery is more P
	62.11	But] Pms; ¶ ~ P
	62.24	*lets*] Pms; lets P
	62.34	architect] Pms; Architect P
	63.15	krisses] Pms; knives P
	63.20	Yet it] Pms-a; Yet after all, it P 49
	63.29	and] Pms; And P
	65.1	gentleman, not] P; gentleman, in the true sense, not Pms(1); gentleman among gods, not Pms(2); gentleman, among gods, not 49
	65.14	God] P; god 68
	65.15	No god ever dies.] 68; *lacking* P 49
*	65.33-34	wood, in a few minutes, . . . wits.] PE; wood, which would frighten him out of his wits in a few minutes. P; wood, in a few minutes. Which . . . wits$_{\wedge}$ Pms; wood$_{\wedge}$ in a few minutes, which . . . wits. 49 68
*	66.16	seventh] 68; sixth P 49
	66.21	Mona-day] Pms; Moona-day P
*	66.29-30	him? One] 68; *in* P: him?—Yet there are certain current expressions of blasphemous modes of viewing things, as, frequently, when we say, "He is doing a good business," more profane than cursing and swearing. There is sin and death in such words. Let not the children hear them.—My neighbor says that his hill farm is "poor stuff," "only fit to hold the world together,"—and much more to that effect. He deserves that God should give him a better for so free a treating of his gifts, more than if he patiently put up therewith. But perhaps my farmer forgets that his lean soil has sharpened his wits. This is a crop it was good for. ¶ One *dashes after* things, *and* business," *added in* Pms *and* 49
	67.2	upon] P; on 68

	67.6	is not] Pms; isn't P
	67.6	I know not what] Pms; then I don't know what P; then I know not what 49 68
	67.7-8	Christ and the] Pms-a; Christ–the P; Christ,–the Pms 49 68
	67.18	Sepulchre;–a] Pms; Sepulchre⟨.⟩ A P
*	67.34	"God . . . Khu."] 68; *lacking* P 49
	68.2	simple minded sailors] Pms; sailors simple minded, P
	68.15	The] Pms; ¶ ~ P
	68.15	play-house] Pms; play-mouse P; playhouse 68
	68.17	would be] Pms; would as P
*	68.26-29	That would . . . tragedies."] 68; *lacking* P 49
	69.7	Ye gods, . . . scoffer,] Pms(2); (~ ~$_\wedge$ . . . ~;) P; ~ ~$_\wedge$ . . . ~, Pms(1)
	69.32	hear] Pms; bear P
	70.11	rafter] Pms; rafters P
	70.15	standing, still] Pms; ~$_\wedge$~ P
	70.17	me?] Pms; ~! P 49 68
	70.23	Jacob, . . . subtilest] Pms; Jacob$_\wedge$ . . . subtlest P
*	71.9-12	Pythagoras . . . literature.] 68; *lacking* P 49
	72.10	sure that they] Pms; sure they P
	72.17	It] P; ¶ ~ 68
	72.27	more than] 68; but P 49
	73.17	nature] Pms; history P
	73.23	written which is] Pms; written; that is, P
	73.24	any] Pms; some P
	74.8	apostles] P; Apostles 68
	74.15-16	priests inculcate] Pms; priest inculcates P 49
	74.20	not to, monopolize] Pms; ~,~$_\wedge$~ P; ~ ~$_\wedge$~ 68
	75.14	*may*] Pms; may P
	75.28	you] Pms; You P

	76.6	Sabbath] Pms; sabbath P
	76.6-7	on the watch] 68; at work P 49
	76.12	is the ugliest] Pms^{++}; is ugliest P
*	76.15-22	There are . . . work.] 68; *lacking* P 49
	76.25	pray] P; *pray* 68
	76.26	ordained] P; *ordained* 68
	76.28	Sabbath] Pms; sabbath P
	76.34	Snug] P; Sung 68
	76.35	sunny] Pms^{+}; runny P
	77.10	sabbath] P; Sabbath 49 68
	77.18	Pharoah's] P; Pharaoh's 68
	78.1	Earl] Pms; Duke P
	78.26	in] Pms; is P
	78.33	said;] Pms; ~, P 49 68
	79.1	'O] Pms; ∧~ P
	79.8	read: the] Pms; ~. The P; ~;~ 49 68
	79.10	thee!' "] Pms; ~!∧" P
	79.30	he] Pms; we P
	79.32	we] Pms; he P
	80.1	on] Pms; upon P
	80.28	Elliot] P; Eliot 68
	80.33	"being] Pms; ¶ "Being P
	81.8	Merrimak] Pms; Merrimack P
	81.9	Pasaconway] Pms; Pasaconoway P; Pasaconaway 49 68
	81.22	into] Pms; in P
	81.34	Wamesit] Pms; Wameset P
	81.41	Nashoonon] Pms; Nashoonoon P
	82.5	gates] Pms; gate P
	82.7-8	"So," says . . . "we causing] Pms; "So∧∧we," says . . . "causing P
	82.17	gospel] P; Gospel 68
	82.35	he] Pms; be P
	82.36	Mount Hope] P; Montaup 68
	83.15	MERRIMACK] Pms; Merrimack P
	83.16-17	Pemigewasset] Pms; Pemigewassett P
	83.18	Winnepisiogee] P; Winnipiseogee 68
	84.6	pastured] Pms; postured P

	84.6	Ossa] Pms; Osso P
	84.29	Winnepisiogee] P; Winnipiseogee 68
	84.33	Contoocook] Pms; Coutrocook P
	85.6	skirted with] Pms; skirted at intervals with P
	85.15	wind or] Pms; wind to P
	85.24	or] Pms; Or P
	85.28	sea, and behold, as one] Pms; sea, as one P
	85.29	its head waters] Pms; its waters P
*	86.7	rarely or] 68; occasionally and P 49
	86.17	Pemigewasset] Pms; Pemigewassett P
	86.32	Winnepisiogee] Pms; Winnipisiogee P; Winnipiseogee 68
	86.33	Massabesic] Pms; Massaberic P
	87.2	Standing at] Pms-a; Standing here at P 49
	89.3	affect] P; effect 68
	89.10	sport] Pms; report P
	89.24	tree on] Pms; tree, upon P
	90.7	bald] Pms; bold P
	90.8	pleasure] Pms; pleasures P
	90.15	Every thing] Pms^{+}; Everything P 68
	90.25	gemmæ;"] Pms; ∼." P
	90.26	stem;] Pms; ∼. P 68
*	90.27	or] Pms; Or P; *lacking* 68
	91.13	not] Pms; nor P
	91.31	but its] Pms-a; but of its P 49
	91.33	the sun] Pms; The sun P
	92.2	so the child itself] 68; so that childhood itself P 49
	92.21	expense] Pms(2); expanse Pms^{+}(1)
*	92.29	midday meal] PE; morning meal P 49 68
	94.9	not wonder] Pms; not have to wonder P
*	94.12	lifesome.–] Pms; ∼.‸ P; lifelike.– 49 68
	94.17	alone.–] P; ∼:‸ 68

* 94.20	sped us] 68; speed as P; sped as Pms 49
94.23	Minyas] Pms; Mynias P
94.33	were at once the] Pms-a; were the P 49 68
94.33-95.1	earliest and latest] Pms; earliest latest P
95.18	harmony the] Pms; harmony with the P
95.24	of] Pms; on P
96.20	Arjoon] Pms; Argoon P
97.23	authors need not now erase] Pms(2); authors do not now have to erase P; authors have not now to erase Pms(1)
97.24	they write] Pms; they can write P
97.27-28	as others actually raise] Pms; as some really raise P
98.12	*terra firma*] Pms; terra firma P
98.19	me] Pms; we P
98.22	biographies. The] Pms; biographies. In a true biography, any would be great and any small. The P
98.25	and our] Pms(2); and after all P; and, after all, Pms(1)
98.26	kind.] 49; ~, P
99.9-10	We love to think in winter, as we walk . . . pastures, of those] 68; It is pleasant to think in winter, as we walk . . . pastures, of those P 49; As we walk . . . pastures, we think of those Pms-a
100.16	there her] Pms; there here P
100.25	Muses'] Pms; ~‸ P
101.14	year.] P; ~; 68
101.16	From *his*] Pms; *no* ¶ From his P
101.22	It] Pms; ¶ ~ P
101.22-23	Contemporary] Pms; contemporary P
101.29	south-west] Pms(2); sout-heast P; south-east Pms(1); southwest 68
102.4	"That] Pms; ‸~ P
102.4	[or presidents] to] Pms(2); (or presi-dents to P; (or presidents) to Pms(1)

102.8	yet] Pms; Yet P
102.10	*our*] Pms; our P
102.13	The] Pms; ¶ ~ P
102.13	of the poet Daniel] 68; of Samuel, Daniel P; of Samuel Daniel Pms 49
102.18	stores?] Pms; ~! P
102.19	occident] Pms; accident P
102.28	and is the] Pms; and the P
102.28	influence, not] Pms; influence, and not P
102.30	and flows . . . descends.] 68; and descends the faster as it flows more rapidly. P 49
103.12	Pythagoras and Plato, and Jamblichus, halt] Pms; Plato, Jamblichus, and Pythagoras halt P; ~, ~ ~, ~ ~, ~ 49; ~ ~ ~$_{\wedge}$ ~ ~$_{\wedge}$ ~ 68
103.13	slimy] Pms; rhymy P
103.23	thousands] Pms; thousand P; thousand, 49
103.24	Spenser] 49; Spencer P
103.30-31	thither, reader, you and I, at least, will not] 68; thither$_{\wedge}$ you and I, at least, reader, will not P 49
104.4	roundest] Pms; soundest P
* 104.30	sentences] PE; sentence P 49 68
105.11-12	which . . . better] Pms; which could have been better P
105.29	Learn] Pms^{+}; learn P
106.19	struck] Pms; astonished P
* 106.33-107.3	The world . . . god."] 68; *lacking* P 49
107.11	spirits. A sentence] Pms; spirits. We like that a sentence P
107.16-17	effectively] Pms; effectually P
107.31	but will saunter] Pms; but saunter P
107.34	the fruitful kernels] Pms; the kernels P
108.11	ramble] Pms; saunter P
108.19-20	but it is careless country] Pms; but careless countrified P

108.30-31	them. The . . . woods] Pms; them. I like better the . . . wood P
108.32-109.1	axe, is better than] Pms; axe, than P
109.10-11	Charing-cross." He] Pms; Charing-Cross." These are very good and wholesome facts to know of a man, as copious as some modern volumes. He P
109.11	He loved] Pms; he loved P
109.15	then, he said, . . . fellow] Pms; then ‸ he said ‸ . . . fellow P
109.21	a good] Pms; a true P
110.7	*amnis*] Pms; *arunis* P
110.13	banks,"–] Pms; ~." P
110.14	campoque] Pms; Campoque P
110.16	called] 68; call P 49
* 110.22	Westford] 68; Chelmsford P 49
111.17	their own country.] Pms; their country. P
111.23	historian] Pms; Historian P
111.24	although] Pms; though P
111.28	Feb.] P; February, 68
112.12	therein".] Pms; ~‸. P
112.15-16	lands, for fear . . . foes, without] Pms; lands, without P
112.18	am sometimes inclined] Pms; am inclined P
112.19	deserters] Pms; deserter's P
112.34	preferred. But] Pms; preferred; but P
113.2	*it*] Pms; it P
113.3	effort; so] Pms; effort. So P
* 113.13	Island Brook] P; island brook 68
113.31	time. Whether] Pms; time; whether P
114.9	Sturgeon River] Pms; sturgeon river P
114.14	would] Pms; could P
114.19-20	ever . . . his] Pms; even . . . its P
114.21	himself] Pms; itself P
114.25	Scene-shifter] Pms; scene-shifter P
114.26	any unities] Pms; any writers P

114.30	still on] Pms; still upon P
114.30	are on] Pms; are upon P
114.33-34	absorbs . . . reflects . . . seems] Pms; absorb . . . reflect . . . seemed P
115.1	deeper air] Pms; deep air P
115.6	weeds] Pms; weed P
115.11	fin, which] Pms; fin, that P
* 115.26	made. A] Pms; made. One of our buffaloes, which had been cured by the Indians, by stretching it over a smoky fire, and frequently beating and kneading it, was soft and pliable, and much more comfortable than the other. A P
116.5	sucking] Pms; making P
* 116.7	wash] Pms; work P 49
116.23	other happily] Pms; other sailor happily P
116.23	passed a serene] P; passed serene 49
116.23-24	or immortal] Pms; and immortal P
116.26	morning;] Pms; ~, P 49
116.28	Good Genius] Pms; good genius P
* 117.5-7	"The hye . . . *Ballads.*] 68; *lacking* P 49
* 117.8-12	"His shoote . . . *Ballads.*] 68; *lacking* P 49
117.15	*Britania's*] Pms; *Browne's Brittania's* P
* 117.23-30	"All courageous . . . gone."] 68; *lacking* P 49
118.1	us took] Pms; us had to take P
118.7	come] Pms; came P
118.26	night?] Pms; ~, P
118.28	transit;] Pms; ~, P
118.30	Dante] Pms^{+}; Donto P
119.2	horses] Pms; horse P
119.3	gutted, . . . after never with] Pms; gutted‸ . . . after, were with P
119.5	texture;] Pms; ~, P
119.10-11	scraping, . . . travel,–] Pms; ~,– . . . ~,‸ P
119.11	from] P; for 68
119.13	rowed . . . along] Pms; rode . . . ~, P

119.14	Tyngsboro',] Pms; ~'^ P
119.26	woods] Pms; wood P
119.29	Pequawket] Pms; Pigwacket P
119.32	A township] Pms; ¶ ~ ~ P
120.10	there] Pms; here P
* 121.8	halls] Pms; walls P
121.20	brave] P; Brave 68
121.25	it in] Pms; it into P
122.11-12	well,"–how] Pms; ~."^ How P
122.12-13	how it fared with their] P; how fared their 68
123.3	stream, but] Pms; stream, and P
123.6	Occasionally one] Pms; Occasionally we P
123.13	milk, or] Pms; milk, while P
* 123.17	the high banks] P; the banks 68
124.20	lives of men] 68; times P 49
124.27	execution." So] Pms; execution," so P 49
124.27	Veeshnoo] Pms; Veshnoo P
124.34	Suns] Pms; suns P
125.30	subsistence;] Pms; ~, P
126.11	Sabér] Pms; Tabér P
126.17	We thought that we] Pms; It seemed as if we P
126.23	sitting] Pms; setting P
126.27	interested still to] 68; interested to P 49
127.12	do you not] Pms; do n't you P
127.22	Marlboro'] Pms; Marlborough P
127.24	but] P; ~, 68
127.25-26	Will . . . along?"] Pms; Wont . . . along." P
127.27	*dolce-far-niente*] Pms; dolce-far-niente P
127.28	at infinite] Pms; at different P
127.31	of Australian] Pms; of the Australian P
128.4	were] P; was 68
128.21	As] Pms; ¶ ~ P
128.32-33	him who] Pms; him that P
129.1	Be assured] Pms; Be aware P

	129.4	they reach] Pms; they revel P
	129.10	the farmer] Pms; the husbandman P
*	129.11	best tell] P; tell best 68
	129.28	But] P; ¶ ~ 68
	129.31	"The king answered;–At] Pms(2); ‸The king answered,‸ at P; ‸~ ~ ~,– ~ Pms$^+$(1); "~ ~ ~;‸~ 49; "~ ~ ~:‸~ 68
	129.33-130.1	The ex-minister said;] Pms; One ex-minister said, P; ~ ~ ~, 49
	130.3	matters".] Pms; ~‸. P; ~." 49 68
*	130.17	his way] P; the way 68
	130.17-18	way;"–thieves] Pms(2); way."‸ Thieves P; way;" Thieves Pms(1)
	130.19	would] Pms; could P
	130.21	as that] Pms; or that P
	130.25-26	State . . . protection which I] Pms; state . . . protection I P
	131.2	Dragon] Pms; dragon P
	131.10	becomes] Pms; become P
	131.12-13	unkind] Pms; un—kind P
	131.18	derives] Pms; deserves P
	131.18	*pius Æneas*] Pms; pious Æneas P
	131.24	tolerates] Pms$^+$; tolerate P
	131.25	that is he] P; that he 68
	131.26	State] Pms; state P
*	131.28	jailer] Pms-a; jailor Pms$^+$ 49
	132.10	condition of . . . snakes which I] Pms; condition with . . . snakes I P
	132.26	Indian sect of] Pms; Indians of P
*	132.27	West] Pms; west P 49
	132.29	They] Pms; they P
	132.33	"They . . . Lieou-hia-hoei] Pms(2); ‸They . . . Lieou-hia-hoe, P Pms$^+$(1) 49 68
	134.2	hinderance] Pms; hindrance P 49
*	134.2	expediency] Pms; experience P 49
	134.23	do extreme things] Pms; do what is beyond one's sphere P
	134.27	bury] Pms; lie P

134.28	will lie] Pms; will be P
136.20	are there some] Pms; are some P
136.28	within; so] Pms; within. So P
136.34	Brahman] Pms; Brahmin P
137.4	protestants] P; Protestants 68
137.9	beauty merely] 68; pure beauty P 49
137.12	Hindoo] PE; Hindo P 49 68
137.25	that] P; which 68
137.31	their] Pms; them P
138.14-15	begun] Pms; began P
* 138.22	tracks] P; tracts 68
138.30-31	from age to age] Pms-a; from one to another P 49
139.33-34	*Pandeet* . . . undertaking] Pms; *Pandect* . . . understanding P
140.1	Amreeta] Pms; Amrecta P
140.7-8	I . . . my] 68; our . . . we P 49
140.9	which I] 68; which we P 49
140.18	Brahman] Pms; Brahmin P
140.28-29	mind? The duty . . . one.] 68; mind? He speaks of duty, but the duty of which he speaks is it not an arbitrary one? P 49
140.29	Brahman's] Pms; Brahmin's P
140.30	in doing, not right] 68; not in doing right P 49
141.2	It is a] 68; It is in fact a P 49
141.7-8	actions. Behold] 68; actions.—Yet we know not where we should look for a loftier speculative faith. ¶ Behold P 49
141.13	cast] P; caste 68
141.13	faint. It] P; faint; it 68
141.16	bonds, the] P; bonds. The 49
141.21	latter, When] Pms; latter, but when P
141.28	Sanjay] Pms; Salrjay P
142.4	good book to read, Read the] P; good book, read the 68
142.5	Mahabharat] Pms; Mahabbarat P
142.19	mountains] P; Mountains 68

142.20	appears] Pms; seems P
142.21-22	own sympathies and studies,] Pms; own, sympathizes and studies P
142.23	is perceived] Pms; is often perceived P
142.30	have even been] 68; have been P 49
143.1	Goethe wanted] 68; Goethe, one would say, wanted P 49
143.5	and was less] Pms-a; and less P 49
143.13	influenced . . . the] 68; influenced the P 49
143.28	Zoroaster, still] 68; Zoroaster, for instance, still P 49
143.29	translations, alone make] 68; translations, make P 49
* 144.19	into] P; in 68
144.20	breath] Pms; breaths P
144.20	think] P; ~, 68
144.22	this] Pms; the P
144.27-28	solitude, once more rowing] 68; solitude, rowing P 49
144.30	other; from] P; other. From 68
144.31	we scared up] 68; scaring up P 49
145.3	creeping down] Pms; creeping from P
145.12	they would] 68; *lacking* P 49
146.25	stones] P; ~, 68
147.5	pasture,] P; ~$_\wedge$ 68
147.7	hazles] P; hazels 68
147.11	Heetopades] Pms; Hectopades P
147.20	Darfour.] P; ~$_\wedge$ 49
148.2	Angas] Pms; Ungas P
148.4	Puranas] Pms; Purana P
148.7	human."] 49; ~$_\wedge$" P
148.20	Sastra] Pms; Sartra P
148.23	has been] 68; seems to have been P 49
148.25	it was but] 68; it is but P 49
148.26-27	supplied . . . directed] 68; supplies . . . directs P 49
148.29	freemen] Pms; free men P

148.30	cast] P; caste 68
148.34	modes in which] Pms; in modes which P
149.9	mountains] Pms; mounts P; Mountains 68
149.15	inclinations renders] 68; inclinations seems to render P 49
149.17-18	Though the sentences] 68; The sentences P 49
149.19-20	flower, they] 68; flower, yet they P 49
150.1	are dabbling] Pms-a; seem to be dabbling P 49
150.6	questions] Pms; question P
150.6-7	intimate with us even] 68; intimate even P 49
150.14-15	it addresses,] 68; does it address P 49
150.25	wood, and its] 68; wood. Its P 49
150.26	ether, sweeps] Pms; ether, seems to sweep P
150.27	country. The] 68; country, and the P 49
150.32-33	east. While we are reading these sentences, this] 68; east. This P 49
150.33	seems] 68; is Pms
150.35	Culluca] Pms; Cullucca P
151.3-4	ordeal] Pms; ideal P
151.23	revealed,] Pms; $\sim_\wedge$ P
151.26	lakes in] Pms; lakes on P
152.12	lichens] Pms; Lichens P
152.14	Brahmans] Pms; Brahmins P
152.18-19	Pythagoras] Pms; Pythagorus P 49
152.21	them] 68; these P 49
152.28	Brahmans] Pms(2); Brahmens P; Brahmins Pms+(1)
153.2	at a] Pms; at the P
153.17	Sanscrit] Pms; sanscrit P
153.22	Sibyls] Pms; Sybils P
154.2	ground which we walk on] Pms; ground we walk upon P

* 154.3	leaves that] P; leaves which 68
154.21	hue] Pms; line P
* 154.29	that] P; which 68
155.2	trees] Pms; tree P
155.9	began] Pms; ~, P 49 68
* 155.9	Alwákidi's] PE; Aleakidis' P; Alwákidis' Pms 49 68
155.10	*Almatîn*] PE; *Almatin* P 49 68
155.11	*Alámiri*] Pms; *Alamiri* P
155.12	*Jabalah*] PE; *Fbalah* P; *Fabalah* Pms 49 68
155.12	*Alchátgami*] PE; *Alahâtquarmi* P; *Alchâtquarmi* Pms 49 68
155.13	*Thabet*] Pms; *Shabet* P
156.7	us–] Pms; ~‸ P
157.18	Always] 68; always P 49
157.36-158.1	appears."– these] Pms; appears."‸ ¶ These P; appears."‸ These 68
158.7	affairs] Pms; events P
158.17-18	However, we] Pms; But after all, we P; But we 49; ¶ But we 68
159.14-15	sounding-boards of piano-fortes and] 68; *lacking* P 49
159.17	Baskets . . . twigs.] 68; *lacking* P 49
160.10	stretch] 49; sketch P; stretchtch Pms
160.21	creels] Pms; weeds P
160.27	those] Pms; these P 49
161.14	brook,] Pms; ~‸ P
161.22	swathe] P; swath 68
161.23	Lovewell's] 68; Loevwell's P 49
161.26	Pequawket] Pms; Pigwacket P
161.28	was] P; is 68
161.30	Sept.] P; September 68
162.4	pond] P; Pond 68
162.12	Mountain] Pms; mountain P
162.25	them.– There] Pms; them;–there P
163.11	Peterboro'] P; Peterborough 68
163.17	emprise] Pms; comprise P
163.38	ye lie] Pms; ye be P
164.17	Were] Pms; Was P

165.12	know'st] Pms; knowest P
165.21	Cleaving] Pms; Clearing P
165.35-36	We have since made] Pms; Since then, we have made P
* 166.10	gristly] P; grisly 68
166.15	Ten] Pms; Eleven P
166.22	first who] Pms; first that P
167.11	a row] P; a-row 68
167.12	Nottingham] Pms; ¶ ~ P
167.14	Memento] Pms; memento P
167.15	"departed this] Pms; ‸~"~ P
167.18-19	this grave . . . the Indians] Pms(2); This grave . . . The Indiens Pms(1)
167.20	The] Pms; ¶ ~ P
167.22	nine] Pms; ten P
167.32	History] Pms; history P
168.7	Philip's] Pms; Phillip's P
168.15	appears] Pms; seems P
168.19	related, he left] Pms; related, left P 49
168.29	that] Pms; *lacking* P 49
169.5	high road] P; high-road 68
169.20	one, it] Pms-a; one, and stands upright, pointing to the skies, it P 49
169.24	"star-y-pointing,"] Pms; ‸star-y-pointing,‸ P
170.3	perpetuate] 68; commemorate P 49
170.30-31	Hood, and reflecting favorably on his character, that] 68; Hood, that P 49; Hood, reflecting favorably on the character of his life that Pms-a
* 171.15	of what is now Nashville, by] Pms-a; of Nashua by P; of Nashville, by 49
* 171.18	overhead] Pms-a; over head P 49
171.30	asserts] Pms; assert P
172.5	sights which we] Pms-a; sights we P 49
173.27	God] P; ~, 68
173.27	live.–] Pms; ~.‸ P 68
174.14	bought] Pms; brought P
174.17	Time] Pms^{+}; time P

174.26	speech, is music!] 68; speech! P 49
* 175.2-11	We feel . . . existence."] 68; *lacking* P 49
176.11	in the] Pms; in thy P
176.20	Jamblichus] Pms; Gamblichus P
177.14	it hinted] Pms; it united P
178.7	babbling] Pms; bubbling P
178.21	bucklers'] Pms; buckler's P
178.26	Heaven] Pms; Hearer P
179.3	wold] Pms; world P
179.10	sang] Pms; sung P
179.20	mist] Pms; fog P
180.1	sure] Pms; rare P
180.26	six hundred] Pms; *lacking* P
180.29	Bellows] Pms; Billows P
181.4	gates] Pms+; gate P
* 181.16	Hugunots] Pms; Hugenots P; Huguenots 68
181.20	on a] Pms; on an P
181.22	Hugunots] Pms; Hugenots P; Huguenots 68
181.28	Hugunots'] Pms; Hugenot's P; Huguenot's 68
182.31-32	had at first] Pms; at first had P 49 68
183.7	though] Pms; but P
183.8	but that nobody] Pms; but nobody P 49
183.17	I at once] Pms; I directly P
183.24	forest,] Pms-a; forest, and P 49 68
183.28	takes only] Pms; only takes P
184.2	evil] Pms; evils P
184.23	at once] Pms; directly P 49 68
184.26	tracks] Pms; track P
184.31	scale;] Pms; scale; but P
185.30	afterward] Pms; after P 49 68
186.3	attempt; as if the] P; attempt; the 68
186.11	Guano, and Logwood] P; Guano, Logwood 68

186.29	managing even] Pms; and even managed P
187.21	would be] Pms-a; would really be P 49
187.33	there before] P; ~,~ 68
188.1	Long-wharf] P; Long‸Wharf 49 68
188.5	by chance reached up] 68; reached up by chance P 49
188.12-13	terra-firma] Pms; terra‸firma P
188.14	places] Pms; place P
188.20	swell] Pms; swells P
188.23-24	pastures,] Pms; ~‸ P 49
188.27	windings] Pms; winding P
188.28	Amazon or Orinoko] Pms; amazon or orinoco P
189.1	this] Pms; the P
189.14	Sun's] Pms; sun's P
189.15	its] Pms; his P
189.18	under-side] Pms; under-sides P
189.27	eye, * * *] Pms; ~, ‸‸‸ P
189.29	himself. But] P; himself. ¶ But 68
190.4	Sun] Pms; sun P 68
190.4	visage.–] P; ~,– 68
190.25	"away!] P; "Away! 68
191.2	motion. One] Pms; motion, one P
191.17	fays] Pms; fogs P
191.19	daisied] Pms; dazied P
192.2	book] P; Book 68
192.6	small-featured] Pms-a; small‸featured P 49
192.28	river] Pms; ~, P 49
193.7	rowed] Pms; rode P
193.27	imagine] Pms; imagined P
193.32	banks] Pms; bank P
194.21	has] Pms; had P
194.33	water's] Pms; waters' P
195.8	equals, the] Pms; equals. The P
195.17	mountain] Pms; Mountain P
195.24	forenoon.] Pms; ~, P

* 195.26-27	(*Tamias Lysteri*, Aud.)] 68; *lacking* P 49
* 196.2	beside] P; besides 68
196.3	breadth. As] P; breadth,–as 68
196.6-7	tail; and] Pms; ~,~ P; tail. And 68
196.7	dives] Pms; drives P
* 196.10	*sciurus*] PE; *striurus* P 49; *Scriurus* 68
* 197.12-15	In the New . . . preserved."] 68; *lacking* P 49
197.20	Indians] Pms; Indian P
* 197.27-29	raised, a small hole . . . taken.] 68; raised a sum of money was found. P 49
* 198.6	to go work] P; to go to work 68
198.28	fleas] 68; flies P 49
199.13	Company] P; company 68
199.15	seemed] Pms; seems P
199.30	than] Pms; than a P
200.5	September, and pitch] P; September, pitch 68
200.16	masons'] Pms; mason's P
200.26	sea side] Pms; sea-side P
201.7-8	maple of the mountain] 68; mountain maple P 49
201.29	fruits] Pms; prints P
202.7	off,] Pms; ~‸ P
202.20	teamsters'] Pms; teamster's P
202.22-23	along musing, and enchanted] P; ~, ~‸ ~ ~, 68
203.19	"What] Pms; "what P 68
203.24	this] Pms; the P
* 203.28	"in] Pms; "In P 68
* 204.8	and inquired] P; and I inquired 68
206.32	sweet wild . . . would not] Pms; sweet, mild . . . could not P
207.13	told him] Pms; said P
208.12	Before] Pms; But before P
208.18	–"his] P; ‸"His 68
208.24-25	presently,] Pms; ~‸ P

208.34	(meaning me,)] Pms^{++}; ‸~ ~,‸ P
209.30-31	out-door] 49; out-of-door P; out- -door Pms
210.5	pointed] 68; shod P 49
210.11-12	wood or bricks,– . . . cords of wood, . . . thousand bricks,] 68; bricks or wood,– . . . thousand bricks, . . . cords of wood, P 49
210.13	two or three] 49; three or four P; 2 or 3 Pms
* 210.19	nature] Pms; Nature P
210.24	moveable] P; movable 68
211.15	causes] Pms; assists P
211.21-22	stealing] Pms; steering P
212.4	swathes] P; swaths 68
212.7	We admired] Pms-a; We used to admire P 49
212.14	imagined to what . . . put.] 49; imagined what infinite uses it might be put to. P; ~ ~.~ . . . ~‸ Pms
212.15	appeared] Pms; seemed P
212.35	sun?–As] Pms^{+}; ~,–~ P; sun?–as 68
213.2-3	recognised] P; recognized 68
213.6-7	Pacific] Pms; pacific P
213.14	ray] Pms; ~, P 49
213.33	on this river] Pms; on the Merrimack P
213.35	Hooksett] Pms; Hookset P
213.36-214.2	in a week, . . . weather, . . . way.] 68; from Merrimack to Lowell and back, about twenty-five miles each way, in a week, according to wind and weather. P 49; in a week, . . . weather. . . . way, Pms-a
214.9	gets] Pms; get P
214.11	"hand,"] Pms; ‸~,‸ P
214.22	circulated] Pms; circulates P
215.5-6	appeared] Pms; seemed P
216.16-20	ships; *quæque* . . . I. 133.) We] 68; ships. We P 49

216.20	well] Pms; better P
216.20-23	the traveller / instead of finding / of Henry the] 49; ⟨*faintly inked*⟩ P
216.32	faggots or sheep] Pms-a; faggots, or on sheep P 49
217.11	lethean] P; Lethean 68
217.17	air-water] Pms; air, water P
218.4	busy-ness] PE; busi-/ness P 68; busy-/ness Pms 49
218.15	Navigator] P; "∼" 68
218.17	We] P; ¶ ∼ 68
218.23	Hudson's] P; Hudson 68
218.23	Ottaway] Pms; Otawa P
219.33	Babboosuck] Pms; Babbooruck P
220.27-28	*sunt*? In] 68; *sunt*? Where are they now?–In P 49
220.29	or else a] 68; or P 49
221.7	If your] Pms; If you P
221.10	power.–] 49; ∼‸– P
221.15	Signed] P; ¶ ∼ 68
223.25	further] 68; farther P 49
224.6	these] Pms; those P
224.9	about; yet] P; about. Yet 68
224.29	could] P; would 68
225.11	cerealian] Pms; cerulian P
* 225.23	but] P; for 68
225.29	poetic] Pms; *lacking* P
225.32	Ibycus] Pms; Ilycus P
225.32	Stesichorus] Pms; Steschorus P
226.28	only] P; but 68
226.29	would] Pms; could P
227.8	tread] Pms; walk P
227.15	These are some of the best] 68; Perhaps these are the best P 49
227.18	Atridæ] Pms; Atridal P
228.13	vines] Pms; wines P
228.38	this] Pms; the P
229.2	He'll] 49; He ll P
230.11	men] Pms; man P
231.21	long] P; along 68
231.21	one] Pms; our P
232.19	shadow] P; shadows 68

232.28-29	widow's wood-lot . . . wilder,] Pms; widdow's woodlot . . . wilder$_{\wedge}$ P; widow's woodlot . . . wilder$_{\wedge}$ Pms^{+}
233.2-3	probably . . . day] Pms-a; unknown to any human inhabitant probably to this day. P 49; probably unknown to any human inhabitant to this day. Pms; without the knowledge of any human inhabitant probably to this day. 68
233.35-234.1	to put . . . appeared] 68; as it appeared, to put her straw asoak P 49
234.15	adventures] P; adventure 68
234.26	us that we] Pms-a; us we P 49
235.10	their path] P; the path 68
236.23	at the] Pms; at P
236.26	Massabesic] Pms; Massabesie P
237.26	Indian's] Pms; Indians' P
238.5	heave-yoing] Pms; heave-going P
238.23	for] Pms; far P
239.33	counting] Pms^{++}; courting P
239.35	this] Pms; the P
240.6	over] Pms; on P
240.29	night] Pms; sight P
241.9	'tis] Pms; is P
243.3	"*sua* . . . ,"] Pms-a; $_{\wedge}$~ . . . ,$_{\wedge}$ P 49 68
243.4	or] Pms-a; nor P 49 68
243.15	were passed] 68; occurred P 49
243.22	There is commonly such a one at] 68; It is commonly the offspring of P 49
* 243.26	far-fetched] P; far-stretched 68
244.7	Stretching hand to hand,] Pms; *lacking* P
244.22	"Springing] P; "springing 68
244.25	–"The] Pms; –"the P
244.26	Genial] P; genial 68
245.13	stone, to] Pms-a; stone, probably to P 49 68
245.29	now, as . . . told,] Pms-a; now after nine years, as . . . told$_{\wedge}$ P; now, after nine years, as . . . told$_{\wedge}$ 49

* 245.30	fourteen] 68; sixteen P 49; fifteen Pms
245.32	have seen] Pms-a; have since seen P 49
245.35	fields; and] 68; fields to get a draught of water. And P; fields to get a draught of water; and Pms 49
246.1	museum] P; Museum 68
246.25	Bellows'] Pms; Bellows P
246.30	Pemigewasset] Pms; Pemmawasset P
248.10-13	period. In deepening . . . river, and there] 68; period. There P 49
249.13	Roman] Pms; Romans P
249.20	old world] P; Old World 68
250.22	satisfactory] 68; unanswerable P 49
250.25	lichens] 68; moss P 49
252.11	this present] P; the present 68
252.18-19	Passaconaway] P; Pasaconaway 68
252.27-28	one, and . . . miracles." In] 68; one." In P 49
253.33	prospect] Pms; prospect for P
254.3	of whom . . . heard?] Pms; whom you have never heard of? P
254.4	Passaconaway] P; Pasaconaway 68
254.13	"The] Pms; ¶ "~ P 68
254.16	Merrimac,–] P; Merrimack: 68
254.34	Matthew] Pms; Mathew P
255.7	whom had] P; them had 68
255.18	guide-post on which were the words,] 68; guide-board which said P 49
255.20	But] Pms; ¶ ~ P
255.25-29	It is . . . climbed.] 68; *lacking* P 49
256.20-21	herb, but] Pms-a; herb that grows, but P 49
257.31-32	one school as] Pms; one as P
257.3	doctor's] Pms; Doctor's P
257.17	It is] P; Is it 68
257.23	stools] P; souls 68
258.5	lunch. Though] Pms; lunch, though P
* 258.13	one-winged] Pms; one winged P

258.21	spoken] Pms; spoken of P
258.28	sails] Pms; sail P
258.33	tow," to] Pms; tow," at P
259.1	and passed] 68; *lacking* P 49
259.12-15	True kindness . . . station.] 68; *lacking* P 49
260.9	crockery but] Pms-a; crockery in my life but P 49 68
260.14	Virtue's] 68; Virtues' P 49
260.30	subtil] Pms; subtle P; subtile 68
260.32	works] Pms; work, P
261.18	strain] Pms; strains P
262.23	Only] P; Scarcely 68
* 263.16	Friend] Pms; friend P
* 264.13-18	Mencius . . . all."] 68; *lacking* P 49
264.24	ground which] Pms-a; ground P 49 68
264.28	they can] 68; they P 49
265.23	use] Pms; are P
265.23	disposition] P; dispositions 68
265.28	farewell] Pms; Farewell P
266.30-267.2	For the . . . him.] 68; *lacking* P 49
* 267.5-6	"He that . . . doe."] 68; *lacking* P 49
267.7	It will] 68; *no* ¶ P 49
267.12	And it . . . poet,] 68; *lacking* P 49
267.24-27	Only . . . civility.] 68; *lacking* P 49
267.30-31	Though we . . . copper.] 68; *lacking* P 49
268.3-4	no . . . be,] P; "~ . . . ~," 68
268.14-15	neighborhood and the family] 68; family and the neighborhood P 49
268.17	that is] P; ~ ~, 68
268.26	heaven] P; Heaven 68
268.30	this old] P; the old 68
268.31	universe?] Pms; ~; P
268.32	exist.] Pms; ~? P
269.5	repeat them] P; repeat these 68
269.24-25	to some extent] 68; in one sense P 49

270.22	this] Pms; the P
270.28	each other] 68; one another P 49
271.20-21	"And love . . . nobleman."] 68; Love equals swift and slow, / And high and low, / Racer and lame, / The hunter and his game. P 49
271.25	man that] P; man who 68
272.8-15	There are . . . root.] 68; *lacking* P 49
273.3	it. The] P; ~. ¶ ~ 68
273.7-8	hesitancy, or end;] Pms; hesitance, or end, P
* 273.14	know of] P; know 68
273.18	thing.] Pms; ~? P
* 273.30-33	Yet reserve . . . harmonious.] 68; *lacking* P 49
274.21-28	castles. It is not . . . embrace." The] 68; cities. ¶ The P 49
276.2	two who are more] Pms-a; two more P 49 68
276.20	afford] Pms; afford to P
278.3	finely appreciated] Pms; finely heard and appreciated P
278.27	speak to] Pms; approach P
278.27	expector] P; expecter 68
* 280.31	Few . . . than] 68; ¶ Nothing is so difficult as Pms P 49
281.3	with whom he deals] 68; whom he deals with P 49
282.32	a precipice,–] P; ~ ~.‸ 68
282.34	better,"] Pms; better,' ⟨*ink cancellation*⟩ P
283.18	True] P; ¶ True 68
284.2-3	the rock] P; a rock 68
284.11	unaltered] Pms; united P
284.23	My] P; ¶ ~ 68
* 284.27-30	It says, . . . together."] 68; *lacking* P 49
286.8-9	as monuments . . . graveyard.] 68; as their monuments are overgrown with moss. P 49

286.12	Acquaintances,] Pms; Acquaintance P
286.23	then] Pms; them P
287.15	pansy] Pms; tansy P
289.12	teazed] P; teased 68
289.33	duck] Pms; ducks P
290.24	host's] Pms; hosts P
291.25	tap] Pms; top P
292.16	In other words] P; In short 68
292.19	feebler] Pms; feeble P
292.20	canvass] P; canvas 68
292.28	wanting?] Pms; ~. P
292.35	natures] Pms; nature P
293.7	*them*] Pms; them P
* 293.16	any] P; anything 68
293.29	clothes] Pms; ~, P
294.13	secure it a] 68; secure a P 49
294.19	seasons] Pms; reasons P
295.9	streams] 49; streams patient P
295.29	in] Pms; on P
296.11	human] P; man 68
296.12	drought] Pms; draught P
296.15	sing] Pms; ring P
296.22	contributary] Pms; contributory P
297.6	use] Pms; used P
297.10	our grief] Pms; your grief P
297.11	measures inversely the] Pms; measured inversely, the P; measures the 68
297.16	has not] P; had not 68
297.28	winde] Pms; wind P
297.29	swowne] Pms; swoone P
* 298.24	chip-sparrow] PE; tree-sparrow P 49; hair-bird 68
* 298.26	quire] P; choir 68
300.11	woods] Pms; woods a P
300.13	there] Pms; there in P
* 300.14	leaves or] P; leaves of 68
300.29	hummock!] Pms; ~. P 49 68
301.18	was] P; were 68
301.20	men.] P; ~‸ 68

302.13	sun] Pms; Sun P
303.1	Concord in New] Pms; Concord, New P 68
303.11	Concord in New] Pms; Concord, in New P; Concord, New 68
* 303.28	grist-mill] PE; saw-mill P 49 68
303.36	city] P; City 68
304.4	"men] P; "Men 68
304.32	at times] 68; frequently P 49
305.8	come] P; Come 68
306.16	other] P; *lacking* 68
306.22-23	legs, . . . last. The] 68; legs. The P 49
307.16	or] 49; and P; ord Pms
307.31	sybil] P; sibyl 68
309.16	saint's] Pms; saints' P
309.29	sentences] Pms; sentence P
310.5	who] Pms; that P
312.17	spoil] Pms; injure P
313.8	dank] Pms; dark P
313.22	road; deep] Pms; road. Deep P
314.4	wrestled] Pms; wrastled P
314.5	get off] Pms; got off P
315.5	wished] 68; pleased P 49
315.6	state] Pms; State P
315.10	gentlemen] Pms; gentleman P
315.28	sound] P; sounds 68
316.4	Ægean] Pms; Ægian P
317.21	Pythagoras] Pms; Pythagorus P
318.21-22	where there is] Pms; where is P
* 318.24	single-spruce] 68; double-spruce P 49
320.33	Dustan,] Pms; Dunstan$_\wedge$ P
321.12	neighbors' dwellings] Pms; neighbor's dwelling P
322.6	proofs] Pms; proof P
322.15	these] Pms; those P
322.32	exercise. For] Pms; exercise; for P
322.33	in] Pms; on P
323.5	clangor;] Pms; $\sim_\wedge$ P
324.1	later] Pms; late P
325.1	at] Pms$^+$; as P

325.23	—"old] P; ‸"Old 68
326.1	excellencies] P; excellences 68
326.2-3	he was . . . appeared] Pms-a; he is . . . appear P 49
326.12-13	and scene] Pms(2); and a scene Pms+(1)
326.22	gathered] Pms+; gather P
327.18-19	its merely artistic] 68; its artistic P 49
327.35	external] Pms; eternal P
328.13	Art.] P; ~." 68
328.17	demonic] Pms; demoniac P
328.21	whether of man or nature] Pms; whether Art or Nature P
329.21	the paper] Pms; it P
329.24	than an] Pms; than P
329.29	Brenner] Pms; Brenmer P
330.9	light] Pms; tight P
331.18	gulf as] Pms; gulf, a P
331.21	loth] P; loath 68
332.7	conversing and] Pms; conversing, P
335.3	look-out] Pms; lookout P 68; look‸ out 49
336.6	Cattle-Show] Pms; Cattle‸Show P 49
* 336.18	base] P; bass 68
337.9	Running] Pms; Pursuing P
337.20	fruits] Pms; fruit P
337.32	Bacchantes] Pms; Bacchannals P
339.9	many men are] 68; many are P 49
339.15	oar] Pms; oars P
340.5	body, may impede] P; body, impede 68
340.14	fairy] Pms; fancy P
340.19	beauty] Pms; Beauty P
340.34	after; the rest] P; after. The rest 68
341.9	foresee into what . . . fall.] 49; foresee what . . . fall into. P; ~ ~. ~ . . . ~‸ Pms
342.1	with his] Pms; with the P
342.20	fed like] Pms-a; fed simply like P 49

344.4	we but worship] P; we worship but 68
* 344.7	and we are] P; and are 68
344.13	eras,] Pms; $\sim_{\wedge}$ P
344.13-14	Indian] Pms; Indians P
344.34	live; they] Pms; live. They P
344.35	furniture. They] Pms; furniture; they P
345.32	stands] P; stand 68
348.21	wall] P; walls 68
348.23	Even] P; *no* ¶ ~ 68
349.32	center] Pms; centre P 68
350.1	immense] Pms; enormous P
350.24	fruits] Pms; fruit P
351.9-10	and pry . . . moss,] Pms; *lacking* P
352.22	spirit; this is his grief; let] P; spirit. This is his grief. Let 68
352.31	side] Pms; ride P
353.8	days'] P; day's 68
353.29-30	and blue-curls (*Trichostema dichotoma*)] 68; and the *trichostema dichotoma* P 49
354.17	Day-god's] Pms^{++}; Day-gods' P
354.21	moon light] Pms; noon light P
355.10	with its irregular] Pms; with irregular P
* 356.5-7	According . . . 1818.] 68; *lacking* P 49
356.26	tell as] Pms; tell us P
357.34	native] Pms; wild P
* 358.20	supposed] P; suspected 68
359.4	subtil] P; subtile 68
359.13	highway] Pms; higher P
360.8	faces] Pms; face P
360.32	heel] Pms; keel P
361.3	wings] Pms; wing P
361.9	contrived] 49; continued P; contcontrived Pms
361.20	busy-ness] Pms; *busy-ness* P
361.30	*the principle*] P; *The principle* 68
362.21	Knowledge . . . Knowledge] Pms; knowledge . . . knowledge P

362.28	larger] Pms; longer P
364.21	residue] Pms; residues P
365.13	We] Pms; Me P
365.15	Ross'] Pms; Ross's P 68
365.30	covering, . . . beholder] Pms^{++}; ~∧ . . . ~, P
365.32	reviewer] Pms; Reviewer P
365.34	20', and by] Pms; 20', by P
366.1-2	(ground! . . . ground?)] 68; *lacking* P 49
366.10	Cuviers. We] P; Cuviers; we 68
366.15	Concord, . . . row] Pms^{++}; ~∧ . . . ~, P
368.20	spring] Pms; Spring P
368.21	even] Pms; ever P
371.4	Third, and] 49; Third, P; Third, & Pms
371.8	possessed] Pms; possesses P
372.2	invent] Pms; invert P
372.27	man.] Pms; ~, P
374.35	envelope] P; envelop 68
376.8	dressed] Pms; decreed P
377.18	Autumn] Pms; autumn P
* 377.23-26	winter . . . field of a] P; *lacking* 49
377.23	subside. We] P; subside; we 68
378.11	run;] Pms; ~, P
378.13	bowers?] Pms; ~! P
378.30	on] Pms; in P
379.27	Gods'] Pms; God's P
379.31-380.1	Where is . . . theatre?] 68; *lacking* P 49
381.18	fragrance,] Pms; ~∧ P 49 68
382.27	develope] P; develop 68
382.31	profanity?] P; ~. 68
384.17	woe] 68; wo P 49
385.2	What after all do] P; What do 68
387.10	Slave] Pms; slave P 49 68
387.17	walks] Pms; walk P
388.23	"Yesterday] Pms; *no* ¶ "~ P 49 68
* 390.2	Two herons, *Ardea herodias*] 68; The blue herons, *ardeæ herodiades* P;

	Two blue-herons, *ardea herodias* Pms 49
390.5	silent] Pms; violent P
390.11	meadow] Pms; meridian P
390.12	storks] Pms; stork P
390.30	toward] Pms; towards P
391.3	"Pulsæ] Pms; "Pulrae P
391.31	Silence] 68; silence P 49
392.1	contrast] Pms; contract P
392.7	as after] Pms; as P
393.2	said," "*ἔφη*," "*ἔ*."] Pms; ~," "*εφη*," ‸~.‸ P; ~," "~," ‸~.‸ 49; ~," ‸~,‸ ‸~.‸ 68
393.6	interpret] P; interrupt 68
393.28-29	wild apple-tree] Pms^{+}; wild-apple‸tree P

Table of Emendations

THE Table lists all emendations of copy-text from a later authority: 49, 68, or the present editor. Emendations marked PE are unique to the Princeton Edition, appearing on the editor's authority. Principles of emendation are discussed in the TI, pp. 536-542. For abbreviations used, see the List of Abbreviations, pp. 427-431. Entries marked with an asterisk (*) are discussed in the TNs.

The PE reading appears before a bracket, followed by the source, and then by the copy-text reading. For other rejected readings, see TV. Thus, "*245.30 fourteen] 68; fifteen" means that PE adopts 68 "fourteen" as an emendation of copy-text "fifteen," for reasons explained in a TN. PE has no silent emendations; for a discussion of regularized design features, see TI, pp. 542-543.

	3.10	lands, new] 68; lands new
	4.1-9	Fluminaque . . . banks.] 68; *lacking*
	7.30	aground on] 49; aground on on
	8.20	plowing] 49; plouwing
	10.17-11.17	Let us here read . . . towns to winter."] 68; *lacking*
*	10.33	5 and 20] PE; 5 to 20
*	15.3	*Christ's Invitation*] 68; *Invitation*
*	19.14-17	On Ponkawtasset . . . day.] 68; On Ponkawtasset, since, with such delay, / Down this still stream we took our meadowy way, / . . . Doth twinkle oft . . . day.
	20.18-19	(*Salix Purshiana*)] 68; *lacking*
	20.21	small] 68; *lacking*
	20.24	in front of] 68; in the midst of
	21.5	purple Gerardia, the] 68; *lacking*
	21.9	still] 68; *lacking*

*	21.10	past] 68; in
	27.34	From time to time] 49; from time to time
*	29.14-16	Old Josselyn . . . Partridge.] 68; *lacking*
	31.5-6	which Josselyn . . . Wolf,] 68; *lacking*
	32.25	of eel] 68; *lacking*
	34.16	creditably] 68; creditaby
	35.26-27	is the] 68; was the
	35.30	after] 49; afterfte
	40.10	we] 68; he
	46.2-4	Sabbath, and we fancied . . . day. The air] 68; Sabbath. The air
*	46.13-14	holiday] 68; holyday
	50.5-7	dotage, named . . . Shawshine. I] 68; dotage. I
	52.20	plot. He] 68; plot. And thus he plants a town. He
	52.32-33	And thus . . . town.] 68; *lacking*
	59.24	from west] 68; from to west
*	60.6	Hodeyda] PE; Hodyeda
	60.35	genealogy] 68; geneaology
	62.32	kingfisher] 49; king fisher
	65.15	No god ever dies.] 68; *lacking*
*	65.33	wood, in] PE; $\sim_{\wedge} \sim$
*	66.16	seventh] 68; sixth
*	66.29-30	him? One] PE; him?– ¶ ⟨*underlined*⟩ One
*	67.34	"God . . . Khu."] 68; *lacking*
*	68.26-29	That would . . . tragedies."] 68; *lacking*
*	71.9-12	Pythagoras . . . literature.] 68; *lacking*
	72.27	more than] 68; but
	76.6-7	on the watch] 68; at work
*	76.15-22	There are . . . work.] 68; *lacking*
*	86.7	rarely or] 68; occasionally and
	87.33	Virginia] 68; Virgiania
	92.2	so the child itself] 68; so that childhood itself
*	92.29	midday meal] PE; morning meal
*	94.20	sped us] 68; sped as

98.26	kind.] 49; ~,
99.9-10	We love to think in winter, as we walk . . . pastures, of those] 68; As we walk over the snowy pastures, we think of those
102.13	of the poet Daniel] 68; of Samuel Daniel
102.30	and flows . . . descends.] 68; and descends the faster as it flows more rapidly.
103.24	Spenser] 49; Spencer
103.30-31	thither, reader, you and I, at least, will not] 68; thither you and I, at least, reader, will not
* 104.30	sentences] PE; sentence
* 106.33-107.3	The world . . . god."] 68; *lacking*
110.16	called] 68; call
* 110.22	Westford] 68; Chelmsford
112.12	therein."] 49; ~".
* 117.5-7	"The hye . . . *Ballads*.] 68; *lacking*
* 117.8-12	"His shoote . . . *Ballads*.] 68; *lacking*
* 117.23-30	"All courageous . . . gone."] 68; *lacking*
* 117.26	fone] PE; foue
124.20	lives of men] 68; times
126.27	interested still to] 68; interested to
137.9	beauty merely] 68; pure beauty
137.12	Hindoo] PE; Hindo
140.7-8	my . . . I] 68; our . . . we
140.9	which I] 68; which we
140.28-29	mind? The duty . . . one.] 68; mind? He speaks of duty, but the duty of which he speaks is it not an arbitrary one?
140.30	in doing, not right] 68; not in doing right
141.2	It is a] 68; It is in fact a
141.7-8	actions.] 68; actions.—Yet we know not where we should look for a loftier speculative faith.
142.30	have even been] 68; have been
143.1	Goethe wanted] 68; Goethe, one would say, wanted

143.13	influenced . . . the] 68; influenced the
143.28	Zoroaster, still] 68; Zoroaster, for instance, still
143.29	translations, alone make] 68; translations, make
144.27-28	solitude, once more rowing] 68; solitude, rowing
144.31	we scared up] 68; scaring up
145.12	they would] 68; *lacking*
148.7	human."] 49; ~‸"
148.23	has been] 68; seems to have been
148.25	it was but] 68; it is but
148.26-27	supplied . . . directed] 68; supplies . . . directs
149.15	inclinations renders] 68; inclinations seems to render
149.17-18	Though the sentences] 68; The sentences
149.19-20	flower, they] 68; flower, yet they
150.6-7	intimate with us even] 68; intimate even
150.14-15	it addresses,] 68; does it address
150.25	wood, and its] 68; wood. Its
150.27	country. The] 68; country, and the
150.32-33	east. While . . . this] 68; east. This
150.33	seems] 68; is
152.21	them] 68; these
153.22	Sibyls] 49; Sibybls
* 155.9	Alwákidi's] PE; Alwákidis'
155.10	*Almatîn*] PE; *Almatin*
155.12	*Jabalah*] PE; *Fabalah*
155.12	*Alchátgami*] PE; *Alchâtquarmi*
157.18	Always] 68; always
159.14-15	sounding-boards of piano-fortes and] 68; *lacking*
159.17	Baskets . . . twigs.] 68; *lacking*
160.10	stretch] 49; stretchtch
161.23	Lovewell's] 68; Loevwell's
163.9	Tumultuous] 68; Tumultous
165.15	canst] 68; can'st
166.16	their] 49; the r

170.3	perpetuate] 68; commemorate
170.30-31	Hood, and reflecting favorably on his character, that] 68; Hood, reflecting favorably on the character of his life that
174.26	speech, is music!] 68; speech!
* 175.2-11	We feel . . . existence."] 68; *lacking*
177.13	carry] 68; carrry
185.35	singular] 68; singlar
188.5	by chance reached up] 68; reached up by chance
* 195.26-27	(*Tamias Lysteri,* Aud.)] 68; *lacking*
* 196.10	*sciurus Hudsonius*] PE; *striurus Hudsonius*
* 197.12-15	In the New . . . preserved."] 68; *lacking*
* 197.27-29	raised, a small hole . . . taken.] 68; raised a sum of money was found.
198.28	fleas] 68; flies
201.7-8	maple of the mountain] 68; mountain maple
209.30-31	out-door] 49; out- -door
210.5	pointed] 68; shod
210.11-12	wood or bricks,— . . . cords of wood, . . . thousand bricks,] 68; bricks or wood, — . . . thousand bricks, . . . cords of wood,
210.13	two or three] 49; 2 or 3
212.14	imagined to what . . . put.] 49; ~ ~. ~ . . . ~∧
213.36-214.2	in a week, . . . weather, . . . way.] 68; in a week, . . . ~. . . . ~,
216.16-20	ships; *quæque* . . . I. 133.) We] 68; ships. We
216.20-23	the traveller / instead of finding / of Henry the] 49; ⟨*faintly inked*⟩
218.4	busy-ness] PE; busy-/ness
220.27-28	*sunt*? In] 68; *sunt*? Where are they now?—In
220.29	or else a] 68; or
221.10	power.—] 49; ~∧—
223.25	further] 68; farther

227.7	lightness] 68; lightnesss
* 227.15	These are some of the best] 68; Perhaps these are the best
229.2	He'll] 49; He ll
233.35-234.1	to put . . . appeared,] 68; as it appeared, to put her straw asoak
236.34-35	Merrimack have] 68; Merrimac have
243.15	were passed] 68; occurred
243.22	There is commonly such a one at] 68; It is commonly the offspring of
* 245.30	fourteen] 68; fifteen
245.35	fields; and] 68; fields to get a draught of water; and
248.10-13	period. In deepening . . . river, and there] 68; period. There
250.22	satisfactory] 68; unanswerable
250.25	lichens] 68; moss
252.27-28	one, and . . . miracles." In] 68; one." In
254.3	descendants] 68; descndants
255.18	guide-post on which were the words,] 68; guide-board which said
255.25-29	It is . . . climbed.] 68; *lacking*
259.1	and passed] 68; *lacking*
259.12-15	True kindness . . . station.] 68; *lacking*
* 260.14	Virtue's] 68; Virtues'
* 264.13-18	Mencius . . . all."] 68; *lacking*
264.28	they can] 68; they
266.30-267.2	For the . . . him.] 68; *lacking*
* 267.5-6	"He that . . . doe."] 68; *lacking*
267.7	It will] 68; *no* ¶
267.12	And it . . . poet,] 68; *lacking*
267.24-27	Only . . . civility.] 68; *lacking*
267.30-31	Though we . . . copper.] 68; *lacking*
268.14-15	neighborhood and the family] 68; family and the neighborhood
268.23	passages] 68; passsages
269.24-25	to some extent] 68; in one sense
270.28	each other] 68; one another
271.20-21	"And love . . . nobleman."] 68; Love equals swift and slow, / And high

	and low, / Racer and lame, / The hunter and his game.
272.8-15	There are . . . root.] 68; *lacking*
* 273.30-33	Yet reserve . . . harmonious.] 68; *lacking*
274.21-28	castles. It is not . . . embrace." The] 68; cities. ¶ The
* 280.31	Few . . . than] 68; ¶ Nothing is so difficult as
281.3	with whom he deals] 68; whom he deals with
* 284.27-30	It says, . . . together."] 68; *lacking*
286.8-9	as monuments . . . graveyard.] 68; as their monuments are overgrown with moss.
292.31	heroic] 68; heoric
294.13	secure it a] 68; secure a
295.9	streams] 49; streams patient
* 298.24	chip-sparrow] PE; tree-sparrow
300.13	microscopic] 68; miscroscopic
303.17	Capt.] 49; Capt
* 303.28	grist-mill] PE; saw-mill
304.32	at times] 68; frequently
306.22-23	legs, . . . last. The] 68; legs. The
307.16	or] 49; ord
315.5	wished] 68; pleased
317.21	peculiar] 68; pecular
* 318.24	single-spruce] 68; double-spruce
327.18-19	its merely artistic] 68; its artistic
339.9	many men are] 68; many are
341.9	foresee into what . . . fall.] 49; ∼ ∼. ∼ . . . ∼‸
347.14	wood,] 68; wood ⟨*comma possibly period*⟩
353.29-30	and blue-curls (*Trichostema dichotoma*),] 68; and the *trichostema dichotoma*,
* 356.5-7	According . . . 1818.] 68; *lacking*
358.3-4	paradisiacal] PE; paradisaical
361.9	contrived] 49; contcontrived
366.1-2	(ground! . . . ground?)] 68; *lacking*
371.4	Third, and] 49; Third, &

	379.31-380.1	Where is . . . theatre?] 68; *lacking*
	384.17	woe] 68; wo
	385.24	clearly] 68; elearly
*	390.2	Two herons, *Ardea herodias*] 68; Two blue-herons, *ardea herodias*
	391.31	Silence] 68; silence

End-of-Line Hyphenation

COMPOUND words that are hyphenated at the ends of lines in copy-text have been resolved to hyphenated or closed forms in PE, as recorded on Table A. Some special cases of retained hyphens are also included. Table B records hyphenated compound words that are coincidentally hyphenated at the ends of lines by the PE typesetting. Persons copying or quoting PE should adopt the forms of Table B. For a discussion, see TI, p. 542.

TABLE A

7.7	Nine-Acre-Corner	51.16	selectmen
7.31	pipe-grass	52.23	muskrat
8.4	blue-winged	52.30	themselves
10.25	Allwifes	53.20	weather-stained
11.21	north-east	54.5	school-house
12.21	lowlands	55.25	short-lived
15.18	bullrushes	58.19	understanding
17.4	russet-clad	58.27	understanding
20.29	themselves	61.5	sometimes
21.6	ladies'-tresses	62.30	herself
22.13	afternoon	64.24	lifetime
22.15-16	play-fellows	66.20	blameless
24.1	meanwhile	68.33	undertake
25.3	low-roofed	73.13-14	so-called
30.29	something	82.36	bearskins
31.32	sometimes	85.11	fishermen
34.7	elsewhere	88.12	Nile-like
35.24	alewives	91.4	anything
36.10-11	able-bodied	107.29	themselves
38.14	sometimes	109.1	mealy-mouthed
38.23	without new	111.32	watchhouse
46.23	limitless	114.29	Sunday
49.2	themselves	128.16	supernatural
50.9	meeting-house	128.25	stealthy-paced
		128.33	overtake

135.31	himself
137.17	Chairman
145.16	themselves
148.24	resting-place
149.6-7	table-land
151.7-8	understand
153.16	Methinks
160.16	railroad
160.22	fishermen's
165.34	ourselves
167.14	churchyard
169.4-5	overgrown
170.32	whetstones
171.1	grave-yards
173.23	skylight
175.31	artfully
180.21	sometimes
184.5	himself
186.16	logwood
188.1	hogshead
189.16	far-darting
194.17	boatmen
194.35-195.1	hearth-stone
195.35	hide-and-seek
197.18	arrow-heads
201.12-13	ear-shot
202.23	sugar-maples
207.7	mankind
211.8	meanwhile
212.27	somewhere
213.2	ourselves
224.33	mankind
225.13	wholesome
225.27	bookshop
226.13	highway
227.4	flower-like
233.16	otherwise
235.20	sunrise
236.14	sunshine
238.8	sometimes
238.25	overhanging
242.16	Yankee-Hindoo
242.29	Sometimes
243.11	forenoon
246.14	hereabouts
247.2	pot-holes
247.15	Sisyphus-like
251.19	hoary-headed
255.26	north-easternmost
255.31	fourteen
256.15	*something*
257.2	everywhere
265.6	Nevertheless
266.7	town-meeting
266.19	foresees
270.26	another
271.17	fountain-head
273.17	forgotten
275.8-9	fellow-countrymen
284.2	firebrand
289.29	white-pine
293.2	cannot
296.31	ourselves
297.17	ourselves
299.21	however
306.28	themselves
310.16	himself
311.31	notwithstanding
318.6	another
318.7	hill-top
320.2	tit-for-tat
320.23	forty-two
323.3	fish-hawk
324.27	war-path
326.12	fatherland
330.1	another
344.6-7	somewhat
351.12-13	something
352.29-30	ourselves

353.31	harebell
354.9	hill-side
355.9	witch-hazel
356.6-7	high-water
356.30	apple-tree
357.11	churchyard
359.7	daylight
364.16	herself
368.18	highway
370.20	without
373.17	without
377.29	sunsets
380.10	earth-born
381.30	rainbow's
382.9	without
386.26	cannot
389.27	south-west

TABLE B

6.28-29	cut-grass
7.21-22	hay-stacks
10.1-2	moss-bed
20.21-22	rose-colored
21.1-2	soap-wort
22.15-16	play-fellows
33.11-12	sea-floor
34.4-5	fish-ways
36.10-11	able-bodied
40.10-11	hill-side
50.3-4	moss-grown
60.17-18	to-day
73.13-14	so-called
83.20-21	seventy-eight
83.21-22	thirty-five
86.33-34	mill-ponds
89.1-2	head-waters
92.18-19	ægis-bearing
93.26-27	fair-throned
98.32-33	horse-rake
103.1-2	shore-craft
115.34-35	corn-field
116.2-3	meadow-mice
116.6-7	sea-board
118.14-15	jail-birds
124.24-25	to-day
140.12-13	pencil-maker
149.6-7	table-land
153.32-33	pulse-beat
188.12-13	terra-firma
194.35-195.1	hearth-stone
195.24-25	fish-hawk
200.10-11	moss-like
201.12-13	ear-shot
201.19-20	sap-wood
206.14-15	day-light
209.20-21	well-being
209.30-31	out-door
209.31-32	pen-knife
211.31-32	river-men
215.8-9	great-grand-father
216.10-11	boat-building
217.3-4	mud-wasps
219.19-20	fur-trader
237.22-23	reed-birds
241.25-26	lock-men's
242.20-21	white-scoured
246.23-24	pot-holes
251.13-14	red-maple
275.8-9	fellow-countrymen
287.4-5	horse-pond
327.1-2	good-will
338.6-7	to-day
345.33-346.1	blue-eyed

349.33-34	hill-top	357.26-27	apple-tree
351.2-3	wild-apple	357.34-35	apple-trees
355.15-16	fairy-land	361.17-18	out-doors
356.6-7	high-water	378.26-27	golden-rods
356.11-12	apple-tree	386.1-2	so-called

Blank Lines

THOREAU used blank lines to indicate divisions of text within chapters. At the following junctures copy-text has blank lines which coincidentally fall at the bottoms of pages in the PE typesetting: pp. 38-39, 146-147, and 330-331.

Library of Congress Cataloging in Publication Data

Thoreau, Henry David, 1817-1862.
A week on the Concord and Merrimack Rivers.

(The Writings of Henry D. Thoreau)
Includes index.
1. Merrimack River—Description and travel.
2. Concord River—Description and travel. 3. Thoreau, Henry David, 1817-1862. I. Hovde, Carl. II. Title.
F72.M7T5 1979 974.2'72 78-51201
ISBN 0-691-06376-1